Cognition, Emotion and Psychopathology

Theoretical, empirical and clinical directions

Edited by

Jenny Yiend

CAMBRIDGE
UNIVERSITY PRESS

PUBLISHED BY THE PRESS SYNDICATE OF THE UNIVERSITY OF CAMBRIDGE
The Pitt Building, Trumpington Street, Cambridge, United Kingdom

CAMBRIDGE UNIVERSITY PRESS
The Edinburgh Building, Cambridge, CB2 2RU, UK
40 West 20th Street, New York, NY 10011–4211, USA
477 Williamstown Road, Port Melbourne, VIC 3207, Australia
Ruiz de Alarcón 13, 28014 Madrid, Spain
Dock House, The Waterfront, Cape Town 8001, South Africa

http://www.cambridge.org

First published 2004

Printed in the United Kingdom at the University Press, Cambridge

Typeface Plantin 10/12 pt.   *System* LaTeX 2$_\varepsilon$ [TB]

A catalogue record for this book is available from the British Library

Library of Congress cataloguing in publication data

Cognition, emotion, and psychopathology : theoretical, empirical,
and clinical approaches/edited by Jenny Yiend.
    p.   cm.
Includes bibliographical references and index.
ISBN 0 521 83391 4 (hardback) – ISBN 0 521 54174 3 (paperback)
1. Cognition.   2. Emotions.   3. Anxiety.   4. Psychology, Pathological.
5. Clinical psychology.   I. Yiend, Jenny.   II. Mathews, Andrew M.
BF311.C548735   2004
153 – dc22   2004047295

ISBN 0 521 83391 4 hardback
ISBN 0 521 54174 3 paperback

Contents

List of contributors

THOMAS D. BORKOVEC is Distinguished Professor of Psychology, The Pennsylvania State University.

BRENDAN P. BRADLEY is Professor of Psychology at the Centre for the Study of Emotion and Motivation, University of Southampton.

GILLIAN BUTLER is Consultant Clinical Psychologist at the Warneford Hospital, Oxford.

ANDREW J. CALDER is a Researcher at the MRC Cognition and Brain Sciences Unit, Cambridge.

LYNLEE CAMPBELL is an Australian Research Council funded Research Officer at The University of Western Australia.

DAVID M. CLARK is Professor of Psychology and Head of Department at the Institute of Psychiatry, King's College, University of London.

MICHAEL W. EYSENCK is Professor of Psychology and Head of Department, Royal Holloway College, University of London.

EDNA B. FOA is Professor of Clinical Psychology in Psychiatry at the University of Pennsylvania, and Director of the Center for the Treatment and Study of Anxiety.

ELAINE FOX is Professor in Psychology at the University of Essex.

PAULA HERTEL is Professor of Psychology, Trinity University.

COLETTE R. HIRSCH is a clinical psychologist and lecturer in the Department of Psychology at the Institute of Psychiatry, King's College, University of London.

JONATHAN D. HUPPERT is Assistant Professor of Psychology at the University of Pennsylvania Medical School and a clinical psychologist at the Center for the Treatment and Study of Anxiety.

ANDREW D. LAWRENCE is a Researcher at the MRC Cognition and Brain Sciences Unit, Cambridge.

BUNDY MACKINTOSH is Lecturer in Psychology at the Open University and a Visiting Scientist at the MRC Cognition and Brain Sciences Unit, Cambridge.

COLIN MACLEOD is Professor of Psychology at the University of Western Australia.

SUSAN MINEKA is Professor of Psychology and Director of Clinical Training at Northwestern University.

KARIN MOGG is Professor of Psychology at the Centre for the Study of Emotion and Motivation, University of Southampton.

FIONNUALA MURPHY is a Research Support Scientist at the MRC Cognition and Brain Sciences Unit, Cambridge.

ANNE RICHARDS is a Senior Lecturer in the School of Psychology, Birkbeck College, University of London.

ELIZABETH RUTHERFORD is an Australian Research Council funded Research Officer at The University of Western Australia.

JOHN D. TEASDALE holds a Special Scientific Appointment at the MRC Cognition and Brain Sciences Unit, Cambridge and is a Fellow of the British Academy.

J. MARK G. WILLIAMS is Wellcome Principal Research Fellow in the Department of Psychiatry, University of Oxford.

EDWARD WILSON is a Ph.D. student at The University of Western Australia.

JENNY YIEND is a Research Fellow in the Department of Psychiatry, University of Oxford.

An introduction and synthesis

Jenny Yiend

It will not escape the reader's notice that the inspiration for this volume is our friend and colleague, Andrew Mathews. It was my intention at the outset of the project to bring together a collection of researchers in the field of cognition and emotion who have been taught by, worked with or been heavily influenced by Andrew. The enthusiasm and readiness to participate that I encountered is testament itself to the high esteem in which Andrew is held, and this is also reflected in the many personal tributes scattered throughout the book. For those less familiar with Andrew's history, Tom Borkovec, a long-standing colleague and friend, provides a fascinating and more personal overview of Andrew's contributions to the field, from his clinically oriented early work, through his seminal findings and theorizing on cognitive biases, to his latest theory and present interests in the experimental modification of biased processing.

It is a tribute to the extent of Andrew's influence that contributors to this volume span a wide range of approaches. This is reflected in the structure of the book, which is organized around the scientific progression from theoretical conception, through experimental verification, to application in the clinic. These divisions are inevitably somewhat arbitrary, given that in this field most of us are typically concerned with all three domains. Indeed, some contributions would sit equally comfortably in any section. Thus, rather than being at all exclusive, the structure is instead intended to reflect authors' primary orientations towards the field, be it clinical, theoretical or empirical.

Scope of this volume

A glance at the current peer-reviewed literature shows that the field has indeed moved on, not merely in time, but crucially in content. There is a wealth of new information to be assimilated. In Part I (Theoretical approaches) Mineka starts by presenting a new theoretical model of generalized anxiety disorder (GAD), which draws together the literature on worry and the animal work on conditioned fear and avoidance. Eysenck

1

considers the relative contributions of trait anxiety and repression to the cognitive bias literature and proposes new refinements to his 1997 model. Mogg and Bradley review their recent cognitive-motivational account of mood disorders and discuss relevant new data from their laboratory. Finally, Fox summarizes data in support of her ideas about the mechanisms underlying attentional biases.

Part II (Empirical directions) focuses on recent work reporting important new findings that have the potential eventually to impinge in both directions, upon theoretical models as well as on clinical practice. Hertel opens with some fascinating new data from her own laboratory, demonstrating the elusive memory bias in anxiety following an interpretative training manipulation. She follows this up with a theoretical discussion addressing, amongst other things, why memory biases may have proven hard to find in anxiety, but not depression. Using a transfer-appropriate processing framework, she suggests that a critical factor may be the use of tasks that are sensitive to cognitive habits. Richards focuses too on the resolution of ambiguity and sets this within the wider literature on text comprehension. She describes the recent expansion of this work to explore more ecologically valid materials, such as facial expressions, as well as the influence of the context or setting within which such interpretations occur. The increasing application of functional imaging techniques is set to be a growth area within our field, as in many others, and the chapter by Lawrence, Murphy and Calder reflects this. They describe both functional imaging and neuropsychological data relevant to the processing of fear and disgust, and highlight the implications of these data for current theoretical approaches to emotion. The last two contributions to this section cover the burgeoning work on experimental modification of cognitive biases that Andrew Mathews has himself been heavily involved in over recent years. These new 'training' methodologies are allowing us to assess directly for the first time the causal status of cognitive biases. This is described in the MacLeod, Campbell, Rutherford and Wilson chapter, where they review the evidence for a causal link between biased processing and cognitive disorder, in the light of these new data. Finally, Yiend and Mackintosh outline the ongoing programme of research into interpretative bias modification that Mathews' lab has been engaged in over recent years.

Part III (Clinical perspectives) concentrates on research and theory that is approached from a primarily clinical angle. Many of the contributions in this section provide examples of the transfer of ideas from research into practice. For example, Huppert and Foa discuss how their emotional processing theory might be integrated with Mathews' own latest model and applied to the treatment of social anxiety disorder. Staying with social anxiety, Hirsch and Clark describe recent work exploring the seemingly powerful role of mental imagery in treatment. Williams gives an overview of over-general autobiographical memory and its implications for clinical practice. Teasdale gives a summary of mindfulness-based cognitive therapy, as well as an update on the latest treatment trial results. In the final chapter, Butler rounds off by presenting a clinician's view of current research priorities. She highlights several areas, including comorbidity and treatment-failure rates, which can be overlooked by non-practising academics, but which need to inform the future research agenda.

Emergent themes

The overall scientific goal of the book is to provide an account of current research in cognition and emotion, particularly that having implications for clinical conditions, and to set out an agenda for productive future work in the field. In keeping with this purpose, I will attempt, in the latter half of this introduction, to draw out some common themes arising from the many excellent contributions in this volume that researchers might focus on over the coming years.

There are several theoretical themes running through a number of chapters. The most general of these is the trend to focus on issues of *process*, as opposed to, say, the content of material undergoing that process. Delineating the precise nature and characteristics of the cognitive processing undertaken by the individual appears crucial to current thinking. That is, a given cognitive operation may be performed in a number of different ways, or be made up of different specific elements, which researchers need to delineate. There are many examples of this in the present volume. Conceptualizing attention as a series of operations involving, for example, engaging and disengaging is a case in point. Fox's chapter is an elegant example of how such an approach can reap rewards in terms of a more detailed characterization of the nature of, in this case, anxiety-related processing differences. Similarly Hertel, in her discussion of memory bias, shows that in our experimental design we might inadvertently constrain processing, such that memory biases in anxiety, but not depression, for example, remain unobserved. Mathews' own work on training has thrown up an apparently important distinction of process, such that different techniques of encoding – generative or passive – have different clinically relevant mood consequences.

That the nature of cognitive processing matters is of no surprise to cognitive psychologists, but the issue is more specific than this. We need to focus more research effort on characterizing the components and mediators of cognitive operations and on understanding how these lead to clinically important differences in mental products. Imagery, for example (see Hirsch and Clark), has the potential to produce effects across cognitive domains and could therefore be important in a variety of operations, including attention, encoding and memory. Teasdale's notion of mindful attention also illustrates the point. Here, it is the *manner* in which attention is deployed towards unpleasant information that determines whether the consequences for vulnerable individuals will be beneficial or detrimental. One of the challenges for future years, then, will be to continue to identify the precise aspects of a given process that are critical to an emotionally relevant outcome and to identify how to conceptualize and measure these features.

Another broad topic that is likely to become increasingly prominent is the issue of *cognitive control*. In previous years, there has been considerable interest in the degree of automaticity of cognitive biases, especially within attention. Now that we have a corpus of literature exploring the extent to which biases operate automatically, interest is shifting towards the degree to which they can be controlled. The emergence of attentional and interpretive training paradigms, from the laboratories of MacLeod, Mathews and others, demonstrates that biases are amenable to control and raise questions about the mechanisms underlying those changes. Similarly, Teasdale's application of mindfulness to relapse prevention in depression implies a level of cognitive control that warrants further characterization. Imagery (see Hirsch and Clark) is another example of a process that can be influenced by simple instruction and presumably the effects are mediated by conscious intent. As psychologists in general are becoming less afraid to address the 'last frontier' of consciousness, so too can cognitive clinical researchers begin to consider similar questions in the context of processing in emotional disorders. This will doubtless be assisted by the availability of functional imaging, which allows us for the first time directly to observe and quantify concepts such as mental resources, effort and intent.

A third, related, but somewhat more specific, theme that looks set to develop further over coming years concerns the potential importance of *avoidance* in emotional processing. Mogg and Bradley provide us with the most detailed discussion of this issue in the present volume. They explicitly consider the possibility of reversal of attentional biases for threat in the context of their cognitive-motivational model and explore possible factors that might mediate this, such as effort (see above), and the evolutionary need for escape. Cognitive avoidance has been found in specific phobias, social anxiety, repressors and low anxious individuals, and the need to incorporate these data into our theoretical understanding of processing biases is increasing as the data continue to accumulate. Indeed,

Eysenck's four factor theory already predicts that in responding to ambiguity repressors show a vigilant-avoidant pattern. Interestingly, in this volume, he goes on to speculate that this pattern may account for repressors' paradoxical autonomic versus experiential profile: initial vigilance could lead to behavioural and physiological anxiety, while subsequent avoidance might be responsible for the absence of any conscious experience of distress. The relevance of avoidant processing is picked up again by Teasdale. In discussing mindfulness, he proposes that in disorder, attention to negative material may be driven by an underlying motivation to avoid the associated unpleasantness. In contrast, one mechanism of mindfulness may be to teach an approach motivation, involving positive orientation towards such material, one that promotes acceptance rather than avoidance. Avoidance is also an important component in Mineka's new learning theory perspective on GAD. She suggests that we can better understand the persistent and uncontrollable nature of worry in this disorder by conceptualizing worry as a cognitive avoidance response, which is then both negatively reinforced (for example, by a reduction in somatic symptoms) and punished. Consideration of the learning theory literature suggests that punishing an *avoidant* response leads to a paradoxical increase in that behaviour, which, in the case of GAD, is consistent with increased worry and the perception of uncontrollability. Thus, both theoretically and empirically, the role of avoidance in cognitive processing is likely to be a recurring feature in future work.

Another emerging issue is the potential importance of the *context* in which cognitive operations occur. In the rigorously controlled environment of the laboratory it can be too easy to forget that real world cognition occurs within a contextual setting, which may or may not have the power to influence processes and their outcomes. Richards' work on contextual effects of ambiguity resolution gives us an excellent example of how important context might actually be, finding, as she does, that context effects can in fact override individual differences. Similarly, as training methodologies move further towards clinical application, it becomes increasingly important to examine their efficacy outside of the laboratory. Likewise, Huppert and Foa's discussion of social anxiety acknowledges the importance of invoking multiple contexts to achieve maximally effective treatment outcome. Future work is very likely to continue this trend for a broader perspective on cognitive–emotional interactions.

Comparisons between *different emotions* is a topic as old as any within psychology. Nevertheless, it is acquiring renewed interest within the cognitive–emotional literature, as the chapter by Lawrence, Murphy and Calder illustrates. In turn, this trend is likely to impact upon the clinical-cognitive field. Whereas our earlier focus was on issues of content specificity, such as whether attentional biases applied uniformly to negative material or uniquely to threat, we are now starting to focus on more discrete emotion categories. This is complemented by methodological shifts, such as an increasing use of facial expressions as stimuli. Fox, for example, speculates that angry and fearful facial expressions both constitute a threat to the observer, but have different directional implications, with anger being directed towards the observer and fear being directed towards the environment. The implications of this for cognitive processing remain to be determined. It is also likely that other emotions, such as disgust, which to date have been largely ignored within cognition and emotion may become more prominent, especially given links such as that between disgust and obsessive-compulsive disorder (OCD). Lawrence et al. provide a good starting-point for the interested researcher.

The importance of prior *trauma* in the genesis of emotional disorder is another topic of widening interest. Here, this is represented by, for example, Hirsch and Clark's discussion of early traumatic social episodes. They suggest that such trauma may be the original source material from which the potent negative imagery is constructed, and that subsequent avoidance (see above) may prevent updating in the presence of disconfirmatory information. Williams also highlights the role of trauma in producing the over-general autobiographical memory associated with depression. He concludes from the data that previous traumatic experience is necessary, but not sufficient, to produce the effect, but also points out that over-generality could be a vulnerability factor, pre-dating the trauma itself. Either way, the severity of the trauma appears to be the critical factor mediating the degree of subsequent over-generality. Could it be that trauma, and the individual's response to it, may turn out to have a crucial role in a range of pathologies, in addition to post-traumatic stress disorder (PTSD)? More research is clearly needed, but if we could identify such a substrate linking ostensibly different pathologies, then we would be making a significant step forward.

This leads us to the question of *comorbidity*. As Butler points out, practising clinicians have to confront this reality and its attendant problems on a daily basis. However, it has not historically been at the forefront of the research agenda. The time is right to redress this. Mogg and Bradley are heading in this direction by attempting to explain the paradoxical absence of attentional biases in comorbid anxiety and depression. They describe the interaction between the putative processes of valence evaluation and goal engagement in their cognitive-motivational model. They suggest that the amotivational state associated with depression leads to poor goal engagement, so that the attentional consequences of negative valence evaluations are not displayed, despite the attendant anxiety. Although there is clearly still a long way to go, the potential gains of understanding comorbid presentations are large. After well over a decade of characterizing the cognitive processing of specific pathologies, researchers should now be in a position to explore the reasons for, and implications of, the widespread co-occurrence of apparently different pathologies.

As this last point demonstrates, there is a continued need for a synthesis between clinical and research priorities. Practising clinicians need to stay in touch with advances in relevant cognitive research and apply them where they can. Similarly, researchers need to be aware of the needs and concerns arising from the clinic. One of the aims of this edited collection is to encourage this synthesis, by representing views from a variety of perspectives. In doing so, it also provides an up-to-date picture of the field today. Finally, it is hoped that this volume will, in some small way, assist in marking out a path for researchers and clinicians over the next decade.

Andrew Mathews: a brief history of a clinical scientist

T. D. Borkovec

On a cold, cloudy, dreary day in June of 1939, Andrew Mathews was born in Farnborough Hospital, just outside of London. No one suspected at the time that he was destined to become one of the leading clinical scientists of his generation. I am guessing about the meteorological conditions of his first appearance on earth, but I lived in London while working at the Institute of Psychiatry for three summer months in 1978, during which time I saw the sun on exactly three days. So I am fairly confident about the cold, cloudy, dreary bit. Everything else is certainly true.

I am uncertain about the cosmic significance, if any, of that particular summer spent in London, but I do know that the brightest spot in my stay involved meeting Andrew for the first time. He was Chair of the British Association for Behavioural Psychotherapy, and I had written to ask whether I might come to the Association's annual meeting in Sterling, Scotland, so that I could present some of my research and have the opportunity to meet British clinical psychologists at the beginning of my stay in England. He graciously agreed to schedule something for me. So began a cherished friendship and collaboration that has lasted for a quarter of a century.

Andrew grew up educationally at the University of London, where he received his B.Sc., Dip.Psych. (Clinical Qualification, Institute of Psychiatry) and Ph.D. From 1969 to 1976, he was a Senior Research Psychologist in the Department of Psychiatry at the University of Oxford, where he had a lovely vineyard in his backyard, whose wine was not too bad. He held the position of Chair of the Department of Psychology at St George's Hospital Medical School from 1976 to 1988, living in a lovely home on the Thames. This home would later play a significant role in both of our histories. From 1988 to 1992 he was a Professor of Psychology at Louisiana State University. He returned to the United Kingdom in 1992, as a Medical Research Council Senior Scientist at the Cognition and Brain Sciences Unit (formerly, the Applied Psychology Unit) in Cambridge, where he has been ever since. The external world has recognized the significance of his work with two prestigious awards:

The British Psychological Society's President's Award for Distinguished Scientific Contributions to Psychology (1993) and The American Psychological Association, Society for the Science of Clinical Psychology, Distinguished Scientist Award (1995). The basis of such awards can be found within the 5 books, 18 book chapters and 106 journal articles that he has produced during his career thus far. I am getting ahead of myself, however.

Andrew and I are from the same generational cohort. We became graduate students in clinical psychology at the dawn of behaviour therapy, so we have had the privilege of observing and periodically participating in nearly its entire history. The 1960s were wonderfully exciting times, because everything seemed possible from this new point of view, and there were seemingly unlimited opportunities for research and treatment development from this new perspective.

Early behaviour therapy rested on two important and fundamental ideas. First, it insisted that the best way to understand psychological problems and to develop effective therapies based on such understandings resided in the application of known principles of human behaviour. It just happened to be the case that the best-known principles at that time came from the operant and classical conditioning literatures. Second, this movement committed itself to the experimental evaluation of the efficacy of newly developed therapy techniques. Within the prevailing psychodynamic and experiential traditions of this time, both of these were remarkably radical ideas. And they were ideas that eventually yielded very important results. It now seems amazing that, when Andrew and I were graduate students, the practising community considered panic attacks and obsessive compulsive disorder to be untreatable! The relative success of the subsequent work based on these early behaviour therapy ideas is clearly evident in the current existence of several empirically supported treatments (e.g. Chambless & Ollendick, 2001), the majority of which are grounded in applications of those very same, early-learning principles. Exposure therapies and operant reinforcement and extinction procedures make up the bulk of methods contained in these validated approaches. This is an important point to which I will much later return in commentary about Andrew's significant contributions to our field.

Andrew's research career really has two distinct phases. The first phase lasted until the mid-1980s. I will call this phase 'Andrew's Wanderings in the Desert'. There was so much to do in the early days and so many questions to address with research. In terms of overall approach, his work during this time was reflective of behaviour therapy's original empirical commitment, in that it was characterized by an ideal combination of therapy outcome studies and laboratory studies designed to acquire basic knowledge about the nature and mechanisms of psychological disorders. In terms of content, Andrew's passion focused on anxiety and behavioural medicine. Although some of his earliest work involved investigations of epilepsy (Scott, Moffett, Mathews & Ettlinger, 1967), tics and Gilles de la Tourette's syndrome (Connell, Corbett, Horne & Mathews, 1967; Corbett, Mathews, Connell & Shapiro, 1969), he was already showing signs of a systematic and programmatic interest in the anxiety disorders. At first, working with Malcolm Lader and Michael Gelder, that interest had a decidedly physiological thrust in both theory development (Lader & Mathews, 1968) and empirical work (Lader & Mathews, 1968, 1970a, 1970b, 1971; Mathews & Gelder, 1969; Mathews & Lader, 1971), culminating in his brilliant *Psychological Bulletin* article on the psychophysiological mechanisms of systematic desensitization (Mathews, 1971). One of his conclusions from that review of the extant literature on desensitization was that the presence of a relaxed state during phobic imagery presentations likely produced three important effects facilitative of extinction process: increased vividness of the imagery, augmentation of the autonomic effects of the imagery, and maximization of response decrement to repeated exposures to the feared stimuli. It is striking to recognize how similar this perspective was in significant ways to the highly influential neo-behaviouristic model of fear reduction via emotional processing proposed fifteen years later by Foa and Kozak (1986). Andrew's article also had a profound effect on my way of thinking about desensitization and the kind of research that I would pursue for the next few years. Our group's series of investigations culminated in a component control study designed explicitly to test Andrew's conclusions by contrasting hierarchical imaginal exposures during contiguous relaxation, exposures with noncontiguous relaxation, exposures alone and no-treatment, while heart rate reactions to the images were monitored during the five sessions of therapy for speech anxiety. The results unequivocally supported all three of Andrew's hypothesized effects of relaxation (Borkovec & Sides, 1979). I presented these results for the first time at the British Association for Behavioural Psychotherapy in Sterling, Scotland, June, 1978.

Andrew's research and writing during the mid-1970s and early 1980s continued to focus on basic research on anxiety disorders, as well as on clinical descriptions of exposure-based therapies and on experimental outcome investigations of their efficacy. This work primarily involved phobias (e.g. Mathews & Rezin, 1977; Mathews & Shaw, 1973) and especially agoraphobia (e.g. Cobb, Mathews, Childs-Clarke & Blowers 1984; Johnston, Lancashire, Mathews, Munby, Shaw & Gelder, 1976; Mathews, 1977a, 1977b, 1984; Mathews, Johnston, Lancashire, Munby, Shaw & Gelder, 1976; Mathews, Teasdale, Munby, Johnston & Shaw,

1977; Teasdale, Walsh, Lancashire & Mathews, 1977). He also continued to explore, from both basic and applied perspectives, additional behavioural medicine problems, including sexual dysfunction (e.g. Bancroft & Mathews, 1971; Carney, Bancroft & Mathews, 1978; Mathews, 1982, 1983; Mathews, Bancroft & Slater, 1972; Mathews, Bancroft, Whitehead, Hackmann, Julier, Bancroft, Gath & Shaw, 1976; Mathews, Whitehead & Kellett, 1983; Whitehead & Mathews, 1977, 1986), tension headaches (Martin & Mathews, 1978) and, in collaboration with his soon-to-be wife, Valerie, recovery from surgery (e.g. Mathews & Ridgeway, 1981, 1984; Ridgeway & Mathews, 1982). Several of his books ultimately emerged from this period of thinking and empirical work: in collaboration with Andrew Steptoe, Andrew edited two texts (Mathews & Steptoe, 1982; Steptoe & Mathews, 1984) and wrote another (Mathew & Steptoe, 1988) in the areas of behavioural medicine and the psychology of medical practice, and he, along with colleagues Michael Gelder and Derek Johnston, wrote a very significant book on the nature and treatment of agoraphobia (Mathews, Gelder & Johnston, 1981).

Near the end of this phase, a significant event happened that would dramatically change both of our lives. We had been talking about collaborating on research for a long time, and we finally decided to seek funding together from the National Institute of Mental Health (NIMH) for a therapy outcome investigation on the cognitive behavioural treatment of generalized anxiety disorder (GAD). Although some outcome studies had previously been conducted with diffuse anxiety problems (including a dismal failure to use thought-stopping techniques; Mathews & Shaw, 1977), there had not yet been a controlled clinical trial of any form of psychotherapy for this recently defined DSM-III (American Psychiatric Association, 1980) disorder. I flew to London to spend a week in Andrew and Valerie's home on the Thames in April 1983, so that we could work on creating this joint project. Racking our small brains continuously in his living-room (with periodic breaks to allow me to huddle over his electric heater), we were able to outline the basic elements of a multi-site investigation. Half of the clients would be treated at Andrew's department, and half would be seen at my department. The project was ultimately funded, but NIMH at that time did not yet see the wisdom of multi-site studies (although it currently does; it was the one instance in my life in which I was ahead of my time). So only the US site received support. We ultimately published two outcome studies with this support (Borkovec, Mathews, Chambers, Ebrahimi, Lytle & Nelson, 1987; Borkovec & Mathews, 1988). It is hard to say whether the funding of Andrew's site, had it occurred, would have made a difference to the focus of his future research. It is quite possible that he might have continued to conduct large-scale, time-consuming, emotionally exhausting clinical outcome trials. That certainly was the consequence of these initial studies for me. Starting with this collaborative grant with Andrew, I have spent eighteen wondrously happy years doing therapy research with generalized anxiety disorder, with frequent and sage advice from my original co-principal investigator, without whose contributions to that first grant none of the ensuing studies would ever have occurred. Fortunately for the field, however, Andrew was not as crazy as me to choose this research path, and he made a major shift in his research agenda, entering the second phase of his research career, the phase which the reader has no doubt anticipated and which I will call 'Andrew's Discovery of the Promised Land'.

He and I have over the years spent countless hours together brainstorming about important topics (like the natures of anxiety, depression, human behaviour in general), trivial topics (like the nature of reality) and extremely important topics (like whether or not Douglas Adams did indeed have a profound insight into the ultimate question about life, the universe, and everything with Deep Thought's answer '42' – which many people believe is ASCII code for 'insufficient information'). One of the things about which we became quite sure was this: human behaviour involves interactive multi-system processes over time. In response to a significant stimulus, humans enact a sequence of responses, and the process and content of that sequence determine the future 'meaning' of that stimulus upon its next occasion. So whether the meaning (or functional value) of a significant event changes, is maintained or is further strengthened will be a function of exactly how we sequentially respond in all of our information processing systems (cognitive, physiological, affective, behavioural) upon each occurrence of the event. Action (at any and all levels of responding) is meaning, a view reminiscent of the James–Lange theory of emotion and contained as well in Mowrer's (1947) seminal two-stage theory of fear conditioning. At the molar level in my development of cognitive-behavioural approaches to the treatment of generalised anxiety disorder, this has partly meant an emphasis on teaching our clients early in therapy to monitor objectively their responding in daily life, to detect the very first occurrence of a movement in the direction of anxious responding, and to learn to emit new cognitive, affective and behavioural responses that will change the meaning of the situation to one that is less threatening (Borkovec & Sharpless, in press). To Andrew, it meant that the specific, molecular, sequential processes characteristic of anxious responding, from the moment of threat-cue detection through subsequent automatic and strategic processing (attention–perception–interpretation), are what need to be researched and understood. And it meant that the starting-point of the sequence (and therefore of a research programme devoted to the elucidation of the sequence) had to be at the moment when attention was first captured.

Although there were growing signs of this interest in cognitive factors in some of his earlier work on emotional disorders (e.g. Bradley & Mathews, 1988; Butler & Mathews, 1987; Mathews & Shaw, 1977), it was his collaborations with Colin MacLeod on attentional bias in anxiety in the mid-1980s (MacLeod, Mathews & Tata, 1986; Mathews & MacLeod, 1985, 1986) that gave birth to an explosion of systematic and ingenious research that has contributed so enormously to our detailed, current understanding of the nature of anxious process. In Andrew's own words:

As for starting on information-processing, I don't think I ever had any great insights – these things just evolve, don't they? I remember towards the end of the time at Oxford (so around 1975), we were still working on treatment of agoraphobia and related topics and wondering if people who did not respond so well to exposure and had more general anxiety may have thoughts of the kind Beck described in his paper on ideational components of anxiety neurosis (Beck, Laude & Bohnert, 1974). John Teasdale came to Oxford and was working with us on phobias but was interested in depressive thinking, so that may have started me thinking that anxiety might be similar. But we didn't do much on it, except for pilot studies on techniques like thought-stopping, before moving to St George's Hospital, where the job involved lots of reading in cognitive and social psychology when planning the medical student course. I started supervising clinical Ph.D. students, like Brendan Bradley and Karin Mogg, on memory bias in depression and anxiety, and Gillian Butler on heuristics and subjective risk, a bit later. It didn't really all come together until writing a grant proposal on whether GAD clients showed biases in processing threat. The intention was to test Beck's ideas, using methods from social cognition from people like Bargh and Kahneman. I was looking for a research assistant for the grant and was recommended to Colin who was just completing clinical training at the Institute of Psychiatry. Once he joined the group, it just took off. The two of us started visiting the Applied Psychology Unit in Cambridge to have meetings with Fraser Watts and Mark Williams, who gave us lots of ideas (e.g. to use the Stroop task). Then Michael Eysenck made contact, and we picked up the idea for the dot probe method from his student, Chris Haliopoulos. I certainly remember that being a really fun time.

Because much of this volume is devoted to information-processing analyses of cognition and emotion in emotional disorders, I will highlight some of his significant discoveries and thinking below but will not describe in detail the large body of empirical work on this topic that Andrew has generated with his students and colleagues over the past two decades. Many of those studies will be reviewed or cited in the upcoming chapters, and it will become very clear to the reader how Andrew's theoretical thinking and laboratory research have so strongly influenced the direction, content and methods of this domain of psychological science. The work described in this volume by the various authors is extremely important (in and of itself and as a shining example of the very best in scientific approaches to psychological phenomena), because it is devoted to understanding psychopathology on the basis of identifying the best-known principles of human behaviour (the original commitment of early behaviour therapy). My remaining task instead will be to comment on the qualities that I see in Andrew's work over this period of time, qualities which are the reason why he is one of the leading clinical scientists of his generation.

The fundamental quality of his work, upon which all of his other qualities rest, is that it embodies the Strong Inference approach to scientific investigation. Platt (1964, p. 347) eloquently describes this approach as follows:

Why should there be such rapid advances in some fields and not in others? . . . I have begun to believe that the primary factor in scientific advance is an intellectual one. These rapidly moving fields are fields where a particular method of doing scientific research is systematically used and taught, an accumulative method of inductive inference that is so effective that I think it should be given the name 'strong inference' . . . Strong inference consists of applying the following steps to every problem in science, formally and explicitly and regularly:
1. Devising alternative hypotheses;
2. Devising a crucial experiment (or several of them), with alternative possible outcomes, each of which will, as nearly as possible, exclude one or more of the hypotheses;
3. Carrying out the experiment so as to get a clean result;
4. Recycling the procedure, making subhypotheses or sequential hypotheses to refine the possibilities that remain, and so on.

To Platt, strong inference is to inductive reasoning as syllogism is to deductive reasoning, and it provides a consistent procedure for coming to firm inductive conclusions, one after another, as fast as possible. Indeed, he felt that no more rapid way to acquire scientific knowledge exists in any area or any discipline than by following this approach, and this is especially true in poorly advanced areas where so much is unknown. Popperian knowledge progresses through falsification. What is relatively true emerges by strong inference from the sequential and unequivocal determination of what is not true. Put another way, we adopt a relative truth at that point at which multiple rival hypotheses have been clearly ruled out. We consider the remaining, as yet unrejected, hypothesis to contain temporarily a relative truth, even though it too will ultimately be rejected and replaced by another relative truth that contains more knowledge than its predecessor. In addition to providing the most rapid approach to knowledge acquisition within science, strong inference and its multiple-rival-hypotheses method provide scientists with another advantage: it is much less likely that we will become attached to our hypotheses (or our theory) if we force ourselves to maintain several rival ones until the empirical data provide us with a basis for dispassionately (but with great joy and excitement in the quest) rejecting some of them (Chamberlain, cited in Platt, 1964). Science becomes a conflict of ideas rather than a conflict of scientists (Platt, 1964).

Within clear theoretical contexts from both clinical and cognitive psychology, Andrew's research has been devoted to the pursuit of causal mechanisms and has done so by applications of strong inference within his entire programmatic series of investigations from 1985 to the present. His empirical studies are typified by the generation of multiple-rival hypotheses (prospectively in their published introductions as well as retrospectively in their discussions) about the nature of the phenomena under investigation and the deployment of experimental designs, methodologies and measures to rule out unequivocally one or more of these alternative explanations. He has variously drawn from the theoretical positions of others (e.g. Beck and Clark, 1988; Bower, 1981; Eysenck, 1982; Fox, 1994; Öhman, 1993; Wells & G. Mathews, 1994) as well as from his own prior models (e.g. Williams, Watts, MacLeod & Mathews, 1988), to deduce logically the (often contrasting) implications from each position, pointing out ways in which specific empirical results cannot be handled by those positions and creating his next studies to test rival conceptualizations derived from them. At times, he has even had strong versus weak versions of a theoretical account (e.g. Dalgleish, Mathews & Wood, 1999). A single publication will frequently include a series of multiple experiments, each leading to the next in a logical and progressive fashion in their sequential attempt to rule out further alternative hypotheses and to go more deeply each time towards a more thorough understanding of the phenomenon. Through his application of strong inference, his body of work has led to highly significant discoveries about the nature of anxiety process, and his emerging, current theoretical model (see Figure a; Mathews & Mackintosh, 1998; Mathews & MacLeod, 2002) has allowed him to capture previously known empirical results as well as to explain anomalies that prior models were unable to handle. Anxious people do not show evidence of attentional bias to a singularly presented stimulus; there must be a competition among multiple stimuli in the environment to evoke such a bias. This suggests that stimuli are processed in parallel and compete for attention until the activation of the representation of one of them is sufficient to inhibit other representations and emerge into awareness, at which time strategic processes in response to the detected

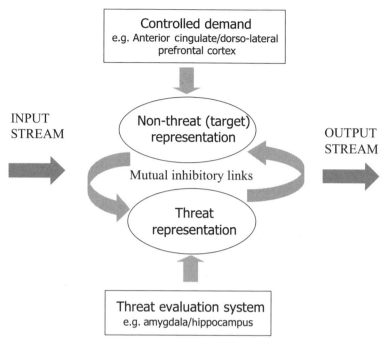

Figure a Automatic (bottom-up) and strategic (top-down) processes in emotional bias. See Mathews and Mackintosh (1998).

cue can take place. In the case of anxiety, the matching of one of the stimuli to representations within the threat-evaluation system results in the allocation of resources to the threatening cue. Remarkably, non-anxious people actually *avoid* threat cues when such cues are mild or moderate in danger-signal value; it requires highly threatening information before the threshold between avoidance and vigilance is exceeded and the conscious perception of danger occurs. For anxious people, this threshold is set lower, affected both by their predisposing vulnerability and by state conditions that increment anxious experience. Although top-down voluntary control in an effort to attend to task-related cues can potentially counteract the effects of activated representations from the threat-evaluation system, the presence of stressful events or cognitive load in anxiety-vulnerable individuals can overwhelm such attempts at strategic control and can lead to an inability to inhibit these threat representations and to the intrusion of anxious process. Importantly, detection of threat can occur automatically and thus at non-conscious levels. An analogous process occurs at the next stage of processing, the interpretive stage. Multiple possible meanings are potentially activated upon cue detection (especially in response to ambiguous material), and the same type of competition occurs. Although there is some degree of control over this stage of processing, in anxious individuals in an anxious state, the input from the threat-evaluation system activates stored meanings that further activate the perceived threat. Hypothetically, both the attentional biases and interpretive biases displayed by anxious individuals contribute to the maintenance of anxiety disorders. The absence of clear evidence for memory bias in anxiety disorders (in contrast to the negatively biased recall in depression) finds its explanation in the difference in encoding modes (see Hertel, this volume). Anxiety largely has to do with non-conscious, perceptual processing that leads to avoidance or escape and is driven by a threat-evaluation system that does not make use of verbal encoding, whereas the encoding mode in depression involves higher-order conceptual and verbal processing, more closely matching the verbal report basis of recall tasks.

Again depending upon generation and ruling out of rival hypotheses, Andrew has pursued the question of causal mechanisms potentially present in cognitive processes and the possible therapeutic implications of such causal determinants, should they be shown to exist. He repeatedly warned, in his earlier work, that there had not yet been an unambiguous demonstration that a cognitive factor could actually be a cause of anxiety (e.g. Mathews, 1990). It is truly remarkable that cognitive behavioural therapy has been around for so many years and yet its most fundamental assumption (that certain cognitions can cause anxiety and that therefore changing cognitions can reduce or eliminate anxiety) had never been adequately tested. Andrew has found the Holy Grail, however. Attentional and interpretive biases have now been demonstrated to be learnable through mere repeated exposure (Mathews & MacLeod, 2002; Yiend & Mathews, 2002). And such induced biases do indeed directly elicit anxiety, but only when they are used in the processing of emotionally significant information (Mathews & MacLeod, 2002). Specifically, the person has to actively generate (not merely passively observe) the biased response. Moreover, multi-session training in avoiding threat information or interpreting ambiguous scenarios in non-threatening ways leads to significant reductions in trait anxiety.

Further exemplary of strong inference, his work is also characterized by ingenious discriminations of process and content with equally ingenious uses of methodologies and measures (borrowed from other brilliant researchers or created on his own) to isolate where truth resides. Although verbal representations and processes have been an important focus of his attention, searching for causal connections in other systems has provided him with opportunities to investigate similarities and differences across differing information processing systems. The use of pictorial stimuli allows him to draw conclusions about the operation of perceptual and imaginal systems (e.g. Yiend & Mathews, 2001), while the use of novel line drawings allows him to create a history of evaluative learning in participants unaffected by certain critical aspects of prior learning, thus pointing in the direction of the potential identification of aetiological factors in the development of anxiety disorders (Mackintosh & Mathews, 2003; Yiend & Macintosh, this volume). Duration of stimulus presentation and use of masking procedures allow him to isolate the millisecond moments at which specific internal events occur. Such procedures also allow the investigation, as mentioned above, of the role of automatic and strategic processes and the necessity or not of conscious and non-conscious experience in the unfolding sequence of human responses to discrete events. Most recently, Andrew and his colleagues have obtained remarkable findings regarding automatic and strategic processing of threat using functional Magnetic Resonance Imaging (fMRI) (Mathews, Lawrence & Yiend, in press). Fear-related and neutral pictures were presented under emotional encoding and non-emotional encoding conditions. Striking evidence was found for both:

1. Obligatory differential fear reactions throughout the whole of the hierarchical defensive system (importantly including the amygdala), even when encoding the information in a non-emotional way, but
2. Modulation of fear-related activation by optional, top-down encoding processes involving attentional control. Moreover, individual differences in subjectively reported vulnerability to anxiety correlated significantly with the degree to which many of these events occurred.

Including various dispositional groups (e.g. GAD, depression, social phobia, normal control) within his designs allows him to rule out certain rival hypotheses concerning what is distinctive and what is not in each disorder. His periodic inclusion of recovered GAD clients (see Mathews, Mogg, Kentish & Eysenck, 1995) allows him to draw conclusions about sites of effect of intervention, documentation in information-processing tasks that clinical improvement reflects more than merely client self-report, and the identification of specific potential vulnerabilities that may remain despite clinical improvement. Often examining both pre-existing traits and experimentally or naturally occurring induced states, he has been able to unpack the frequent interaction of these factors to provide a more complete account of a phenomenon, like the necessary conditions for low-threshold attentional bias towards threat in anxious individuals and the remarkable protective functions of positive or non-threat bias in non-anxious folks (see Mathews & Mackintosh, 1998).

Throughout this work, Andrew has been equally critical of his own previous thinking as he is of others when the data indicate that he was wrong or when logic indicates that there remain crucial problems that need to be sorted out with his conceptualizations at a particular moment in time. Listen to examples of this self-critical stance in Andrew's own published voice: 'Depressed patients can show attentional vigilance effects (contrary to our own previous published results)' (Mathews, Ridgeway & Williamson, 1996, p. 703). 'In neither this, nor alternative views (see Mathews & Mackintosh, 1998), was there any provision for how such biases can be induced, and whether or how they might influence proneness to anxiety' (Mathews & MacLeod, 2002, p. 349). 'One problem with the original version of this model (Williams, Watts, MacLeod & Mathews, 1988) was that it did not explain the critical role of competition in attentional effects' (Mathews & Mackintosh, 1998, p. 540).

Finally, two critical elements in Andrew's research programme are that he is very rigorous in the details of his methodologies and conduct of his individual studies, and that he requires of himself replication of results before taking them seriously at the theoretical level. His exquisite methodological rigour reduces error variance, resulting in greater ability to detect effects, while his commitment to replication, integrity in his thinking and the careful conduct of experimental protocols guarantee that his results can be trusted.

Epilogue

Andrew's thinking has had a tremendous effect on my own work. His detailed description of anxious process at the microscopic level has richly informed my molar views on worry and GAD. And he reinforces our early behaviour therapy perspective that the very best way to develop increasingly effective modes of intervention resides within the identification of fundamental laws of behaviour. His work has laid the foundation for the creation of types of cognitive therapy that are powerfully focused on the actual processes involved in the development and maintenance of anxiety disorders. If, as I predict, major advances in psychotherapy occur in the future because of his work, it will be the first time that this has happened since the application of classical and operant conditioning principles in the 1960s.

Andrew and I differ in one additional way. He represents the epitome of critical and logical thinking. I, on the other hand, have a tendency to think divergently, a tendency that sometimes leads me to the absurd. For example, in his attempts to isolate the very beginnings of anxious process, he has frequently pointed out the critical role of the construct

'I THINK YOU SHOULD BE MORE EXPLICIT HERE IN STEP TWO.'

Figure b

of the 'self.' Evolutionarily, threat-detection systems maximize survival. For most modern humans, however, it is the psychological survival of the 'self', the maintenance of one's own image of oneself, that is most frequently at stake and the source of anxiety. This suggests to me that the very beginnings of anxious process can be traced back earlier in the sequence, prior to the moment of attention. If the 'self' is the source of anxiety, then reducing or eliminating that 'self' would reduce or eliminate anxiety. As the comedic character, Father Guido Sarducci, suggests, the answer to the ultimate question about life is: 'Don't take life personally.'

Andrew and I have for many years jokingly ridiculed the extreme versions of each other's tendencies, but in fact we have always recognized how complementary we have been to each other. The bonds between us are strong partly because of the joy and importance of play in the work and partly because of the seriousness of our goals in our joint pursuit of knowledge. Our relationship is wonderfully characterized by a cartoon that depicts the essence of Andrew and me (see Figure b).

In every science, at the cutting edge of its knowledge, the next step is always a miracle. Every well-conducted experiment answers some questions and helps to elucidate the miracle but at the same time generates an even larger number of questions that we were not aware of beforehand. As knowledge thus increases linearly, awareness of the unknown increases geometrically. The more we know, the more we know that we don't know. What was previously unknowable becomes the definable unknown to be pursued until it becomes known. Andrew's systematic work has been elucidating miracles. This is why he is one of the leading clinical scientists of his generation. This is why I am so proud of him. This is partly why I am so happy that he is my dear friend.

ACKNOWLEDGMENT

Preparation of this chapter was supported in part by National Institute of Mental Health Research Grant RO1 MH58593. Correspondence can be addressed to T. D. Borkovec, Department of Psychology, The Pennsylvania State University, University Park, PA 16802, USA. Electronic mail may be sent to tdb@psu.edu.

REFERENCES

American Psychiatric Association (1980). *Diagnostic and Statistical Manual, 3rd edn.* Washington, DC: American Psychiatric Association.

Bancroft, J. H. & Mathews, A. (1971). Autonomic correlates of penile erection. *Journal of Psychosomatic Research, 15,* 159–167.

Beck, A. T. & Clark, D. A. (1988). Anxiety and depression: an information-processing perspective. *Anxiety Research, 1,* 23–36.

Beck, A. T., Laude, R. & Bohnert, M. (1974). Ideational components of anxiety neurosis. *Archives of General Psychiatry, 31,* 319–325.

Borkovec, T. D. & Mathews, A. M. (1988). Treatment of non-phobic anxiety disorders: a comparison of nondirective, cognitive, and coping desensitization therapy. *Journal of Consulting and Clinical Psychology, 56,* 877–884.

Borkovec, T. D., Mathews, A., Chambers, A., Ebrahimi, S., Lytle, R. & Nelson, R. (1987). The effects of relaxation plus cognitive therapy and relaxation plus non-directive therapy in the treatment of generalized anxiety and the role of relaxation-induced anxiety. *Journal of Consulting and Clinical Psychology*, *55*, 883–888.

Borkovec, T. D. & Sharpless, B. (in press). Cognitive behavioral therapy for generalized anxiety disorder: living in the present. In S. Hayes, V. Follette & M. Linehan (Eds.), *New Directions in Behavior Therapy*. New York: Guilford.

Borkovec, T. D. & Sides, J. K. (1979). The contribution of relaxation and expectancy to fear reduction via graded, imaginal exposure to feared stimuli. *Behaviour Research and Therapy*, *17*, 529–540.

Bower, G. H. (1981). Mood and memory. *American Psychologist*, *36*, 129–148.

Bradley, B. & Mathews, A. (1988). Memory bias in recovered clinical depressives. *Cognition and Emotion*, *2*, 235–245.

Butler, G. & Mathews, A. (1987). Anticipatory anxiety and risk estimation. *Cognitive Therapy and Research*, *5*, 551–565.

Carney, A., Bancroft, J. & Mathews, A. (1978). Combination of hormonal and psychological treatment for female sexual unresponsiveness: a comparative study. *British Journal of Psychiatry*, *133*, 339–346.

Chambless, D. L. & Ollendick, T. H. (2001). Empirically supported psychological interventions: controversies and evidence. *Annual Review of Psychology*, *52*, 685–716.

Cobb, J. P., Mathews, A., Childs-Clarke, A. & Blowers, C. M. (1984). The spouse as co-therapist in the treatment of agoraphobia. *British Journal of Psychiatry*, *144*, 282–287.

Connell, P. H., Corbett, J. A., Horne, D. J. & Mathews, A. (1967). Drug treatment of adolescent ticquers. A double-blind trial of Diazepam and Maloperidol. *British Journal of Psychiatry*, *113*, 375–381.

Corbett, J. A., Mathews, A., Connell, P. H. & Shapiro, D. A. (1969). Tics and Gilles de la Tourette's syndrome: a follow-up study and critical review. *British Journal of Psychiatry*, *115*, 1229–1241.

Dalgleish, T., Mathews, A. & Wood, J. (1999). Inhibition processes in cognition and emotion: a special case. In T. Dalgleish & M. Power (Eds.), *Handbook of Cognition and Emotion*, 243–266. Chichester: Wiley.

Eysenck, M. W. (1982). *Attention and Arousal: Cognition and Performance*. Berlin: Springer.

Fox, E. (1994). Attentional bias in anxiety: a defective inhibition hypothesis. *Cognition and Emotion*, *8*, 165–195.

Foa, E. B. & Kozak, M. J. (1986). Emotional processing of fear: exposure to corrective information. *Psychological Bulletin*, *99*, 20–35.

Johnston, D. W., Lancashire, M., Mathews, A., Munby, M., Shaw, P. M. & Gelder, M. G. (1976). Imaginal flooding and exposure to real phobic situations: changes during treatment. *British Journal of Psychiatry*, *129*, 372–377.

Lader, M. H. & Mathews, A. (1968). A physiological model of phobic anxiety and desensitisation. *Behaviour Research and Therapy*, *6*, 411–421.

Lader, M. H. & Mathews, A. (1970a). Physiological changes during spontaneous panic attacks. *Journal of Psychosomatic Research*, *14*, 377–382.

Lader, M. H. & Mathews, A. (1970b). Comparisons of methods of relaxation using physiological measures. *Behaviour Research and Therapy*, *8*, 331–337.

Lader, M. & Mathews, A. (1971). Electromyographic studies of tension. *Journal of Psychosomatic Research*, *15*, 479–486.

Mackintosh, B. & Mathews, A. (2003). Don't look now: attentional avoidance of emotionally-valenced cues. *Cognition and Emotion*, *17*, 623–646.

MacLeod, C., Mathews, A. & Tata, C. (1986). Attentional bias in emotional disorders. *Journal of Abnormal Psychology*, *95*, 15–20.

Martin, P. & Mathews, A. (1978). Tension headaches: psychophysiological investigation and treatment. *Journal of Psychosomatic Research*, *22*, 389–399.

Mathews, A. (1971). Psychophysiological approaches to the investigation of desensitisation and related procedures. *Psychological Bulletin*, *76*, 73–91.

Mathews, A. (1977a). Recent developments in the treatment of agoraphobia. *Behavioural Analysis and Modification*, *2*, 64–75.

Mathews, A. (1977b). Behavioural treatment of agoraphobia; new findings, new problems. In: J. C. Boulougouris and A. D. Rabavilas (Eds.), *The Treatment of Phobic and Obsessive Compulsive Disorders*. Oxford: Pergamon.

Mathews, A. (1982). Treatment of female sexual dysfunction. In J. Boulougouris (Ed.), *Learning Theory Approaches to Psychiatry*. Chichester: Wiley.

Mathews, A. (1983). Progress in the treatment of female sexual dysfunction. *Journal of Psychosomatic Research*, *27*, 165–173.

Mathews, A. (1984). Anxiety and its management. In Gaind, Fawzy, Hudson & Pasnau (Eds.), *Current Themes in Psychiatry, vol. III*. New York: SP Publications.

Mathews, A. (1990). Why worry? The cognitive function of anxiety. *Behaviour Research and Therapy*, *28*, 455–468.

Mathews, A., Bancroft, J. H. J. & Slater, P. (1972). The principal components of sexual preference. *British Journal of Social Clinical Psychology*, *11*, 35–43.

Mathews, A., Bancroft, J. H. J., Whitehead, A., Hackmann, A., Julier, D., Bancroft, J., Gath, D. & Shaw, P. M. (1976). The behavioural treatment of sexual inadequacy: a comparative study. *Behaviour Research and Therapy*, *14*, 427–436.

Mathews, A. & Gelder, M. G. (1969). Psychophysiological investigations of brief relaxation training. *Journal of Psychosomatic Research*, *13*, 1–12.

Mathews, A., Gelder, M. G. & Johnston, D. W. (1981). *Agoraphobia: Nature and Treatment*. New York: Guilford and London: Tavistock.

Mathews, A., Johnston, D. W., Lancashire, M., Munby, M., Shaw, P. M. & Gelder, M. G. (1976). Imaginal flooding and exposure to real phobic situations: treatment outcome with agoraphobic patients. *British Journal of Psychiatry*, *129*, 362–371.

Mathews, A. & Lader, M. H. (1971). An evaluation of forearm blood flow as a psychophysiological measure. *Psychophysiology*, *8*, 509–524.

Mathews, A. & Mackintosh, B. (1998). A cognitive model of selective processing in anxiety. *Cognitive Therapy and Research*, *22*, 539–560.

Mathews, A. & MacLeod, C. (1985). Selective processing of threat cues in anxiety states. *Behaviour Research and Therapy*, *5*, 563–569.

Mathews, A. & MacLeod, C. (1986). Discrimination of threat cues without awareness in anxiety states. *Journal of Abnormal Psychology*, *95*, 131–138.

Mathews A. & MacLeod, C. (2002). Induced processing biases have causal effects on anxiety. *Cognition and Emotion*, *16*, 310–315.

Mathews, A., Mogg, K., Kentish, J. & Eysenck, M. (1995). Effect of psychological treatment on cognitive bias in generalized anxiety disorder. *Behaviour Research and Therapy*, *33*, 293–303.

Mathews, A. & Rezin, V. (1977). Treatment of dental fears by imaginal flooding and rehearsal of coping behaviour. *Behaviour Research and Therapy*, *15*, 321–328.

Mathews, A. & Ridgeway, V. (1981). Personality and recovery from surgery. *British Journal of Clinical Psychology*, *20*, 243–260.

Mathews, A. & Ridgeway, V. (1984). Psychological preparation for surgery. In A. Steptoe and A. M. Mathews (Eds.), *Health Care and Human Behaviour*. London: Academic Press.

Mathews, A., Ridgeway, V. & Williamson, D. (1996). Evidence for attention to threatening stimuli in depression. *Behaviour Research and Therapy*, *34*, 695–705.

Mathews, A. & Shaw, P. M. (1973). Emotional arousal and persuasion effects in flooding. *Behaviour Research and Therapy*, *11*, 587–598.

Mathews, A. & Shaw, P. M. (1977). Cognitions related to anxiety: a pilot study of treatment. *Behaviour Research and Therapy*, *15*, 503–505.

Mathews, A. & Steptoe, A. (Eds.) (1982). *Behavioural Medicine*. British Psychological Society.

Mathews, A. & Steptoe, A. (1988). *Essentials of Psychology for Medical Practice*. London: Churchill Livingston.

Mathews, A., Teasdale, J., Munby, M., Johnston, D. W. & Shaw, P. M. (1977). A home-based treatment programme for agoraphobia. *Behavior Therapy*, *8*, 915–924.

Mathews, A., Whitehead, A. & Kellett, J. (1983). Psychological and hormonal factors in the treatment of female sexual dysfunction. *Psychological Medicine*, *13*, 83–92.

Mathews, A., Yiend, J. & Lawrence, A. D. (in press). Individual differences in the modulation of fear-related brain activation by attentional control. *Journal of Cognitive Neuroscience*.

Mowrer, O. H. (1947). On the dual nature of learning: a re-interpretation of 'conditioning' and 'problem-solving'. *Harvard Educational Review*, *17*, 102–148.

Öhman, A. (1993). Fear and anxiety as emotional phenomena. In M. Lewis & J. Haviland (Eds.), *Handbook of Emotions*, 511–536. New York: Guilford.

Platt, J. R. (1964). Strong inference. *Science*, *146*, 347–353.

Ridgeway, V. & Mathews, A. (1982). Psychological preparation for surgery: a comparison of methods. *British Journal of Clinical Psychology*, *21*, 271–280.

Scott, D. F., Moffett, A., Mathews, A. & Ettlinger, G. (1967). The effect of epileptic discharge on learning and memory in patients. *Epilepsia*, *8*, 188–194.

Steptoe, A. & Mathews, A. (Eds.) (1984). *Health Care and Human Behaviour*. London: Academic Press.

Teasdale, J., Walsh, P. A., Lancashire, M. & Mathews, A. (1977). Group exposure for agoraphobics: a replication study. *British Journal of Psychiatry*, *130*, 186–193.

Wells, A. & Mathews, G. (1994). *Attention and Emotion: A Clinical Perspective.* Hove: Erlbaum.

Whitehead, A. & Mathews, A. (1977). Attitude change during behavioural treatment of sexual inadequacy. *British Journal of Social Clinical Psychology, 16,* 275–281.

Whitehead, A. & Mathews, A. (1986). Factors related to successful outcome in treatment of sexually unresponsive women. *Psychological Medicine, 16,* 373–378.

Williams, J. M., Watts, F. N., MacLeod, C. & Mathews, A. (1988). *Cognitive Psychology and Emotional Disorders.* Chichester: Wiley.

Yiend, J. & Mathews, A. (2001). Anxiety and attention to threatening pictures. *Quarterly Journal of Experimental Psychology, 54,* 665–681.

Yiend, J. & Mathews, A. (2002). Induced biases in the processing of emotional information. In S. P. Shohov (Ed.), *Advances in Psychology Research,* vol. 13, 43–68. New York: Nova Science Publishers, Inc.

Part I

Theoretical approaches

1 The positive and negative consequences of worry in the aetiology of generalized anxiety disorder: a learning theory perspective

Susan Mineka

Two very important lines of work in the past twenty years have contributed substantially to our understanding of many factors involved in the aetiology and maintenance of generalized anxiety disorder (GAD). One of these lines of work was initiated by the pioneering studies of Andrew Mathews, Colin MacLeod and their colleagues in the mid-1980s on individuals with GAD. In numerous studies, such individuals have demonstrated prominent automatic attentional biases for threatening information, and interpretive biases for ambiguous information that could be threatening or non-threatening (see Mathews & MacLeod, 1994; Mineka, Rafaeli & Yovel, 2003; Williams et al., 1997). It is now known that such biases seem to serve as vulnerability factors for anxiety during periods of stress and to serve a likely role in the maintenance of anxiety once it has developed (e.g. MacLeod et al., this volume; Mathews & MacLeod, 2002).

The other line of work contributing substantially to our understanding of GAD was that initiated by Borkovec and his colleagues in the mid-1980s on the nature, functions and consequences of the worry process, which is seen as so central to current formulations of GAD. Worry is often considered to be the primary cognitive component of anxiety and Borkovec's work has focused on understanding why worry is so excessive and persistent in individuals with GAD. Mathews (1990) published an important and widely cited paper linking these two lines of research by arguing that worry functions to maintain hypervigilance to threatening cues. Borkovec and colleagues (Borkovec, Alcaine & Behar, in press) have also linked these two lines of work by noting that the attentional and interpretive biases for threatening information that are shown by generally anxious individuals seem to provide further sources of input or triggers for the worry process.

The current chapter addresses what two former students (Iftah Yovel and Suzanne Pineles) and I consider to be a theoretical paradox that seems to characterize research findings on the nature and consequences of worry (Mineka, Yovel & Pineles, 2002). In our view, this theoretical paradox has not yet been clearly recognized in the literature, and has certainly not yet been satisfactorily resolved. Briefly, as we shall see, the worry process seems to have both positive and negative consequences. In light of the negative consequences, why does worry persist and become so excessive and uncontrollable for those who develop the pathological worry characteristic of GAD? We hope that by highlighting the major features of this paradox, and then suggesting a possible theoretical mechanism to help resolve it, we can further our understanding of the aetiology and maintenance of pathological worry in GAD (Mineka et al., 2002). We also attempt to integrate these ideas with research on cognitive biases associated with generalized anxiety.

Prominent characteristics of generalized anxiety disorder

According to DSM-IV (Diagnostic and Statistical Manual of Mental Disorders, Fourth Edition, 1994), the central feature of GAD is excessive anxiety and worry about a number of events and activities (such as health, work, interpersonal relationships). The worry and anxiety must occur on more days than not for at least six months, and the individual must find it difficult to control the worry. In addition, three or more out of six other symptoms of tension, irritability, difficulty concentrating, etc. must also be present. People with GAD are not, however, characterized by excessive autonomic arousal symptoms, as was once thought; rather, they show significant autonomic inflexibility (associated with reduced vagal tone) and sometimes suppression of autonomic reactivity (e.g. Brown et al., 1998; Thayer et al., 1996).

From the standpoint of structural models of emotions and emotional disorders, individuals with both GAD and major depressive disorder are characterized by high levels of negative affect – a broad basic dimension of affect, including a variety of negative mood states, such as fear, sadness, anger. Individuals with major depressive disorder differ from those with GAD primarily in terms of their levels of positive affect – the second basic dimension of affect, including the experience of positive feelings, such as joy, enthusiasm and energy. Positive affect is unrelated to GAD but is negatively correlated with major depressive disorder, that is, depressed individuals usually have low levels of positive affect and anhedonic symptoms (Brown et al., 1998; Clark & Watson, 1991).

Neuroticism or negative affectivity is a broad personality trait that makes people prone to high levels of negative affect. People with high levels of neuroticism (referred to here as N) are known to be at increased risk for developing a variety of anxiety and mood disorders (e.g. Clark et al., 1994; Hayward et al., 2000). But clearly not everyone with high levels of N develops one or more of these emotional disorders. So what are the psychological processes that make certain people with high N develop any specific one (or more) of these disorders?

The present chapter will address why only a subset of individuals with high N develop the *uncontrollable worry* which is thought to be so central to GAD (Mineka et al., 2002). Most people with high N probably worry to some degree, but what leads some people to develop such excessive worry that it comes to be perceived as uncontrollable? People also tend to find worry to be an unpleasant activity (Borkovec et al., in press) so why should it be so difficult for some people to control it? As we will see, the answer may well be related to findings by Borkovec and others indicating that worry produces some beneficial effects. However, worry also has negative consequences and, if so, why shouldn't the negative consequences help to extinguish the worry process, or at least keep it in check rather than letting it become excessive (see Mineka et al., 2002)? Before turning our attention to a potential mechanism for uncontrollable worry, we must first review a few highlights of the two lines of research mentioned at the outset on cognitive biases for threat and on the functions of worry.

Mood-congruent biases for threat in generalized anxiety

In the past twenty to twenty-five years, interest in how our moods and emotions, such as anxiety and depression (as well as personality traits associated with them), affect the processing of emotional information has expanded tremendously. For GAD, the most widely studied bias involves a tendency to have one's attention directed toward threatening information in the environment (verbal or pictorial) when a mixture of threatening and non-threatening information is available; non-anxious individuals, if anything, show the opposite kind of bias (Mathews & MacLeod, 1994; Williams et al., 1997). A number of these studies have indicated that these biases seem to occur automatically or preconsciously, that is, without the subject's conscious awareness (e.g. Mogg, Bradley et al., 1993). Several studies have also shown that individuals who are simply high in trait anxiety (without full-blown GAD) also exhibit these preconscious attentional biases – especially when under stress (e.g. Mathews & MacLeod, 2002; Mineka et al., 2003).

Attentional biases for threatening material are believed to be important because they may serve as vulnerability factors for anxiety disorders, and they may also play a role in maintenance of anxiety (see Mathews & MacLeod, 2002). For example, if someone is already anxious and his or her attention is automatically drawn towards threatening information, this should serve to maintain or even exacerbate his or her level of anxiety. Moreover, exciting new evidence shows that attentional biases play a causal role in increased anxiety in response to stress. In an elegant series of studies, MacLeod and colleagues showed that with extensive training unselected students show an induced attentional bias towards threat, which increases their vulnerability to state anxiety in response to a stress task. Moreover, high trait anxious subjects who were trained extensively to attend away from threat showed a substantial drop in trait anxiety. (See MacLeod et al., this volume for more details.)

Three other studies also suggest that naturally occurring attentional biases for threat serve as risk factors for the development of anxiety in response to naturalistic stressors. In each of these studies, a group of individuals facing a potentially stressful situation were given a subliminal emotional Stroop task to assess their attentional bias towards threat. In each study, individuals who showed subliminal threat interference were more likely to show high levels of emotional distress in response to the stressful situation (e.g. MacLeod & Hagan, 1992; MacLeod, 1999; Pury, 2002). These results are particularly striking given that they occurred in very different samples experiencing very different stressors.

Individuals with generalized anxiety, relative to controls, also show an interpretive bias for ambiguous information that has both a threatening and a non-threatening meaning. Generally anxious and high trait anxious individuals tend to interpret such ambiguous information as having the threatening meaning, relative to controls. As with attentional biases, these interpretive biases are thought to play a role in maintaining or exacerbating anxiety. Moreover, exciting new evidence shows they may play an aetiological role as well (e.g. Mathews & MacLeod, 2002; see also MacLeod et al., this volume).

The perceived benefits and positive functions of worry

Borkovec and colleagues developed another independent line of research on the benefits and functions of worry, and this has also led to important insights into both the nature of the worry process itself and why it is so persistent. When integrated together, these two lines of research by Borkovec and colleagues, and by Mathews, MacLeod and colleagues, begin to help us build a model of how worry can become excessive and uncontrollable in certain individuals high in neuroticism and trait anxiety who go on to develop GAD.

Before examining what positive functions worry may actually serve, it is interesting to consider what people simply think the benefits of worry

are. Several investigators have asked people with GAD what they believed were the most common benefits of worrying. The five most commonly listed benefits were:
1. Superstitious avoidance of catastrophe;
2. Actual avoidance of catastrophe by generating ways to prevent it;
3. Avoidance of deeper emotional topics by distraction from them;
4. Coping and preparation for a negative event, and
5. Motivating device to accomplish what needs to be done (Borkovec, 1994; see also Wells, 1999).

For the most part, non-anxious controls also believe worry serves the same functions (e.g. Dugas et al., 1998). Although the actual functions of worry are somewhat different than these, simply expecting or believing worry serves these functions may help explain why it becomes a favoured strategy of coping for some people.

But what are the actual functions that the worry process serves, and how might these help further explain why worry becomes such a self-sustaining process? First, Borkovec and colleagues (in press) believe worry serves as a coping response which suppresses physiological and emotional responses that would ordinarily be aroused by the perception of threat. For example, when someone verbally articulates (or worries about) threatening material, they show very little cardiovascular reactivity compared to when they imagine the same threat material (Borkovec & Hu, 1990; Vrana et al., 1986). Moreover, the somatic arousal which occurs in other anxiety disorders, even during a resting baseline, is not present with chronic worry, which is instead associated with reduced autonomic flexibility that indicates either sympathetic inhibition or deficient parasympathetic tone (e.g. Hoehn-Saric et al., 1989; Thayer et al., 1996).

Borkovec has further argued that this decreased sympathetic activation during worry serves to negatively reinforce (and therefore increases the probability of) the worry process. Moreover, because the suppression of somatic arousal is associated with a person not fully processing or experiencing the topic that is being worried about, the anxiety associated with that topic will not extinguish as it would if full emotional processing were allowed (Borkovec et al., in press; Foa & Kozak, 1986). The threatening meaning of the topic is therefore maintained. These features of the worry process have led Borkovec and colleagues to propose that worry serves as a *cognitive avoidance response* which is repeatedly negatively reinforced because of the reduction of psychological and physiological emotional responses that occurs during and following worry. These individuals often cannot use more typical overt behavioural avoidance responses (although they do use some subtle ones) because the threats they worry about are often rather remote and distal.

Finally, Borkovec and colleagues proposed that the worry process is also superstitiously reinforced because the vast majority of things people worry about never actually happen (or if they do, they are usually far less catastrophic than anticipated). For example, in one study both individuals with GAD and non-anxious controls were asked to keep diaries of the topics they worried about for two weeks, and also to record whether or not these things actually happened. Results indicated that for those with GAD, 85 per cent of the topics they worried about turned out better than expected (70 per cent for non-anxious controls) (Borkovec et al., 1999). Thus, whether or not worry actually does prevent bad outcomes, it is clearly superstitiously negatively reinforced as if it does prevent them the vast majority of the time.

Important characteristics of cognitive and behavioural avoidance responses

To date, very little is known about important characteristics of cognitive avoidance responses, but there is a large literature on behavioural avoidance learning in animals, some of which has been replicated with humans (e.g. Mineka, 1979; Seligman & Johnston, 1973). It is tempting, therefore, to consider that some of the important characteristics of behavioural avoidance responses might also apply to cognitive avoidance responses. One well-studied and important characteristic of avoidance learning is that once learned, such responses are often very resistant to extinction. To understand this phenemenon, it is important to consider the hypothesized mechanisms that motivate and reinforce behavioural avoidance responses.

Early on in a typical experiment on avoidance learning, human or non-human animals are presented with a discriminative stimulus (S^D) (that will later set the occasion for avoidance responding) that is followed some seconds later by an aversive stimulus, like a loud noise or an electric shock; this sets the stage for classical conditioning of fear to the S^D. The experimental contingencies are arranged such that if the animal makes a designated response (R) after the shock begins, it will be able to escape it (escape learning) and turn off the S^D, which terminates the conditioned fear. (See Figure 1.1. – Early.) As more fear gets conditioned to the S^D on subsequent escape trials, the fear comes to motivate the animal to respond to the S^D alone (before the shock begins); this first avoidance response is reinforced by termination of the fear induced by the S^D (as well as by avoidance of the shock). Thus, a well-trained animal rarely, if ever, receives the shock any longer because it is successfully avoided by responding soon after the onset of the S^D. This seems to parallel what is

I. Avoidance learning

(1) Early learning

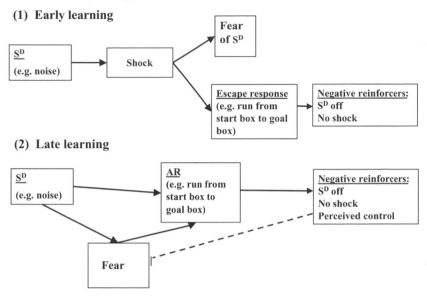

(2) Late learning

Figure 1.1 Early and late phases of avoidance learning. Note: solid line with an arrow indicates one box leads to (or increases the likelihood of) the other. Dashed line with a bar indicates one box inhibits (or decreases the likelihood of) the other.

thought to happen with non-pathological worry, where the person often begins to worry (the avoidance response) whenever a potentially threatening situation (no matter how remote) arises (referred to here as the trigger topic).[1] Many believe worrying helps them to cope, and the process is reinforced by reduction in the emotional and somatic arousal that occurs. In addition, because the catastrophic outcome rarely occurs (just as the aversive stimulus does not occur in animals), the worry response is reinforced by the non-occurrence of bad outcomes.

Another important characteristic of behavioural avoidance responses (ARs) is that as they become well learned, a sense of control over the situation develops and this sense of control is associated with an attenuation of fear of the S^D (although fear is not eliminated; Cook et al., 1987; Mineka & Kelly, 1989). (Figure 1.1. – Late.) This increased sense of control may be one of the negative reinforcers of well-learned ARs. By analogy, individuals who worry occasionally and experience the forms of negative reinforcement noted above may well develop a sense of perceived control over the situation about which they are worrying. Having a sense of perceived control reduces anxiety (see Mineka & Kelly, 1989; Mineka & Zinbarg, 1996).

Once well learned, ARs are usually highly resistant to extinction once the aversive stimulus is turned off by the experimenter, so that the animal no longer needs to respond to avoid it. When this happens, animals typically respond for prolonged periods of time even though responding is no longer necessary to avoid the shock, presumably because the AR continues to be reinforced by fear reduction (and by the non-occurrence of the aversive stimulus and the sense of perceived control associated with the AR; see Mineka, 1979; Cook et al., 1987). If similar effects occur with human cognitive avoidance responses such as worry, one might also expect them to be very resistant to extinction even in the face of non-occurrence of catastrophic outcomes. This is, of course, consistent with the persistent nature of worry in some individuals (e.g. Borkovec et al., in press).

Summarizing so far, for many non-pathological worriers, worry (at least in part) seems to serve as a cognitive avoidance response that may be negatively reinforced in at least the four ways enumerated above, each of which have important parallels to those seen with well-learned ARs in animals (Figure 1.1. – Late and the four bolded boxes of Figure 1.3). We believe these interrelationships also apply to those with *pathological worry* who often qualify for a diagnosis of GAD but that *additional processes are crucial in determining which individuals with non-pathological worry go on to develop GAD.*

For example, we do not believe that these sources of negative re-inforcement for worry can explain why worry comes to be perceived as an *uncontrollable* activity for those individuals with a diagnosis of GAD (Mineka et al., 2002). This is in contrast to a proposal by Wells and Butler (1997) that 'the immediate anxiety-reducing or anxiety-controlling properties of worry will lead to a loss of control of the activity as it is reinforced' (p. 163). This latter proposal is not compelling when one considers what happens to other human (or animal) activities that are reinforced by negative or positive reinforcement. Indeed, the only kinds of reinforced activities that people and animals sometimes do lose control over are those seen with addictive substances (Mineka et al., 2002). For example, taking the trash out regularly to avoid rotten smells does not make one become a compulsive cleaner, and being praised or paid for a job well done does not make one become a workaholic. Moreover, it seems even less likely that loss of control over positively or negatively reinforced activities would occur when the nature of the activity itself is generally considered to be somewhat unpleasant to begin with, as is the case with worry (e.g. Borkovec et al., in press).

We believe that we must next consider some of the negative consequences of worry to understand why individuals who develop pathological worry as seen in GAD feel that they have lost control over their worrying (Mineka et al., 2002).

The negative consequences of worry

Several lines of research on worry reveal that it can also have negative consequences. For example, Wells (1999) noted that worry may lead to a greater sense of anxiety and danger because the person who is worrying is generating a variety of possible catastrophic outcomes (many of which may not have been present before worrying began), and these in turn may serve as further trigger topics for more worry. In addition, people who worry about some situation, relative to those who do not worry, later tend to have more intrusive thoughts about that situation. For example, several studies found that normal participants had more negative intrusive thoughts following a short period of induced worry than following a control period (e.g. Borkovec et al., 1983; York, Borkovec et al., 1987).[2]

In a somewhat more clinically relevant example, Wells and Papageorgiou (1995) had several groups of students watch an eight-minute gruesome film about a workshop accident. Two groups were then told to worry for four minutes (either about the film itself, or about their usual worries), and another group was told to relax for four minutes. Then all three groups were asked to keep a diary for three days, in which they recorded the occurrence of intrusive images about the film. Results indicated that the two worry groups had more intrusive thoughts about the film over the next three days than did the relaxation group. Thus, worrying for a brief period following a gruesome film clip increased the number of intrusive thoughts over a period of three days (see also Butler et al., 1995). Such studies led Wells and Butler (1997) to suggest that 'individuals who are prone to worry, in particular those that use worry as a coping strategy, perhaps to avoid images, are likely to engage in an activity that pollutes the stream of consciousness with an increasing frequency of intrusive thoughts' (p. 165). These intrusive thoughts may serve as trigger topics for further worries and for increasing anxiety more generally.

If one conceptualizes worry as a cognitive avoidance response that is negatively reinforced in several ways, then the two negative consequences of worry considered here might be conceptualized as serving as *punishments* for worrying. These punishing consequences of worry should also be considered in light of the fact that the worry process itself is considered negative in nature. If worry is an unpleasant activity that can lead to generating more catastrophic outcomes and to further worry and intrusive thoughts, it becomes more difficult to understand why worry is so persistent in spite of some of its negatively reinforcing consequences.

However, before considering this theoretical paradox, it is important to consider an additional negative and punishing consequence of worry that may sometimes occur if a person attempts to control or suppress his or her worrying. Evidence for this additional negative consequence should be considered tentative because there are somewhat mixed results in the literature (e.g. see Abramowitz et al., 2001; Purdon, 1999, for reviews that come to rather different conclusions). Research on mental control has shown that people asked to suppress a particular (neutral) thought (e.g. white bears) may actually show an increase in thinking about that topic when the suppression period is over and they are asked to think about anything (e.g. Wegner, 1994). There have been many replications of this basic *rebound* effect (although not all studies obtain the effect) and its implications for understanding GAD and OCD (obsessive-compulsive disorder) have begun to be explored by examining the effects of trying to control one's emotional thoughts, worries or obsessions rather than simply neutral topics like white bears. Wells and Butler (1997; Wells, 1999) summarized research showing that when people attempt to control their thoughts and their worry, pernicious effects may occur, in which they experience increased intrusive thoughts and a perception that they are unable to control them.

Indeed, a recent meta-analysis (Abramowitz et al., 2001) reviewed the results of twenty-eight such studies on thought suppression and found that the average effect size was .30 (small to moderate) for a rebound effect following a thought suppression period. Interestingly, the effect size was significantly larger when the suppressed thought was nondiscrete (e.g. a story) than when it was discrete (e.g. a white bear); worries are clearly not usually discrete. However, there were no significant effects suggesting that the valence or personal relevance of the suppressed thoughts influenced the magnitude of rebound effects. Moreover, there was no suggestion that distressed groups of subjects (such as those with several anxiety and mood disorders) showed larger or smaller rebound effects. Thus, it seems quite likely that individuals with GAD will show such rebound effects, although of course the findings need to be replicated in such a sample to be sure.

Summarizing the negative consequences of worry, we have reviewed evidence that:

1. Worry is not only an unpleasant linguistic activity but also one that generates a variety of possible catastrophic outcomes;
2. Worry can lead to more worry and intrusive thoughts, and

3. Attempts to suppress negative intrusive thoughts and worry may be relatively ineffective (relative to suppressing neutral thoughts; Mathews & Milroy, 1994). Moreover, attempts at suppression often lead to an increase in those thoughts, and perhaps to increased depressed or anxious mood, relative to what would occur if those thoughts and worries were not suppressed in the first place. It is important to note that chronic worriers may not actually be aware of these contingencies between their worrying and any negative consequences, just as they also may not be aware of the positive (i.e. negatively reinforcing) functions of worry.

If we conceptualize each of these negative consequences of worry as possibly serving as punishments for the worry process, we are left with a situation in which worry is both negatively reinforced because of the positive functions it serves, but also punished because of the negative consequences of worry. Negatively reinforced responses generally are strengthened, but punished responses very often extinguish. Thus, worry as an attempted coping response might be expected to diminish, rather than to persist and come to be perceived as uncontrollable.

The effects of punishing avoidance responses

Study of punishment has largely focused on punishment of positively reinforced behavioural responses in both animals and humans (especially children). For years, it has been known that punishment can be highly effective in eliminating such responses if parameters of the punishment include the following (among others):
1. It is delivered immediately.
2. It is fairly intense from the outset.
3. A rewarded alternative response is available (e.g. Church, 1969; Walters & Grusec, 1977).

However, in the case of worry as a cognitive avoidance response, the punishing consequences of worry are presumably operating on negatively reinforced responses rather than positively reinforced ones. It is well known in the learning literature that punishment of avoidance responses is often (although not always) highly *ineffective* in helping to extinguish avoidance responses, instead often leading to paradoxical *increases* in avoidance responding that may persist for very prolonged periods of time (e.g. Brown, 1969; Mackintosh, 1974). These effects have been observed in rats, monkeys and humans. (See Dean & Pittman, 1991, for a more recent review.)

As noted earlier, during avoidance learning, animals learn to make an avoidance response (AR) when the S^D is presented. The AR is thought to be motivated by the fear of the S^D conditioned during escape trials, and reinforced, in part, by termination of the S^D. (See Figure 1.1 – Late.) Well-learned ARs can be extraordinarily resistant to extinction, continuing for prolonged periods with no aversive stimuli occurring (Solomon et al., 1953). In essence, from a cognitive perspective, the animal never waits around long enough to discover that the avoidance response is no longer required (Seligman & Johnston, 1973).

At least half a century ago, researchers interested in avoidance learning (which was thought to resemble neurotic behaviour) began to explore ways to eliminate these persistent avoidance responses (and, by analogy, neurotic behaviour). Because punishment was known to extinguish positively reinforced responses, researchers tried punishing animals for making the ARs. Specifically, rather than negatively reinforcing the AR by non-occurrence of the aversive stimulus, any AR made was now actively punished with a brief shock. Dozens of experiments using a variety of paradigms and several species found the opposite of what had originally been anticipated.[3] That is, animals showed paradoxical increases rather than decreases in avoidance responding, a phenomenon often called *vicious circle behaviour* (or sometimes, self-punitive behaviour). Probably the most influential theoretical explanation of this phenomenon proposes that when a punishing shock occurs two important things happen:

1. The punishing shock reinstates fear of the S^D and the context (which has diminished substantially as the response becomes well learned).
2. Because in the past the S^D was eliminated and fear was reduced when the AR was made, the same response is now made again in order to reduce the newly reinstated fear of the S^D (see Figure 1.2).

A vicious circle then develops, in which each AR leads to another brief shock, continuing to reinstate fear of the S^D, which in turn motivates further ARs that had been negatively reinforced during acquisition.

Several other important aspects of this vicious circle behaviour are important to note. First, punishment does not need to occur on every trial – indeed, the tendency for vicious circle behaviour to occur *increases* when the punishing stimulus is delivered only occasionally, rather than every time the AR is made; this may happen in part because the AR–punishment contingency is less obvious with intermittent punishment. Second, the punishing stimulus need not be of the same modality as the original aversive stimulus. So, for example, loud noise as a punishing stimulus can be as effective at increasing avoidance responding to avoid shock as is shock itself, and vice versa (e.g. Melvin & Martin, 1966). Third, the 'punishing stimulus' need not be delivered contingent on the occurrence of the AR. Rather, occasional random delivery of an aversive stimulus can also support vicious circle behaviour (see Mackintosh, 1974,

II. Paradoxical effects of punishment on extinction of avoidance learning

(1) With an AR:

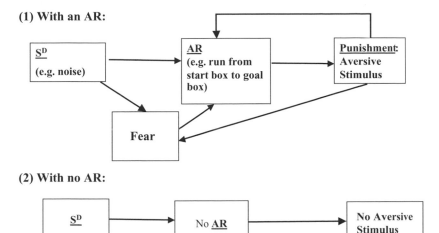

(2) With no AR:

Figure 1.2 Paradoxical effect of punishment on extinction of avoidance learning: sequence of events when an AR is made and when no AR is made.

for a review). Finally, vicious circle behaviour is most likely to develop when the punishing stimulus can be escaped from by making the AR.

So why does worry persist if it is both punished and reinforced? A possible resolution of this apparent paradox

How does understanding the effects of punishment of avoidance responses help illuminate the persistent and uncontrollable quality of worry in GAD? As noted earlier, the worry response as a cognitive AR is, in part, negatively reinforced (and therefore strengthened), but it also often leads to negative consequences, which could be considered as punishments. Thus, given consideration of the punishment of avoidance learning literature, one might expect the worry response to be further strengthened rather than weakened or eliminated.

III. Pathological worry in GAD

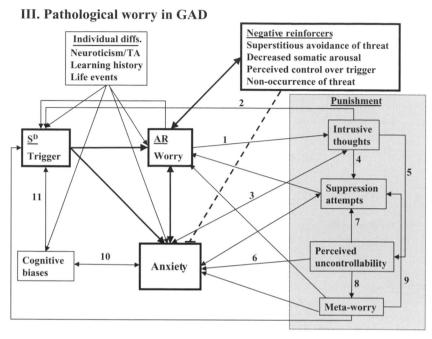

Figure 1.3 The psychological processes that underlie pathological worry in GAD.

Let us now spell out this analogy in more detail. As illustrated in Figure 1.3, sometimes worry as a cognitive avoidance response leads to more worry and intrusive thoughts (arrow 1), which in turn can lead to the generation of more trigger topics (arrow 2). Worry is negatively reinforced because of decreased somatic arousal, superstitious avoidance of threat etc. But, as described above, the increased worry and intrusive thoughts may also serve as sources of punishment (contingent or non-contingent) for the worry process (although the worrier may not be aware of this). As seen in avoidance learning, punishment serves to reinstate anxiety (arrow 3 from intrusive thoughts to anxiety), and worry through a positive feedback process. Because these punishing effects do not always occur, and because these punishing effects can be escaped from temporarily by further worry, the positive feedback process may be greater, such as occurs when punishing ARs in animals (see Mackintosh, 1974).

The occurrence of intrusive thoughts and more worry following a particular worry episode may also lead to attempts to suppress these thoughts (arrow 4) and begin to lead to a sense of uncontrollability over the worry process (arrow 5); perceived uncontrollability is a necessary criterion for

GAD. As noted earlier, both animal and human research has demonstrated that uncontrollable aversive events lead to a greater sense of anxiety than do comparable aversive events that are controllable (e.g. see Mineka & Kelly, 1989; Mineka & Zinbarg, 1996). Thus, perceived uncontrollability over the worry process would also be expected to lead to more anxiety (arrow 6) and worry.

The development of perceived uncontrollability over worry may also have two further consequences. First, perceived uncontrollability may sometimes lead to an attempt to control or suppress further worrying (arrow 7). As reviewed above, evidence from a recent meta-analysis shows that attempting to suppress non-discrete thoughts may lead to an increase in those thoughts later. Second, perceived uncontrollability may also lead to what Wells and Butler have termed meta-worry (worry about worry) (arrow 8). Meta-worry is thought to develop because of the human tendency to evaluate and appraise topics of personal concern (e.g. Wells & Butler, 1997). In other words, if worry is experienced as leading to intrusive thoughts and perceived uncontrollability, individuals may begin to worry (and become more generally anxious) about feeling they are losing control over certain aspects of their mind and develop fears of having a mental breakdown (cf. Wells & Carter, 1999). The self-reported tendency to engage in meta-worry does indeed discriminate people who are non-clinical worriers from those with GAD (see Wells, 1999). Wells has also suggested that those who develop meta-worry may try especially hard to suppress this worry so they can regain a sense of perceived control (arrow 9), but attempts to suppress worry may have paradoxical effects.

The increased anxiety and worry that may occur because of the punishing quality of the intrusive thoughts, the perceived uncontrollability over worry, and the meta-worry that may develop are also associated with the cognitive biases for threatening material (arrow 10) discussed earlier. Specifically, increased state anxiety occurring this way in trait anxious individuals may potentiate their attentional bias for threatening cues in the environment (MacLeod & Mathews, 1988). Further attention towards threat, in combination with the tendency of anxious people to interpret ambiguous information in a threatening manner, serves to provide yet further trigger topics for worry and anxiety (arrow 11).

Individual differences in the tendency to get into this vicious circle

Finally, why do only some individuals who worry get into the vicious circles described above? Several personality and experiential variables probably influence substantially which individuals develop the pathological uncontrollable worry seen in GAD. For example, people who have high levels of neuroticism and trait anxiety (a facet of neuroticism) are by definition inherently more prone to becoming anxious and worrying. Moreover, trait anxiety is also associated with a tendency to exhibit the attentional and interpretive biases for threatening information reviewed above. Thus, highly trait anxious individuals are more likely to get into the vicious circle described above, at least in part, because these cognitive biases lead them to have more trigger topics for worry (arrow 11).

A second individual difference variable contributing to the tendency to get into this vicious circle involves an individual's learning history. Children who grow up with parents who are worriers (including those with GAD) are likely to learn vicariously the tendency to think this way about potentially threatening topics. Although not yet studied in GAD, parallel effects have been observed in individuals with panic disorder who tend to report histories of having had parents who had had more chronic illnesses when they were children, as well as more panic symptoms (Ehlers, 1993). Similar effects also occur in medical illness. For example, Turkat (1982) found that adult diabetics who had observed in childhood their parents engage in sick role behaviour when temporarily ill were more likely to engage in illness-related avoidance themselves as adults than diabetics whose parents had not engaged in sick role behaviour when they were children. In addition to vicarious learning of the tendency to worry per se, evidence shows that attentional and interpretive biases can be trained in normal individuals and that such training results in increased susceptibility to anxiety in stressful situations (e.g. MacLeod et al., this volume; Yiend & Mackintosh, this volume). Whether such training occurs in everyday life circumstances just as it does in the laboratory remains to be determined, but the possibility is an intriguing one that should be investigated.

Finally, a third individual difference variable that may influence which individuals are most prone to getting into this vicious circle involves the occurrence of negative or stressful life events. Both distal and proximal negative life events provide further trigger topics (S^D) for worry and also promote a general sense of perceived uncontrollability in life (not just over worry). (See Borkovec et al., in press; Mineka & Zinbarg, 1996.)

Conclusions

We have reviewed a variety of lines of research that we believe enhance our understanding of some important aspects of the aetiology of the excessive, persistent and uncontrollable worry seen in GAD. Generalized and high trait anxiety are clearly associated with attentional and interpretive biases for threatening material, which in turn provide further trigger topics for the worry process, as well as serving as vulnerability factors for increased anxiety during stressful periods. Furthermore, worry may be negatively reinforced as a cognitive avoidance response because of some of the benefits worrying may provide, and this seems to parallel what is known about behavioural avoidance learning. But worrying clearly also sometimes has negative or punishing consequences that may accrue at approximately the same time. We have suggested that, although the worrier may not be aware of it, these punishing consequences may lead to a positive feedback process in which worry leads to more worry and anxiety, which in turn may lead to a sense of perceived uncontrollability over the worry process. Once worry is experienced as uncontrollable, meta-worry may also develop. Clinically, this might suggest that teaching individuals (through the use of their own examples and homework exercises) about the negative vicious circles that their worry activities can get them into may be beneficial (as it is in the cognitive treatment of panic disorder). Cognitive restructuring about the illusory (superstitious) relationships between their worrying and the non-occurrence of their feared catastrophes may also help them to attend to these negative vicious circles rather than their presumed avoidance of catastrophes from worrying. Finally, through prolonged worry exposure exercises, anxiety and some of the punishing consequences of worry should habituate.

In our model, we propose that the punishing consequences of worry as a cognitive avoidance response may operate in a parallel manner to what often happens when behavioural avoidance responses are punished and avoidance responding paradoxically increases in strength. Specifically, these punishing consequences may create a vicious circle in which the increased anxiety generated by punishment simply leads to more worry because it is the coping response that has been learned to reduce anxiety. In addition, certain important personality and experiential variables, such as trait anxiety and one's vicarious reinforcement history, may facilitate certain individuals getting into this vicious circle.

NOTES

1. One step that is not necessary in humans is the initial step of conditioning of fear to the trigger topic because this has generally been taught or acquired earlier in life.
2. It should be noted that Mathews and Milroy (1994) did not find a similar effect in an older community sample of high worriers. However, in addition to using different subject populations the Mathews and Milroy study also used a different method of worry induction, so it is difficult to determine why the results differed.
3. There are several paradigms where punishment of ARs does facilitate their extinction.

REFERENCES

Abramowitz, J. S., Tolin, D. F. & Street, G. P. (2001). Paradoxical effects of thought suppression: a meta-analysis of controlled studies. *Clinical Psychology Review*, *21*, 683–703.

APA (1994). *Diagnostic and Statistical Manual of Mental Disorders*, 4th edn. Washington, DC: American Psychiatric Association.

Borkovec, T. D. (1994). The nature, functions, and origins of worry. In G. C. Davey & F. Tallis (Eds.), *Worrying: Perspectives on Theory, Assessment and Treatment*, 5–33. New York: Wiley.

Borkovec, T. D., Alcaine, O. & Behar, E. (in press). Avoidance theory of worry and generalized anxiety disorder. In R. G. Heimberg, C. L. Turk & D. S. Mennin (Eds.), *Generalized Anxiety Disorder: Advances in Research and Practice*. New York: Guilford.

Borkovec, T. D., Hazlett-Stevens, H. & Diaz, M. L. (1999). The role of positive beliefs about worry in generalized anxiety disorder and its treatment. *Clinical Psychology and Psychotherapy*, *6*, 126–138.

Borkovec, T. D. & Hu, S. (1990). The effect of worry on cardiovascular response to phobic imagery, *Behaviour Research and Therapy*, *28*, 69–73.

Borkovec, T. D., Robinson, E., Pruzinsky, T. & De Pree, J. A. (1983). Preliminary exploration of worry: some characteristics and processes. *Behaviour Research and Therapy*, *21*, 9–16.

Brown, J. S. (1969). Factors affecting self-punitive locomotor behavior. In B. Campbell & R. Church (Eds.), *Punishment and Aversive Behavior*, 467–514. New York: Appleton Century Crofts.

Brown, T. A., Chorpita, B. & Barlow, D. H. (1998). Structural relationships among dimensions of the DSM-IV anxiety and mood disorders and dimensions of negative affect, positive affect, and autonomic arousal. *Journal of Abnormal Psychology*, *107*, 179–192.

Butler, G., Wells, A. & Dewick, H. (1995). Differential effects of worry and imagery after exposure to a stressful stimulus: a pilot study. *Behavioural and Cognitive Psychotherapy*, *23*, 45–56.

Church, R. M. (1969). Response suppression. In B. Campbell & R. Church (Eds.), *Punishment and Aversive Behavior*, New York: Appleton Century Crofts.

Clark, L. A. & Watson, D. (1991). Tripartite model of anxiety and depression: psychometric evidence and taxonomic implications. *Journal of Abnormal Psychology*, *100*, 316–336.

Clark, L. A., Watson, D. & Mineka, S. (1994). Temperament, personality, and the mood and anxiety disorders. *Journal of Abnormal Psychology*, *103*, 103–116.

Cook, M., Mineka, S. & Trumble, D. (1987). The role of response-produced and exteroceptive feedback in the attenuation of fear over the course of avoidance learning. *Journal of Experimental Psychology: Animal Behavior Processes*, *13*, 239–249.

Dean, S. J. & Pittman, C. M. (1991). Self-punitive behavior: a revised analysis. In M. R. Denny (Ed.), *Fear, Avoidance, and Phobias: A Fundamental Analysis*, 259–284. Hillsdale, NJ: Erlbaum.

Dugas, M. J., Gagnon, F., Ladouceur, R. & Freeston, M. H. (1998). Generalized anxiety disorder: a preliminary test of a conceptual model, *Behaviour Research and Therapy*, *36*, 215–226.

Ehlers, A. (1993). Somatic symptoms and panic attacks: a retrospective study of learning experiences. *Behaviour Research and Therapy*, *31*, 269–278.

Foa, E. B. & Kozak, M. J. (1986). Emotional processing of fear: exposure to corrective information. *Psycholological Bulletin*, *99*, 20–35.

Hayward, C., Killen, J. D., Kraemer, H. C. & Taylor, C. B. (2000). Predictors of panic attacks in adolescence. *Journal of the American Academy of Child and Adolescent Psychiatry*, *39*, 207–214.

Hoehn-Saric, R., McLeod, D. R. & Zimmerli, W. D. (1989). Somatic manifestations in women with generalized anxiety disorder. *Archives of General Psychiatry*, *46*, 1113–1119.

Mackintosh, N. J. (1974). *The Psychology of Animal Learning*. New York: Academic Press.

MacLeod, C. (1999). Anxiety and anxiety disorders. In T. Dalgleish & M. J. Power (Eds.), *Handbook of Cognition and Emotion*, 447–477. Chichester: Wiley.

MacLeod, C. & Hagan, R. (1992). Individual differences in the selective processing of threatening information, and emotional responses to a stressful life event. *Behaviour Research and Therapy*, *30*, 151–161.

MacLeod, C. & Mathews, A. (1988). Anxiety and the allocation of attention to threat. *Quarterly Journal of Experimental Psychology. A: Human Experimental Psychology*, *40*(4–A), 653–670.

Mathews, A. (1990). Why worry? The cognitive function of worry. *Behaviour Research and Therapy*, *28*, 455–468.

Mathews, A. & MacLeod, C. (1994). Cognitive approaches to emotion and emotional disorders. *Annual Review of Psychology*, *45*, 25–50.

Mathews, A. & MacLeod, C. (2002). Induced processing biases have causal effects on anxiety. *Cognition and Emotion*, *16*, 331–354.

Mathews A. & Milroy, R. (1994). Effects of priming and suppression of worry. *Behaviour Research and Therapy*, *32*, 843–850.

Melvin, K. B. & Martin, R. C. (1966). Facilitative effects of two modes of punishment on resistance to extinction. *Journal of Comparative and Physiological Psychology*, *62*, 491–494.

Mineka, S. (1979). The role of fear in theories of avoidance learning, flooding, and extinction. *Psychological Bulletin*, *86*, 985–1010.

Mineka, S. & Kelly, K. (1989). The relationship between anxiety, lack of control, and loss of control. In A. Steptoe (Ed.), *Stress, Personal Control and Health*, 163–191. New York: Wiley.

Mineka, S., Rafaeli, E. & Yovel, I. (2003). Cognitive biases in emotional disorders: social-cognitive and information processing perspectives. In R. Davidson, H. Goldsmith & K. Scherer (Eds.), *Handbook of Affective Science*. New York: Oxford University Press.

Mineka, S., Yovel, I. & Pineles, S. (2002). Toward a psychological model of the etiology of generalized anxiety disorder. In D. J. Nutt, K. Rickels & D. J. Stein (Eds.), *Generalized Anxiety Disorder: Symptomatology, Pathogenesis and Management*. London: Martin Dunitz Ltd.

Mineka, S. & Zinbarg, R. (1996). Conditioning and ethological models of anxiety disorders: stress-in-dynamic-context anxiety models. In D. Hope (Ed.), *Nebraska Symposium on Motivation, 1996: Perspectives on Anxiety, Panic, and Fear. Current Theory and Research in Motivation, 43,* 135–210. Lincoln, NE: University of Nebraska Press.

Mogg, K., Bradley, B. P., Williams, R. & Mathews, A. (1993). Subliminal processing of emotional information in anxiety and depression. *Journal of Abnormal Psychology, 102,* 304–311.

Purdon, C. (1999). Thought suppression and psychopathology, *Behaviour Research and Therapy, 37,* 129–154.

Pury, C. (2002). Information-processing predictors of emotional response to stress. *Cognition and Emotion, 16,* 667–683.

Seligman, M. E. P. & Johnston, J. (1973). A cognitive theory of avoidance learning. In F. S. McGuigan & D. Lumsden (Eds.), *Contemporary Approaches to Conditioning and Learning.* Washington, DC: V. H. Winston & Sons.

Solomon, R. L., Kamin, L. J. & Wynne, L. C. (1953). Traumatic avoidance learning: the outcomes of several extinction procedures with dogs. *Journal of Abnormal and Social Psychology, 48,* 291–302.

Thayer, J. F., Friedman, B. H. & Borkovec, T. D. (1996). Autonomic characteristics of generalized anxiety disorder and worry. *Biological Psychiatry, 39,* 255–266.

Turkat, I. (1982). An investigation of parental modeling in the etiology of diabetic illness behavior. *Behaviour Research and Therapy, 20,* 547–552.

Vrana, S. R., Cuthbert, B. N. & Lang, P. J. (1986). Fear imagery and text processing. *Psychophysiology, 23,* 247–253.

Walters, G. C. & Grusec, J. E. (1977). *Punishment.* San Francisco: Freeman & Co.

Wegner, D. (1994). Ironic processes of mental control. *Psychological Review, 10,* 34–52.

Wells, A. (1999). A cognitive model of generalized anxiety disorder. *Behavior Modification, 23,* 526–555.

Wells, A. & Butler, G. (1997). Generalized anxiety disorder. In D. M. Clark & C. G. Fairburn (Eds.), *Science and Practice of Cognitive Behaviour Therapy,* 155–178. New York: Oxford University Press.

Wells, A. & Carter, K. (1999). Preliminary tests of a cognitive model of generalized anxiety disorder. *Behaviour Research and Therapy, 37,* 585–594.

Wells, A. & Papageorgiou, C. (1995). Worry and the incubation of intrusive images following stress. *Behaviour Research and Therapy, 33,* 579–583.

Williams, J. M., Watts, F. N., MacLeod, C. & Mathews, A. (1997). *Cognitive Psychology and Emotional Disorders,* 2nd edn. Chichester: Wiley.

York, D., Borkovec, T. D., Vasey, M. & Stern, R. (1987). Effects of worry and somatic anxiety induction on thoughts, emotion and physiological activity. *Behaviour Research and Therapy, 25,* 523–526.

2 Trait anxiety, repressors and cognitive biases

Michael W. Eysenck

Introduction

The main emphasis of this chapter is on the personality dimension of trait anxiety, which is concerned with individual differences in the tendency to experience anxiety and related negative emotional states. There is general agreement among personality researchers and theorists that trait anxiety (or neuroticism) is one of the most important personality dimensions. Most researchers focusing on the structure of human personality (e.g. McCrae & Costa, 1985) accept there are five main personality dimensions or factors (often called the Big Five), of which neuroticism or trait anxiety is one. Thus, there is considerable consensus at the level of description. Note that the terms 'trait anxiety' and 'neuroticism' will be used more or less interchangeably in what follows. This is justifiable for two reasons. First, the two personality dimensions typically correlate about +0.7 with each other (H. J. Eysenck & Eysenck, 1985; the name 'Eysenck' on its own refers to the author of this chapter). Second, there is considerable evidence that trait anxiety and neuroticism are both relatively pure measures of a broad personality dimension known as negative affectivity (Watson & Clark, 1984). However, it should be noted that neuroticism is typically orthogonal to the personality dimension of extraversion, whereas there is a small negative correlation between trait anxiety and extraversion (H. J. Eysenck & Eysenck, 1985).

There has been significantly less progress at the level of explanation than at the level of description. In other words, the nature of the mechanisms underlying individual differences in trait anxiety or neuroticism remain unclear. Some of the main theoretical approaches are discussed in this section. Thereafter, the emphasis will be on a theory of trait anxiety proposed by Eysenck (1997).

Biological approach

Historically, several attempts to understand individual differences in trait anxiety or neuroticism focused on biological factors. More specifically,

49

H. J. Eysenck (1967) and Gray (1982) argued that genetic factors play an important role in producing individual differences in trait anxiety or neuroticism. The most relevant research on this issue has involved twin studies, with numerous such studies having been carried out in several countries. The relevant literature has been reviewed several times (e.g. Eysenck, 1992), so no attempt will be made here to provide a full account. However, mention should be made of the study by Pedersen et al. (1988), which is the most comprehensive attempt to address this issue. They obtained data from large numbers of monozygotic and dizygotic twin pairs brought up together and apart. The conclusion which they came to was that genetic factors account for approximately 31 per cent of individual differences in neuroticism. That estimate of the contribution of genetic factors is similar to those stemming from other twin studies (see Eysenck, 1992).

A second prediction from the biological approach has not always fared well. H. J. Eysenck (1967) assumed that individuals high and low in trait anxiety or neuroticism differ in terms of physiological reactivity or responsiveness. He argued that these differences involve the visceral brain, which consists of the hippocampus, amygdala, cingulum, septum and hypothalamus. In contrast, Gray (1982) argued that the septo-hippocampal system was of prime importance. According to H. J. Eysenck, individuals high in trait anxiety or neuroticism should exhibit greater physiological responsiveness than those low in trait anxiety or neuroticism on a range of physiological measures, and this should be especially the case under stressful conditions. The relevant evidence was reviewed by Fahrenberg (1992), a leading expert in this area. His conclusions were unequivocal: 'Over many decades research has failed to substantiate the physiological correlates that are assumed for emotionality and trait anxiety. There is virtually no distinct finding that has been reliably replicated across studies and laboratories' (Fahrenberg, 1992, pp. 212–213). Non-significant findings have consistently been reported in non-stressful, moderately stressful and highly stressful conditions.

How can we explain the lack of association between trait anxiety or neuroticism on the one hand and physiological responsiveness on the other hand? There are three major explanatory possibilities. First, it could, of course, be the case that the theory is incorrect. Second, the preferred explanation for many years was that the physiological measures used in most studies are insensitive and provide only a very indirect reflection of underlying brain activity. Gray (1982) and Gray and McNaughton (2000) endorsed this view, arguing that more direct measures of brain activity are needed. Some support for this theoretical position has been obtained. For example, Mathews, Yiend and Lawrence (in press) using fMRI found predicted individual differences in brain activity in response to fear-related pictures. Third, as is emphasized in this chapter, it is possible that trait anxiety or neuroticism is more complex than allowed for in conventional forms of assessment.

Weinberger, Schwartz and Davidson (1979) provided the first convincing evidence in support of the third explanation. They proposed a fourfold classification based on trait anxiety and defensiveness (assessed by the Marlowe–Crowne Social Desirability Scale). High scorers on both dimensions were labelled defensive high anxious, and those high on trait anxiety and low on defensiveness were labelled high anxious. Of more relevance here, Weinberger et al. argued that those obtaining low scores on measures of trait anxiety form a heterogeneous group. More specifically, Weinberger et al. distinguished between two types of individual scoring low on trait anxiety:

1. The truly low anxious, who have low defensiveness scores and claim to enjoy life and to be generally relaxed.
2. Repressors, who have high defensiveness scores and claim that they experience little anxiety because they are highly controlled and do not allow emotions to disrupt their everyday lives. It may be noted in passing that there appear to be important health implications associated with being a repressor. For example, there is evidence that children with cancer are more likely to be repressors than would be expected by chance (Phipps et al., 2001).

Weinberger et al. (1979) obtained evidence that there are important differences between the truly low anxious and repressors. When participants were placed in a moderately stressful situation, the physiological and behavioural responses of repressors were indicative of much higher levels of anxiety than was the case for the truly low anxious. Indeed, the physiological and behavioural responses of repressors were comparable to those of the high anxious (high scorers on trait anxiety). Thus, the prediction that physiological responsiveness should be greater among those high in trait anxiety or neuroticism than among low scorers was supported empirically if high anxious individuals were compared with the truly low anxious. However, data from the repressor group were very much contrary to the prediction of the biological approach: repressors had low levels of self-reported anxiety but high levels of physiological responsiveness.

Similar findings have been obtained in several other studies (e.g. Brown et al., 1996; Derakshan & Eysenck, 2001b; Newton & Contrada, 1992). The findings of Brown et al. (1996) are of particular interest. They obtained measures of salivary cortisol from participants who were placed in a stressful situation. When the data were analysed in the traditional way by comparing all low scorers on trait anxiety with all high scorers, there was no significant difference between the two groups in salivary cortisol. However, when the low scorers on trait anxiety were divided into truly low anxious and repressor groups, the truly low anxious had lower levels of salivary cortisol than did the high anxious. Thus, it was the data from the repressor group which were inconsistent with the predictions of the biological approach. A potential explanation for the findings with repressors was offered by Eysenck (1997), and will be discussed shortly.

There are other important limitations associated with the biological approach. It appears to predict that any given individual's level of trait anxiety or neuroticism will remain constant over time, and it predicts that individuals who experience relatively high levels of anxiety in one situation will also experience relatively high levels of anxiety in other situations. Consistency over time was studied by Conley (1984). He found that trait anxiety or neuroticism was moderately consistent over time. However, it was significantly less consistent than intelligence, and there were fairly large changes in trait anxiety or neuroticism over long periods of time.

The notion that individuals are characteristically relatively anxious or non-anxious across numerous situations is a considerable oversimplification. Endler (e.g. 1983) proposed instead that trait anxiety consists of various domains or facets (e.g. social evaluation; physical danger; ambiguous). For any given individual, experienced anxiety will be greatest when there is congruence or agreement between the nature of the threat posed by the environment and the most salient domain or facet of trait anxiety possessed by him/her. There is much empirical evidence in support of this interactionist perspective (Endler, 1983).

In sum, it is clear that the biological approach has contributed much to our understanding of trait anxiety or neuroticism. Individual differences in trait anxiety do depend in part on genetic factors and on differences in physiological responsiveness. However, environmental factors presumably influence changes in trait anxiety over time and cross-situational inconsistencies in experienced anxiety, and such environmental factors are not considered in detail within the biological approach. In addition, the relationship between trait anxiety and physiological responsiveness is more complex than is assumed by the biological approach.

Cognitive approach

The notion that individual differences in trait anxiety depend in part on various cognitive processes and structures is one that became influential during the 1980s and 1990s. It was in early 1984 that I first met Andrew Mathews, who rapidly convinced me of the value of a cognitive approach to understanding individual differences in trait anxiety. More specifically, he argued that individuals high and low in trait anxiety differ importantly in the schemas and other information contained in long-term memory, which still seems an excellent starting-point for theorizing about trait anxiety. The cognitive approach to trait anxiety was first proposed in a systematic way in a book by Williams, Watts, MacLeod and Mathews (1988), although their primary concern was with the anxiety disorders. Their approach was subsequently developed and extended (Williams, Watts, MacLeod & Mathews, 1997), and a related approach was proposed by Eysenck (1992).

The central theoretical assumption of the cognitive approach is that individuals high in trait anxiety or neuroticism experience higher levels of anxiety than those low in trait anxiety because they possess various cognitive biases. The two most important cognitive biases are attentional bias (the tendency to attend selectively to threat-related rather than neutral stimuli) and interpretive bias (the tendency to interpret ambiguous stimuli and situations in a threatening fashion). These two biases together mean that individuals high in trait anxiety regard the environment as more threatening than do individuals low in trait anxiety.

In addition, two memory biases (explicit memory bias and implicit memory bias) have been identified, both of which involve the disproportionate retrieval of threat-related words. The two biases differ in that explicit memory involves the conscious recollection of information, whereas implicit memory involves assessing retrieval indirectly in ways not involving conscious recollection. According to Williams et al. (1988, 1997), high anxiety is associated with an implicit memory bias but not with an explicit memory bias.

The voluminous evidence relating to trait anxiety and cognitive biases has been reviewed several times (e.g. Eysenck, 1992; Mathews & MacLeod, 1994; Williams, Mathews & MacLeod, 1996), and will not be considered in detail here. However, one important issue which has only recently received the attention it deserves will be mentioned briefly. Most of the relevant evidence is correlational, in that an association has been found between reporting high levels of anxiety and the existence of various cognitive biases. What has not been clear is whether (as predicted theoretically) cognitive biases produce anxiety. Alternative views are that anxiety produces cognitive biases, or that there are bi-directional effects of cognitive biases on anxiety and of anxiety on cognitive biases.

Convincing evidence on the causality issue has been reported recently. For example, MacLeod, Rutherford, Campbell, Ebsworthy and Holker (2002) found that a long training programme designed to reduce attentional bias produced a reduction in anxiety. Derakshan and Eysenck (2001a) manipulated the extent to which individuals focused their attention on themselves. All groups of participants, including those obtaining high and low scores on trait anxiety, showed substantial increases in state anxiety in the self-focus condition, compared to a control condition.

Mathews and Mackintosh (2000) investigated the effects of altering individuals' interpretive bias. They found that manipulations designed to increase interpretive bias produced an increase in state anxiety. Thus, it seems from the available evidence that cognitive biases do exert causal influence on experienced anxiety (for reviews, see Mathews & MacLeod, 2002; MacLeod et al., this volume; Yiend & Mathews, 2002). Of course, this leaves open the possibility that there is an additional causal pathway going in the opposite direction.

In spite of the numerous contributions of the cognitive approach developed in the 1980s and 1990s, it possesses several significant limitations. Some of the main limitations are as follows. First, most advocates of that approach (e.g. Eysenck, 1992; Williams et al., 1988, 1997) assumed that all individuals scoring low on trait anxiety constitute a homogenous group. As we have already seen, there is convincing evidence (e.g. Weinberger et al., 1979) that that assumption is an oversimplification and should be replaced with a division of low scorers on trait anxiety into truly low anxious and repressor groups.

Second, the emphasis in this approach was on cognitive biases applied to environmental or external stimuli. It may well be that the cognitive biases possessed by individuals high in trait anxiety are most often applied to external stimuli, but there is increasing evidence (see below) that their cognitive biases are also applied to various internal stimuli. The participants in research in the 1980s and 1990s on cognitive biases associated with anxiety were sometimes presented with words relating to internal physiological symptoms or diseases, but the findings from such research may well be relatively uninformative with respect to attentional and interpretive biases for internal stimuli.

Third, the cognitive approach discussed above is limited because insufficient attention is paid to the fact that several different response systems are involved in anxiety. For example, Lang (e.g. 1985) identified three response systems: verbal, physiological and behavioural. It would perhaps be less important to consider all three response systems if there were concordance or agreement among them. In fact, however, lack of concordance among the three response systems is the rule rather than the exception (see Eysenck, 1997), as exemplified by the data on repressive low-anxious individuals. Accordingly, it is of theoretical importance to understand the reasons for failures of concordance, but this issue cannot readily be considered within the scope of the cognitive theories proposed in the 1980s and early 1990s.

Eysenck's four-factor theory

Most theories build on the endeavours of previous theorists, and that is certainly the case with the four-factor theory proposed by Eysenck (1997). Three previous theoretical contributions which strongly influenced the development of that theory were those of Parkinson (1994), Weinberger (1990) and Williams et al. (1988). However, the four-factor theory is clearly broader in scope than the theories on which it is partly based.

One of the main starting-points for the theory was the notion that an adequate theory of trait anxiety should consider fully anxiety as an emotional state. More specifically, such a theory should address an issue which has been insufficiently addressed in the personality literature: what are the sources of information determining any given individual's experience of anxiety? According to Eysenck's (1997) theory, the emotional experience of anxiety depends on four sources of information (discussed below). More precisely, experienced anxiety depends on the extent to which information from these four sources is attended to, and on the ways in which such information is interpreted.

First, and undoubtedly most importantly, there is information about the external environment, which has played a central role in most theories of emotion (e.g. Lazarus, 1991). Second, there is information about the individual's own physiological activity (e.g. heart rate), which was emphasized in the James–Lange theory of emotion. Third, there is information about the individual's own behaviour. Fourth, there are cognitions (e.g. worries) about possible negative future events.

The empirical evidence indicating that each of these sources of information influences experienced anxiety is discussed in detail by Eysenck (1997, 2000). In general, the available evidence indicates that the amount of anxiety experienced depends on all four sources of information.

Cognitive biases

Anxiety depends on four different sources of information. According to the four-factor theory, high anxious individuals, repressors and low anxious individuals differ with respect to their processing of all four kinds of information, and this is especially the case in stressful situations. High anxious individuals have attentional and interpretive biases in all four domains. These biases mean that high anxious individuals typically exaggerate the threat of external and internal stimuli, as a result of which they experience high levels of state or experienced anxiety.

Repressors have an opposite attentional bias (probably in all four domains), which is the tendency to avoid attending to threat-related external and internal stimuli when presented concurrently with neutral stimuli. They also have an opposite interpretive bias, which is the tendency to interpret ambiguous stimuli and situations in a non-threatening fashion. These biases mean that repressors typically minimize the threat of external and internal stimuli, as a result of which they experience low levels of state or experienced anxiety.

Low anxious individuals are assumed not to have attentional or interpretive biases. In other words, they do not systematically attend to (or avoid attending to) threat-related external and internal stimuli. In addition, they do not show a strong tendency to interpret ambiguous stimuli and situations in either a threatening or a non-threatening fashion. This prediction may seem inconsistent with studies showing that individuals low in trait anxiety have an opposite interpretive bias. However, such studies have not typically distinguished between the truly low anxious and repressors, and so do not disprove the prediction.

It was assumed in the four-factor theory (Eysenck, 1997) that attentional and interpretive biases are of more importance to anxiety than are memory biases (i.e. explicit memory bias or implicit memory bias). However, as predicted by Williams et al. (1988, 1997), there is some evidence that individuals high in trait anxiety show an implicit memory bias. For example, Eysenck and Byrne (1994) found that high anxious participants had an implicit memory bias, as revealed by a word-stem completion task. Other research has fairly consistently failed to provide convincing evidence for an implicit memory bias in individuals high in trait anxiety, especially when reasonably stringent criteria are used to define the presence of such a bias (Russo, Fox & Bowles, 1999), but see Hertel, this volume, for a different perspective.

Empirical evidence

Numerous predictions follow from the four-factor theory. Much of the relevant research evidence relating to high anxious individuals has been reviewed several times previously (e.g. Eysenck, 1997, 2000), and will not be repeated here. Two of the distinctive features of the four-factor theory are that it is predicted that repressors possess opposite cognitive biases and that this constitutes an important difference between them and the truly low anxious, who do not possess any systematic cognitive biases. Thus, avoidance of threat by individuals scoring low on trait anxiety is attributed to the repressors among them. The brief, selective review which follows is concerned with research addressing those two predictions.

Derakshan and Eysenck (1997) investigated cognitive biases with respect to one's own social behaviour. Students were videotaped while they gave a short public talk about psychology in front of a small group of their peers. Over a week later, they watched the video recording of themselves, and completed a detailed measure of various symptoms associated with behavioural anxiety. In order to decide whether the participants' assessments of their own level of behavioural anxiety were biased, these assessments were compared against ratings of their behavioural anxiety made by independent judges, who watched the same video recordings. As predicted, the repressors showed an opposite interpretive bias, with their ratings of their own behavioural anxiety being much lower than the ratings of their behavioural anxiety provided by the independent judges. In contrast, truly low anxious participants did not show any interpretive bias for their own behavioural anxiety.

Eysenck and Derakshan (1997) assessed interpretive bias for future cognitions in a study on university students; the students completed a questionnaire concerning their negative expectations about their examination performance in examinations which were due to take place approximately five or six weeks thereafter. In order to assess interpretive bias, the students completed the questionnaire for a second time, but this time they filled it in as they thought a typical student would. Repressors had an opposite interpretive bias, because they had significantly fewer negative expectations about their own examination performance than about the examination performance of a typical student. In contrast, the truly low anxious had no interpretive bias, because their negative expectations about their own future examination performance were neither more positive nor more negative than those relating to a typical student.

Schill and Althoff (1968) assessed perception of auditorily presented sentences masked by noise. There were three categories of sentences: sexual, aggressive and neutral. The repressors performed significantly worse than the truly low anxious or the high anxious in perceiving the sexual sentences, which are arguably threatening.

Bonanno, Davis, Singer and Schwartz (1991) gave their participants a dichotic listening task, with a number of threat-related words being presented on the unattended channel. The participants were subsequently given an unexpected recognition test for these threat-related words. Repressors recognized fewer threat-related words than did the truly low anxious (46 per cent versus 61 per cent), which is consistent with the notion that only the repressors had an opposite attentional bias for the threat-related words.

Fox (1993) assessed attentional biases in truly low anxious, repressor and high anxious groups of participants, who had to respond as rapidly as possible to a probe which replaced either a threat-related or a neutral word. Fox used both social and physical threat words, but the key findings were obtained with the social threat words. Repressors showed an opposite attentional bias for social threat, systematically attending to the neutral word rather than the social threat word. In contrast, the truly low anxious did not show any attentional bias towards or away from social threat.

Failures of concordance

As was discussed earlier, there are frequent failures of concordance among measures of anxiety taken from different domains (self-report or verbal; behavioural; and physiological). Evidence from several studies (e.g. Derakshan & Eysenck, 2001b; Newton & Contrada, 1992; Weinberger et al., 1979) indicates that repressors' relative levels of self-reported anxiety are significantly lower than their relative levels of physiological responsiveness.

Additional information was reported by Derakshan and Eysenck (2001b), who found that repressors' relative level of self-reported anxiety was significantly lower than their relative level of behavioural anxiety in a moderately stressful situation, as assessed by independent judges. In similar fashion, Fox, O'Boyle, Barry and McCreary (1989) found that independent ratings of behavioural anxiety among patients undergoing stressful dental surgery indicated that repressors were significantly more behaviourally anxious than the truly low anxious. However, repressors about to undergo colonoscopy had significantly lower self-reported anxiety than truly low anxious patients in the same situation (Fox, O'Boyle, Lennon & Keeling, 1989).

How can we explain the consistent pattern that repressors in stressful situations have relatively low levels of self-reported anxiety but relatively high levels of behavioural anxiety and physiological responsiveness? According to Eysenck's (1997) four-factor theory, repressors have little conscious experience of anxiety because their opposite attentional and interpretive biases minimize the perceived threat of external and internal stimuli. However, there is a simple alternative explanation which needs to be considered. If repressors actually experience relatively high levels of anxiety but deliberately distort their self-reports of anxious experience, then this same pattern of behavioural, physiological and self-report measures would emerge.

This alternative explanation was tested by Derakshan and Eysenck (1998). Since it is extremely difficult to decide whether someone's self-reported anxiety is accurate or distorted, they decided to assess the level of experienced anxiety in an indirect fashion. In essence, MacLeod and Donnellan (1993) found that the performance of individuals high in trait anxiety on a reasoning task was impaired much more than that of individuals low in trait anxiety when a concurrent memory task had to be performed. The individuals high in trait anxiety experienced more state anxiety than those low in trait anxiety, and this impaired their ability to perform the reasoning task effectively. The logic used by Derakshan and Eysenck (1998) was as follows: if repressors deliberately under-state their experienced level of anxiety and actually experience much anxiety in stressful situations, then their performance with the concurrent memory load should resemble that of the high anxious participants in the study by MacLeod and Donnellan (1993). In contrast, if their self-reported low level of state anxiety in stressful situations is genuine, their performance with the concurrent memory load should be similar to that of truly low anxious participants. The findings of Derakshan and Eysenck were unequivocal. Repressors' performance was very similar to that of truly low anxious participants, and very different from that of high anxious participants. The implication of these findings is that repressors' actual state anxiety is comparable to that of the truly low anxious rather than that of the high anxious.

The same conclusion follows from a study on the same issue by Derakshan and Eysenck (1999). They asked their participants to complete the measure of trait anxiety from the Spielberger State-Trait Anxiety Inventory on two occasions separated by approximately two months. On the first occasion, the questionnaire was completed under standard conditions. On the second occasion, in contrast, the questionnaire was completed while using the 'bogus pipeline'. The bogus pipeline consists of an impressive-looking piece of equipment which the participants are led to believe will detect any lying on their part. The bogus pipeline has proved effective in persuading people to produce more honest answers on numerous issues. For example, Tourangeau, Smith and Rasinski (1997) found that use of the bogus pipeline led people to admit to cocaine use, frequent oral sex and excessive drinking.

What did Derakshan and Eysenck (1999) find when they compared trait-anxiety scores under standard and bogus-pipeline conditions? The mean score for trait anxiety in repressors was slightly (but non-significantly) greater with the bogus pipeline than under standard conditions. Under bogus-pipeline conditions, the mean trait anxiety score of repressors was comparable to that of the truly low anxious. Thus, the findings provided little or no evidence that repressors deliberately understate their level of anxiety, suggesting that they genuinely have limited conscious experience of anxiety.

Clinical relevance

Eysenck's (1997) four-factor theory was designed in part to address issues over and above those discussed so far. For example, it addresses the theoretically important (but strangely neglected) issue of *why* it is that there are the particular anxiety disorders which are observed in therapeutic practice. According to the four-factor theory, we might anticipate that there would be four major anxiety disorders, each one involving cognitive biases associated with one of the four sources of information influencing experienced anxiety. Such an approach (see below) may possibly prove a useful starting-point for more systematic theorizing.

The anxiety disorder which is most obviously related to cognitive biases for one's own physiological symptoms is panic disorder. The anxiety disorder most closely related to cognitive biases for one's own behaviour is social phobia, when people with social phobia greatly exaggerate the inadequate nature of their social behaviour. The anxiety disorder most related to cognitive biases for possible future negative events is obsessive-compulsive disorder, especially those patients who much exaggerate the probability that their actions will be followed by dire consequences for which they will be held personally responsible. Finally, cognitive biases for environmental stimuli are probably present in virtually all anxiety disorders, but are of central importance in specific phobia. We may speculate that patients with generalized anxiety possess cognitive biases for most or all four sources of information.

Of course, the above suggestions are speculative and are in need of considerable refinement. However, it seems reasonable to assume that a theoretical understanding of why certain anxiety disorders exist needs to be considered in conjunction with an analysis of the various factors associated with the experience of anxiety.

It would seem in principle to be valuable to consider possible associations between repressors and anxiety disorders. However, to the best of my knowledge there has been no systematic research on such associations. In some ways, it could be argued that repressors' use of cognitive biases which minimize the threat of external and internal stimuli suggests that they engage in a form of self-administered therapy. An interesting (but unresolved) issue is whether these attempts at self-administered therapy are typically successful in preventing the development of clinical anxiety.

Theoretical limitations and extensions

In the years that have passed since Eysenck (1997) put forward his four-factor theory, various empirical and theoretical limitations have become apparent, and some of these limitations will be discussed in this section. The first limitation relates to the assessment of anxiety at the physiological level. In the great majority of studies in which physiological measures of anxiety have been obtained, these measures have been indirect reflections of autonomic system activity (e.g. heart rate or galvanic skin response). However, these measures are very non-specific, and often do not reflect an emotional response. As Gray (1994, p. 243) pointed out with respect to the autonomic and endocrine systems, 'These systems are concerned with housekeeping functions, energy metabolism, tissue repair, and the like. It would be surprising if these functions bore any specific relation to particular emotional states, since energy requirements, for example, are likely to be the same whenever an animal undertakes vigorous action, whatever the emotional significance of the action.'

How should researchers approach the issue of assessing anxiety at a physiological level? A very useful starting-point is the research of LeDoux (1992, 1996). He claims (with much supporting evidence) that two different brain circuits are involved in fear or anxiety. First, there is a slow-acting thalamus-to-cortex circuit, which is based on detailed analysis of sensory information. Second, there is a fast-acting thalamus–amygdala circuit, which bypasses the cortex and is based on simple stimulus features (e.g. intensity). A more detailed account of the physiological response to threat-related stimuli in the truly low anxious, repressors and the high-anxious could be obtained by assessing activity in these brain circuits. Partial relevant evidence has been obtained by Mathews et al. (in press).

Another limitation in the available empirical evidence relates to the distinction between trait anxiety and state anxiety. As yet, there have been relatively few empirical attempts to distinguish between the effects of trait anxiety and state anxiety on cognitive biases. According to the four-factor theory, attentional and interpretive biases should be greatest among individuals high in trait anxiety and state anxiety, and the available evidence broadly supports that prediction (e.g. MacLeod & Mathews, 1988). However, the effects of high and low state anxiety on the opposite biases exhibited by repressors have not been investigated systematically, and it may prove difficult to find situations in which repressors experience high levels of state anxiety. More generally, there have been very few attempts to assess the effects of manipulating situational stress on repressors' opposite cognitive biases. It will be important theoretically to establish the conditions in which opposite cognitive biases are likely to be strongest.

Finally, we turn to a more detailed consideration of the account of cognitive processes in repressors provided by Eysenck (1997). In essence, the existence of opposite cognitive biases in repressors is relevant to accounting for the findings that their relative level of self-reported anxiety is typically much less than their relative levels of behavioural anxiety and physiological activation (Derakshan & Eysenck, 2001b). However, the theory manifestly fails to provide an explanation for the further findings that repressors have relatively high levels of behavioural anxiety and physiological activation in stressful conditions (e.g. Derakshan & Eysenck, 2001b; Newton & Contrada, 1992).

Calvo and Eysenck (2000) carried out a study on interpretive bias which may be of relevance to understanding the above findings. In their study, the participants named as rapidly as possible target words which confirmed or disconfirmed the consequences implied by previous ambiguous sentences. The time interval between the sentence and the target word was varied, in order to make it possible to assess the time course for the activation of threat-related and neutral target words. So far as the low anxious participants were concerned, there was no evidence of any interpretive bias at any of the time intervals. So far as the high anxious participants were concerned, there was clear evidence of an interpretive bias at the longer time intervals. However, the key finding involved the repressors. In essence, they showed an interpretive bias when the interval of time between the ambiguous sentence and the target word was short, but there was no evidence of any interpretive bias at a longer interval.

Calvo and Eysenck (2000) accounted for the findings from repressors by assuming that repressors initially respond to an ambiguous stimulus or situation by being vigilant and processing threat-related interpretations of that stimulus or situation. This first vigilant phase is followed by a second phase of processing, which is characterized by avoidance. Speculatively, it is possible that the failures of concordance shown by repressors can be accounted for within this two-phase approach. Suppose that the first or vigilant phase serves to trigger repressors' physiological and behavioural responses to ambiguous situations, whereas the second or avoidant phase is more important in influencing the conscious experience of anxiety. As a consequence, repressors would show high levels of anxiety within the behavioural and physiological response systems, but would have low levels of experienced anxiety. Of course, it would require replication and extension of Calvo and Eysenck's (2000) findings to make this theoretical account less speculative. It would also require on-line assessment of the three response systems, to see whether the physiological and behavioural systems respond as rapidly to ambiguous stimuli as is implied by Calvo and Eysenck's account.

The notion that there may be two phases in response to threat-related stimuli can be related to the development of various multi-level theories, such as the Schematic Propositional and Analogical Representational Systems (SPAARS) approach proposed by Power and Dalgleish (1997). In essence, it is assumed within SPAARS that there are two main ways in which emotions are produced. First, emotion can occur via thorough cognitive processing involving the schematic system, in which information about the self and about the world is combined with information about the individual's current goals in order to generate an internal representation of the immediate situation. If this analysis reveals that the individual's current goals are being thwarted, then an emotional response will be generated.

Second, emotion can be produced automatically via the associative system, which was described in the following terms by Dalgleish (1998, p. 492): 'If the same event is repeatedly processed in the same way at the schematic level, then an associative representation will be formed such that, on future encounters of the same event, the relevant emotion will be *automatically* elicited.' With respect to repressors, it could be argued that their vigilance response occurs via the associative system, whereas their avoidant response occurs via the schematic system.

According to the four-factor theory, high anxious individuals have attentional and interpretive biases, whereas repressors have opposite attentional and interpretive biases. As we have seen, there is empirical support for these theoretical assumptions. However, the evidence is more extensive and more convincing with respect to the predicted cognitive biases for high anxious individuals than for repressors. Why are opposite attentional and interpretive biases not found reliably and consistently in repressors? The answer to that question is currently unclear. However, there seems to be more evidence of opposite cognitive biases in repressors when stimuli are of clear personal and/or social relevance than when they are not. More specifically, opposite attentional and/or interpretive biases in repressors have been found when the stimuli in question relate to the repressors' own behaviour in stressful situations (e.g. Derakshan & Eysenck, 1997) or their negative cognitions about their own future examination performance (Eysenck & Derakshan, 1997). However, no evidence of an opposite interpretive bias in repressors was found when they were presented with homophones having a threat-related and a neutral meaning (Mogg, Bradley, Miller, Potts, Glenwright & Kentish, 1994). In similar fashion, repressors did not have an opposite interpretive bias when they were presented with ambiguous sentences (Calvo & Eysenck, 2000).

There is a final limitation which is common to the four-factor theory and to other cognitive theories of trait anxiety, which is that it has not proved possible as yet to accommodate elements of the biological approach. More specifically, there is compelling evidence that genetic factors play a role in producing individual differences in trait anxiety, but the details of how these genetic factors influence the development of various cognitive biases remain totally unclear. In other words, what will ultimately be needed is a synthesis of the cognitive and biological approaches. Such a synthesis (e.g. Gray & McNaughton, 2000) could potentially provide a more complete understanding of individual differences in trait anxiety than is achievable by either approach on its own.

REFERENCES

Bonanno, G. A., Davis, P. J., Singer, J. L. & Schwartz, G. E. (1991). The repressor personality and avoidant information processing: a dichotic listening study. *Journal of Research in Personality*, *25*, 386–401.

Brown, L. L., Tomarken, A. J., Orth, D. N., Loosen, P. T., Kalin, N. H. & Davidson, R. J. (1996). Individual differences in repressive-defensiveness predict basal salivary cortisol levels. *Journal of Personality and Social Psychology*, *70*, 362–371.

Calvo, M. G. & Eysenck, M. W. (2000). Early vigilance and late avoidance of threat processing: repressive coping vs. low/high anxiety. *Cognition and Emotion*, *14*, 763–787.

Conley, J. J. (1984). The hierarchy of consistency: a review and model of longitudinal findings on adult individual differences in intelligence, personality and self-opinion. *Personality and Individual Differences*, *5*, 11–25.

Dalgleish, T. (1998). Emotion. In M. W. Eysenck (Ed.), *Psychology: an Integrated Approach*. Harlow: Longman.

Derakshan, N. & Eysenck, M. W. (1997). Interpretive biases for one's own behaviour and physiology in high trait anxious individuals and repressors. *Journal of Personality and Social Psychology*, *73*, 816–825.

Derakshan, N. & Eysenck, M. W. (1998). Working memory capacity in high trait anxious and repressor groups. *Cognition and Emotion*, *12*, 697–713.

Derakshan, N. & Eysenck, M. W. (1999). Are repressors self-deceivers or other-deceivers? *Cognition and Emotion*, *13*, 1–17.

Derakshan, N. & Eysenck, M. W. (2001a). Manipulation of focus of attention and its effects on anxiety in high-anxious individuals and repressors. *Anxiety, Stress, and Coping*, *14*, 173–191.

Derakshan, N. & Eysenck, M. W. (2001b). Effects of locus of attention on physiological, behavioural, and reported state anxiety in repressors, low-anxious, high-anxious, and defensive high-anxious individuals. *Anxiety, Stress, and Coping*, *14*, 285–299.

Endler, N. S. (1983). Interactionism: a personality model, but not yet a theory. In M. M. Page (Ed.), *Nebraska Symposium on Motivation: Personality – Current Theory and Research*. Lincoln, NE: University of Nebraska Press.

Eysenck, H. J. (1967). *The Biological Basis of Personality*. Springfield, IL: C. C. Thomas.

Eysenck, H. J. & Eysenck, M. W. (1985). *Personality and Individual Differences*. New York: Plenum.

Eysenck, M. W. (1992). *Anxiety: The Cognitive Perspective*. Hove: Erlbaum.

Eysenck, M. W. (1997). *Anxiety and Cognition: a Unified Theory*. Hove: Psychology Press.

Eysenck, M. W. (2000). A cognitive approach to trait anxiety. *European Journal of Personality*, *14*, 463–476.

Eysenck, M. W. & Byrne, A. (1994). Implicit memory bias, explicit memory bias and anxiety. *Cognition and Emotion*, *8*, 415–432.

Eysenck, M. W. & Derakshan, N. (1997). Cognitive biases for future negative events as a function of trait anxiety and social desirability. *Personality and Individual Differences*, *22*, 597–605.

Fahrenberg, J. (1992). Psychophysiology of neuroticism and emotionality. In A. Gale & M. W. Eysenck (Eds.), *Individual Differences: Biological Perspectives*. Chichester: Wiley.

Fox, E. (1993). Allocation of visual attention and anxiety. *Cognition and Emotion*, *7*, 207–215.

Fox, E., O'Boyle, C., Barry, H. & McCreary, C. (1989). Repressive coping style and anxiety in stressful dental surgery. *British Journal of Medical Psychology*, *62*, 371–380.

Fox, E., O'Boyle, C., Lennon, J. & Keeling, P. W. (1989). Trait anxiety and coping style as predictors of pre-operative anxiety. *British Journal of Clinical Psychology*, *28*, 89–90.

Gray, J. A. (1982). *The Neuropsychology of Anxiety*. Oxford: Clarendon.

Gray, J. A. (1994). Three fundamental emotion systems. In P. Ekman & R. J. Davidson (Eds.), *The Nature of Emotion: Fundamental Questions*. Oxford: Oxford University Press.

Gray, J. A. & McNaughton, N. (2000). *The Neuropsychology of Anxiety*, 2nd edn. Oxford: Oxford University Press.

Lang, P. J. (1985). The cognitive neuropsychology of emotion: fear and anxiety. In A. H. Tuma & J. Maser (Eds.), *Anxiety and the Anxiety Disorders*. Hillsdale, NJ: Erlbaum.

Lazarus, R. S. (1991). *Emotion and Adaptation*. Oxford: Oxford University Press.

LeDoux, J. E. (1992). Brain mechanisms of emotion and emotional learning. *Current Opinions in Neurobiology*, *2*, 191–198.

LeDoux, J. E. (1996). *The Emotional Brain: The Mysterious Underpinnings of Emotional Life*. New York: Simon & Schuster.

MacLeod, C. & Donnellan, A. M. (1993). Individual differences in anxiety and the restriction of working memory capacity. *Personality and Individual Differences*, *15*, 163–173.

MacLeod, C. & Mathews, A. (1988). Anxiety and the allocation of attention to threat. *Quarterly Journal of Experimental Psychology*, *38A*, 659–670.

MacLeod, C., Rutherford, E., Campbell, L., Ebsworthy, G. & Holker, L. (2002). Selective attention and emotional vulnerability: assessing the causal basis of their association through the experimental manipulation of attentional bias. *Journal of Abnormal Psychology, 111*, 107–123.

Mathews, A. & Mackintosh, B. (2000). Induced emotional interpretation bias and anxiety. *Journal of Abnormal Psychology, 109*, 602–615.

Mathews, A. & MacLeod, C. (1994). Cognitive approaches to emotion and emotional disorders. *Annual Review of Psychology, 45*, 25–50.

Mathews, A. & MacLeod, C. (2002). Induced processing biases have causal effects on anxiety. *Cognition and Emotion, 16*, 331–354.

Mathews, A., Yiend, J. & Lawrence, A. D. (in press). Individual differences in the modulation of fear-related brain activation by attentional control. *Journal of Cognitive Neuroscience.*

McCrae, R. R. & Costa, P. T. (1985). Updating Norman's 'adequate taxonomy': intelligence and personality dimensions in natural language and in questionnaires. *Journal of Personality and Social Psychology, 49*, 710–721.

Mogg, K., Bradley, B. P., Miller, T., Potts, H., Glenwright, J. & Kentish, J. (1994). Interpretation of homophones related to threat: anxiety response bias effects. *Cognitive Therapy and Research, 18*, 461–475.

Newton, T. L. & Contrada, R. J. (1992). Repressive coping and verbal autonomic response dissociation: the influence of social context. *Journal of Personality and Social Psychology, 62*, 159–167.

Parkinson, B. (1994). Emotion. In A. M. Colman (Ed.), *Companion Encyclopaedia of Psychology*, vol. II. London: Routledge.

Pedersen, N. L., Plomin, R., McClearn, G. E. & Friberg, L. (1988). Neuroticism, extraversion, and related traits in adult twins reared apart and reared together. *Journal of Personality and Social Psychology, 55*, 950–957.

Phipps, S., Steele, R. G., Hall, K. & Leigh, L. (2001). Repressive adaptation in children with cancer: a replication and extension. *Health Psychology, 20*, 445–451.

Power, M. J. & Dalgleish, T. (1997). *Cognition and Emotion: From Order to Disorder.* Hove: Psychology Press.

Russo, R., Fox, E. & Bowles, R. J. (1999). On the status of implicit memory bias in anxiety. *Cognition and Emotion, 13*, 435–456.

Schill, T. & Althoff, M. (1968). Auditory perceptual thresholds for sensitizers, defensive and non-defensive repressors. *Perceptual and Motor Skills, 27*, 935–938.

Tourangeau, R., Smith, T. W. & Rasinski, K. A. (1997). Motivation to report sensitive behaviours on surveys: evidence from a bogus pipeline experiment. *Journal of Applied Social Psychology, 27*, 209–222.

Watson, D. & Clark, L. A. (1984). Negative affectivity: the disposition to experience aversive emotional states. *Psychological Bulletin, 96*, 465–490.

Weinberger, D. A. (1990). The construct validity of the repressive coping style. In J. L. Singer (Ed.), *Repression and Dissociation: Implications for Personality Theory, Psychopathology, and Health.* Chicago, IL: University of Chicago Press.

Weinberger, D. A., Schwartz, G. E. & Davidson, J. R. (1979). Low-anxious, high-anxious, and repressive coping styles: psychometric patterns and behavioural and physiological responses to threat. *Journal of Abnormal Psychology, 88*, 369–380.

Williams, J. M. G., Mathews, A. & MacLeod, C. (1996). The emotional Stroop task and psychopathology. *Psychological Bulletin, 120*, 3–24.

Williams, J. M. G., Watts, F. N., MacLeod, C. & Mathews, A. (1988). *Cognitive Psychology and Emotional Disorders*. Chichester: Wiley.

Williams, J. M. G., Watts, F. N., MacLeod, C. & Mathews, A. (1997). *Cognitive Psychology and Emotional Disorders*, 2nd edn. Chichester: Wiley.

Yiend, J. & Mathews, A. (2002). Induced biases in the processing of emotional information. In S. P. Shohov (Ed.), *Advances in Psychology Research*, vol. XIII. New York: Nova Science Publishers Inc.

3   A cognitive-motivational perspective on the processing of threat information and anxiety

Karin Mogg and Brendan P. Bradley

We are pleased to contribute a chapter describing our work to this Festschrift for Andrew Mathews, who has made a major contribution to the evaluation and development of cognitive theories of anxiety, as well as being among the first to apply paradigms from cognitive-experimental psychology to the study of cognitive biases in clinical and non-clinical anxiety. Indeed, research by Andrew and his colleagues has been particularly influential in this field during the last twenty or so years (e.g. Mathews, 1990; Mathews & MacLeod, 1985, 1994, 2002; MacLeod, Mathews & Tata, 1986; Mathews & Mackintosh, 1998, 2000). Such research has addressed a variety of questions. For example:

1. Do biases for threat information operate throughout information processing, or only in specific cognitive operations (e.g. stimulus evaluation, selective attention, memory)?
2. Do cognitive biases operate automatically, independently of awareness?
3. Do cognitive biases play a role in causing and/or maintaining clinical anxiety states? If so, which specific biases (e.g. biases in evaluative or attentional processes) play such a role?
4. What is the nature of cognitive biases in non-clinical anxiety, and how do they differ from biases associated with clinical anxiety?
5. Do different types of cognitive bias operate in different anxiety disorders (e.g. generalized anxiety disorder (GAD) versus social phobia)?
6. Are anxiety and depression characterized by different patterns of cognitive bias?

Although there have been considerable advances, answers to many of these questions remain incomplete. In this chapter, because of space limitations, we will only be able to consider a few notable issues mainly arising from research into attentional biases in anxiety, as this has been a core aspect of the research carried out by Andrew and his colleagues. However, before doing so, we will outline the development of some key theoretical ideas in this field, as these have been of fundamental importance in directing the empirical work carried out to date.

Theoretical frameworks guiding research into cognitive biases in anxiety

In our 1998 review, we outlined various cognitive models of anxiety which have been influential in this field (Mogg & Bradley, 1998), so we will not repeat the details here. However, it is helpful to note some of the key issues which are relevant to research questions that remain unresolved. For example, during the 1980s, there was growing evidence of attentional biases for threat cues in generalized anxiety (e.g. MacLeod et al., 1986) and memory biases for negative information in depression (e.g. Bradley & Mathews, 1983, 1988; Mathews & Bradley, 1983), but there was less persuasive evidence of attentional biases in depression, or of memory biases in anxiety (e.g. MacLeod et al., 1986; Mogg, Mathews & Weinman, 1987).

Such discrepant findings are of contemporary theoretical relevance within clinical psychology because of the difficulty in explaining them in terms of Beck's schema model (1976), as this assumed that cognitive biases operate throughout the cognitive system in both anxiety and depression. Thus, they highlight a continuing dissociation between the clinical value of cognitive models of anxiety (e.g. providing a basis for clinical formulation and treatment) versus the scientific value of such models in providing an accurate and complete account of cognitive processes in emotional disorders (see Mogg, Stopa & Bradley, 2001, for more detailed discussion of this issue). Beck's schema model has been of seminal importance in developing effective treatments for anxiety, and continues to have considerable heuristic value in clinical practice. It also stimulated much research into cognitive biases in emotional disorders; this in turn led to a search for better cognitive models, which could account for those findings that could not be explained by schema theory (e.g. different pattern of biases found in anxiety and depression). Another driving force behind much research in this field is that a more accurate understanding of cognitive processes in non-clinical and clinical anxiety may help, in the longer term, in developing treatments that are even more effective than those available today. Indeed, in a recent review of therapies for anxiety, Ballenger (1999) concluded that, although cognitive behaviour therapy is effective in reducing anxiety, only a minority of patients attain normal functioning. This highlights the need to develop more effective interventions based on more accurate models of anxiety.

Several cognitive models of anxiety during the last fifteen years have reflected an increasing integration of theoretical ideas from cognitive and clinical psychology, and have emphasized the role of attentional processes in anxiety (Mathews & MacLeod, 1994; Eysenck, 1992; Williams, Watts,

MacLeod & Mathews, 1988, 1997). Other cognitive models of anxiety and fear have been more strongly influenced by evolutionary considerations. For example, Oatley and Johnson-Laird (1987) discussed the functional value of emotions and also highlighted the role of attentional processes in anxiety, in suggesting that a key function of anxiety is its associated vigilant mode of processing, which facilitates the detection of potential threat cues in the environment. Similarly, evolutionary considerations played an important role in Öhman's (1993, 1996) models of fear and anxiety. He proposed that 'threat feature detectors' operate at a very early stage of processing (i.e. before stimuli have entered awareness) and that these detectors are sensitive to basic threat cues which have acquired biological relevance over evolutionary development (e.g. spiders, snakes, angry faces). Once activated by a threat cue, such detectors send output to other components of the cognitive system, such as those responsible for increasing autonomic arousal (e.g. increased heart rate), which in turn facilitate behavioural responding to potential threats (e.g. running away). Thus, according to this model, the cognitive system has evolved to be highly sensitive in detecting and responding rapidly to biologically fear-relevant stimuli in the environment. Öhman's theoretical views seemed to be complemented by developments in cognitive neuroscience. For example, LeDoux (1996) argued from animal and neuroanatomical research that there were two pathways for processing threat cues: one pathway, largely involving sub-cortical structures (especially the thalamus and amygdala), supported rapid, non-conscious processing of simple threat-related stimulus features (e.g. loud noises, snakes), while the other pathway, mediated by cortical regions of the brain, was responsible for slower, conscious and more detailed processing of complex stimuli. Thus, both Öhman's and LeDoux's models described specialized mechanisms responsible for rapid non-conscious detection of biologically relevant threat cues.

Although there are common themes across these various models (e.g. the role of anxiety in threat detection), there are also important distinctive features. For example, models by Williams et al. (1988, 1997) proposed not only that anxiety is primarily characterized by an attentional bias for threat cues, but also that this bias operates in very early aspects of processing, i.e. prior to awareness. They further argued that individual differences in the direction of the attentional bias underlie vulnerability to anxiety. That is, an anxiety-prone person has an enduring tendency to allocate attentional resources towards threat cues, whereas a low trait anxious person has the opposite bias: i.e. a tendency to be avoidant of threat. This model not only suggests that attentional biases play a causal role in anxiety, but also that attentional retraining (i.e. training an anxious person to direct attention away from threat cues) is likely to be an effective treatment for anxiety. However, this model seems to have difficulty explaining findings which suggest that dissociation can occur between the attentional bias and anxiety. For example, individuals with mixed diagnoses of anxiety and depression often have high levels of anxiety but no attentional bias, which suggests that the bias is unlikely to be a primary cause of anxiety (e.g. Bradley, Mogg, Millar & White, 1995; see review by Mogg & Bradley, 1998). The model by Williams et al. also predicts that, as the threat value of stimuli increases, high trait anxious individuals become more vigilant, whereas low trait anxious individuals become more avoidant of the threat. However, the latter prediction seems problematic because it seems unlikely (and substantially maladaptive) that low anxious individuals would show increasing avoidance of threat cues which signal increasingly greater danger.

These concerns led us to put forward a cognitive-motivational analysis of anxiety (Mogg & Bradley, 1998) that was influenced by a variety of empirical findings and theoretical views regarding the cognitive and motivational properties of anxiety, as well as functional and evolutionary considerations (e.g. Mathews & MacLeod, 1994; Lang et al., 1990; Oatley & Johnson-Laird, 1987; Öhman, 1993; Williams et al., 1988). Accordingly, anxiety is conceptualized as an aversive motivational state, which is triggered by potential threat cues and which is characterized by a mode of cognitive processing that facilitates rapid response to threat, including heightened attention to external threat cues and increased autonomic activation. More specifically, we suggested that biases in the evaluation of threat cues, rather than attentional biases, underlie vulnerability to anxiety. That is, individuals who tend to overestimate the threat value of stimuli are more likely to be anxiety prone, compared with those who do not have such a bias in evaluating threat stimuli. We also proposed that the extent to which attention is initially allocated to a threat cue depends on the appraisal of the degree of threat, as reflected by output from stimulus-evaluation processes, which feed into 'goal-engagement' processes that control attention. Thus, if a stimulus is evaluated as highly threatening, attention will be diverted away from ongoing goals and activities, and allocated towards the threat. However, if the output from the initial evaluation processes indicates that a distracting stimulus has minimal threat value, attention will remain preferentially on ongoing activities rather than the distracting stimulus (see Figure 3.1 for a schematic illustration of the mechanisms involved in initial orienting to threat in anxiety). Another feature of our model is that it incorporated the vigilance-avoidance hypothesis (Mogg et al., 1987, 1997), discussed later.

We soon discovered that other researchers shared our concerns about the emphasis of the model by Williams et al. (1997) on the primary role of attentional biases in causing anxiety. Indeed, Mathews and Mackintosh

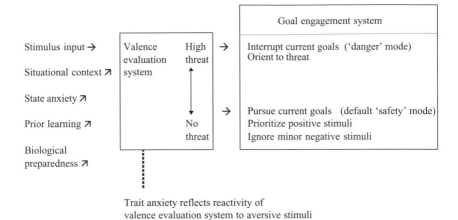

Figure 3.1 Cognitive mechanisms underlying biases in initial allocation of attention towards threat cues in anxiety. (Reprinted from Mogg, K., & Bradley, B. P. (1998). A cognitive-motivational analysis of anxiety. *Behaviour Research and Therapy*, *36*, 809–848. With permission from Elsevier.)

(1998) made a similar criticism of this model, in particular, regarding the counter-intuitive nature of its prediction that low anxious individuals would become increasingly more avoidant of threat cues as their threat value increases, and they also suggested that individual differences in trait anxiety arise largely from biases in stimulus evaluation. Hence, there seems to be growing tension between those models which emphasize the role of attentional biases (e.g. Williams et al., 1988, 1997) versus evaluative biases (e.g. Mogg & Bradley, 1998; Mathews & Mackintosh, 1998) in underlying vulnerability to anxiety.

Subsequently, several studies have directly tested the differing predictions from these models. For example, two studies in our laboratory (Mogg, McNamara et al., 2000) assessed attentional biases for pictorial stimuli that had either high or mild threat value to address the following questions:

1. Do both high and low trait anxious individuals show a greater attentional bias for stimuli with higher threat value, as predicted by the cognitive-motivational model (Mogg & Bradley, 1998), or
2. Do they show different patterns of attentional bias as stimulus threat value increases (i.e. greater vigilance for high threat in the high anxious, but increased avoidance in low anxious), as predicted by the model by Williams et al. (1988, 1997)?

The results supported the cognitive-motivational model. Wilson and MacLeod (2003) also directly compared predictions from these models by examining attentional responses to faces that varied from very low to very high anger, which had been created by morphing techniques. Their results showed that individuals tended to orient attention away from very low anger and toward high anger faces, with a greater attentional bias for moderate anger faces being found in high than low trait anxious individuals. They concluded that 'the pattern of results fully supports . . . and lends credence to models, such as those developed by Mathews and Mackintosh (1998) and Mogg and Bradley (1998)'. Other findings that have been interpreted as consistent with the cognitive-motivational model include those from studies of attention to somatic sensations and interpretive biases for ambiguous information (e.g. Stegen, Van Diest, Van de Woestijne & Van den Bergh, 2001; Calvo & Castillo, 2001).

The tension between these theoretical models raises the question of whether attentional or evaluative biases play a causal role in anxiety. This issue has been addressed in a series of studies which have experimentally manipulated these cognitive biases, recently reviewed by Mathews and MacLeod (2002); see also MacLeod et al., this volume. This issue is important because of its implications for the development of effective interventions for treating and preventing anxiety.

Do different types of cognitive bias operate in different anxiety disorders?

A major theme of the work of Andrew Mathews and his colleagues has been the study of attentional biases in generalized anxiety in both non-clinical and clinical populations (i.e. high trait anxiety, GAD). A notable contribution has been the modification of paradigms from experimental-cognitive psychology to assess attentional biases. The most widely used tasks have been the modified Stroop and visual probe tasks. In the modified Stroop task, participants are shown words written in different colours and are required to name the colour as quickly as possible and to disregard the word meaning. Typically, anxious individuals take longer to name the colours of threatening words, compared with controls (e.g. Mathews & MacLeod, 1985; Mathews, Mogg, Kentish & Eysenck, 1995; see Williams, Mathews & MacLeod, 1996, for a review). Such results suggest that anxious individuals preferentially allocate attention to the threat content. Moreover, this bias appears to operate outside awareness (e.g. MacLeod & Rutherford, 1992; Mogg, Bradley, Williams & Mathews, 1993).

The visual probe task was developed by MacLeod, Mathews and Tata (1986) from research indicating that individuals respond faster to a probe stimulus which is presented in an attended rather than unattended region of a display (e.g. Posner, Snyder & Davidson, 1980). In a typical version of the visual probe task, a series of word pairs is presented on a computer screen and, on critical trials, one word of each pair is emotion-related (e.g. a threat word) and the other neutral. Each pair is presented fairly briefly (e.g. 500–1,000 ms), and when the words disappear, a probe (e.g. dot or arrow) appears in the location previously occupied by one of the words. Participants are required to respond as quickly as possible to the probe. Individuals with GAD are faster to respond to probes replacing threat words rather than neutral words, compared with normal controls; this is consistent with an attentional bias for threat in GAD (e.g. MacLeod et al., 1986; Mogg, Bradley & Williams, 1995).

The task has been modified in several ways, e.g. using masked presentations to investigate preconscious biases (Mogg et al., 1995; Mathews, Ridgeway & Williamson, 1996); using pictorial stimuli, rather than single words (e.g. Bradley et al., 1997); and different response options (see Mogg & Bradley, 1999, for discussion of methodological issues). The exposure duration of the stimulus pairs has also been manipulated to investigate whether biases operate in initial orienting or in the maintenance of attention (e.g. Bradley, Mogg, Falla & Hamilton, 1998). A feature of the visual probe task (which also applies to the modified Stroop task) is that it presents only a snapshot view of attentional bias, which depends on the presentation time of the stimulus pair. To address this, complementary measures of attentional bias can be obtained during the visual probe task, for example, by assessing the direction and latency of eye movements to the emotional stimuli (e.g. Bradley, Mogg & Millar, 2000; Mogg, Millar & Bradley, 2000).

These paradigms have yielded considerable evidence that individuals with generalized anxiety selectively allocate their attentional resources to threat-related information (see Mathews & MacLeod, 1994; Williams et al., 1997; Mogg & Bradley, 1998, for reviews). Attentional biases have also been studied in other anxiety conditions, such as social anxiety and specific fears. There is considerable evidence indicating that socially anxious individuals have an attentional bias favouring social-threat stimuli, such as angry faces and social-threat words (e.g. Maidenberg, Chen, Craske, Bohn & Bystritsky 1996; Gilboa-Schechtman, Foa & Amir, 1999; Mogg & Bradley, 2002; Mogg, Philippot & Bradley, 2004; Heinrichs & Hofmann, 2001), which is consistent with similar findings of attentional biases for angry faces in high generalized anxiety (e.g. Bradley et al., 1998; Bradley, Mogg, White, Groom & de Bono, 1999). However, two studies indicated attentional avoidance of negative faces, relative to inanimate objects, in socially anxious individuals (Mansell, Clark, Ehlers & Chen, 1999; Chen, Ehlers, Clark & Mansell, 2002). Such apparently discrepant findings raise important questions about the cognitive mechanisms that underlie attentional biases (i.e. vigilance versus avoidance), which we will return to later.

Similarly, the evidence of attentional biases in specific fears (e.g. fear of spiders), has been mixed. Results from modified Stroop tasks typically show that individuals with spider phobia are slower in colour-naming spider-related than neutral words, which is commonly interpreted as vigilance for fear-relevant information (e.g. Lavy & van den Hout, 1993; Kindt & Brosschot, 1997). However, the interpretation of such interference effects has been questioned, as they may not necessarily reflect an attentional bias for threat, but may instead reflect an attempt to avoid processing the aversive information (De-Ruiter & Brosschot, 1994). At least four studies, using a variety of other attentional tasks, failed to find evidence of enhanced vigilance for spider-relevant stimuli in individuals with spider phobia, relative to non-fearful controls (Merckelbach, Kenemans, Dijkstra & Schouten, 1993; Wenzel & Holt, 1999; Tolin, Lohr, Lee & Sawchuk, 1999; Hermans, Vansteenwegen & Eelen, 1999). Moreover, the latter two studies found evidence of enhanced avoidance in spiderfear. Tolin et al. (1999) reported that individuals with spider phobia spent relatively less time viewing spider pictures than control pictures. In an eye movement study, Hermans et al. (1999) found that, after initial orienting, individuals with spider phobia were more likely to avert their gaze from spiders, compared with controls. However, enhanced vigilance for fearrelevant stimuli has been demonstrated on a visual search task (Öhman, Flykt & Esteves, 2001) and visual probe task using brief stimulus presentations (Mogg & Bradley, in press a). Thus, some studies suggest enhanced attention to threat stimuli in specific fears, while others suggest avoidance.

Another source of discrepant findings has emerged from research into the effects of stressors on attentional biases. For example, several studies found that anxiety-related attentional biases for threat cues are enhanced under stressful conditions (e.g. MacLeod & Mathews, 1988; Mogg, Bradley & Hallowell, 1994), whereas others found that such biases are reduced in the presence of a stressor (e.g. Mathews & Sebastian, 1993; Amir et al., 1996). Thus, although an enhanced attentional bias for threat cues appears to be a fairly consistent feature of generalized anxiety states (e.g. high trait anxiety, GAD), it does not appear to be reliably found in all anxiety conditions (e.g. social anxiety, specific fears). Moreover, there is evidence that attentional biases for threat cues in GAD may be suppressed under certain conditions, for example if the GAD is accompanied by a clinical diagnosis of depression (e.g. Bradley et al., 1995; Mogg et al., 2000; see review by Mogg & Bradley, in press b). In the next section, we will consider the theoretical implications of these findings.

Competing cognitive mechanisms determining vigilance versus avoidance of threat

Given that an increasing number of studies indicate that anxiety-related attentional biases for threat cues may be suppressed or even reversed under certain circumstances, we will next consider some mechanisms that might be responsible for this. Mathews and Mackintosh (1998) suggested three effects which may explain an absence of attentional bias in anxiety-prone individuals:

1. If state anxiety levels are low.
2. If individuals have had corrective experiences, or psychological treatment, which reduce the threat value of the cues.
3. 'Override', whereby individuals can override or suppress the attentional bias to threat cues by making strenuous efforts to perform the primary task, such as colour-naming (Mathews & Sebastian, 1993).

Williams et al. (1996) suggested that override effects are primarily found in non-clinical samples and are not observed in clinical samples, because considerable effort is required to counteract the automatic attentional bias towards threat. These override effects are of particular relevance in explaining the apparent ability of stressors to suppress attentional biases in paradigms where the processing of distracting threat information directly competes with the processing of the primary task, such as in modified Stroop tasks (Mathews & Sebastian, 1993; Amir et al., 1996). However, given that such override effects are proposed to involve a high level of effort and pertain mainly to non-clinical samples, additional explanations seem to be required to account for the lack of reliable attentional bias in individuals with comorbid clinical depression and anxiety.

In our cognitive-motivational model, we suggested that the absence of biases in the initial allocation of attentional resources in comorbid clinical anxiety and depression may be due to a deficit in the operation of attentional engagement processes (Mogg & Bradley, 1998). This would be consistent with depression being commonly viewed as an amotivational state associated with increased apathy and reduced interest in external goals and activities. While the lack of an attentional bias in depression can be accommodated within our model, it remains problematic for other cognitive models, which suggests that the attentional bias plays a primary role in causing anxiety. This is because such findings suggest that high levels of anxiety can be dissociated from attentional biases for threat. This in turn implies that reduction of the attentional bias (e.g. by attention training) might not necessarily result in a reduction in anxiety levels (see Mogg & Bradley, in press, for further discussion of these issues, including the importance of stimulus presentation conditions in revealing attentional biases in depression).

Another approach to explaining the suppression, or reversal, of attentional biases for threat involves other competing mechanisms, which may be evolution-driven (rather than task-driven). For example, Öhman's (1996) model of fear proposes that the automatic capture of attention by feared stimuli is a key feature of an innate defence system, which allows rapid identification of potential threats. However, the cardinal function of this system is to prompt avoidance of, or escape from, stimuli that may endanger the organism. In our 1998 model, we discussed the role of avoidance or escape responses in opposing attentional biases for threat in the context of the 'vigilance – avoidance' hypothesis. This suggests that, if the threat cue is highly aversive, attention is likely to be initially allocated towards it, but may subsequently be diverted away from it, in an attempt to reduce subjective discomfort elicited by the threat, or to reduce the degree of danger of the situation (e.g. avert gaze from aversive scene, escape; Mogg & Bradley, 1998, p. 820). This hypothesis may be helpful in accounting for the suppression of attentional biases for high threat cues, particularly in specific fears. Several studies in our laboratory, which have examined the time course of such biases, suggest a bias in anxious individuals to allocate attention initially towards mild threat cues, without subsequent avoidance (e.g. Bradley et al., 1998; Mogg, Bradley, de Bono & Painter, 1997). In specific fear, this initial bias towards threat seems to dissipate quickly (within a second or so), and may switch to avoidance, particularly if participants find the stimuli highly aversive, such as pictures relevant to blood-injury fear (Mogg & Bradley, in press a; Mogg, Bradley, Miles & Dixon, in press; see also Hermans et al., 1999; Rohner, 2002).

Competing mechanisms underlying vigilance and avoidance responses have also been discussed in relation to attentional biases in social anxiety. Rapee and Heimberg's (1997) model of social anxiety proposes that socially anxious individuals show enhanced selective attention to threat cues, such as signals of social disapproval or criticism. In contrast, Clark and Wells (1995) proposed that, in response to social threat, socially anxious individuals direct attention away from external social threat cues and engage in detailed monitoring of themselves; i.e. attention becomes self-focused. Consequently, the latter view does not predict an attentional bias for external cues relevant to social threat, and Clark (1999) further suggested that 'in social phobia . . . attention away from threat cues may play an important role in the maintenance of this disorder' (p. 10). Most studies showing avoidance of social-threat cues in social phobia have used household objects, rather than neutral faces, as the control stimuli (e.g. Chen et al., 2002; Mansell et al., 1999). Consequently, Chen et al. (2002) suggested that when there is an option of attending to either social-threat cues (e.g. faces) or non-social cues (objects), socially anxious individuals will attend preferentially to the latter. They proposed that avoidance of faces (relative to non-social cues) may serve to reduce some aspects of the threatening situation for social phobics (e.g. by providing psychological escape from social situations) and it may also reflect an appeasement gesture, where, for example, in evolutionary terms, a subordinate individual in a social group may avert their gaze from the face of a dominant individual. However, when there is no competition for attention between social and non-social cues (e.g. if the stimuli consist entirely of faces), then socially anxious individuals will selectively attend to the more threatening cue which is present. However, Clark and McManus (2002) suggested that, in naturally occurring situations, the attentional bias towards external threat cues may be less significant for individuals with social phobia, relative to their tendency to avoid social cues and to have enhanced self-focused attention.

We have been carrying out eye movement studies with Matthew Garner to examine some of these issues, and preliminary findings suggest that, under no stress conditions, socially anxious individuals preferentially direct their gaze towards faces rather than objects, but when under social stress, this bias for social cues is reduced (Garner, Mogg & Bradley, 2004). Moreover, socially anxious individuals under stress maintained their gaze for less time on angry faces, compared with low socially anxious individuals. Such studies indicate a complex pattern of attentional biases in social anxiety, which vary as a function of stress and the time course of attentional responses, and indeed suggest that more than one mechanism may be contributing to such biases.

Another possible competing mechanism is suggested by research that has distinguished between two primary aversive motivational states which underlie cognitive and behavioural responses to threat, namely, 'fear' versus 'anxiety' (Blanchard, Yudko, Rodgers & Blanchard, 1993; Lang et al., 2000; MacNaughton & Gray, 2000; Bouton, Mineka & Barlow, 2001). According to this distinction, fear is characterized by defensive avoidance, which facilitates escape from dangerous situations. In contrast, anxiety reflects a defensive approach state, which occurs when an approach goal state of 'risk-assessment' (i.e. vigilance for threat cues) conflicts with avoidance of threat (MacNaughton & Gray, 2000). Social phobia may reflect a combination of both aversive motivational states, as it is associated not only with high levels of generalized trait anxiety, but also with high levels of phobic avoidance. Activation of anxiety would trigger vigilant monitoring of the environment for threat, which may conflict with the effect of activating fear mechanisms, which can trigger rapid, automatic escape responses, as well as more complex, strategic avoidance behaviours (MacNaughton & Gray, 2000). Thus, the extent to which attentional vigilance or avoidance is observed in anxious individuals may depend on the extent to which the specific circumstances provoke anxiety and/or fear states.

However, it may not be necessary to distinguish between anxiety and fear as two distinct aversive motivational states. Instead, there may be a single aversive motivational system that produces different patterns of cognitive and behavioural responses, depending on its level of activation, as influenced by output from stimulus evaluation processes. So, for example, if a stimulus is evaluated as a mild to moderate threat, it may trigger attentional monitoring of the threat (i.e. a state of vigilance) and moderate autonomic arousal. However, if the stimulus is evaluated as an imminent, extreme threat, it would instead trigger attentional and behavioural avoidance and escape responses. This account makes similar predictions to those from models which suggest two separate aversive motivational systems, but would seem conceptually simpler, in that it only requires one aversive motivational system, which produces different types of response output depending on its level of activation.

Motivational influences on selective attention

Another unresolved question is whether there is a specialized psychological mechanism that is involved in processing threat-related information, which underlies cognitive biases in aversive motivational states (e.g. anxiety, fear), or whether such biases may be partly controlled by more general motivational mechanisms. Indeed, there is growing evidence of corresponding cognitive biases in appetitive motivational states, such as addiction and hunger (e.g. Mogg, Bradley, Hyare & Lee, 1998). Research in addiction had been stimulated by influential theories (e.g. Robinson & Berridge, 1993) which propose that drug-taking behaviour is mediated by a dopamine-based incentive system, which causes drug-related stimuli to be perceived as highly attractive, to 'grab attention' and to elicit approach behaviours. These processes are presumed to operate automatically, outside awareness. In support of such theories, there is evidence of attentional biases for drug-related cues in a range of drug users, including opiate addicts, cigarette smokers and cannabis users (e.g. Lubman et al.,

2000; Bradley, Mogg, Wright & Field, 2003; Field, Mogg & Bradley, 2004a). Such attentional biases seem to operate not only in initial orienting, but also in attentional dwell time, as assessed by the duration of gaze in smokers (Mogg, Bradley, Field & de Houwer, 2003; Field, Mogg & Bradley, 2004b); although it is less clear whether such biases operate outside awareness (Bradley, Field, Mogg & de Houwer, 2004). Evidence has also been found of a relationship between attentional and evaluative biases (Mogg et al., 2003), as the bias to look longer at motivationally salient cues (gaze dwell time) was associated with increased positive evaluations of the cues on both implicit and explicit measures of stimulus valence, as predicted by incentive models of addiction.

Such findings have implications for research into anxiety. For example, they raise the question of whether an anxiety-related bias against disengaging attention from threat cues (Fox, Russo, Bowles and Dutton, 2001; Derryberry & Reed, 1994) is mediated by a specific threat-processing mechanism, or by a more general motivational mechanism, which causes attention to be 'grabbed' by and maintained on motivationally salient stimuli (irrespective of whether the stimuli are appetitive or aversive). It also raises the question of whether, with respect to attentional biases, anxiety may have more in common with addiction than with other emotional disorders such as depression. That is, anxiety and addiction are both motivational states (aversive and appetitive, respectively), which are both associated with attentional biases for motivationally relevant stimuli, whereas depression is an 'amotivational' state that does not seem to be consistently characterized by attentional biases. Furthermore, given that cognitive theories of emotional disorders propose that attentional biases may play either a causal or a maintaining role in anxiety (e.g. Williams et al., 1997; Mogg & Bradley, 1998), it would seem helpful to clarify several unresolved issues. These include the precise nature of the attentional biases (e.g. initial shift, disengagement, maintained attention), the specificity of the underlying mechanisms (e.g. anxiety-specific versus general motivational processes), as well as the relationship between biases in attention and stimulus evaluation processes, since the latter may in fact play a more important role in underlying anxiety vulnerability (Mogg & Bradley, 1998). Such research should advance further our knowledge of the fundamental psychological and neural mechanisms that underlie the relationships between cognitive processes and emotional and motivational states and disorders.

Concluding comments

We are pleased that we have been able to contribute to this Festschrift for Andrew Mathews. Important features of his legacy in this research field include the application of rigorous logical analysis, incisive theorizing and exceptional expertise in research, design and experimental innovation. We have tried to illustrate here the stimulating effects of his theoretical and empirical work in one aspect of this research field. His work has been a source of inspiration for experimental psychopathologists and clinical psychologists, who are trying to answer fundamental questions concerning the cognitive mechanisms that cause and maintain anxiety, because an improved understanding of such basic psychological processes should lead in the future to more effective interventions.

AUTHOR NOTE

Our research has largely been supported by the Wellcome Trust. Karin Mogg holds a Wellcome Senior Research Fellowship in Basic Biomedical Science. This chapter has been adapted from: Mogg, K., & Bradley, B. P. (2004). A cognitive-motivational analysis of anxiety: current status and unresolved issues.

REFERENCES

Amir, N., NcNally, R. J., Riemann, B. C., Burns, J., Lorenz, M. & Mullen, J. T. (1996). Suppression of the emotional Stroop effect by increased anxiety in patients with social phobia. *Behaviour Research and Therapy*, *34*, 945–948.

Ballenger, J. C. (1999). Current treatments of anxiety disorders in adults. *Biological Psychiatry*, *46*, 1579–1594.

Beck, A. T. (1976). *Cognitive Therapy and the Emotional Disorders*. New York: International Universities Press.

Blanchard, R. J., Yudko, E. B., Rodgers, R. J. & Blanchard, D. C. (1993). Defense system psychopharmacology: an ethological approach to the pharmacology of fear and anxiety. *Behavioural Brain Research*, *58*, 155–165.

Bouton, M. E., Mineka, S. & Barlow, D. H. (2001). A modern learning theory perspective on the etiology of panic disorder. *Psychological Review*, *108*, 4–32.

Bradley, B. P., Field, M., Mogg, K. & de Houwer, J. (2004). Attentional and evaluative biases for smoking cues in nicotine dependence: component processes of biases in visual orienting. *Behavioural Pharmacology*, *15*, 29–36.

Bradley, B. P. & Mathews, A. (1983). Negative self-schemata in clinical depression. *British Journal of Clinical Psychology*, *22*, 173–181.

Bradley, B. P. & Mathews, A. (1988). Memory bias in recovered clinical depressives. *Cognition and Emotion*, *2*, 235–245.

Bradley, B. P., Mogg, K., Falla, S. J. & Hamilton, L. R. (1998). Attentional bias for threatening facial expressions in anxiety: manipulation of stimulus duration. *Cognition and Emotion*, *12*, 737–753.

Bradley, B. P., Mogg, K. & Millar, N. (2000). Biases in overt and covert orienting to emotional facial expressions. *Cognition and Emotion*, *14*, 789–808.

Bradley, B. P., Mogg, K., Millar, N., Bonham-Carter, C., Fergusson, E., Jenkins, J. & Parr, M. (1997). Attentional biases for emotional faces. *Cognition and Emotion*, *11*, 25–42.

Bradley, B. P., Mogg, K., Millar, N. & White, J. (1995). Selective processing of negative information: effects of clinical anxiety, concurrent depression, and awareness. *Journal of Abnormal Psychology, 104* (3), 532–536.

Bradley, B. P., Mogg, K., White, J., Groom, C. & de Bono, J. (1999). Attentional bias for emotional faces in generalized anxiety disorder. *British Journal of Clinical Psychology, 38*, 267–278.

Bradley, B. P., Mogg, K., Wright, T. & Field, M. (2003). Attentional bias in drug dependence: vigilance for cigarette-related cues in smokers. *Psychology of Addictive Behaviors, 17*, 66–72.

Calvo, M. G. & Castillo, M. D. (2001). Selective interpretation in anxiety: uncertainty for threatening events. *Cognition and Emotion, 15*, 299–320.

Chen, Y. P., Ehlers, A., Clark, D. M. & Mansell, W. (2002). Patients with social phobia direct their attention away from faces. *Behaviour Research and Therapy, 40*, 677–687.

Clark, D. M. (1999). Anxiety disorders: why they persist and how to treat them. *Behaviour Research and Therapy, 37*, S5–S27.

Clark, D. & McManus, F. (2002). Information processing in social phobia. *Biological Psychiatry, 51*, 92–100.

Clark, D. M. & Wells, A. (1995). A cognitive model of social phobia. In R. Heimberg, M. Liebowitz, D. A. Hope & F. R. Schneier, *Social Phobia: Diagnosis, Assessment and Treatment*. New York: Guilford.

De-Ruiter, C. & Brosschot, J. F. (1994). The emotional Stroop interference in anxiety: attentional bias or cognitive avoidance. *Behaviour Research and Therapy, 32*, 315–319.

Derryberry, D. & Reed, M. A. (1994). Temperament and attention: orienting toward and away from positive and negative signals. *Journal of Personality and Social Psychology, 66*, 1128–1139.

Eysenck, M. W. (1992). *Anxiety: the Cognitive Perspective*. Hove: Erlbaum.

Field, M., Mogg, K. & Bradley, B. P. (2004a). Cognitive bias and drug craving in recreational cannabis users. *Drug and Alcohol Dependence, 74*, 105–111.

Field, M., Mogg, K. & Bradley, B. P. (2004b). Eye movements to smoking-related cues: effects of nicotine deprivation. *Psychopharmacology, 173*, 116–123.

Fox, E., Russo, R., Bowles, R. & Dutton, K. (2001). Do threatening stimuli draw or hold visual attention in subclinical anxiety. *Journal of Experimental Psychology: General, 130*, 681–700.

Garner, M. J., Mogg, K. & Bradley, B. P. (2004). Orienting and maintenance of gaze to facial expressions in social anxiety (submitted).

Gilboa-Schechtman, E., Foa, E. B. & Amir, N. (1999). Attentional biases for facial expressions in social phobia: the face-in-the-crowd paradigm. *Cognition and Emotion, 13*, 305–318.

Heinrichs, N. & Hofmann, S. G. (2001). Information processing in social phobia. *Clinical Psychology Review, 21*, 751–770.

Hermans, D., Vansteenwegen, D. & Eelen, P. (1999). Eye movement registration as a continuous index of attention deployment: data from a group of spider anxious students. *Cognition and Emotion, 13*, 419–434.

Kindt, M. & Brosschot, J. F. (1997). Phobia-related cognitive bias for pictorial and linguistic stimuli. *Journal of Abnormal Psychology, 106*, 644–648.

Lang, P. J., Bradley, M. M. & Cuthbert, B. N. (1990). Emotion, attention and the startle reflex. *Psychological Review*, *97*, 377–398.

Lang, P. J., Davis, M. & Öhman, A. (2000). Fear and anxiety: animal models and human cognitive psychopharmacology. *Journal of Affective Disorders*, *61*, 137–159.

Lavy, E. & van den Hout, M. (1993). Selective attention evidenced by pictorial and linguistic Stroop tasks. *Behaviour Therapy*, *24*, 645–657.

LeDoux, J. E. (1996). *The Emotional Brain*. New York: Simon & Schuster.

Lubman, D. I., Peters, L. A., Mogg, K., Bradley, B. P. & Deakin, J. F. W. (2000). Attentional bias for drug cues in opiate dependence. *Psychological Medicine*, *30*, 169–175.

MacLeod, C. & Mathews, A. (1988). Anxiety and the allocation of attention to threat. *Quarterly Journal of Experimental Psychology*, *40*, 653–670.

MacLeod, C., Mathews, A. & Tata, P. (1986). Attentional bias in emotional disorders. *Journal of Abnormal Psychology*, *95*, 15–20.

MacLeod, C. & Rutherford, E. M. (1992). Anxiety and the selective processing of emotional information: mediating roles of awareness, trait and state variables, and personal relevance of stimulus materials. *Behaviour Research and Therapy*, *30*, 479–491.

MacNaughton, N. & Gray, J. A. (2000). Anxiolytic action on the behavioural inhibition system implies multiple types of arousal contribute to anxiety. *Journal of Affective Disorders*, *61*, 161–176.

Maidenberg, E., Chen, E., Craske, M., Bohn, P. & Bystritsky, A. (1996). Specificity of attentional bias in panic disorder and social phobia. *Journal of Anxiety Disorders*, *10*, 529–541.

Mansell, W., Clark, D. M., Ehlers, A. & Chen, Y. P. (1999). Social anxiety and attention away from emotional faces. *Cognition and Emotion*, *13*, 673–690.

Mathews, A. (1990). Why worry? The cognitive function of anxiety. *Behaviour Research and Therapy*, *28*, 455–468.

Mathews, A. & Bradley, B. P. (1983). Mood and the self-reference bias in recall. *Behaviour Research and Therapy*, *21*, 233–239.

Mathews, A. & Mackintosh, B. (1998). A cognitive model of selective processing in anxiety. *Cognitive Therapy and Research*, *22*, 539–560.

Mathews, A. & Mackintosh, B. (2000). Induced emotional interpretation bias and anxiety. *Journal of Abnormal Psychology*, *109*, 602–615.

Mathews, A. & MacLeod, C. (1985). Selective processing of threat cues in anxiety states. *Behaviour Research and Therapy*, *23*, 563–569.

Mathews, A. & MacLeod, C. (1994). Cognitive approaches to emotion and emotional disorders. *Annual Review of Psychology*, *45*, 25–50.

Mathews, A. & MacLeod, C. (2002). Induced processing biases have causal effects on anxiety. *Cognition and Emotion*, *16*, 331–354.

Mathews, A., Mogg, K., Kentish, J. & Eysenck, M. (1995). Effects of psychological treatment on cognitive bias in generalized anxiety disorder. *Behaviour Research and Therapy*, *33*, 293–303.

Mathews, A., Ridgeway, V. & Williamson, D. A. (1996). Evidence for attention to threatening stimuli in depression. *Behaviour Research and Therapy*, *34*, 695–705.

Mathews, A. & Sebastian, S. (1993). Suppression of emotional Stroop effects by fear arousal. *Cognition and Emotion*, *7*, 517–530.

Merckelbach, H., Kenemans, J. L., Dijkstra, A. & Schouten, E., (1993). No attentional bias for pictoral stimuli in spider-fearful subjects. *Journal of Psychopathology and Behavioral Assessment*, *15*, 197–206.

Mogg, K. & Bradley, B. P. (1998). A cognitive-motivational analysis of anxiety. *Behaviour Research and Therapy*, *36*, 809–848.

Mogg, K. & Bradley, B. P. (1999). Some methodological issues in assessing attentional biases for threatening faces in anxiety: a replication study using a modified version of the probe detection task. *Behaviour Research and Therapy*, *37*, 595–604.

Mogg, K. & Bradley, B. P. (2002). Selective orienting to masked threat faces in social anxiety. *Behaviour Research and Therapy*, *40*, 1403–1414.

Mogg, K. & Bradley, B. P. (in press a). Time course of attentional bias for fear-relevant pictures in spider-fearful individuals. *Behaviour Research and Therapy*.

Mogg, K. & Bradley, B. P. (in press b). Attentional bias in generalized anxiety disorder versus depressive disorder. *Cognitive Therapy and Research*.

Mogg, K., Bradley, B. P., de Bono, J. & Painter, M. (1997). Time course of attentional bias for threat information in non-clinical anxiety. *Behaviour Research and Therapy*, *35*, 297–303.

Mogg, K., Bradley, B. P., Field, M. & de Houwer, J. (2003). Eye movements to smoking-related pictures in smokers: relationship between attentional biases and implicit and explicit measures of stimulus valence. *Addiction*, *98*, 825–836.

Mogg, K., Bradley, B. P. & Hallowell, N. (1994). Attentional bias to threat: roles of trait anxiety, stressful events, and awareness. *Quarterly Journal of Experimental Psychology*, *47A*, 841–864.

Mogg, K., Bradley, B. P., Hyare, H. & Lee, S. (1998). Selective attention to food-related stimuli in hunger: are attentional biases specific to emotional and psychopathological states, or are they also found in normal drive states? *Behaviour Research and Therapy*, *36*, 227–237.

Mogg, K., Bradley, B. P., Miles, F. & Dixon, R. (in press). Time course of attentional bias for threat scenes: testing the vigilance-avoidance hypothesis. *Cognition and Emotion*.

Mogg, K., Bradley, B. P. & Williams, R. (1995). Attentional bias in anxiety and depression: the role of awareness. *British Journal of Clinical Psychology*, *34*, 17–36.

Mogg, K., Bradley, B. P., Williams, R. & Mathews, A. (1993). Subliminal processing of emotional information in anxiety and depression. *Journal of Abnormal Psychology*, *102*, 304–311.

Mogg, K., Mathews, A. & Weinman, J. (1987). Memory bias in clinical anxiety. *Journal of Abnormal Psychology*, *96*, 94–98.

Mogg, K., McNamara, J., Powys, M., Rawlinson, H., Sieffer, A. & Bradley, B. P. (2000). Selective attention to threat: a test of two cognitive models. *Cognition and Emotion*, *14*, 375–399.

Mogg, K., Millar, N. & Bradley, B. P. (2000). Biases in eye movements to threatening facial expressions in generalized anxiety disorder and depressive disorder. *Journal of Abnormal Psychology, 19*, 695–704.

Mogg, K., Philippot, P. & Bradley, B. P. (2004). Selective attention to angry faces in clinical social phobia. *Journal of Abnormal Psychology, 113*, 160–165.

Mogg, K., Stopa, L. & Bradley, B. P. (2001). 'From the conscious to the unconscious': what can cognitive theories of psychopathology learn from Freudian theory? *Psychological Inquiry, 12*, 139–143.

Oatley, K. & Johnson-Laird, P. (1987). Towards a cognitive theory of emotions. *Cognition and Emotion, 1*, 29–50.

Öhman, A. (1993). Fear and anxiety as emotional phenomena: clinical phenomenology, evolutionary perspectives, and information processing mechanisms. In M. Lewis & J. M. Haviland (Eds.), *Handbook of Emotions*. New York: Guilford.

Öhman, A. (1996). Preferential preattentive processing of threat in anxiety: preparedness and attentional biases. In R. M. Rapee (Ed.), *Current Controversies in the Anxiety Disorders*. New York: Guilford.

Öhman, A., Flykt, A. & Esteves, F. (2001). Emotion drives attention: detecting the snake in the grass. *Journal of Experimental Psychology: General, 130*, 466–478.

Posner, M. I., Snyder, C. R. & Davidson, B. J. (1980). Attention and the detection of signals. *Journal of Experimental Psychology: General, 109*, 160–174.

Rapee, R. M. & Heimberg, R. G. (1997). A model of social phobia. *Behaviour Research and Therapy, 35*, 741–756.

Robinson, T. E. & Berridge, K. E. (1993). The neural basis of drug craving: an incentive-sensitisation theory of addiction. *Brain Research Review, 18*, 247–291.

Rohner, J.-C. (2002). The time-course of visual threat processing: high trait anxious individuals eventually avert their gaze from angry faces. *Cognition and Emotion, 16*, 837–844.

Stegen, K., Van Diest, I., Van de Woestijne, K. P. & Van den Bergh, O. (2001). Do persons with negative affect have an attentional bias to bodily sensations? *Cognition and Emotion, 15*, 813–830.

Tolin, D. F., Lohr, J. M., Lee, T. C. & Sawchuk, C. N. (1999). Visual avoidance in specific phobia. *Behaviour Research and Therapy, 37*, 63–70.

Wenzel, A. & Holt, C. S. (1999). Dot probe performance in two specific phobias. *British Journal of Clinical Psychology, 38*, 407–410.

Williams, J. M. G., Mathews, A. & MacLeod, C. (1996). The emotional Stroop task and psychopathology. *Psychological Bulletin, 120*, 3–24.

Williams, J. M. G., Watts, F. N., MacLeod, C. & Mathews, A. (1988). *Cognitive Psychology and Emotional Disorders*. Chichester: Wiley.

Williams, J. M. G., Watts, F. N., MacLeod, C. & Mathews, A. (1997). *Cognitive Psychology and Emotional Disorders*, 2nd edn. Chichester: Wiley.

Wilson E. & MacLeod, C. (2003). Contrasting two accounts of anxiety-linked attentional bias: selective attention to varying levels of threat intensity. *Journal of Abnormal Psychology, 112*, 212–218.

4 Maintenance or capture of attention in anxiety-related biases?

Elaine Fox

Maintenance or capture of attention in anxiety-related biases?

Anxiety is a complex experience, which serves as a biological warning system and is generally activated by the perception of danger in the environment. Normal levels of anxiety, while somewhat difficult to quantify, allow for the rapid identification of potential threat and the preparation of an appropriate response. However, anxiety levels can become abnormal when the intensity and duration of anxious episodes are disproportional to the potential for harm, or when they occur without any clear threat. In the last two decades, significant advances have been made in the understanding of how a variety of cognitive processes (e.g. attention and memory) are affected in emotional disorders. In particular, the work of Andrew Mathews and his colleagues has been influential in promoting the idea that fundamental biases in the way in which information is processed may underlie many of the characteristic problems of anxiety and depression (e.g. Mathews & Bradley, 1983; Mathews & MacLeod, 1985; Mathews, Mogg, May & Eysenck, 1989). This empirical research programme has resulted in the development of a coherent and influential framework for the understanding of emotional disorders (e.g. Mathews & MacLeod, 1994; Williams, Watts, MacLeod & Mathews, 1988, 1997). It is a great pleasure to contribute a chapter to this Festschrift for Andrew. From my very first submitted paper to *Cognition and Emotion* (for which Andrew was the action editor) to more recent direct collaborations, my own research and thinking have been strongly influenced by Andrew's depth of knowledge and understanding of the cognitive processes involved in emotion and emotional disorders. In this chapter, I would like to outline my own programme of research, which has attempted to examine the nature of attentional bias in anxiety and takes the approach that the relations between particular emotions and cognitive processes arise to a large extent from the biological and social functions served by different emotions (Oatley & Johnson-Laird, 1987; Williams et al., 1997).

Detection of threat-relevant stimuli using the visual search task

Eysenck (1992) has argued that one of the most important functions of anxiety may be to facilitate the early detection of threat in potentially dangerous environments. If this is correct, then a natural consequence would be to find a hypervigilant attentional system in anxious states. Moreover, it might be expected that any attentional hypervigilance would be especially finely tuned to biologically threat-relevant stimuli (Öhman & Mineka, 2001). Evidence that snakes and spiders, for example, may hold a special status in terms of capturing the attentional system of humans comes from experiments using the visual search task, in which photographs of snakes and spiders were detected more rapidly than photographs of flowers and mushrooms (Öhman, Flykt & Esteves, 2001). Moreover, the speed of finding the snake or spider stimuli was not slowed to any great extent by the presentation of extra distractor stimuli, while the speed of detecting flower and mushroom stimuli was considerably slowed when the display size increased. This suggests that the biologically threat-relevant stimuli were detected fairly automatically and 'popped out' of the visual array. The most interesting finding in this study for the present purposes was that people with a phobic fear of snakes (or spiders) showed an enhanced ability to detect the appropriate fear-relevant stimuli (snakes or spiders) compared to people with a low level of fear for snakes and spiders (Öhman, Flykt & Esteves, 2001). This supports the notion that the attentional system of these anxious individuals was sensitized so that threat-relevant stimuli were detected especially fast.

Another category of stimuli that may activate an evolved fear module is threat-related facial expressions. In our early ancestral environment, the rapid detection of danger was vital for survival, and facial expressions of fear or anger would have been clear signals of imminent danger. Therefore, the ability to recognize threat-related facial expressions quickly would have conferred a distinct survival advantage. It is interesting to note that while an 'angry' or aggressive facial display represents a clear threat signal, a 'fearful' facial expression may also represent a strong threat signal (Whalen, 1998). While a fearful expression clearly indicates potential danger in the environment, it is ambiguous with regard to where the danger is coming from. Indeed, if the eyes of the fearful face are looking directly at the observer, then the implication is that the person is afraid of YOU. Whalen (1998) argues, however, that it is highly adaptive to maintain attention on the fearful expression, in case of a sudden change to the closely related defensive attack mode. Thus, the term 'threat-related' will be used in this chapter to refer to either fearful or angry expressions.

Hansen and Hansen (1988) found that angry facial expressions were detected more quickly than happy expressions when people had to search through crowds of distractor faces for the 'different' face. Importantly, this study found that while the speed of detection of angry expressions was not affected by increasing the display size, detection speed for a happy expression was influenced to a large extent by the display size. Thus, just as with snake and spider stimuli (Öhman, Flykt & Esteves, 2001), threat-related facial expressions appeared to 'pop out' of the display. However, it was subsequently discovered that the stimuli used by Hansen and Hansen contained dimples and other visual artifacts that may have led to the faster detection times for the angry faces (Purcell, Stewart & Skov, 1996). This prompted us to re-examine the threat-superiority effect for angry faces by using schematic cartoon-like faces that did not have these potential confounds (Fox, Lester, Russo, Bowles, Pichler & Dutton, 2000). We presented a visual search task using schematic 'angry', 'happy' and 'neutral' expressions, and found that the 'angry' expressions were consistently detected more quickly than the 'happy' expressions. One experiment demonstrated that this threat-superiority effect did not occur when the faces were inverted, suggesting that low-level visual artefacts were unlikely to be producing the effect. Instead, it is more likely that the facial expression of emotion was driving the results. It is of interest to note, however, that the angry faces did not 'pop out' of the crowd, in the sense that increasing the display size did impair the efficiency of detection. Nevertheless, the degree of impairment as measured by the slope of the search function was statistically less (16 milliseconds) than that found when searching for 'happy' targets (29 ms: Fox et al., 2000). A very similar result has been reported recently, showing that the slope of the search function was around 13 ms per item for locating a negative facial expression in displays containing up to thirty faces and this increased significantly to around 21 ms for locating positive facial expressions (Eastwood, Smilek & Merikle, 2001). Öhman, Lundqvist and Esteves (2001) have also found a threat-superiority effect for schematic angry expressions relative to happy expressions. Of particular importance was their demonstration that the negative expression of 'sadness' did *not* lead to faster detection times. This result is an indicator that it was indeed the threat value of the expression of the face that produced the faster detection times, rather than the negative valence. Thus, these studies using the visual search paradigm suggest that threat-related facial expressions are indeed detected faster than other facial expressions (sad, happy or neutral) and can guide visual attention to the location of the face.

As with individuals with snake and spider phobia, it might be expected that the threat-superiority effect would be enhanced even further for anxious individuals. In one study, an enhanced threat superiority effect (for angry facial expressions) has indeed been found in a group of people with social phobia relative to matched controls (Gilboa-Schechtman, Foa & Amir, 1999). However, the evidence with non-clinical anxiety is not clear. Byrne and Eysenck (1995) did find that a high trait anxious group was faster at detecting angry faces relative to a low trait anxious group. However, while the high anxious group was faster than the low anxious group in detecting the angry faces, they were not any faster in detecting angry relative to happy faces in a within-subjects comparison. This does not provide strong support for an anxiety-related hypervigilance for threat-related facial expressions. In our own visual search work, we examined high and low trait anxious groups in four out of the five published experiments (Fox et al., 2000). In all cases, there was no difference in the magnitude of the threat-superiority effect between the two groups. Other unpublished studies in our lab also found strong threat superiority effects but no difference between high and low trait anxious groups, even when they were tested under conditions of high state anxiety (e.g. close to final year examinations). However, recently we have conducted a series of experiments using just the eye regions of angry, happy and neutral faces in a visual search task (Fox & Damjanovic, submitted) and found that the eye regions were sufficient to produce strong threat-superiority effects. In any given experiment, we did not find an enhanced threat-superiority effect in high trait anxious groups relative to low trait anxious groups. However, when we combined the data across several experiments giving a sample size of sixty-two participants per group (and a statistical power of over .80) we did find the elusive interaction between trait anxiety and target type. The results showed that the overall speeding with 'angry' compared to 'happy' targets was greater for the high trait anxious group (mean = 81 ms) than for the low trait-anxious group (mean = 44 ms; t (122) = 2.09, p <.036, p <.018). Thus, it seems that there is some evidence that high levels of trait anxiety can indeed increase the propensity to detect threat-relevant stimuli rapidly. However, the effect size is small, and large numbers (over sixty per group) are required to detect a significant interaction. It is also likely that matching the target stimuli to an individual's particular concerns is crucial. Nevertheless, the general difficulty in demonstrating an enhanced threat-superiority effect for angry facial expressions in high anxiety groups is not consistent with the assumption that anxiety is associated with an increased propensity to detect threat-related stimuli in the environment.

Does the Stroop task measure shifting or disengagement of attention?

One of the most consistent findings with anxious populations is that they take longer to name the colours of threat-related words relative to neutral or positive words (see Williams et al., 1996, for review). One interpretation of this emotional Stroop effect is that the presence of a threat-related word draws attention towards itself, thus interfering with the colour-naming response. This interpretation is consistent with the notion that anxious people are hypervigilant for threat and detect potential threat in the environment more rapidly than less anxious people. However, given the nature of the Stroop task (the integration of word and colour), it is impossible to separate out a variety of different mechanisms that may lead to slower colour-naming times (e.g. De-Ruiter & Brosschot, 1994; Fox, 1993). An alternative interpretation of the emotional Stroop effect, for example, is that the slower colour-naming times may be due to a delay in *disengaging* attention from the threat-related word.

This question was addressed in a series of experiments in which the neutral task (colour naming) and the to-be-ignored threat-related stimuli (threat-related words) were either integrated or separated. In one study, high and low trait anxious groups named the colours of words which were printed on A4 cards (Fox, 1993). As predicted, anxious people took longer to name the colours of threat-related words relative to positive or neutral words. The more interesting comparison was on another set of cards, in which the threat-related words were presented above or below a colour patch. The task was to name the colour patch whilst ignoring the words. While the magnitude of the emotional Stroop effect was reduced relative to the integrated condition, there was still a statistically significant effect that differed across anxiety groups, even in this separated condition (Fox, 1993). This finding of a threat-related Stroop effect, even though the words were not centrally attended, is consistent with the hypothesis that anxious people may be hypervigilant and constantly scanning their environment for signs of potential threat.

It was still not clear, however, why we could not demonstrate an enhanced threat-superiority effect in anxious groups using the visual search task, which seems a more direct measure of hypervigilance for environmental threat. One possibility was that the presentation of Stroop words on cards might be problematic, since participants could scan the entire card before beginning. In particular, there is no way of ensuring attentional focus on the colour patches with this design. Thus, further experiments were conducted in which the separated Stroop task was presented trial by trial on a computer screen. Under these conditions, no

Table 4.1 *Mean correct colour naming times for high and low trait anxious groups when words were separated from colour patches (standard deviations are in brackets)*

	Threat-related	Positive	Neutral
Traditional Stroop task			
High trait anxious (n = 20)	582 (57.3)	562 (54.7)	556 (54.3)
Low trait anxious (n = 20)	546 (52.0)	542 (53.6)	548 (50.2)
Separated Stroop task			
High trait anxious (n = 20)	579 (51.6)	571 (50.2)	566 (52.4)
Low trait anxious (n = 20)	554 (48.7)	542 (44.6)	539 (43.2)

evidence for an emotional Stroop effect could be found (Fox, 1994). A problem, however, was that no emotional Stroop effect was observed on the traditional integrated Stroop task either (Fox, 1994, Experiment 1). Thus, this experiment may not have been sensitive enough to detect emotional effects.

To address this, a more recent experiment was conducted in an undergraduate laboratory class. Both the traditional Stroop (coloured words) and the separated Stroop (colour patch and colour words) were presented to twenty people reporting trait anxiety scores of more than fifty on the State Trait Anxiety Inventory (STAI) (high trait anxious) and twenty people reporting less that thirty on the same scale (low trait anxious). Threat-related (e.g. cancer), positively valenced (e.g. lucky) and neutral (e.g. house) words were carefully matched for both word frequency and length and presented individually on a computer screen for 200 ms each. The participant's task was to name either the colour of the word (traditional task), or a centrally located colour patch (red, green, blue or yellow) as quickly as possible while ignoring a word that was presented above and below the colour patch (separated task). The separated and integrated tasks were presented in separate blocks and the order of presentation of these blocks was fully counterbalanced. The mean correct naming times are presented in Table 4.1.

For the traditional task, high trait anxious (but not low trait anxious, $t\,(19) < 1$) participants took longer to name the colours of threat-related words relative to either positive ($t\,(19) = 2.1, p < .05$) or neutral ($t\,(19) = 2.4, p < .05$) words. However, in the separated task there was no hint of an interaction between anxiety group and word valence ($F\,(1, 39) < 1$). This failure of threat-related words to induce Stroop-like interference effects on the separated task does not seem to fit very well with the notion that anxious people are drawn towards threat stimuli in their visual environment, even when they are not attending to the location of the threat. When a threat word was presented just 1.5 degrees of visual angle from the colour patch, no interference was found. In contrast, when the colour words themselves had to be named there was significant interference from threat words for the high trait anxious participants. This line of research is more consistent with the notion that the emotional Stroop effect may be indexing the delay in *disengaging* from the threat content of words, rather than a measure of the movement of attention towards the source of threat.

What about the dot-probe task?

While the emotional Stroop task may be ambiguous with regard to the aspect of attention that is being assessed, the dot-probe task seems a much clearer demonstration that anxious people shift their attention towards the location of threat-related stimuli. In the traditional version of this task, two words are presented on a computer screen for 500 ms and the observer is instructed to attend to the word in the upper location. Following the offset of this display a probe is presented in the location of one of the words and the task is to detect the dot by pressing a button as quickly as possible. On critical trials, a pair of frequency-matched threat-related and neutral words is presented, and it has consistently been found that anxious people are faster to detect the probe when it occurs in the location of the threat word while the opposite pattern is often found in low anxious groups (see Mathews & MacLeod, 1994; Williams et al., 1988, 1997, for reviews). This pattern of results has been interpreted as evidence that anxious individuals are preferentially processing threat relative to non-threat at that particular moment in time. A problem with the original form of this task is that participants are asked to attend to the word in the upper location but the results are generally not reported for upper and lower locations separately. Thus, it might be the case that anxious people are faster in detecting the probe only following a threat word in the upper location (indicating delayed disengagement from threat), or only following a threat word in the lower location (indicating enhanced shifting of attention towards threat). Indeed, when the data from some classic studies were examined in this way the pattern of results supported a delayed disengagement hypothesis (i.e. faster probe detection times following threat words only seemed to occur when the probes and the words appeared in the *attended* upper location: Wells & Matthews, 1994).

However, subsequent research has circumvented this problem by instructing people to attend to a central fixation point when the word pair is presented (one above and one below fixation) and the task is to categorize the probe (Bradley, Mogg, Falla & Hamilton, 1998). Under these conditions, clear anxiety-related effects have been found, which suggest that anxious people are indeed orienting their attention towards the source of threat (e.g. Bradley et al., 1998; Fox, 2002; Mogg & Bradley, 1999b). However, to play devil's advocate again, since the word pairs are generally presented for about 500 ms, it is possible that participants switch attention several times between the two locations, and it might be the case that faster probe detection times occur *only* following words that have been attended. This again would support a delayed disengagement hypothesis and would be consistent with the failure to find enhanced threat-superiority effects for anxious people in the visual search paradigm. Consistent with this interpretation, recent work in my lab has found anxiety-related speeding of probe categorization following threat-related facial expressions only when the face pairs are presented for 500 ms or 700 ms, and not when they are presented for 50 ms or 200 ms. This pattern of results suggests that the enhanced ability to detect a probe when it occurs in the location of threat only develops with a presentation time of 500 ms or longer. However, against this vigilance effects have been reported on the dot-probe task at durations of just 100 ms (Mogg et al., 1997). Moreover, there are several intriguing findings of anxiety-related effects on the dot-probe task with masked stimuli (e.g. Mogg & Bradley, 1999b; Fox, 2002). These results indicate that anxiety may be influencing attention at a very early (preconscious) point, which seems difficult to reconcile with the notion that anxiety is only having an effect when attention is disengaging from a stimulus. It is difficult to be clear on this issue, however, until we know more about the attentional mechanisms that might be involved in the processing of stimuli of which people are not aware.

Measuring the disengagement of attention

It is clear that results from both Stroop and dot-probe tasks could be due *either* to a tendency to move attention towards the location of unattended threat-related stimuli *or* to a tendency to delay the disengagement of attention from threat-related stimuli. Of course, the pattern of results may well be due to a mixture of both of these tendencies. In the case of the dot-probe task, for example, the sudden onset of two items is likely to result in the allocation of attention to *both* locations, making it very difficult to determine if any differential response is due to the drawing and/or to the holding of attention (see Fox, Russo, Bowles & Dutton, 2001, for further discussion).

In order to examine the speed of disengagement more directly, we adapted the Posner cueing task (Posner, 1980). In the original version of this task, one of two boxes on the left- and right-hand side of fixation was cued briefly by a short flickering of one of the boxes. This was followed by the presentation of a target which had to be detected in either the valid (cued) or the invalid (uncued) location. The typical findings are that responses to targets appearing in the valid location are *facilitated*, whereas targets appearing in the invalid location are *impaired* relative to a neutral baseline. The general interpretation of this pattern of responding is that attention is reflexively allocated to the cue, so that when the target appears in the invalid location this necessitates a disengagement of attention from the cued location, the subsequent movement of attention to the uncued location, and finally a re-engagement of attention to the target. We modified this task, by using either words or faces as cues (Fox et al., 2001). The logic was that the movement of attention towards a neutral target as well as the re-engagement of attention with a neutral target should be equivalent across all conditions. Therefore, we should be able to examine directly the speed of *disengagement* from threat-related, positive and neutral cues. To illustrate, if a single word or face is presented on either the left- or right-hand side of the screen, we know that attention will be reflexively oriented to that object. Thus, on invalid trials, the disengagement of attention from threat-related, positive or neutral stimuli can then be directly compared. A typical trial in our studies is presented in Figure 4.1.

In our first experiment, we presented threat-related, positively valenced or neutral words as cues, and each cue was presented for 100 ms, followed by a blank screen for 50 ms. The target was then presented in either the cued or the uncued location, giving a cue-target onset asynchrony of 150 ms. Most of the trials (75 per cent) were valid, while the remaining 25 per cent were invalid. This was done to ensure a build-up of expectation of the target appearing at the cued location, so that disengagement from this location could be measured. It was found that participants did indeed take longer to disengage from the threat-related (375 ms) relative to either positive (369 ms) or neutral (370 ms) cues (Fox et al., 2001, Experiment 1). It is interesting to note, however, that there was no difference between high and low anxious groups. In a second experiment, we used schematic faces with 'angry', 'happy' or 'neutral' expressions. As before, with a 100 ms cue presentation (but with the Stimulus Onset Asynchrony (SOA) increased to 300 ms by inserting a 200 ms gap prior to target onset) we again found a general delay in disengaging attention from the 'angry' faces relative to the happy or neutral faces, with no differences between anxiety groups. However, when the cue duration

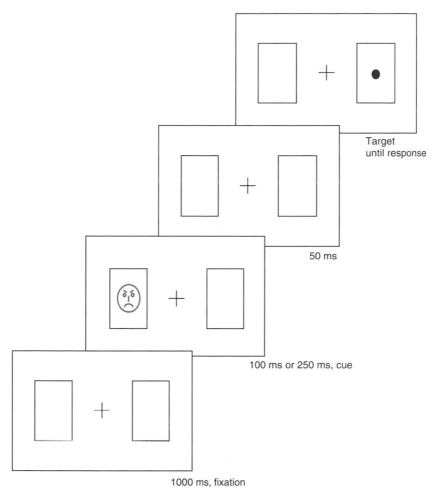

Target
until response

50 ms

100 ms or 250 ms, cue

1000 ms, fixation

Figure 4.1 Typical trial in the modified cueing paradigm, as used in Fox et al. (2001). This example shows an invalid trial with an angry schematic face cue.

was increased to 250 ms (still with a cue-target SOA of 300 ms) we now found a cue validity x cue valence x state anxiety interaction, such that the delayed disengagement from 'angry' faces now occurred only for those with high levels of state anxiety. Similar trends were found when participants were divided on the basis of trait anxiety scores, but these did not generally reach conventional levels of statistical significance. The results for state anxiety, which are adapted from Fox et al. (2001: Table 3,

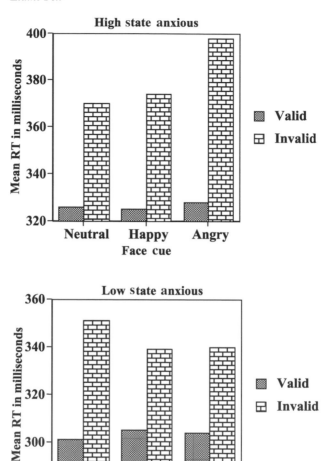

Figure 4.2 Pattern of results for high (n = 17) and low (n = 19) state anxious groups on the Posner cueing task with 'angry', 'happy' and 'neutral' schematic face cues. These results are adapted from Fox et al. (2001: Table 3, p. 689).

p. 689), are presented in Figure 4.2. As can be seen, high levels of state anxiety were associated with a tendency to delay disengagement from threat-related facial expressions, at least when the cue was presented for 250 ms. The results with 100 ms cue presentation imply that there may be an initial tendency for everyone, regardless of anxiety level, to dwell on threat-related stimuli when presented for a brief period. However, with a longer processing time, low anxious people seem to disengage equally quickly from threat-related, positive and neutral stimuli, while the high state anxious people tend to maintain their attention in the location of the threat material. In subsequent experiments, we replicated this tendency for high state anxious people to take longer to disengage from angry facial expressions relative to happy and neutral expressions (Fox et al., 2001). While we did not find consistent effects for variations in *trait anxiety* in these initial studies, other research using adaptations of the Posner cueing task have found that high trait anxious people take longer to disengage from threat-related pictures relative to neutral pictures (Yiend & Mathews, 2001), and from locations associated with losing points (negative), relative to locations associated with gaining points (positive: Derryberry & Reed, 1994, 2002). Thus, it seems that both trait and state anxiety may be related to a general tendency for attention to dwell on threat-related material.

We have tested this hypothesis further in the Posner cueing task by investigating the impact of threat-related stimuli on the *inhibition of return effect* (IOR: Posner & Cohen, 1984). IOR is the demonstration that responding to a target takes *longer* following a validly cued trial, relative to an invalidly cued trial, once attention has shifted away from that location, for example by re-orienting to fixation (Posner & Cohen, 1984). Posner and Cohen (1984) have suggested that IOR is a reflection of a mechanism that serves to favour *novelty* in the visual environment. The idea is that visual attention is inhibited from returning to an already attended location, thus biasing the system towards new information. We considered that this effect would be ideal to further assess anxiety-related delayed disengagement. First, given that threat-related stimuli may pose a potential danger it would make little sense to inhibit the return of attention to the location of potential danger (e.g. a predator). Therefore, we might expect that IOR would be severely reduced by the presentation of threat-related cues, especially for anxious individuals. In an initial study, we found that angry schematic faces did indeed reduce IOR, while normal levels of IOR occurred for both happy and neutral face cues (Fox, Russo & Dutton, 2002: Experiment 2). While there was a hint of a greater disruption for those with high levels of trait and state anxiety, this did not reach conventional levels of statistical significance. In a follow-up experiment, we induced increased levels of state anxiety (by asking participants to rate unpleasant photographs) in high and low trait anxious groups, and now did find a differential effect between these groups. For the high trait anxious group IOR of about -19 ms (i.e. slower reaction times on valid relative to invalid trials) was found with neutral face cues ($p < .001$), which was reduced to a non-significant $+3$ ms with angry face cues.

In contrast, for the low trait anxious group IOR effects of –12 ms and –22 ms were found for neutral and angry face cues, respectively (Fox et al., 2002: Experiment 3). These results suggest that the angry faces were particularly effective in holding the attention of the high trait anxious participants, resulting in a disruption of the development of IOR.

The temporal dynamics of the IOR paradigm are critical to test further the disengage hypothesis. For example, while we have evidence that anxious individuals may take longer to disengage from threat-related stimuli, we have little idea of how much longer. With the IOR task, for example, it is possible to miss differences between anxiety groups if the SOA is too short. It is important to note that this potential to 'miss' the critical moment where the groups differ is also a feature of the dot-probe and the disengage paradigms (see Mogg & Bradley, this volume, for further discussion of this issue). To illustrate, for the IOR paradigm, let us imagine that anxious people take about 600 ms to disengage from an angry face, whereas low anxious people disengage from angry faces in about 300 ms. This difference between groups would not be detected if the SOA was 1,000 ms. In other words, equivalent IOR may have built up by 1,000 ms so that the magnitude of IOR looks equivalent between the two groups. Ongoing research in my laboratory is attempting to determine the timescale of IOR in this paradigm. Using photographs of real facial expressions, we have found that high trait anxious people do show less IOR with angry face cues when the SOA is 500 ms or 600 ms while low trait anxious people show comparable levels of IOR across these SOAs. However, as the SOA gets longer (1,500 ms and upwards) the tendency is for the anxiety-related disruption of IOR by angry faces to dissipate. We are currently in the process of attempting to replicate this result (Fox, Carmona, Noguera & Vaquero, in preparation). If these results turn out to be reliable, they would support the view that trait anxiety is associated with a tendency to dwell for a longer period on threat-related material relative to low anxious people.

We have also asked the more detailed question of whether delayed disengagement really is specific to threat-related material (Georgiou, Bleakley, Hayward, Russo, Dutton, Eltiti & Fox, in press). To illustrate, all of the previous research has used threat-relevant material, such as negative feedback, angry faces or threat-related pictures (Derryberry & Reed, 2002; Fox et al., 2001, 2002; Yiend & Mathews, 2001). Therefore, it is quite possible that the results may reflect a general tendency for anxious people to dwell on *negative* stimuli, which may not be specific to threat. Using a task in which participants had to focus on a centrally located face and categorize a letter that appeared briefly either above, below, to the left or to the right of the face, it was found that high trait anxious individuals took longer to respond to the target when a *fearful* expression was presented at fixation, relative to either a *sad* or a *neutral* facial expression (Georgiou et al., in press). These results are consistent with the evolutionary hypothesis that delayed disengagement might be specific to threat-relevant stimuli (e.g. fearful facial expressions) and not to generally negative stimuli (e.g. sad facial expressions).

The functional significance and implications of delayed disengagement from threat

A tendency to delay disengaging attention from threat may have important clinical implications in terms of flowing through the cognitive system and escalating in increased negative rumination and worry (Fox et al., 2001). The idea is that these fairly automatic attention effects may feed forward and influence other cognitive processes, which then may enter conscious awareness. Worry is, of course, a key feature of clinical anxiety (Mathews, 1990) and may well be related to what seem like fairly minor delays (e.g. 10–20 ms on average) in disengaging from threat-related stimuli. We are currently examining this question in more detail in a series of experiments. Our working hypothesis is that worry and memory bias for negative material may be the end-product of delayed attentional disengagement from threat. Data from an initial study support this contention. In a previous experiment (Fox et al., 2001: Experiment 5) eighty high and low anxious students fixated on a word that could be threat-related, neutral or positive. While fixating on the word, they had to categorize a neutral target that briefly appeared above, below, to the left or right of the fixated word. The results showed that high anxious people took longer to disengage from the negative words, but not from the positive or neutral words. While we did not report the results in the paper, we then calculated a post-hoc 'worry' score based on answers to three questions from the Spielberger Trait Anxiety scale that explicitly relate to worry (Questions 29, 37 and 40). We also calculated a *disengagement* cost for the negative (mean RT negative words – mean RT neutral words) and positive words (mean RT positive words – mean RT neutral words) for each of our participants. A regression analysis was conducted with scores on 'worry' as the dependent variable. When positive costs were entered into the regression equation, these did not explain a significance portion of the variance on the 'worry' score ($R^2 = .018$). However, when the negative costs were added, a significance portion of the variance in 'worry' scores was now accounted for ($R^2 = .133$, $F(2, 77) = 5.9$, $p < .004$). In addition, the 'worry' score provided the best predictor of disengagement from threat (negative cost) in a subsequent analysis ($R^2 = .152$,

F (3, 76) = 4.5, $p < .006$), while entering both state and trait anxiety scores did not add to the amount of variance explained. These results provide support for our hypothesis that disengagement from threat may be a good predictor of subsequent worry and negative rumination. We are currently conducting follow-up experiments using a wider range of anxiety and worry questionnaires. This will allow us more directly to assess the relationship between self-reported worry and an objective measure of attentional disengagement. In addition, we are conducting a cognitive training study (see Mathews & MacLeod, 2002) to determine whether inducing selective disengagement from threat-related material may be an effective means of reducing worry.

What is the evidence for anxiety-related enhanced engagement with threat?

The previous section demonstrated that high levels of trait and state anxiety are associated with a delay in *disengaging* attentional resources from threat-related material. The question of whether anxiety improves the initial detection of threat has been approached by means of the visual search task, which has been discussed previously (Byrne & Eysenck, 1995; Fox et al., 2000). In collaboration with Andrew, we have modified the gaze-cueing task in order to address the question of whether anxiety enhances the *engagement* of attention with threat-related stimuli subsequent to detection (Mathews, Fox, Yiend & Calder, 2003). Previous research has shown that eye-gaze with neutral faces can act as a powerful cue. For example, if a target is to be detected on the right or the left of a face, responses are much faster if the eyes are looking in the direction of the target (congruent gaze), relative to when they are looking in the opposite direction (Driver et al., 1999; Friesen & Kingstone, 1998; Langton & Bruce, 1999). We modified the emotional expressions of the central face and found that if the face had a *fearful* expression, the gaze-congruency effect was greater than that found with a *neutral* expression, but *only* for those with high levels of trait-anxiety (Mathews et al., 2003). Thus, high trait anxious people may be more likely to engage the location indicated by a fearful expression. A problem with this interpretation, however, is that the baseline condition presented faces looking straight ahead, and this produced very slow responses, making it difficult to determine whether the increased congruency effects were due to congruent speeding or incongruent slowing. We are continuing this line of research by using a variety of different baseline conditions that may be less attention-grabbing (e.g. closed eyes) to try and determine whether congruent speeding or incongruent slowing is at the heart of the enhanced gaze-cueing effects with fearful expressions. Nevertheless, these results are an interesting starting-point and, assuming that another's fearful gaze acts as a directional signal for possible danger, then the finding of differential congruency effects is at least consistent with greater attentional engagement at potential threat locations. By this argument, anxious individuals may be more likely than are others to have their attention guided by signals associated with threat, and to engage locations cued by those signals.

Summary and future research

Fundamental biases in the attentional system of anxious individuals have long been considered to determine anxiety vulnerability (e.g. Eysenck, 1992; Mogg & Bradley, 1999a; Williams et al., 1988). Recent research has attempted to refine what specific attentional mechanisms might underlie this selective processing of threat. Several research groups have converged on the notion that a delay in disengaging from threat-relevant stimuli may be the primary attentional difference between high and low anxious individuals (Derryberry & Reed, 2002; Fox et al., 2001, 2002; Yiend & Mathews, 2001). Fox et al. (2001) outlined a framework suggesting that anxiety has little impact on the initial detection of threat but has a stronger effect in terms of modulating the *maintenance* of attention on the source of threat. As shown in Figure 4.3, the speed of *detecting* an object in a visual array can be influenced by the threat significance of that object (e.g. angry facial expressions are easier to detect than are happy facial expressions, Fox et al., 2000; Hansen & Hansen, 1988). However, the individual's level of self-reported trait anxiety does not seem to enhance this detection to any great extent (Fox et al., 2000; but see Byrne & Eysenck, 1995). In contrast, the level of self-reported trait (and state) anxiety does have a strong influence in terms of *maintaining* attentional resources on the source of threat (Derryberry & Reed, 1994; 2002; Fox et al., 2001, 2002; Georgiou et al., 2003; Yiend & Mathews, 2001).

This pattern may not be true for specific phobias, where the evidence for an enhanced threat-superiority effect is stronger (Gilboa-Schechtman et al., 1999; Öhman, Flykt & Esteves, 2001). The enhanced threat-superiority effect in social phobia (Gilboa-Schechtman et al., 1999) is particularly interesting in light of the finding that people with social phobia tend selectively to *avoid* negative (and positive) faces in the dot-probe task, at least under conditions of social-evaluative threat (Chen et al., 2002; Mansell, Clark, Ehlers & Chen, 1999). Thus, in social phobias an increased ability to detect threat-appropriate stimuli may be followed by an attentional avoidance of these stimuli. However, with high trait anxiety

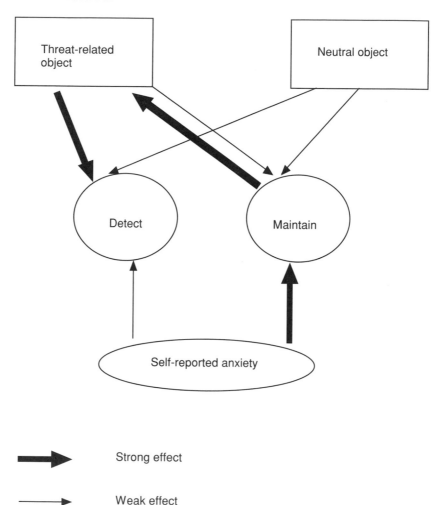

Figure 4.3 A model of how the nature of stimuli (e.g. threat-related versus neutral) and individual differences in self-reported anxiety may differentially affect the *detection* and *maintenance* mechanisms of attention.

(and perhaps other more general anxiety disorders) the detection of threat-relevant stimuli may be enhanced to only a small extent, although it may be that we are not sampling stimuli that are of prime concern to high trait anxious people. What is clearer is that high levels of trait anxiety are strongly associated with a delayed *disengagement* of attention from threat-relevant stimuli (Derryberry & Reed, 2002; Fox et al., 2001, 2002; Yiend & Mathews, 2001). We are currently testing for delayed disengagement effects (as well as enhanced detection of threat) in groups of clinically anxious people, and it will be especially interesting to establish whether delayed disengagement is a feature of phobic conditions as well as in generalized anxiety disorder. Another interesting avenue for future research, especially in terms of differentiating among clinical groups, is to assess the *vigilance-avoidance* pattern that may be characteristic of specific phobias, and the *vigilance-maintenance* pattern that may be characteristic of general anxiety disorders.

AUTHOR NOTE

The work reported in this chapter was supported by The Wellcome Trust.

REFERENCES

Bradley, B. P., Mogg, K., Falla, S. J. & Hamilton, L. R. (1998). Attentional bias for threatening facial expressions in anxiety: manipulation of stimulus duration. *Cognition and Emotion, 6,* 737–753.

Byrne, A. & Eysenck, M. W. (1995). Trait anxiety, anxious mood, and threat detection. *Cognition and Emotion, 9,* 549–562.

Chen, Y. P., Ehlers, A., Clark, D. M. & Mansell, W. (2002). Patients with generalized social phobia direct their attention away from faces. *Behavior Research and Therapy, 40,* 677–687.

Derryberry, D. & Reed, M. A. (1994). Temperament and attention: orienting toward and away from positive and negative signals. *Journal of Personality and Social Psychology, 66,* 1128–1139.

Derryberry, D. & Reed, M. A. (2002). Anxiety-related attentional biases and their regulation by attentional control. *Journal of Abnormal Psychology, 111,* 225–236.

De-Ruiter, C. & Brosschot, J. F. (1994). The emotional Stroop interference effect in anxiety: attentional bias or cognitive avoidance? *Behavior Research and Therapy, 32,* 315–319.

Driver, J., Davies, G., Riciardelli, P., Kidd, P., Maxwell, E. & Baron-Cohen, S. (1999). Gaze perception triggers reflexive visuospatial orienting. *Visual Cognition, 6,* 509–540.

Eastwood, J. D., Smilek, D. & Merikle, P. M. (2001). Differential attentional guidance by unattended faces expressing positive and negative emotion. *Perception and Psychophysics, 63,* 1004–1013.

Eysenck, M. W. (1992). *Anxiety: The Cognitive Perspective.* Hove: Erlbaum.

Fox, E. (1993). Attentional bias in anxiety: selective or not? *Behaviour Research and Therapy, 31,* 487–493.

Fox, E. (1994). Attentional bias in anxiety: a defective inhibition hypothesis. *Cognition and Emotion, 8,* 165–195.

Fox, E. (2002). Processing emotional facial expressions: the role of anxiety and awareness. *Cognitive, Affective, and Behavioural Neuroscience, 2,* 52–63.

Fox, E., E. Carmona, C. Noguera & J. Vaquero (in preparation).

Fox, E. & Damjanovic, L. (submitted). Anxiety and attentional processing of threat-related facial expressions.

Fox, E., Lester, V., Russo, R., Bowles, R. J., Pichler, A. & Dutton, K. (2000). Facial expressions of emotion: are angry faces detected more efficiently? *Cognition and Emotion, 14*, 61–92.

Fox, E., Russo, R., Bowles, R. J. & Dutton, K. (2001). Do threatening stimuli draw or hold visual attention in sub-clinical anxiety? *Journal of Experimental Psychology: General, 130*, 681–700.

Fox, E., Russo, R. & Dutton, K. (2002). Attentional bias for threat: evidence for delayed disengagement from emotional faces. *Cognition and Emotion, 16*, 355–379.

Friesen, C. K. & Kingstone, A. (1998). The eyes have it! Reflexive orienting is triggered by nonpredictive gaze. *Psychonomic Bulletin and Review, 5*, 490–495.

Georgiou, G., Bleakley, C., Hayward, J., Russo, R., Dutton, K., Eltiti, S. & Fox, E. (in press). Focusing on fear: attentional disengagement from emotional faces. *Visual Cognition*.

Gilboa-Schechtman, E., Foa, E. B. & Amir, N. (1999). Attentional biases for facial expressions in social phobia: the face-in-the-crowd paradigm. *Cognition and Emotion, 13*, 305–318.

Hansen, C. H. & Hansen, R. D. (1988). Finding the face in the crowd: an anger superiority effect. *Journal of Personality and Social Psychology, 54*, 917–924.

Langton, S. R. H. & Bruce, V. (1999). Reflexive visual orienting in response to the social attention of others. *Visual Cognition, 6*, 541–567.

Mansell, W., Clark, D. M., Ehlers, A. & Chen, Y. P. (1999). Social anxiety and attention away from emotional faces. *Cognition and Emotion, 13*, 673–690.

Mathews, A. (1990). Why worry? The cognitive function of anxiety *Behavioural Research and Therapy, 28*, 455–468.

Mathews, A. & Bradley, B. (1983). Mood and the self-reference bias in recall. *Behavioural Research and Therapy, 21*, 233–239.

Mathews, A., Fox, E., Yiend, J. & Calder, A. (2003). The face of fear: effects of eye gaze and emotion on visual attention. *Visual Cognition, 10*, 823–835.

Mathews, A. & MacLeod, C. (1985). Selective processing of threat cues in anxiety states. *Behavioural Research and Therapy, 23*, 563–569.

Mathews, A. & MacLeod, C. (1994). Cognitive approaches to emotion and emotional disorders. *Annual Review of Psychology, 45*, 25–50.

Mathews, A. & MacLeod, C. (2002). Induced processing biases have causal effects on anxiety. *Cognition and Emotion, 16*, 331–354.

Mathews, A., Mogg, K., May, J. & Eysenck, M. W. (1989). Memory bias in anxiety. *Journal of Abnormal Psychology, 98*, 236–240.

Mogg, K. & Bradley, B. (1999a). Selective attention and anxiety: a cognitive-motivational perspective. In T. Dalgleish and M. Power (Eds.), *Handbook of Cognition and Emotion*, 145–170. Chichester: Wiley.

Mogg, K. & Bradley, B. (1999b). Orienting of attention to threatening facial expressions presented under conditions of restricted awareness. *Cognition and Emotion, 13*, 713–740.

Mogg, K., Bradley, B., De Bono, J. & Painter, M. (1997). Time course of attentional bias for threat information in non-clinical anxiety. *Behavior Research and Therapy*, *35*, 297–303.

Oatley, K. & Johnson-Laird, P. (1987). Towards a cognitive theory of emotions. *Cognition and Emotion*, *1*, 29–50.

Öhman, A., Flykt, A. & Esteves, F. (2001). Emotion drives attention: detecting the snake in the grass. *Journal of Experimental Psychology: General*, *130*, 466–478.

Öhman, A., Lundqvist, D. & Esteves, F. (2001). The face in the crowd revisited: a threat advantage with schematic stimuli. *Journal of Personality and Social Psychology*, *80*, 381–396.

Öhman, A. & Mineka, S. (2001). Fears, phobias, and preparedness: towards an evolved module of fear and fear learning. *Psychological Review*, *108*, 483–522.

Posner, M. I. (1980). Orienting of attention. *Quarterly Journal of Experimental Psychology*, *32A*, 3–25.

Posner, M. I. & Cohen, Y. (1984). Components of visual orienting. In H. Bouma & D. Bowhuis (Eds.), *Attention and Performance X*, 531–556. Hove: Erlbaum.

Purcell, D. G., Stewart, A. L. & Skov, R. B. (1996). It takes a confounded face to pop out of a crowd. *Perception*, *25*, 1091–1108.

Wells, A. & Matthews, G. (1994). *Attention and Emotion: A Clinical Perspective.* Hove: Erlbaum.

Whalen, P. J. (1998). Fear, vigilance and ambiguity: initial neuroimaging studies of the human amygdala. *Current Directions in Psychological Science*, *7*, 177–188.

Williams, J. M. G., Mathews, A. & MacLeod, C. (1996). The emotional Stroop task and psychopathology. *Psychological Bulletin*, *120*, 3–24.

Williams, J. M. G., Watts, F. N., MacLeod, C. & Mathews, A. (1988; 2nd edn, 1997). *Cognitive Psychology and Emotional Disorders.* Chichester: Wiley.

Yiend, J. & Mathews, A. (2001). Anxiety and attention to threatening pictures. *Quarterly Journal of Experimental Psychology*, *54A*, 665–681.

Part II

Empirical directions

5   Habits of thought produce memory biases in anxiety and depression

Paula Hertel

Explanations of the mental lives of emotionally disordered people are sought by coping with special challenges. Although we can predict differences on a variety of cognitive tasks, we cannot – or should not – gain complete experimental control of the conditions that *seem* to produce those differences, the anxious and depressed states. Toward the goal of characterizing differences, Andrew Mathews and his colleagues have accumulated several decades of evidence about the cognitive processes associated with anxiety, occasionally distinguishing them from those associated with depression. And recently they have done the next best thing to gaining control of emotionally disordered states, by experimentally establishing in non-anxious people the kinds of biases observed in the performance of naturally anxious people (see Macleod et al., this volume, and Yiend & Mackintosh, this volume – Ed.). In this chapter, I report results that extend the effects of training interpretive biases to performance on a subsequent test of remembering. Biased or mood-congruent memory (MCM), however, is much more typical of depression than anxiety. Therefore, the report of this simulation of MCM sets the stage for reconsideration of the distinction between anxiety and depression with respect to biases in remembering – a distinction that corresponds to different personal concerns and habits of thought. Through viewing memory biases as the product of cognitive habits, it is possible to question the implicit assumption in much of the literature on emotionally disordered memory – that *emotional* aspects of anxiety or depression are responsible for biased recall.

Transfer of training interpretations

A substantial body of research has established that anxious people, be they dispositionally anxious or clinically diagnosed, are drawn to events that have potentially threatening features (e.g. MacLeod & Mathews, 1988), dwell on those events relative to others (e.g. Fox, Russo, Bowles & Dutton, 2001) and interpret semantically ambiguous events in a threatening direction (e.g. Mathews, Richards & Eysenck, 1989). In the course of this research, investigators have inquired about the nature of the relation between anxiety and the tendency to 'favour' threatening events. Does an anxious disposition or state trigger the bias toward threat; does sensitivity to threat set the stage for anxious affect, or are both directions involved? Recent attempts to sort out these issues suggest a causal role for cognitive biases in establishing and maintaining anxiety (see the review by Mathews & MacLeod, 2002). In these lines of research, attentional and interpretive biases are manipulated during a training task, and subsequent effects on emotional state, as well as continued biases on subsequent tasks, are observed. The latter type of effect is similar to what in former decades was called *transfer of training* or *transfer of learning* (see Ellis, 1965, for an early review). Experiments on transfer of training compared performance between conditions that varied according to the similarity between the two tasks; the question concerned whether those with a similar prior task performed better or worse than controls (positive versus negative transfer, respectively).

In the experiments reviewed by Mathews and MacLeod (2002), the question instead concerns qualitatively different performances as a function of prior experience. The main feature of the method is a training phase in which, for example, threat interpretations of ambiguous events are encouraged by the structure of the task. Many such trials in a threat-training condition should establish a processing bias in non-anxious participants that mimics the one that occurs naturally in anxious participants. In very simple terms, a new cognitive habit or propensity is established during the training trials.

Recently, evidence for transfer of training interpretative biases has been extended across very different kinds of tasks (Hertel, Mathews, Peterson & Kintner, 2003). Non-anxious students were randomly assigned to the threat-training, non-threat-training or (in Experiment 1 only) the no-training condition. Training took the form of 200 trials of a semantic relatedness task, based on the procedures developed by Grey and Mathews (2000, Experiment 3). Each trial consisted of two successively presented words, the second of which was often a critical homograph – a homograph (such as *stalk*) with at least one threatening and one non-threatening interpretation. The word that preceded each critical homograph disambiguated it in either the threatening or the non-threatening direction (*follow* versus *celery*), consistently across trials, depending on the training condition to which the participant was assigned. The task was to judge whether the two words on each trial were meaningfully related.

The transfer task was described as a pilot study. We asked the participants to provide ratings for materials to be used in future experiments.

On each trial of this transfer task, an individual word appeared on the computer screen and the participants were instructed to form a mental image of themselves interacting with whatever the word described, and then to rate either the emotional value (in Experiment 1) or the vividness (in Experiment 2) of that image. Half of the words were homographs with both threatening and non-threatening meaning, and all of these were novel homographs – not ones that had been used in the training phase. So, our measure of transfer of training was the number of trials in the rating task during which the participants constructed threat-related images. This measure was obtained from a tape recording of the participants' image descriptions while they were alone during this task. They were asked to form each image and then to describe it aloud, after being assured that someone other than the experimenter would later listen to the tape. To the word *beat*, for example, one participant said, 'I am having trouble dancing to the beat', whereas another said, 'My father is threatening to beat me with his belt.' (Agreement between independent raters was high.)

The results of both experiments showed transfer of training. Although all training conditions more frequently produced threat-unrelated interpretations than threat-related interpretations, this difference was significantly lower for those in the threat-trained condition, compared to the other training conditions. Viewed another way, the number of images that implicated the threatening meaning of the homographs was significantly greater for those assigned to the threat-trained condition. (Figure 5.1 depicts another replication of these results in the context of the study described next.)

Training memory bias by training interpretations

Much of the laboratory evidence for MCM – at least with respect to depression and depressed mood – implicates so-called encoding biases, or biased recall that presumably results from particular attention to mood-congruent materials during the initial-exposure phases of experiments. Indeed, in the reviews by Williams, Watts, MacLeod and Mathews (1988, 1997), MCM in depression was attributed to biased elaborative processing during initial encounter. The idea is that materials and events of the same emotional valence as one's own emotional state are elaborated more thoroughly and thereby are advantaged during attempts to recall. It stands to reason that this sort of elaborative bias could result from the habit of thinking relationally about negative events, as depressed people are prone to do while ruminating about their own experiences (see Teasdale, this volume – Ed.). Although some anxious people also ruminate (see

Nolen-Hoeksema, 2000), anxiety disorders are uncommonly associated with MCM patterns that depend on differential elaboration (see MacLeod & Mathews, 2004). Therefore, an attempt to model anxiety-related biases through differentially elaborative processing of threatening versus non-threatening materials would not be the logical method to choose. Instead, the method should reflect the findings that anxious people show interpretive biases. On this account, I reasoned that the interpretive biases trained by Hertel et al. (2003) should carry over to a subsequent task of free recall, in a manner analogous to the potentially differential effects of elaboration obtained in typical MCM experiments. I anticipated that, compared to other participants, threat-trained participants would recall more threat-related words, not because they constructed more elaborative or relational images during initial exposure, but because they interpreted more words in a threatening direction in the first place. This point of view is atypical of reasoning about MCM. Some of the objections that might come to mind are addressed following the description of the experiment. My main intent, however, is to offer this approach as a bridge to rethinking the conditions necessary to the production of MCM.

First, the experiment: university students were selectively recruited on the basis of low trait scores (less than 40) on the State Trait Anxiety Inventory (STAI; Spielberger, Gorsuch, Lushene, Vagg & Jacobs, 1983), obtained earlier during the semester. Under the constraints of equal cell sizes for each gender and balanced trait scores, fifty-four students were randomly assigned to training conditions (threat, non-threat and no-training control). The training phase and the orienting task for the transfer phase were both replicates of Experiment 2 in Hertel et al. (2003): participants were trained on the semantic relatedness task and then asked to describe and rate for vividness the images they formed of themselves interacting with each of sixteen homographs and sixteen non-homographs (more precisely, with the concepts to which the words referred). The thirty-two trials were randomly arranged, and the descriptions of participants' images were tape-recorded. Later, independent observers categorized the descriptions of the sixteen homographs as ones that reflected the threatening meanings, the non-threatening meanings or ambiguous meanings. The subsequent test of free recall was not announced in advance and not expected, according to end-of-session interviews. After the test, the participants filled out the state version of the STAI.[1]

Figure 5.1 presents the mean number of homographs interpreted in the threatening versus non-threatening direction. Compared to no-training controls, the threat-trained participants, but not the non-threat-trained participants, interpreted more homographs as threatening. The

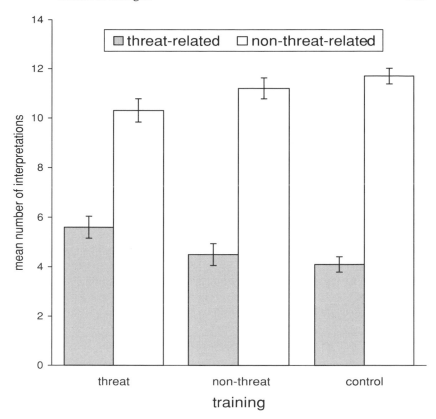

Figure 5.1 Mean number of the sixteen homographs interpreted in the threat-related or non-threat-related direction by participants in each condition of the training task (threat, non-threat and no-training control).

threat-trained group, but not the non-threat-trained group, also interpreted fewer homographs in the non-threatening direction. Therefore, the results obtained by Hertel et al. (2003) were replicated. In this experiment, however, the primary purpose for determining the meanings of the homographs was to classify the interpretations of words to be recalled.

Training-congruent recall

Participants in the three training conditions recalled similar numbers of non-homographs and intrusions.[2] The number of homographs recalled was scored according to whether the participants had interpreted their meanings as threatening or non-threatening. The analysis of variance

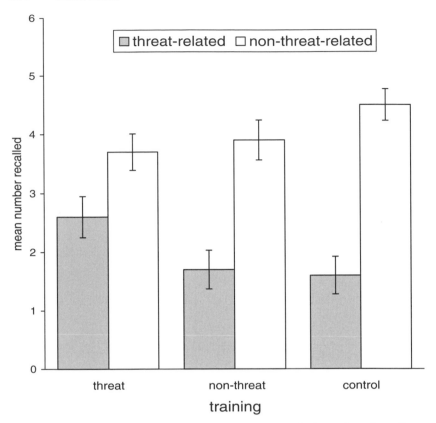

Figure 5.2 Mean number of homographs recalled, as a function of how they had been interpreted initially.

included between-subjects factors for training condition and gender and a within-subjects factor for type of interpretation. Overall, more non-threatening words were recalled, F (1, 48) $= 61.26$, $MSE = 1.90$, $p < .001$. But a significant interaction revealed that this advantage varied according to training condition, $F (2, 48) = 4.02, p < .025$; see Figure 5.2. Comparisons between no-training controls and the non-threat-trained group yielded no significant differences. However, compared to controls, participants who were trained to interpret threat recalled significantly more words that they had interpreted as threatening and fewer words that they had interpreted as non-threatening (although the latter difference was only marginally significant). Because, for example, *beat* is a threatening word only if it was interpreted that way, these results are tantamount to showing that the threat-trained group recalled more threatening words.

If this experiment were designed according to the more traditional procedures for investigating MCM – for example, ones used to examine effects of elaborative processing of valenced words instead of differences according to direction of homograph interpretation – I would score the data as percentages of the words in each valence category that are subsequently recalled. One might think, at first glance, that the comparable way of scoring the present data would be to examine the percentages of threat-interpreted words recalled and expect to find them higher following threat training. This would only be true if the process proposed to account for recall happened to be a process like elaboration. The reasoning would be something like this: threat training should lead to threat interpretations, and threat interpretation should lead to greater elaboration, which would then benefit recall. However, if the hypothesis does not include the postulate about elaboration – as it does not in the account of anxious cognition by Williams et al. (1997) – then the percentage analysis should not be done. Nevertheless, out of curiosity, I did it. None of the effects in the overall design was significant, but the pattern was in the direction corresponding to MCM in studies relying on differential elaboration. The threat-trained participants recalled 45 per cent of the threat-interpreted words and 37 per cent of the non-threatening words. The corresponding means were 38 per cent and 36 per cent for the non-threat-trained group and 36 per cent and 39 per cent for the no-training controls. This pattern hints at the phenomenon that corresponds to better recall for the more fully elaborated or distinctive meanings during orientation. It suggests that the threat-trained participants might have constructed 'threat' images that were more distinctive or vivid, and it raises the question of whether vividness is responsible for the interpretation effect.

Vividness

Does distinctiveness underlie the pattern of recall differences attributed to the nature of the initial interpretation? This issue was first approached by determining whether the images created for threatening interpretations were more vivid in the threat-trained group. To the contrary, as shown in Figure 5.3, the more vivid images were produced for the non-threatening interpretations, $F (1, 43) = 4.29$, $MSE = 0.41$, $p < .05$.[3] Moreover, there was a trend for this unexpected difference to depend on training conditions, $F (2, 43) = 4.84$, $p < .07$. The most vivid images were produced for non-threatening meanings in the control condition, the combination that also produced the highest mean number of words

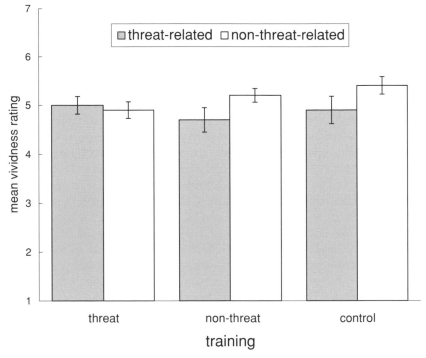

Figure 5.3 Mean rating of image vividness (on a 7-pt scale) for homographs interpreted as threat-related or unrelated by participants in each condition of the training task (threat, non-threat and no-training control).

recalled. In fact, the extent to which the participants made more vivid images for the non-threatening (compared to the threatening) interpretations was significantly correlated with the corresponding advantage of non-threatening words in recall, r (47) = 0.31, p < .05. So, indeed, distinctiveness, as measured by vividness, might have influenced the pattern of data, but not in a manner that could account for the effects of training. This point is underscored by the results of a multiple regression analysis, with the outcome variable being recall bias (number of non-threat meanings minus number of threat meanings recalled) and the predictors being vividness bias (mean ratings for non-threat-related images minus mean ratings for threat-related images) and a training code (threat-trained minus controls). Vividness bias was forced to enter first; then the increase in R^2 with the addition of the training code to the equation was significant, F (1, 46) = 4.80, p < .04.

Other considerations

In summary, the results of this experiment performed with non-anxious students mimic the pattern of interpretive bias typically shown with anxious people, and extend it to the domain of explicit recall. The recall bias likely did not result from processes operating at the point of remembering, if for no other reason than that the interpretations were categorized on the basis of performance on the orienting task. In fact, in the absence of direct assessment of meaning during recall, it is possible to argue that meaning might have changed. To do so seems similar to arguing that words with non-ambiguously negative meaning decrease in negativity between the initial phase and the recall test. Both outcomes, of course, are possible, but somewhat irrelevant because the meaning in the experience of the original event is the real issue (much as it is in the case of MCM by panic-disordered individuals; see McNally, 1999). It is also possible that, even though threat-related images were described (perhaps due to response bias?), threat training influenced the interpretation of *both* meanings and that the multiple meanings facilitated recall. These issues deserve experimental attention, along with the possibility that elaborative processing played a role (as suggested by the percentage analysis described above).

Perhaps the most striking feature of this simulation of interpretive bias and MCM is its relation to the long-documented findings regarding perspective taking and memory. Whether the task is one of recalling the contents of a house from the perspective of a burglar or a homebuyer (Pichert & Anderson, 1977) or recalling a story, the title of which cues a particular theme (Bransford & Johnson, 1972; Sulin & Dooling, 1974), people implicitly use prior knowledge to interpret ambiguous events, and the corresponding bias is revealed at the time of recall. What I have shown is that:
1. Experimentally established perspectives of a *conceptually* emotional nature can take the place of 'prior knowledge' in this formula, and
2. The perspective can operate without instruction or intent (also see Ross & Bradshaw, 1994).

Finally, this experiment constitutes a simulation of anxiety-related biases only because the relevant dimension of meaning – threat – is the most important dimension in the cognitive anxiety literature. One might ask, however, what phenomenon it was intended to simulate, because threat-related biases in recall have been documented infrequently. In the next section, the literature on anxiety and memory is summarized from the perspective of whether it has been sufficiently sensitive to interpretive ambiguity, of the sort that characterizes this experiment. It is the anxious person's habit to interpret ambiguous events in a threatening manner, just as it is the depressed person's habit to dwell on thoughts related to their depressed state. Memory biases should reflect the specificity of these habits of thought (Hertel, 2004).

Memory biases in anxiety and depression

One of the more influential frameworks for understanding cognition in emotionally disordered states is the one described by Williams et al. (1988, 1997) and based on Oatley and Johnson-Laird's (1987) motivational approach to emotion. Anxious people are motivated to avoid threat and thus scan the world for its possibility, whereas depressed people are motivated to resolve the causes of their depression and thereby dwell on personally relevant negative events. Williams et al. argued that these differences are associated with biases in different types of cognitive procedures and tasks. Anxious people show interpretive and other attentional biases, whereas depressed people show biases in tasks that reflect differential elaboration – tests of intentional remembering, in particular. Our understanding of the cognitive biases found in anxiety recently has been revised to incorporate the fact that anxious people tend to dwell longer on threatening information (see Fox, this volume – Ed.). Indeed, the notion of increased dwell time for anxiety-congruent events is not quite so distinct in kind from the dwelling shown by depressed people, but more a matter of degree. The attention of anxious people is focused long enough to identify threatening meaning, whereas the attention of depressed people extends beyond the identification of meaning to a ruminative exploration of meaning. Consider, for example, the early finding that depressed patients choose more often than others to consider their own personal failures when given a choice (Roth & Rehm, 1980). In the case of either depression or anxiety, however, the habit to attend to personally relevant meaning should be reflected in memory for the episode. The difference should lie in whether the test of memory has a chance of reflecting the particular manner or extent that attention is biased during initial exposure.

Anxiety and memory

Recent reviews of the relation of anxiety and memory (MacLeod, 1999; MacLeod & Mathews, 2004) emphasize the many failed attempts to find evidence of MCM in anxious states. Often the failures fit the framework proposed by Williams et al. (1988): anxiety is associated with perceptual vigilance followed by subsequent avoidance or inhibition. A good example is found in the especially poor recall of spider-related words by spider-phobic individuals (e.g. Watts & Dalgleish, 1991), even though such words capture their initial attention especially well. The spider-phobic individual wants to know where the spider is and then, reassured, prefers to dismiss it from mind. Certainly, we should not expect such habits to produce congruent biases on most direct tests of memory, which are prone to effects of elaborative relational processing. Unless the spider 'gets lost', the ambiguity that motivates attention is resolved. Yet when the spider is merely implied, the motivation to attend to clues is sustained and organized and thereby benefits subsequent recall (Rusted & Dighton, 1991).

In addition to reporting the occasional exception – such as the study by Rusted and Dighton – recent reviews have noted particular conditions under which anxiety-related memory biases are found. Although the evidence has been mixed (see MacLeod & Mathews, 2004), several studies have found anxiety-congruent memory through the use of indirect tests (e.g. Mathews, Mogg, May & Eysenck, 1989; Richards & French, 1991). Indirect tests of memory – such as stem or fragment completion – are themselves opportunities for interpretive bias. Typically, each fragment can be completed by more than one word. Completing it with a threat-related word previously attended in the same session is much like having one's attention drawn to threatening meaning. 'Seeing' the word in the fragment (or even hearing the word against background noise, as in Amir, Foa & Coles, 2000) is not dependent on the degree of prior elaboration, merely the extent to which the word itself received prior perceptual attention (or integration). In support, Eysenck and Byrne (1994) found that anxiety-related biases on perceptual indirect tests (like fragment completion) occurred more often following perceptual orienting tasks. This finding, however, does not imply that simple applications of transfer-appropriate processing account for the variety of findings from indirect tests. Sufficient perceptual processing can occur on so-called conceptual orienting tasks – tasks like staring at a word while imagining oneself interacting with its referent (Mathews, Mogg et al., 1989). Full integration is sufficient to produce the bias. Similar post hoc analyses can be constructed for other outcomes, especially if the analysis includes allowances for contamination of performance by intentional recall. A reasonable hypothesis is that the extent to which intentional recall is invited by the context is the extent to which anxiety-biased performance on ostensibly indirect tests will not be observed. The problem, of course, lies in knowing whether contamination has occurred.

A second category of MCM findings in anxiety emerges from cases in which the initial processing episode is free from restriction, according to MacLeod and Mathews (2004). Freedom from restriction (or lack of processing constraint or structure, according to Hertel & Hardin, 1990) permits the self-initiation of processes that benefit performance on later memory tests. MacLeod and Mathews emphasized the initiation of personally relevant relational processing for threatening stimuli by highly anxious individuals. Their examples included experiments in which the initial exposure was long and conceptual processing was not required, beyond the reading of the word (e.g. Friedman, Thayer & Borkovec, 2000; also see Russo, Fox, Bellinger & Nguyen-Van-Tam, 2001). Of equal importance from the current perspective is that unrestricted episodes set the stage for the emergence of cognitive habits (Hertel, 2004) – whether it be the habit personally to evaluate threatening meaning (as MacLeod and Mathews suggested) or to perceive threat in ambiguous situations (as suggested by the experiment reported in this chapter). Interpretations of ambiguity seem to play an important role in MCM shown by panic-disordered individuals. MacLeod and Mathews identified this group as comprising the diagnostic category most likely to show MCM, and the words recalled have often been words that were emotional only for the panic-disordered person (e.g. *street, market*). Similarly, in Burke and Mathews' (1992) study of autobiographical memory (Experiment 1), anxious participants recalled more 'nervous' episodes from their lives than did controls, but independent judgments of the threat value of the recalled events did not differentiate the groups. Indeed, it is possible that lab studies are generally affected by differential interpretations of materials that investigators categorize as negative, neutral and positive.

MacLeod and Mathews also reviewed a few studies documenting bias that occurs as a result of anxious individuals' inhibitory difficulties during initial exposure. For example, in studies of directed forgetting, participants initially attend to items that they subsequently are instructed to forget (by turning attention to other matters). Anxious participants sometimes show MCM, possibly due to the habit to attend to the to-be-forgotten material of a threatening nature.[4]

In summary, the two main categories that have produced evidence for anxiety-related biases in memory are unconstrained or ambiguous conditions of initial exposure and indirect tests, both of which permit the expression of attentional habits. Evidence of MCM in anxiety is most likely to be shown when memory tests are sensitive to prior or current selection and interpretation. Unfortunately, most research designs have been insufficiently sensitive for the purpose of evaluating, even on a post hoc basis, the value of that prediction for direct tests of memory. Memory researchers are accustomed to thinking in terms of the connection between elaboration and recall, even though we fully realize that elaborative and relational processing is not something anxious people are in the habit of doing – that is, unless they are also depressed.

Depression and memory

Although we need more direct evidence that MCM in anxiety is found when memory tests are sensitive to cognitive habits, the case for depression is much clearer. As I have argued previously (Hertel, 2004), habits of thought either facilitate or impair performance on memory tests, depending upon the emotional meaning of events to be remembered and depending on whether sufficient 'room' is made for the habits to emerge. Because ruminative habits kick into gear during unfilled and unstructured intervals, paradigms that include these intervals should be especially sensitive to the relation between the habits and the tasks at hand. Clear examples are provided by evidence that MCM is obtained following self-referential tasks that allow several seconds for the evaluation of whether each word is self-descriptive (e.g. Bradley & Mathews, 1983; Derry & Kuiper, 1981). Even more inviting to habitual thought is the procedure of asking depressed or dysphoric[5] participants to ruminate about themselves for several minutes; this procedure reinstates habits that carry forward to produce negative biases on tests of autobiographical memory (Lyubormirsky, Caldwell & Nolen-Hoeksema, 1998) or deficits in controlled remembering of materials unrelated to the self (Hertel, 1998). Both the facilitation of negative memories and the impairment of neutral memories are possible expressions of transfer of training, from real-world rumination to performance on experimental tasks.

The case for habit influencing memory can be made more easily for depressed or dysphoric people than for anxious people, primarily because typical direct tests of memory are more sensitive to ruminative elaboration than to the interpretation of ambiguity. However, perhaps because dysphoric participants are typically anxious, they too show interpretive biases. For example, dysphoria is associated with interpretive biases during exposure to materials with ambiguous meaning. Lawson, MacLeod and Hammond (2002) found that dysphoric participants were responsive on an indirect measure of attention (a blink reflex to noise) as they imagined situations evoked by negative words. They were similarly responsive in the context of ambiguous words with negative meanings, and more so than in the context of other word types. Wenzlaff and Bates' (1998) dysphoric participants were more likely to unscramble ambiguous word strings to form sentences with negative meaning. If subsequent direct tests of memory for these ambiguous events were to be administered, the quality of the memories should reflect those biases (see Wenzlaff, Meier & Salas, 2002).

Both anxiety and dysphoria seem to be associated with another memory phenomenon: difficulties in forgetting that arise due to failure to inhibit or ignore. When the habit to attend to negative meaning is strong, as in dysphoria, instructions to ignore are more difficult to follow (e.g. in a negative-priming paradigm; Joormann, 2004). Moreover, dysphoria is associated with deficits in forgetting, following a task in which participants were given practice in not thinking about the material to be tested (Hertel & Gerstle, 2003). Forgetting was equally difficult for positive and negative material, as is typical of recall performance in dysphoria (see Matt, Vazquez & Campbell, 1992). However, clinically depressed people might have more trouble forgetting negative words due to arguably stronger habits of thought (see Power, Dalgleish, Claudio, Tata & Kentish, 2000).

When clinical samples have been recruited, differences between depression and anxiety have been found on indirect tests of memory. Anxious participants sometimes show MCM on perceptually oriented tests, whereas biases in clinical depression are sometimes revealed on conceptually oriented tests, which are more likely to reflect prior elaboration, regardless of contamination by intentional recall (e.g. Watkins, Martin & Stern, 2000). These differences implicate the role of differential habits. Another similarly understood difference pertains to evidence for overly general memory, obtained primarily in depressed samples (see the review by Healy & Williams, 1999; also see Williams, this volume – Ed.). Ruminative tendencies encourage the discovery of patterns across individual memories, making them seem fundamentally the same and more easily characterized by schematic descriptions, the hallmark of the overly general memory. Disrupting this habitual mindset, however, can reduce the overly general tendency (Watkins & Teasdale, 2001; see Teasdale, this volume – Ed.).

In order to specify the type of cognitive habit more clearly associated with memory bias, it would be helpful to disentangle the effects associated with anxiety from those associated with depression. This is true even though we know that comorbidity of syndromes and co-occurrence of self-report is high. Again, a reasonable hypothesis is that differences should depend upon the extent to which the tasks are sensitive to initial attentional and interpretive biases (in anxiety) versus prolonged ruminative tendencies (in depression). Dysphoric individuals might indeed show both tendencies. Finally, it is important to notice that biased interpretations and ruminative styles predict subsequent anxious states (see Mathews & MacLeod, 2002) and depressive episodes (e.g. Rude, Wenzlaff, Gibbs, Vane & Whitney, 2002). This type of evidence – that cognitive habits bias performance on later memory tasks *and* influence emotional states – is particularly important because it increases doubt about the primary role of emotional state in causing mood-congruent memory.

MCM from mood induction

The global issue for the training studies reported by Mathews and MacLeod (2002) is whether sensitivity to threat perpetuates itself and increases anxious affect (see also Yiend & Mackintosh, this volume – Ed.). In manipulating cognitive biases to observe changes in mood, the training studies used a method seemingly opposite from a frequently used method in research on mood and memory: the experimental manipulation of mood, particularly depressed mood, to inquire about resulting biases on cognitive tasks. Presumably, this is the opposite side of the causality coin, with the question being whether a particular mood triggers biases in cognitive procedures. Yet, there is reason to suspect that some of the mood-induction techniques are largely manipulations of thought, much like instructions to ruminate, and so they too might more properly be thought of as transfer of training cognitive biases, from one domain or task to another.

Although anxiety is infrequently mimicked by an experimental mood induction (cf. Richards & Whittaker, 1990), depression often is. Many beliefs about MCM in depression seem to be based on manipulations of sad or 'depressed' moods via Velten (1968) mood-induction procedures, or film clips, or autobiographical reflection, or other techniques that instruct or invite thoughts of sad events. Indeed, the thoughts might make the thinker feel sad, but it is not necessarily the case that the sadness itself causes variation in whatever cognitive task follows the manipulation. It is the thought that has been manipulated, and the more parsimonious conclusion for many of these studies is that prior thoughts perpetuate similar thoughts (see Parrott & Hertel, 1999; it is also worth considering that the administration of instruments like the BDI at the beginning of an experimental session can establish the same sort of bias; see Rothkopf & Blaney, 1991). The idea that bias effects in depressed and sad moods might be caused by habits of thought is quite similar to the issues raised in Blaney's (1986) early review, but often ignored in recent years (also see Riskind & Rholes, 1985). Blaney mentioned a plethora of phenomena other than mood that might establish 'affective' memory biases. Cognitive priming effects, particularly through self-referential orientation, seemed most likely to be responsible, but motivational factors also received attention. The motivation of esteem repair, for example, is not unlike the motivational account by Williams et al. (1988) of elaborative processing in depression. Compliance, as another example, refers to the suggestion that 'mood-induced' participants who are aware of the manipulation try to assist it by maintaining the negative cognitive set into the next task. A possible example of this special type of experimental demand is provided by the findings of Seibert and Ellis (1991). Their participants, who were assigned to read and think about negative self-statements (Velten, 1968), produced more off-task thoughts in the next task (in which they were asked to list thoughts unrelated to the task at hand). In terms of the present argument, they were given a temporary habit to think negatively – a propensity assisted by context – and it carried over to a new task. The habit might also have made them temporarily sad (or they might have simply reported sadness due to compliance), but there is no evidence that the sadness itself *caused* intrusive thoughts (and subsequently poor memory for the task material).

An interesting variation on the theme of transfer of training is the case of mood-repair via mood-incongruent memory (Parrott & Sabini, 1990). Having been encouraged to have negative thoughts by experimental manipulations, people sometimes seek to overcome the consequences for their mood by deliberately interfering with the mind-set and recalling positive events from their personal past. Indeed, participants instructed to focus on the events used earlier to induce negative mood have shown MCM, whereas those instructed to reappraise those events positively recalled more incongruent words (Rusting & DeHart, 2000). However, evidence for mood-repairing memory is much more difficult to obtain when the rememberer is naturally depressed and in the habit of thinking negatively (Joormann & Siemer, 2004). Both types of findings clearly underscore the importance of thoughts as precursors to changes in mood states, instead of the role of emotional states as determinants of memory bias. Whereas it is important to acknowledge that some mood induction procedures (perhaps music) might more directly establish biases in memory, it is perhaps even more important for researchers to keep in mind that these studies constitute a small segment of what has passed for documentation of the causal effects of mood on memory.

Conclusions

Emotion, no doubt, exerts a variety of effects on everyone's memory, primarily through the emotion-inducing characteristics of the initial processing episode. Some of these effects reflect the attention-directing properties of arousal (see Reisberg & Heuer, 2004). Some are mediated by chemical changes in the brain and by changes that interact with the altered brain chemistry of emotionally disordered individuals (see Davidson, 2000). These neurochemical differences likely contribute to the development of cognitive habits in emotional disorders. However, habit itself plays an important role in determining what gets remembered.

The experiment that I reported in this chapter suggests that we can simulate habit, independent of mood, and observe its consequences for memory. Other research techniques should also be developed in paradigms that permit the revelation of interpretive biases in anxiety. The overarching goal in doing simulation experiments and developing new memory paradigms is to address the transfer of cognitive habits from one task or set of life events to another. According to this brief reconsideration of the literature, instances of mood-congruent memory quite often seem to be instances of habit-congruent memory.

NOTES

The author acknowledges the contributions of Dimitri Ang and Amanda Rogde, who collected data for the experiment reported in this chapter. Please address correspondence to *phertel@trinity.edu*.

1. Surprisingly, the non-threat-training group reported higher state anxiety than did the controls ($M = 40$ vs. 32), $t (51) = 2.36, SE = 3.13, p < .025$. The threat-trained group did not significantly differ from controls (34 vs. 32), $t < 1.0$. In retrospect, the lack of a measure of state anxiety prior to the training phase makes any sort of interpretation tenuous, although matching groups on trait anxiety might be slightly reassuring about the lack of initial differences. Clearly any pre-training differences would have to be substantial, to overcome the high end-of-session mean in the non-threat-trained group, if evidence for cognitive influences on state anxiety were to have been found. Such influences were actually not expected, for a number of reasons. Unlike the participants in studies summarized by Mathews and MacLeod (2002), these were selected on the basis of low trait scores, and it should be more difficult to make low trait anxious people feel temporarily anxious. Also, these procedures included fewer trials with anxiety-related materials, especially trials during which the participants were required to resolve the direction of meaning themselves. This latter feature might indeed be necessary to the production of state changes (see Mathews & MacLeod, 2002; see also Yiend & Mackintosh, this volume – Ed.).

2. The mean number of non-homographs recalled was 8.3 by the threat-trained group, 7.3 by the non-threat-trained group and 7.9 by controls, $F < 1.0$. The corresponding mean number of intrusions were 1.1, 2.0 and 1.2, $F (1, 51) = 1.43, MSE = 2.96, p < .25$. No significant effects were expected, and none was obtained.

3. Vividness ratings were lost for five participants, due to experimenter error. The ANOVA included a factor for gender, and the main effect of gender was significant, $F (1, 43) = 4.16, MSE = 0.86, p < .05$. (This was the only significant gender difference in the experiment.) The average rating was 5.3 for female students and 5.0 for male.

4. MacLeod and Mathews (2004) reviewed quite a few studies that do not fall neatly into these categories. Some were methodologically flawed. Others – and

we do not know the extent of this problem – found co-occurrence of depressive affect, correlated with the bias.
5. Dysphoria is a term used to denote non-diagnosed, negative affect, of the sort that is tapped by the Beck Depression Inventory.

REFERENCES

Amir, N., Foa, E. B. & Coles, M. (2000). Implicit memory bias for threat-relevant information in individuals with Generalized Social Phobia. *Journal of Abnormal Psychology*, *109*, 713–720.

Blaney, P. H. (1986). Affect and memory: a review. *Psychological Bulletin*, *99*, 229–246.

Bradley, B. & Mathews, A. (1983). Negative self-schemata in clinical depression. *British Journal of Clinical Psychology*, *22*, 173–181.

Bransford, J. D. & Johnson, M. K. (1972). Contextual prerequisites for understanding: some investigations of comprehension and recall. *Journal of Verbal Learning and Verbal Behavior*, *11*, 717–726.

Burke, M. & Mathews, A. (1992). Autobiographical memory and clinical anxiety. *Cognition and Emotion*, *6*, 23–35.

Davidson, R. J. (2000). Affective style, mood, and anxiety disorders: an affective neuroscience approach. In R. J. Davidson (Ed.), *Anxiety, Depression, and Emotion*, 88–108. New York: Oxford University Press.

Derry, P. A. & Kuiper, N. A. (1981). Schematic processing and self-reference in clinical depression. *Journal of Abnormal Psychology*, *90*, 286–297.

Ellis, H. C. (1965). *The Transfer of Learning*. New York: Macmillan.

Eysenck, M. W. & Byrne, A. (1994). Implicit memory bias, explicit memory bias and anxiety. *Cognition and Emotion*, *8*, 415–432.

Fox, E., Russo, R., Bowles, R. & Dutton, K. (2001). Do threatening stimuli draw or hold visual attention in subclinical anxiety? *Journal of Experimental Psychology: General*, *130*, 681–700.

Friedman, B. H., Thayer, J. F. & Borkovec, T. D. (2000). Explicit memory bias for threat words in generalized anxiety disorder. *Behavior Therapy*, *31*, 745–756.

Grey, S. & Mathews, A. (2000). Effects of training on interpretation of emotional ambiguity. *Quarterly Journal of Experimental Psychology*, *53*, 1143–1162.

Healy, H. & Williams, J. M. G. (1999). Autobiographical memory. In T. Dalgleish & M. Power (Eds.), *The Handbook of Cognition and Emotion*, 229–242. Chichester: Wiley.

Hertel, P. T. (1998). The relationship between rumination and impaired memory in dysphoric moods. *Journal of Abnormal Psychology*, *107*, 166–172.

Hertel, P. T. (2004). Memory for emotional and nonemotional events in depression: a question of habit? In D. Reisberg & P. Hertel (Eds.), *Memory and Emotion*, 186–216. New York: Oxford University Press.

Hertel, P. T. & Gerstle, M. (2003). Depressive deficits in forgetting. *Psychological Science*, *14*, 573–578.

Hertel, P. T. & Hardin, T. S. (1990). Remembering with and without awareness in a depressed mood: Evidence of deficits in initiative. *Journal of Experimental Psychology: General*, *119*, 45–59.

Hertel, P. T., Mathews, A., Peterson, S. & Kintner, K. (2003). Transfer of training emotionally biased interpretations. *Applied Cognitive Psychology, 17,* 755–784.

Joormann, J. (2004). Attentional bias in dysphoria: the role of inhibitory processes. *Cognition and Emotion, 18,* 125–147.

Joormann, J. & Siemer, M. (2004). Memory accessibility, mood regulation and dysphoria: difficulties in repairing sad mood with happy memories? *Journal of Abnormal Psychology, 113,* 179–188.

Lawson, C., MacLeod, C. & Hammond, G. (2002). Interpretation revealed in the blink of an eye: depressive bias in the resolution of ambiguity. *Journal of Abnormal Psychology, 111,* 321–328.

Lyubomirsky, S., Caldwell, N. D. & Nolen-Hoeksema, S. (1998). Effects of ruminative and distracting responses to depressed mood on retrieval of autobiographical memories. *Journal of Personality and Social Psychology, 75,* 166–177.

MacLeod, C. (1999). Anxiety and anxiety disorders. In T. Dalgleish & M. Power (Eds.), *Handbook of Cognition and Emotion,* 447–478. Chichester: Wiley.

MacLeod, C. & Mathews, A. (1988). Anxiety and the allocation of attention to threat. *Quarterly Journal of Experimental Psychology: Human Experimental Psychology, 38,* 659–670.

MacLeod, C. & Mathews, A. (2004). Selective memory effects in anxiety disorders: an overview of research findings and their implications. In D. Reisberg & P. Hertel (Eds.), *Memory and Emotion,* 155–185. New York: Oxford University Press.

Mathews, A. & MacLeod, C. (2002). Induced processing biases have causal effects on anxiety. *Cognition and Emotion, 16,* 331–354.

Mathews, A., Mogg, K., May, J. & Eysenck, M. (1989). Implicit and explicit memory bias in anxiety. *Journal of Abnormal Psychology, 98,* 236–240.

Mathews, A., Richards, A. & Eysenck, M. (1989). Interpretation of homophones related to threat in anxiety states. *Journal of Abnormal Psychology, 98,* 31–34.

Matt, G. E., Vazquez, C. & Campbell, W. K., (1992). Mood-congruent recall of affectively toned stimuli: a meta-analytic review. *Clinical Psychology Review, 12,* 227–255.

McNally, R. J. (1999). Panic and phobias. In T. Dalgleish & M. Power (Eds.), *Handbook of Cognition and Emotion,* 479–496. Chichester: Wiley.

Nolen-Hoeksema, S. (2000). The role of rumination in depressive disorders and mixed anxiety/depressive symptoms. *Journal of Abnormal Psychology, 109,* 504–511.

Oatley, K. & Johnson-Laird, P. (1987). Towards a cognitive theory of emotions. *Cognition and Emotion, 1,* 29–50.

Parrott, W. G. & Hertel, P. T. (1999). Research methods in cognition and emotion. In T. Dalgleish & M. Power (Eds.), *Handbook of Cognition and Emotion,* 61–81. Chichester: Wiley.

Parrott, W. G. & Sabini, J. (1990). Mood and memory under natural conditions: evidence for mood-incongruent recall. *Journal of Personality and Social Psychology, 59,* 321–336.

Pichert, J. W. & Anderson, R. C. (1977). Taking different perspectives on a story. *Journal of Educational Psychology, 69,* 309–315.

Power, M. J., Dalgleish, T., Claudio, V., Tata, P. & Kentish, J. (2000). The directed forgetting task: application to emotionally valent material. *Journal of Affective Disorders, 57,* 147–157.

Reisberg, D. & Heuer, F. (2004). Memory for emotional events. In D. Reisberg & P. Hertel (Eds.), *Memory and Emotion,* 3–41. New York: Oxford University Press.

Richards, A. & French, C. C. (1991). Effects of encoding and anxiety on implicit and explicit memory performance. *Personality and Individual Differences, 12,* 131–139.

Richards, A. & Whittaker, T. M. (1990). Effects of anxiety and mood manipulation in autobiographical memory. *British Journal of Clinical Psychology, 29,* 145–153.

Riskind, J. H. & Rholes, W. S. (1985). The Velten mood induction procedure and cognitive manipulation: our response to Clark (1985). *Behaviour Research and Therapy, 23,* 671–673.

Ross, B. H. & Bradshaw, G. L. (1994). Encoding effects of remindings. *Memory and Cognition, 22,* 591–605.

Roth, D. & Rehm, L. P. (1980). Relationships among self-monitoring processes, memory, and depression. *Cognitive Therapy and Research, 4,* 149–157.

Rothkopf, J. S. & Blaney, P. H. (1991). Mood congruent memory: the role of affective focus and gender. *Cognition and Emotion, 5,* 53–64.

Rude, S. S., Wenzlaff, R. M., Gibbs, B., Vane, J. & Whitney, T. (2002). Negative processing biases predict subsequent depressive symptoms. *Cognition and Emotion, 16,* 423–440.

Russo, R., Fox, E., Bellinger, L. & Nguyen-Van-Tam, D. P. (2001). Mood-congruent free recall bias in anxiety. *Cognition and Emotion, 15,* 419–433.

Rusted, J. L. & Dighton, K. (1991). Selective processing of threat-related material by spider phobics in a prose recall task. *Cognition and Emotion, 5,* 123–132.

Rusting, C. L. & DeHart, T. (2000). Retrieving positive memories to regulate negative mood: consequences for mood-congruent memory. *Journal of Personality and Social Psychology, 78,* 737–752.

Seibert, P. S. & Ellis, H. C. (1991). Irrelevant thoughts, emotional mood states, and cognitive task performance. *Memory and Cognition, 19,* 507–513.

Spielberger, C. D., Gorsuch, R. L., Lushene, R., Vagg, P. R. & Jacobs, G. A. (1983). *Manual for the State-Trait Anxiety Inventory.* Palo Alto, CA: Consulting Psychologists Press.

Sulin, R. A. & Dooling, D. J. (1974). Intrusion of a thematic idea in retention of prose. *Journal of Experimental Psychology, 103,* 255–262.

Velten, E. (1968). A laboratory task for induction of mood states. *Behaviour Research and Therapy, 6,* 473–482.

Watkins, E. & Teasdale, J. D. (2001). Rumination and overgeneral memory in depression: effects of self-focus and analytic thinking. *Journal of Abnormal Psychology, 110,* 333–357.

Watkins, P. C., Martin, C. K. & Stern, L. D. (2000). Unconscious memory bias in depression: perceptual and conceptual processes. *Journal of Abnormal Psychology, 109,* 282–289.

Watts, F. N. & Dalgleish, T. (1991). Memory for phobia-related words in spider phobias. *Cognition and Emotion*, 5, 313–329.

Wenzlaff, R. M. & Bates, D. E. (1998). Unmasking a cognitive vulnerability to depression: how lapses in mental control reveal depressive thinking. *Journal of Personality and Social Psychology*, 75, 1559–1571.

Wenzlaff, R. M., Meier, J. & Salas, D. M. (2002). Thought suppression and memory biases during and after depressive moods. *Cognition and Emotion*, 16, 403–422.

Williams, J. M. G., Watts, F. N., MacLeod, C. & Mathews, A. (1988). *Cognitive Psychology and Emotional Disorders*. New York: Wiley.

Williams, J. M. G., Watts, F. N., MacLeod, C. & Mathews, A. (1997). *Cognitive Psychology and Emotional Disorders*, 2nd edn. New York: Wiley.

Anne Richards

Any complete explanation of human cognition must address the issue of ambiguity resolution. We are constantly confronted by indeterminate stimuli that need to be resolved in order for the cognitive system to function in an efficient and adaptive way. There is copious literature on the resolution of ambiguity in text comprehension, and abundant research on interpersonal processes and deciphering of ambiguous signals. The role of depression and dysphoria in ambiguity resolution has also been examined (e.g. Cane & Gotlib, 1985; Lawson & MacLeod, 1999), but the focus of the present chapter is on the influence of anxiety and anxiety-related disorders on ambiguity resolution. In evolutionary terms, anxiety functions to alert the system to impending danger (e.g. Eysenck, this volume, 1992, 1997; LeDoux, 1996; Öhman, 1996), and this involves correctly interpreting ambiguous signals that could predict harm. There is evidence that an evolved neural substrate may be involved in the recognition of fear and danger, and that the amygdala plays a crucial role (e.g. Adolphs, Tranel, Damasio & Damasio, 1995; Calder, Young, Rowland, Perrett, Hodges & Etcoff, 1996; see also Lawrence, Murphy & Calder, this volume). However, Whalen (1998) proposes that the amygdala is maximally responsive to ambiguous information.

Experiments with verbal stimuli

Early studies into the resolution of ambiguity relied on self-report methodology. Seminal work by Andrew Mathews and colleagues (Butler & Mathews, 1983, 1987) demonstrated that anxious individuals rated negative outcomes of ambiguous scenarios as being subjectively more likely to happen and more costly than did the controls. Similar effects have been observed for depressed (Butler & Mathews, 1983) and socially phobic individuals (Amir, Foa & Coles, 1998; Stopa & Clark, 2000). Although self-report studies have face validity, their usefulness is severely limited by their inability to delineate the cognitive components involved in resolving ambiguity. More recent studies have therefore modified paradigms from mainstream experimental psychology or developed novel techniques to enable the identification of the processes and mechanisms involved. Training people to make threat-related or neutral interpretations of ambiguous information influences their subsequent interpretative bias, suggesting that interpretative bias may play a causal role in the development of vulnerability to anxiety (see MacLeod et al., this volume; Mathews & MacLeod, 2002; Yiend & Mackintosh, this volume).

There are many different forms and levels of verbal ambiguity. In word recognition, there may be lexical ambiguity at the level of the word in the form of homophones (e.g. *brews/bruise*) or semantic ambiguity in the form of homographs (e.g. *stroke* can refer to a *brain haemorrhage* or to a *caress*). Ambiguity can be present in sentences containing words that in themselves are not ambiguous, but the overall meaning of the sentence may be uncertain (see Yiend & Mackintosh, this volume). Investigations into ambiguity resolution have typically used verbal stimuli, either words or sentences, with responses of spelling, recognition, lexical decision, reading times, naming and comprehension.

Robust findings have been obtained using a homophone-spelling task. Here, a series of threat/neutral homophones (e.g. *bruise/brews*) together with filler words are presented auditorially, ostensibly as a standard spelling test. The typical finding is that high trait anxious (Eysenck, MacLeod & Mathews, 1987; Mogg, Bradley, Miller, Potts, Glenwright & Kentish, 1994; Richards & Millwood, 1989) and clinically anxious (Mathews, Richards & Eysenck, 1989) participants produce more threat-related spellings than controls. The homophone task lacks sensitivity (Mogg et al., 1994) and is open to the criticism that the effects could simply be due to response bias, as both spellings may be available to the participant, but one is then consciously selected.

Using a recognition paradigm, Eysenck, Mogg, May, Richards and Mathews (1991) demonstrated mood-congruent interpretative bias for ambiguous sentences that had a potentially threatening interpretation. The recognition test required participants to give similarity ratings for disambiguated versions of the previously seen ambiguous item (see Yiend and Mackintosh, this volume, for examples). Other research has required a lexical decision (i.e. identifying whether an item is a word or a non-word) to targets following homographs (Richards & French, 1992), homophones (Blanchette & Richards, 2003) or ambiguous sentences (Calvo, Eysenck & Estevez, 1994; Hirsch & Mathews, 1997). The interpretation of the ambiguous item can then be inferred by comparing the speed of decisions to unambiguous words reflecting each meaning, with faster decisions implicating selection of that meaning. MacLeod and Cohen (1993) and Calvo, Eysenck and Castillo (1997) examined reading times with a manual response to continuation sentences following ambiguous sentences. Finally, Calvo and Castillo (1997, 2001a, 2001b) used a vocal naming task to targets that were related or unrelated to the threat or neutral interpretations of predictive inferences. In all of these cases, when a bias was obtained, the anxious individuals resolved the ambiguity in line with the more threatening interpretation.

Non-verbal stimuli

In an attempt to examine a possible interpretative bias using more ecologically valid stimuli, several studies have employed facial stimuli. Face perception appears to be a relatively automatic process, as shown by Dimberg, Thunberg and Elmehed (2000), who recorded distinct facial electromyographic reactions in emotion-relevant facial muscles. Although the neural systems mediating recognition of facial expressions may take time to develop (Nelson & de Haan, 1997), infants a couple of months old are able to discriminate emotional expressions (Nelson, 1987). Faces are not only more ecologically valid stimuli than are words, they also have the advantage of expressing different emotions from the same vehicle. A facial expression can change swiftly, in real time, from, for example, a surprised to a happy expression. This quality of faces allows the generation of emotionally ambiguous expressions that can then be used to detect interpretative biases in anxiety. In some of our recent work (Richards, French, Calder, Webb, Fox & Young, 2002), we used computer-interpolated facial images. These 'morphed' images created by Young, Rowland, Calder, Etcoff, Seth and Perrett (1997) from Ekman and Friesen's (1976) series, were produced by arranging the six prototype emotion expressions along a continuum, so that each expression was placed next to the expression with which it was the most confusable. This resulted in the following order: happiness, surprise, fear, sadness, disgust and anger. Each expression was then combined, in varying degrees, with the immediately adjacent expression to create an emotional hexagon with, for example, one continuum comprising images combining anger and happiness (e.g. 10 per cent anger–90 per cent happiness, 30 per cent anger–70 per cent happiness, and so on). We presented these images to high and low socially anxious participants, and found that the high trait anxious participants were more sensitive for fear than the low trait anxious. However, this was a general effect, with the anxious participants detecting fear at *all* percentage levels, but particularly strongly when there was at least 50 per cent fear in the face. The effect we observed seemed to reflect sensitivity for fear specifically, rather than this being a simple response bias effect (Snodgrass & Corwin, 1988). The high trait anxious participants were not simply reporting the more negative of the two emotions for each image. Our findings supported some preliminary evidence from Sprengelmeyer, Young, Pundt, Sprengelmeyer, Calder et al. (1997), suggesting enhanced recognition of fear and anger, and a borderline advantage for sadness in a clinically anxious compared to a control group. In our second experiment, state anxiety was manipulated via a mood-manipulation procedure. Here, we found enhanced detection of fear by the high trait anxiety group, replicating our earlier finding. However, we also found increased sensitivity to anger in those people subjected to the anxiety-provoking mood manipulation. This suggested that sensitivity to anger is prevalent in everyone in a stressful situation, and this would be evolutionarily adaptive. However, mood manipulation did not influence sensitivity to fear, suggesting that a fearful face looking straight at the viewer is not threatening, whereas an angry face is directly threatening. A fearful face with averted eyes may indicate danger (see also Adams, Gordon, Baird et al., 2003) but straight gaze may not. The enhancement of fear detection may represent some sort of empathic response in the anxious group, as they may have been more attuned to detecting fear in another person.

In a recent study (Richards, French, Calder & Young, submitted), we presented morphed images where each of the four negative emotions (fear, anger, disgust and sadness) were morphed with happiness between 30 per cent and 70 per cent, in 10 per cent gradations (e.g. 30 per cent fear–70 per cent happiness to 70 per cent fear–30 per cent happiness). Participants made the same affective decision to each expression (whether the expression was positive or negative), rather than having to classify each face as expressing one of five different emotions. The high socially anxious individuals were more sensitive to fear in an expression than the low socially anxious group, with the high anxious group responding *negative* to the fear–happiness expressions when there was 50 per cent fear in the face. At lower and higher percentages of fear along this continuum, the two groups identified a similar number of expressions as being negative. These effects are unlikely to be due to a response bias, as there were no differences in categorization between the groups for any of the other emotions, showing that the high anxious group was more sensitive to fear along the fear–happiness continuum.

Using morphed facial expressions, Holmes, Green and Richards (in preparation) used the dot-probe methodology to investigate attentional bias for ambiguous facial images. Morphed expressions containing 50 per cent fear–50 per cent neutral, 50 per cent happiness–50 per cent neutral, and 50 per cent fear–50 per cent happiness were presented with a neutral expression (100 per cent neutral). At intervals of 250 ms,

500 ms and 800 ms, a target appeared on the screen, replacing either the emotional morphed expression or the neutral expression. There were no differences between the anxiety groups at either 250 ms or 500 ms, but, as predicted, there were differences at 800 ms, reflecting the influence of strategic processes. At this later Stimulus Onset Asynchrony (SOA), the low state anxious individuals showed avoidance of the emotionally ambiguous, fear–happiness morph, and the high anxiety group showed a trend towards vigilance for the fear–neutral expressions and significant vigilance for the fear–happiness ambiguous expression.

Automatic versus strategic processing

One important issue in the resolution of ambiguity is whether the resolution occurs automatically or strategically. Early views of automatic and strategic processes viewed cognitive processes to be either automatic or strategic (Shiffrin & Schneider, 1977) whereas later more sophisticated accounts propose that cognitive processes may contain both automatic and strategic components (Bargh, 1989, 1992; McNally, 1995). There is evidence to support the idea that ambiguity resolution occurs on-line rather than being the consequence of later reconstructive processes. Calvo and Castillo (2001b) cite evidence from basic reading research that predictive inferences are drawn on-line, but that they are unlikely to be the result of automatic processes. The consensus is that there needs to be a gap of 1s after the context in order for the inference to be drawn (e.g. Calvo, Castillo & Estevez, 1999). Just because an outcome of a process appears to have been subjected to strategic processing does not deny the possibility that anxiety has an automatic impact on the strategic processes (Calvo & Castillo, 2001a; MacLeod, 1999).

Keenan, Potts, Golding and Jennings (1990) proposed that there are two methods for measuring inferencing: memory measures and activation measures. Memory measures (e.g. cued recall, sentence verification, question answering and recognition measures) have typically been preferred by reading researchers on the grounds that they measure a higher level of inferencing. However, such measures do not discriminate the making of on-line inferences drawn during comprehension from those drawn at the end of reading that involve reconstructive processes. Activation measures, such as naming, lexical decision and modified Stroop tasks, detect whether an inference has been made indirectly, by examining whether the inference has primed the target (Keenan et al., 1990).

Many early studies examining ambiguity resolution and emotion used memory measures (e.g. Eysenck et al., 1991), and therefore do not contribute to the issue of on-line versus reconstructive processing or the issue of automatic versus strategic processing. However, recently, these issues have been directly examined with activation methodologies. Several studies have examined the issue of automatic versus strategic processing by manipulating the SOA between the ambiguous prime and the target. These timecourse studies have used the 'time criterion' of automaticity (Wells & Matthews, 1994), where processes occurring within about 500 ms are said to reflect automatic processes whereas longer intervals are more likely to have strategic influences. One important question is whether anxiety influences only the probability of a threat-related inference being made or whether it impacts on the timescale of semantic activation (Calvo & Castillo, 2001b). That is, are mood-congruent inferences initiated more often and are they processed more quickly as a result of anxiety?

One early study used a homograph priming technique to examine the time course of semantic activation for different meanings of threat/neutral homographs (Richards & French, 1992). High and low trait anxiety individuals were presented with homographic primes, followed by a target that was related to the threatening or neutral interpretation or was unrelated to the homograph. So, for example, the homograph *stroke* was followed by *heart* (threat-related target), *cat* (neutral target), *tea* (unrelated neutral target) or *traffic* (unrelated threat target). The SOAs were varied across experiments (500 ms, 750 ms and 1,250 ms). At the short SOA, all participants showed facilitation for both meanings of the homographs. However, at later SOAs differential priming was apparent, with the high trait 'locking onto' the threatening meaning of the homograph and, conversely, the low trait showing priming only for the neutral interpretation. Using a lexical decision paradigm has the advantage of being an activation measure, but it has been shown to be contaminated by post-lexical context checking processes whereby the target is checked against the prime to see if it is related. If it is related, then this speeds up the decision to respond positively (Balota & Chumbley, 1984).

The time course of inference activation was investigated by Calvo and Castillo (1997) using a naming response. Naming requires accessing the lexicon followed by articulation, which is not contaminated by post-lexical checking processes, and is seen as being a purer measure of lexical access (Keenan et al., 1990). However, naming is such a rapid response that, as a result, there may be a lack of sensitivity due to the limited interval in which top-down processes can have any influence (Norris, 1986). A naming response may therefore underestimate the size of lexical activation. In their study, Calvo and Castillo (1997) presented ambiguous prime sentences, word by word in a Rapid Serial Visual Presentation (RSVP) procedure. The pretarget word was presented for 450 ms followed by either a 50 ms interval (producing an SOA of 500 ms) or a 800 ms interval (SOA of 1,250 ms) and then the target word was presented for naming. Consistent with Richards and French (1992), the high anxious were faster at naming the threat-related targets at 1,250 ms but not at 500 ms, again supporting the idea that anxiety has an effect on the resolution of ambiguity at a strategic rather than at an automatic level. Calvo and Castillo (2001b) extended the interval between the offset of the pre-target word and the target word and examined intervals of 50 ms, 550 ms and 1,050 ms (producing SOAs of 500 ms, 1,000 ms and 1,500 ms, respectively) in a predictive inference paradigm in which a context sentence predicting a potential threat or non-threat event is followed by a target word related to either the predicted or unlikely event. The time taken to name the target following a predictive context compared to a control condition indicates whether the inference has been drawn. Again, evidence was obtained that predictive inferences occur on-line but with a delay, with the high anxious being more likely to draw the threat-related inference than the low anxious group. However, anxiety did not speed up the time course, as the high anxious group did not draw inferences earlier than the low anxious group. These effects occurred on-line, but only at a delay of 1,050 ms, and not at the earlier intervals of 50 ms or 550 ms, suggestive of strategic processing. However, differential activation of threat meanings at 100 ms intervals between the offset of the context sentence and the onset of the target have been obtained in social anxiety (Amir, Foa & Coles, 1998) and post-traumatic stress disorder (PTSD) (Amir, Coles & Foa, 2002), suggesting the operation of automatic processes.

Using a dot-probe paradigm with facial expressions, Holmes, Green and Richards (in preparation; see details in previous section) found that high state anxious individuals were vigilant for the fear–happiness ambiguous expression at 800 ms but not at earlier SOAs of 250 ms or 500 ms, suggesting the operation of strategic factors in the processing of threat-related ambiguity.

So, despite the different methodologies employed, the findings typically show that anxiety affects the resolution of ambiguity as a result of strategic processes. However, earlier automatic processes may well have impacted upon these strategic processes. It is apparent that automatic and strategic components can both interact and dissociate, with some non-conscious processes only becoming active after being instigated by some thought or attentional process (Bargh, 1989, 1992; Fox, 1996).

Inhibitory processes and ambiguity resolution

Most research has focused on the activation of threat-related or mood-congruent interpretations of ambiguous stimuli, with very little investigation into possible inhibitory mechanisms that might be involved. When presented with an ambiguous word, both meanings appear to be automatically activated initially (Simpson & Burgess, 1985). Over time, activation of the subdominant meaning of the word dissipates, leaving the dominant meaning active. It is not yet determined whether there is direct inhibition of the subordinate meaning or whether this meaning is simply less active, nor what the influence of anxiety might be on these processes. If it is the case that the interpretative bias and the attentional bias arise from the same underlying processes (Mathews & Mackintosh, 1998; Mathews & MacLeod, 2002), then deficits in the inhibition of threat-related interpretations may be observed. The failure of anxious individuals to disengage attention from a threat-related location in order to attend to a new location (e.g. Fox, Russo & Dutton, 2002) and the proposed defective inhibition in anxiety (Fox, 1994) suggest that there may be a corresponding failure to inhibit threat-related interpretations of ambiguous stimuli. However, interactive activation-based models of ambiguity resolution (McClelland, 1987) propose that if there is no context then the most dominant meaning is activated and the subordinate meaning passively decays to resting levels. If a context is present, then the congruent meaning will simply be activated. There has been support for this passive nature of selection (e.g. Love & Swinney, 1996; Simpson & Krueger, 1991).

Richards and French (1992) examined the time course of semantic activation for threat-related and neutral meanings when participants' interpretations of homographs were not controlled. That is, participants were simply asked to attend to the homograph. It appeared that the neutral meaning of the homographs dissipates for the high anxious group, and although these activation levels (compared with an unrelated neutral target) dipped below the resting levels, in that the reaction times (RTs) to the neutral targets related to the homographic prime trials were longer than RTs to neutral targets unrelated to the prime, the effect was not significant.

Nievas and Mari-Beffa (2002) tested the idea that semantic ambiguity resolution involves the central inhibition of the subordinate (non-selected) meaning of the ambiguous word. They argue that in basic language comprehension research, there is very little evidence for semantic inhibition in lexical ambiguity resolution, as after the initial activation of the subordinate meaning this subsequently dissipates back to resting levels. However, they go on to present some preliminary data showing that when an element of selection was imposed on the homograph then the non-primed interpretation of the homograph was inhibited but only in those participants who responded accurately and slowly. Gernsbacher, Varner and Faust (1990) have also demonstrated inhibition of inappropriate meanings in skilled readers after a delay of 850 ms. At 100 ms SOA, all readers showed facilitation of both meanings of the homograph.

Amir and colleagues (1998, 2002) used Gernsbacher, Varner and Faust's (1990) methodology in order to examine inhibition in clinical samples. Targets were presented after sentences ending with either a homograph or a non-homograph, and participants had to decide whether the target matched the meaning of the sentence. The homograph sentence would prime one meaning of the homograph, and the target could be related to that or the alternative meaning. So, for example, the target *unfriendly* followed either: 'She wrote down the mean' or: 'She wrote down the score'. A slower response to the target following the homograph sentence (interference) implies that both meanings of the homograph were activated. A faster response reflects inhibition of the alternative meaning. Amir, Foa and Coles (1998) found more interference for the anxious than the control group at 100 ms SOA, suggestive of automatic processing, but near-significant inhibition at 850 ms SOA. They interpreted these findings as supporting the initial automatic vigilance for threatening information followed by strategic avoidance. Using the same methodology, Amir, Coles and Foa (2002) found evidence of reduced inhibition in PTSD compared with traumatized but non-PTSD individuals. There have therefore been some preliminary investigations into inhibitory effects in the resolution of ambiguity in some affective disorders, but no direct investigation of generalized or trait anxiety. There is clearly a need for such investigations.

Context effects

Verbal stimuli

Research into ambiguity resolution and emotion has typically been examined in isolation from contextual influence. Where studies have incorporated a wider context, this has been in the form of a sentence or a scenario that is an integral part of the ambiguous unit. Yet, in real life situations, ambiguous information is presented within a wider context. For example, ambiguous facial expressions are clarified by the words that are spoken, or by postural information. Isabelle Blanchette and I have set about examining the influence of contextual information on the interpretation of ambiguity.

It is clear that context is highly influential in disambiguating ambiguous information (see Gaskell & Marslen-Wilson, 2001). There is a wide range of models of lexical ambiguity that posit different degrees of influence of contextual factors on ambiguity resolution. A modular account (Onifer & Swinney, 1981; Swinney, 1979) proposes that all meanings are automatically activated, regardless of context, and followed by contextual integration processes that result in the selection of the most appropriate meaning. Alternatively, interactive models propose that the context has a more influential role much earlier on in the process. These models range from those where the context preselects the appropriate meaning and the other meanings are not activated, to models that enhance the activation of the appropriate meaning but do not eliminate inappropriate meanings (e.g. McClelland, 1987; Simpson & Krueger, 1991; Tabossi, 1988). Whichever model is preferred, Lucas (1999) concluded from a meta-analysis that context-appropriate meanings were preferred to inappropriate meanings.

Blanchette and Richards (2003) examined the resolution of ambiguity in more complex, naturalistic conditions, where external contextual information was available to participants subjected to an anxiety manipulation procedure and to control participants. We were interested in the effect emotion has on the content of people's interpretations, as well as on the processes involved in how these interpretations are made. When presented in isolation, there is robust evidence for mood-congruent resolutions, but does this hold up in more complex environments? It is possible that individuals in anxious states may simply ignore emotion-incongruent evidence and seek out evidence consistent with their mood. There is abundant evidence that anxiety is associated with an attentional bias for threat: Mathews and colleagues devised the dot-probe paradigm (MacLeod, Mathews & Tata, 1986; Yiend & Mathews, 2001) that has been extensively used in this area (see also Mogg and Bradley, this volume). There is also evidence that anxiety is associated with a failure to disengage from threat (Fox, Russo & Dutton, 2002; Yiend & Mathews, 2001). Given this evidence, it seems likely that presenting contextual information that is congruent with the threat-related meaning of the homophone should be detected efficiently in the anxious group.

In the first study in this series, participants listened to threat/neutral and positive/neutral homophones whilst being presented simultaneously with a contextual cue related to one or other meaning. So, for example, a participant might hear the homophone *bury/berry* and see either *ground* (threat-related associate) or *fruit* (neutral-related associate). Using this cross-modal paradigm, we examined contextual influences on homophone spelling, and found that all participants were sensitive to context, as their spellings were congruent with the context, and this effect was even stronger in the anxious than the control group. This meant that for the anxious group, *mood-congruent* interpretations were made when the context primed the threat-related meaning of the threat/neutral homophones, but *mood-incongruent* interpretations were made when, for example, the context primed the neutral meaning. This sensitivity to context was apparent for all homophones, irrespective of their valence. We replicated this effect in a second experiment, albeit to a lesser extent, when the contextual cues were presented subliminally, showing that this sensitivity to context occurs without conscious awareness. In addition, we incorporated neutral/neutral homophones in this subliminal paradigm, to see whether the effect was restricted to homophones with an emotional meaning. We observed anxiety-related context-sensitive effects for all homophones, showing that the sensitivity was indeed a general phenomenon. In the third experiment, we employed a lexical decision paradigm, in which a homophone was heard simultaneously with a contextual cue presented on the computer screen. Following this, a target appeared that was either the correct or incorrect spelling of the homophone. On critical trials, the target spelling was congruent or incongruent with the context. This study required a neutral response and enabled us to rule out response bias as an explanation. Context was found to be important for all participants, but especially so for the anxious group. This context-sensitivity effect could not be accounted for by an increase in priming from the contextual cue of the target, as we incorporated a condition in which the contextual cue was presented without the homophone. In this condition, there was a basic contextual priming effect, in that targets congruent with the context were responded to faster than incongruent ones, but no anxiety effects. In the first two experiments, anxiety was manipulated by videoing the participants as they performed the task, having informed them that their performance was being monitored (see Reidy, 1994; Richards et al., 2002). In the third experiment, a speeded arithmetic test was used for the anxiety manipulation. In sum, using various mood-manipulation techniques, we found that our mood-manipulated anxiety groups were consistently more sensitive to contextual information for both emotional and neutral ambiguous information. This effect only occurred when there was some ambiguity to be resolved, and does not simply reflect the anxious group being generally more susceptible to external information. We also demonstrated the effect at a non-conscious level.

There is evidence that mood manipulations induced experimentally may not generalize to real-life situations. For example, although experimentally induced manipulations typically produce mood-congruent effects in the laboratory (e.g. Blaney, 1988), they may produce *mood-incongruent* effects when the task is performed under more natural mood-manipulating conditions (e.g. more positive memories were elicited during cloudy weather and negative memories when sunny; Parrott &

Sabini, 1990). These data may reflect some sort of 'mood-repair' process that would normally be inhibited under experimentally controlled manipulations (e.g. Clark & Isen, 1982). Such mood-repair effects have been postulated as being the result of automatic processes (Clark & Isen, 1982) or strategic processes (e.g. Forgas, 2000). In light of this, we performed a follow-up study of patients attending an orthodontic clinic awaiting dental treatment (Richards, Blanchette & Munijiza, submitted), to see if comparable effects would be found to those when mood was induced experimentally. Here, we employed the homophone lexical decision paradigm just prior to patients undergoing treatment. Our data supported our earlier study, showing that the anxious group displayed an increase in their sensitivity to context, and this was a general effect, as it was apparent for all homophones, irrespective of valence.

Non-verbal stimuli

The context effect has generalized to non-verbal stimuli (Richards & Blanchette, 2002; Blanchette & Richards, submitted), where morphed facial images were presented along the anger–happiness, anger–neutral, fear–happiness, fear–neutral, neutral–happiness, and surprise–happiness continua simultaneously with either a context word (congruent with one of the two component emotions in the expression) or a row of Xs. For example, for a fear–happiness expression, the context word could be happiness-related (e.g. love), fear-related (e.g. terror) or a row of Xs. Participants made an affective decision on the face.

When in an anxious mood, our participants were more likely to use the contextual cue even when this resolved the ambiguous stimulus in the mood-incongruent manner. When the contextual cue was consistent with the more negative interpretation of the expression, then the anxious individuals were more likely to classify the expression as being negative, compared to the control group. However, when the context was related to the more positive emotion in the expression, the anxious individuals were more likely to opt for the positive emotion, even though this interpretation was mood-incongruent.

There is no evidence that anxious individuals disregard emotion-disconfirming evidence. On the contrary, all of our experiments so far have consistently shown such individuals use external sources of information to resolve emotionally ambiguous facial expressions, even when this evidence is mood disconfirming.

Theoretical accounts of context-sensitivity effect

Our research on context effects to date does not fit with semantic activation models of emotion (e.g. Bower, 1991; Bower & Forgas, 2000), as these models would predict mood-congruent effects. According to these models, a particular mood-state would activate associated nodes, which would then enhance the processing of mood-congruent information. They would predict enhanced processing of threat-related meanings generally, and this effect should be particularly evident when the context was congruent with the threat-related interpretation. The fact that we observed mood-incongruent effects in our anxious groups when presented with a contextual cue priming the more positive meaning rules out activation models as an explanation. Likewise, explanations based on mood-regulation mechanisms are also unwarranted, as such models would predict that the anxious group should show mood-incongruent processing as the mood was being repaired. Again, we observed both mood-congruent and mood-incongruent effects in the same experimental session. We suggested (Blanchette & Richards, 2003; Richards, Blanchette & Munijiza, submitted) that the findings might be explained with reference to Fiedler (2000), who proposed that positive affect induces more top-down processes, whereas negative affect is associated with more data-driven processes. When in a negative state, it is likely to be more adaptive to be hypervigilant and aware of the external environment in order to be in a position to act quickly. Fielder's processing strategy for negative affect is consistent with Eysenck's (1992, 1997) hypervigilance theory (see also Eysenck, this volume). Eysenck proposes that there is a characteristic mode of operation associated with anxiety. This mode of processing includes general hypervigilance, demonstrated by a propensity to attend to any task-irrelevant stimuli, and specific hypervigilance, as shown by an inclination to attend selectively to threat-related rather than neutral stimuli. There is also increased environmental scanning and a broadening of attention prior to the detection of threat, followed by a narrowing of attention when a salient stimulus is being processed. This theory cannot provide a full explanation, as there were mood-incongruent effects when the context primed the more positive interpretation of the homophone.

Reconciliation between context-sensitivity and mood-congruency effects

There is an obvious discrepancy between the literature showing robust mood-congruent effects and the resolution of ambiguity and our recent work showing that these effects may not generalize to more complex situations. Our explanation for this is in terms of automatic and strategic processes. When presented with an ambiguous stimulus in isolation, the only sources of evidence available in order to resolve that ambiguity are internal factors, such as one's emotional state or cognitive vulnerability factors. It is therefore predicted that, in the absence of contextual influence, the typical mood-congruent biases would be found, with the anxious individuals resolving ambiguity in the threat-related manner, and non-anxious individuals opting for the neutral interpretation.

There is good evidence that the resolution of ambiguity involves strategic processes, and that the effect of anxiety on resolution is strategic, as it takes time to develop (e.g. Calvo et al., 1997; Calvo & Castillo, 2001b; Richards & French, 1992). When contextual information is available, this overrides the more strategic influence of anxiety on ambiguity resolution. In two of our studies (Blanchette & Richards, 2003), we employed a homophone-spelling test, and therefore there was the possibility that strategic influences could be apparent in the spelling. In the third study of this series, and in our study of dental patients (Richards et al., submitted), there was much less opportunity for strategic influences on the interpretation of the homophones. However, in all cases, the effect of context was paramount, and any mood-congruent effects were eliminated. It is clear that further research is needed to examine more precisely the relative contributions of internal and external sources of evidence in ambiguity resolution. Although some of our studies (i.e. the homophone spelling studies) *allowed* for the possibility of strategic influences, these need to be examined more systematically. The homophone lexical decision task has the advantage over the homophone-spelling task, as it requires a neutral response to target words, and is an activation rather than a memory measure of inferencing (Keenan et al., 1990). The timing of both the context and the target can be manipulated to examine the time course of context sensitivity. In all of our research to date, we have presented the contextual cue simultaneously with the homophone. By increasing the delay between the homophone and the contextual cue, the influence of contextual information on ambiguity resolution when the preferred inference (congruent with, for example, levels of trait anxiety) has been made could be examined. This, together with manipulations between the homophone, cue and target, provides a flexible tool for examining ambiguity resolution within different contexts.

Summary

There is much evidence to suggest that when presented in isolation, ambiguous information is resolved in mood-congruent directions. Early research used self-report methodologies, and these have now evolved into more sophisticated experimental investigations using both verbal and non-verbal stimuli. The consensus of opinion is that anxiety impacts on ambiguity resolution at a strategic level, with both anxious and non-anxious individuals making both threat-related and neutral interpretations early on. The differential effects in interpretation appear after the influence of strategic processes. However, it may be the case that automatic processes influence these more evident strategic effects, and future research should attend to these issues to determine the interactions and influences of automatic and strategic processes. Research is also needed into inhibitory mechanisms and anxiety. In particular, the role of anxiety on inhibitory processes following the selection of mood-incongruent inferences requires investigation.

Recent research has indicated that mood-congruent interpretive biases may not generalize to more complex situations where ambiguity is presented within some external context. Our research has demonstrated that anxiety increases the extent to which external sources of information are accessed to resolve ambiguity. The proposal that the effect of context on ambiguity resolution operates at an early stage of processing and overrides any inherent interpretative bias, such as internal cognitive vulnerabilities, warrants further research.

REFERENCES

Adams, R. B., Gordon, H. L., Baird, A. A., Ambady, N. & Kleck, R. E. (2003). Effects of gaze on amygdala sensitivity to anger and fear faces. *Science, 300,* 1536–1536.

Adolphs, R., Tranel, D., Damasio, H. & Damasio, A. R. (1995). Fear and the human amygdala. *Journal of Neuroscience, 15,* 5879–5891.

Amir, N., Foa, E. B. & Coles, M. E. (1998). Automatic activation and strategic avoidance of threat-relevant information in social phobia. *Journal of Abnormal Psychology, 107,* 285–290.

Amir, N., Foa, E. B. & Coles, M. E. (2002). Automatic and strategic activation and inhibition of threat-relevant information in posttraumatic stress disorder. *Cognitive Therapy and Research, 26,* 645–655.

Balota, D. A. & Chumbley, J. I. (1984). Are lexical decisions a good measure of lexical access? The role of word frequency in the neglected decision stage. *Journal of Experimental Psychology: Human Perception and Performance, 10,* 340–357.

Bargh, J. A. (1989). Conditional automaticity: varieties of automatic influence in social perception and cognition. In J. A. Bargh & J. S. Uleman (Eds.), *Unintended Thought.* New York: Guilford.

Bargh, J. A. (1992). The ecology of automaticity: toward establishing the conditions needed to produce automatic processing effects. *American Journal of Psychology, 105,* 181–199.

Blanchette, I. & Richards, A. (2003). Anxiety and the interpretation of ambiguous stimuli: beyond the emotion-congruent effect. *Journal of Experimental Psychology: General, 132,* 294–309.

Blanchette, I. & Richards, A. (submitted). Anxiety and the interpretation of ambiguous facial expressions: the influence of contextual cues.

Blaney, P. H. (1986). Affect and memory: a review. *Psychological Bulletin*, *99*, 229–246.

Bower, G. H. (1991). Mood congruity of social judgments. In J. P. Forgas (Ed.), *Emotion and Social Judgments. International Series in Experimental Social Psychology*, 31–53. Elmsford, NY: Pergamon.

Bower, G. H. & Forgas, J. P. (2000). Affect, memory, and social cognition. In E. Eich and J. F. Kihlstrom (Eds.), *Cognition and Emotion*, 87–168. New York: Oxford University Press.

Butler, G. & Mathews, A. (1983). Cognitive processes in anxiety. *Advances in Behaviour Research and Therapy*, *5*, 51–62.

Butler, G. & Mathews, A. (1987). Anticipatory anxiety and risk perception. *Cognitive Therapy and Research*, *5*, 551–565.

Calder, A. J., Young, A. W., Rowland, D., Perrett, D. I., Hodges, J. R. & Etcoff, N. L. (1996). Facial emotion recognition after bilateral amygdala damage: differentially severe impairment of fear. *Cognitive Neuropsychology*, *13*, 699–745.

Calvo, M. G. & Castillo, M. D. (1997). Mood-congruent bias in interpretation of ambiguity: strategic processes and temporary activation. *Quarterly Journal of Experimental Psychology: Human Experimental Psychology*, *50*, 163–182.

Calvo, M. G. & Castillo, M. D. (2001a). Selective interpretation in anxiety: uncertainty for threatening events. *Cognition and Emotion*, *15*, 299–320.

Calvo, M. G. & Castillo, M. D. (2001b). Bias in predictive inferences during reading. *Discourse Processes*, *32*, 43–71.

Calvo, M. G., Castillo, M. D. & Estevez, A. (1999). On-line inferences in reading: processing time *during vs. after* the priming context. *Memory and Cognition*, *27*, 834–843.

Calvo, M. G., Eysenck, M. W. & Castillo, M. D. (1997). Interpretation bias in test anxiety: the time course of predictive inferences. *Cognition and Emotion*, *11*, 43–63.

Calvo, M. G., Eysenck, M. W. & Estevez, A. (1994). Ego-threat interpretive bias in test anxiety: on-line inferences. *Cognition and Emotion*, *8*, 127–146.

Cane, D. B. & Gotlib, I. H. (1985). Depression and the effects of positive and negative feedback on expectations, evaluations and performance. *Cognitive Therapy and Research*, *9*, 145–160.

Clark, M. S. & Isen, A. M. (1982). Toward understanding the relationship between feeling states and social behaviour. In A. H. Hastorf & A. M. Isen (Eds.), *Cognitive Social Psychology*, 73–108. Amsterdam: Elsevier/North-Holland.

Dimberg, U., Thunberg, M. & Elmehed, K. (2000). Unconscious facial reactions to emotional facial expressions. *Psychological Science*, *11*, 86–89.

Ekman, P. & Friesen, W. V. (1976). *Pictures of Facial Affect*. Palo Alto, CA: Consulting Psychologists Press.

Eysenck, M. W. (1992). *Anxiety: The Cognitive Perspective*. Hove: Erlbaum.

Eysenck, M. W. (1997). *Anxiety and Cognition: a Unified Theory*. Hove: Psychology Press.

Eysenck, M. W., Macleod, C. & Matthews, A. (1987). Cognitive functioning and anxiety. *Psychological Research*, *49*, 189–195.

Eysenck, M. W., Mogg, K., May, J., Richards, A. & Mathews, A. (1991). Bias in interpretation of ambiguous sentences related to threat in anxiety. *Journal of Abnormal Psychology*, *100*, 144–150.

Fiedler, K. (2000). Toward an integrative account of affect and cognition phenomena using the BIAS computer algorithm. In J. P. Forgas (Ed.), *Feeling and Thinking. The Role of Affect in Social Cognition*, 223–252. Cambridge: Cambridge University Press.

Forgas, J. P. (2000). Affect and information processing strategies. An interactive relationship. In J. P. Forgas (Ed.), *Feeling and Thinking. The Role of Affect in Social Cognition*, 387–406. Cambridge: Cambridge University Press.

Fox, E. (1994). Attentional bias in anxiety: a defective inhibition hypothesis. *Cognition and Emotion*, *8*, 165–195.

Fox, E. (1996). Selective processing of threatening words in anxiety: the role of awareness. *Cognition and Emotion*, *10*, 449–480.

Fox, E., Russo, R. & Dutton, K. (2002). Attentional bias for threat: evidence for delayed disengagement from emotional faces. *Cognition and Emotion*, *16*, 355–379.

Gaskell, M. G. & Marslen-Wilson, W. D. (2001). Lexical ambiguity resolution and spoken word recognition: bridging the gap. *Journal of Memory and Language*, *44*, 325–349.

Gernsbacher, M. A., Varner, K. R. & Faust, M. E. (1990). Investigating differences in general comprehension skill. *Journal of Experimental Psychology: Learning, Memory, and Cognition*, *16*, 430–445.

Hirsch, C. & Mathews, A. (1997). Interpretive inferences when reading about emotional events. *Behaviour Research and Therapy*, *35*, 1123–1132.

Holmes, A., Green, S. E. & Richards, A. (in preparation). Anxiety and orienting to ambiguous faces.

Keenan, J. M., Potts, G. R., Golding, J. M. & Jennings, T. M. (1990). Which elaborative inferences are drawn during reading? A question of methodologies. In D. A. Balota, G. B. Flores d'Arcais & K. Raynor (Eds.), *Comprehension Processes in Reading*, 377–402. Hillsdale, NJ: Erlbaum.

Lawson, C. & MacLeod, C. (1999). Depression and the interpretation of ambiguity. *Behaviour Research and Therapy*, *37*, 463–474.

LeDoux, J. (1996). *The emotional brain*. New York: Simon & Schuster.

Love, T. & Swinney, D. (1996). Co-reference processing and levels of analysis in object-relative constructions: demonstrations of antecedent reactivation with the cross-modal priming paradigm. *Journal of Psycholinguistic Research*, *25*, 5–24.

Lucas, M. (1999). Context effects in lexical access: a meta-analysis. *Memory and Cognition*, *27*, 385–398.

MacLeod, C. (1999). Anxiety and anxiety disorders. In T. Dalgleish & M. Power (Eds.), *Handbook of Cognition and Emotion*, 447–477. Chichester: Wiley.

MacLeod, C. & Cohen, I. L. (1993). Anxiety and the interpretation of ambiguity: a text comprehension study. *Journal of Abnormal Psychology*, *102*, 238–247.

Macleod, C., Mathews, A. & Tata, P. (1986). Attentional bias in emotional disorders. *Journal of Abnormal Psychology*, 95, 15–20.

Mathews, A. & Mackintosh, B. (1998). A cognitive model of selective processing in anxiety. *Cognitive Therapy and Research*, 22, 539–560.

Mathews, A. & MacLeod, C. (2002). Induced processing biases have causal effects on anxiety. *Cognition and Emotion*, 16, 331–354.

Mathews, A., Richards, A. & Eysenck, M. W. (1989). Interpretation of homophones related to threat in anxiety states. *Journal of Abnormal Psychology*, 98, 31–34.

McClelland, J. L. (1987). The case for interactionism in language processing. In M. Coltheart (Ed.), *Attention and Performance XII: The Psychology of Reading*, 3–36. Hillsdale, NJ: Erlbaum.

McNally, R. J. (1995). Automaticity and the anxiety disorders. *Behaviour Research and Therapy*, 33, 747–754.

Mogg, K., Bradley, B. P., Miller, T., Potts, H., Glenwright, J. & Kentish, J. (1994). Interpretation of homophones related to threat: anxiety or response bias effects? *Cognitive Therapy and Research*, 18, 461–477.

Nelson, C. A. (1987). The recognition of facial expressions in the first two years of life: mechanisms of development. *Child Development*, 58, 889–909.

Nelson, C. A. & de Haan, M. (1997). A neurobiological approach to the recognition of facial expressions in infancy. In J. A. Russell & J. M. Fernandez-Dols (Eds.), *The Psychology of Facial Expressions*, 176–204. Cambridge: Cambridge University Press.

Nievas, F. & Mari-Beffa, P. (2002). Negative priming from non-selected meanings of the homograph. *British Journal of Psychology*, 93, 47–66.

Norris, D. (1986). Word recognition: context effects without priming. *Cognition*, 22, 93–136.

Öhman, A. (1996). Preferential preattentive processing of threat in anxiety: preparedness and attentional bias. In R. M. Rapee (Ed.), *Current Controversies in the Anxiety Disorders*, 253–290. New York: Guilford.

Onifer, W. & Swinney, D. A. (1981). Accessing lexical ambiguities during sentence comprehension: effects of frequency of meaning and contextual bias. *Memory and Cognition*, 9, 225–236.

Parrott, W. G. & Sabini, J. (1990). Mood and memory under natural conditions: evidence for mood incongruent recall. *Journal of Personality and Social Psychology*, 59, 321–336.

Reidy. J. G. (1994). *Anxiety and Explicit Memory for Emotionally Toned Words*. Unpublished doctoral thesis, University of London.

Richards, A. & Blanchette, I. (2002). Interpretation of ambiguous facial expression: effect of anxiety and contextual information. XII Conference of the ISRE, 20–24 July 2002. Cuenca, Spain.

Richards, A., Blanchette, I. & Munijiza, J. (submitted). Contextual influences in the resolution of ambiguity in anxiety.

Richards, A. & French, C. C. (1992). An anxiety-related bias in semantic activation when processing threat/neutral homographs. *Quarterly Journal of Experimental Psychology*, 45, 503–525.

Richards, A., French, C. C., Calder, A. J., Webb, B., Fox, R. & Young, A. W. (2002). Anxiety-related bias in the classification of emotionally ambiguous facial expressions. *Emotion*, 2, 273–287.

Richards, A., French, C. C., Calder, A. & Young, A. W. (submitted). Sensitivity to fear in emotionally ambiguous facial expressions and anxiety.

Richards, A. & Millwood, B. (1989). Colour-identification of differentially valenced words in anxiety. *Cognition and Emotion*, 3, 171–176.

Shiffrin, R. M. & Schneider, W. (1977). Controlled and automatic human processing: perceptual learning, automatic attending, and a general theory. *Psychological Review*, 84, 127–190.

Simpson, G. B. & Burgess, C. (1985). Activation and selection processes in the recognition of ambiguous words. *Journal of Experimental Psychology: Human Perception and Performance*, 11, 28–39.

Simpson, G. B. & Krueger, M. A. (1991). Selective access of homograph meanings in sentence context. *Journal of Memory and Language*, 30, 627–643.

Snodgrass, J. G. & Corwin, J. (1988). Pragmatics of measuring recognition memory: applications to dementia and amnesia. *Journal of Experimental Psychology: General*, 117, 34–50.

Sprengelmeyer, R., Young, A. W., Pundt, I., Sprengelmeyer, A., Calder, A. J., Berrios, G., Winkel, R., Vollmöller, W., Kuhn, W., Sartory, G. & Przuntek, H. (1997). Disgust implicated in obsessive-compulsive disorder. *Proceedings of the Royal Society: Biological Sciences*. 264, 1767–1773.

Stopa, L. & Clark, D. M., (2000). Social phobia and interpretation of social events. *Behaviour Research and Therapy*, 38, 273–283.

Swinney, D. A. (1979). Lexical access during sentence comprehension: (re)consideration of context effects. *Journal of Verbal Learning and Verbal Behavior*, 18, 645–659.

Tabossi, P. (1988). Access lexical ambiguity in different sentential contexts. *Journal of Memory and Language*, 27, 324–340.

Wells, A. & Matthews, G. (1994). *Attention and Emotion*. Hillsdale, NJ: Erlbaum.

Whalen, P. (1998). Fear, vigilance and ambiguity: initial neuroimaging studies of the human amygdala. *Current Directions in Psychological Science*, 7, 177–188.

Yiend, J. & Mathews, A. (2001). Anxiety and attention to threatening pictures. *Quarterly Journal of Experimental Psychology: Human Experimental Psychology*, 54, 665–681.

Young, A. W., Rowland, D., Calder, A. J., Etcoff, N. L., Seth, A. & Perrett, D. I. (1997). Facial expression megamix: tests of dimensional and category accounts of emotion recognition. *Cognition*, 63, 271–313.

7   Dissociating fear and disgust: implications for the structure of emotions

Andrew D. Lawrence, Fionnuala C. Murphy and Andrew J. Calder

Introduction

Several authors have suggested that emotion scientists could fruitfully examine the underlying structure, or functional architecture, of human emotion systems using cognitive neuropsychological techniques (Davidson, 1992; Scherer, 1993; Lane et al., 2000). According to Bub (1994), *'The general methodological problem for neuropsychology is how evidence, in the form of patterns of cognitive deficits, bears on theory, in the form of rival functional architectures'*. Analogously, we can ask how evidence, in the form of patterns of emotion deficits, bears on theory, in the form of rival functional architectures of emotion (Mathews & MacLeod, 1994; Scherer & Peper, 2001).

In collecting evidence, neuropsychologists design experiments to elicit dissociations in task performance. Dissocations can be single (task A normal, task B abnormal), or multiple (tasks A, B normal, tasks C, D abnormal). Double dissociations are obtained when task A is normal, task B abnormal in patient P1; task B normal, task A abnormal in patient P2 (Shallice, 1988). Double dissociation evidence is regarded as the most compelling of all. This is because partial lesions allow dissociations to arise from resource artefacts, as one task demands more of some computational resource of a processing component than another (Shallice, 1988). Resource artefacts can be ruled out by double dissociations, and only systems that contain a high degree of functional specialization can produce strong double dissociations (Shallice, 1988). For this argument to hold, two relatively uncontroversial assumptions must be made:
1. That impaired processing is explicable in terms of the same model as normal processing, except that certain parameters of the model are changed (i.e. processes are not fundamentally reorganized following damage), and
2. That task performance is a monotonically increasing function of the computational resource of any subsystem activated in performing the task (Shallice 1988; Caramazza, 1992).

Below, we outline evidence for selective impairments in the processing of two emotions, fear and disgust, following brain damage. Such deficits encompass not only emotion behaviours and emotion experience, but also the recognition of conspecific emotional expressions. We then discuss the results of a recent meta-analysis of functional neuroimaging studies of emotion, focusing on evidence for regional neural specializations for fear and disgust. Finally, we discuss the implications of these findings for theories of the structure of emotions.

Selective impairments in fear processing following damage to the amygdala

The mammalian amygdala, a complex of nuclei residing in the anterior temporal lobe, plays a critical role in the acquisition and expression of fear behaviours. For example, in the rat, lesions of the amygdala can permanently disrupt fear behaviours such as freezing, tachycardia (rapid heart response), hypertension, hypoalgesia, fear-potentiated startle, and vigilance (Davis, 2000; Fanselow & Gale, 2003). Similarly, in non-human primates, selective excitotoxic amygdala lesions disrupt fear behaviours such as freezing and hypoalgesia, and result in increased approach responses to snakes, unfamiliar inanimate objects and unfamiliar conspecifics (Meunier et al., 1999; Kalin et al., 2001; Emery et al., 2001; Manning et al., 2001; Prather et al., 2001; Meunier & Bachevalier, 2002; Amaral et al., 2003).

Data from observational learning experiments (Mineka & Cook, 1988; Gerull & Rapee, 2002), together with evidence for emotional contagion (Lundqvist & Dimberg, 1995), suggest that conspecific fear expressions (facial, vocal, postural) are powerful elicitors of fear states in the viewer. In addition, a broad class of theories (*simulationist*) argues that the mental (including emotional) states of others are represented by mental simulation, i.e. by generating similar states in oneself (Gallese & Goldman, 1998). These data and theories would predict that the human amygdala may not only be involved in generating fear states, but also in reacting to and recognizing the social expression of fear in conspecifics.

Adolphs et al. (1994, 1995) initially addressed the question of whether the human amygdala is involved in the *recognition* of conspecific fearful facial expressions. They studied one patient, SM, with bilateral amygdala damage resulting from Urbach-Wiethe disease, and six patients with unilateral damage to either the left or right amygdala. Participants rated examples of facial expressions of emotion (happiness, sadness, anger, fear, disgust and surprise), plus neutral expressions on several emotion scales. In comparison to controls with or without neurological damage to areas excluding the amygdala, SM showed abnormal ratings of facial expressions of fear and, to a lesser extent, surprise and anger. By contrast, patients with damage to the right amygdala showed no significant impairments, whereas patients with damage to the left amygdala showed some evidence of abnormal performance, but not for fear. Additional studies in SM have revealed that, across several repetitions of Adolphs' rating task, the most consistent impairment is in processing facial expressions of fear (Adolphs & Tranel, 2000). Anderson et al. (2000) have used an adapted version of Adolphs' task in a group of patients with unilateral antero-medial temporal lobectomies. Patients with lesions encompassing the right, but not left, amygdala, showed abnormal processing of faces expressing fear, sadness, disgust and happiness. Adolphs, Tranel & Damasio (2001) have also shown impaired recognition of facial expressions of fear in patients with right temporal lobectomies encompassing the amygdala.

Adolphs' rating task was also used in a study of nine patients with amygdala damage due to various aetiologies (Adolphs et al., 1999b), which found that, when analysed as a group, fear processing was most affected in these patients, although not every patient showed obvious impairments for fear.

Calder et al. (1996) adopted a forced-choice facial-expression labelling procedure (Frank & Stennett, 2001), in a study of two patients with bilateral amygdala lesions: DR, whose lesions result from a series of stereotaxic operations for intractable epilepsy, and SE, whose lesions are a result of encephalitis. Across two forced-choice labelling tasks, including one comprising morphed (blended) facial expressions, both DR and SE showed impaired fear and, to a lesser extent, anger recognition, thus complementing the original findings of Adolphs et al. Reports of further patients with bilateral amygdala damage have since shown fear-recognition impairments on the same or similar forced-choice tasks (Broks et al., 1998; Schmolck & Squire, 2001; Sato et al., 2002). In certain cases, these can be *highly selective* for fear (Sprengelmeyer et al., 1999). Wang et al. (2002) have reported impaired fear-recognition on forced-choice labelling tasks in a patient with a *unilateral* right amygdala lesion, combined with bilateral anterior cingulate damage.

An important issue concerns the extent to which the role of the amygdala is restricted to processing *facial* expressions of emotion, especially fear, or whether it is involved in processing expressions of emotion from other sensory modalities. In several mammalian species, auditory stimuli are powerful elicitors of amygdala activity. For example, in squirrel monkeys, amygdala activity is seen to conspecific calls, e.g. isolation and alarm peeps, and snake calls (Kling et al., 1987).

In humans, support for the polymodal hypothesis comes primarily from two bilateral amygdala patients – DR and NM. DR showed impaired recognition of fear and anger from both facial and vocal cues, whereas NM's deficits with facial, vocal and postural cues were restricted to fear. These deficits were seen both in tests requiring recognition of fear conveyed by non-linguistic sound patterns (e.g. screams) and by prosodic features (Scott et al., 1997; Sprengelmeyer et al., 1999). By contrast, Adolphs and Tranel (1999b) found that SM and a second bilateral amygdala patient, RH, showed no deficit on a vocal (prosodic) variant of Adolphs' facial expression rating task, despite both showing deficits on the original facial expression task. However, one method of analysing the vocal data (Adolphs & Tranel, 2000) indicated that RH experienced some difficulty with vocal cues of fear and sadness. Anderson and Phelps (1998) have reported intact recognition of vocal (non-linguistic sounds and prosody) but not facial expressions of fear in patient SP, who has bilateral amygdala damage. However, SP's recognition of other vocal expressions, including surprise and disgust, is impaired. Adolphs, Tranel and Damasio (2001) have reported intact recognition of prosodic expressions of fear in patients with unilateral left- and right-temporal lobectomies encompassing the amygdala.

The data on auditory fear recognition are thus less compelling than those on facial expression recognition. Anatomical data (Stefanacci & Amaral, 2000) suggest that there are sensory-specific domains within the amygdala, and so one possibility is that, in patients with spared auditory fear recognition, these regions are intact. SM has rather complete amygdala damage, however, reducing the plausibility of this argument. Nevertheless, we tend to favour the notion that the amygdala is involved in processing fear signals across multiple modalities.

Whilst much empirical research has focused on the role of the human amygdala in conspecific fear recognition, there have been several investigations of fear behaviours and self-report fear experience in patients with amygdala damage.

Consistent with the findings in other mammals, the human amygdala is indeed critical for the acquisition and expression of a variety of fear behaviours. Patients with bilateral amygdala damage show impaired fear conditioning and reduced response to frightening images and stressors, as indexed by electrodermal activity (Bechara et al., 1995; Lee et al., 1998; Phelps et al., 1998; Adolphs & Tranel, 1999a; Asahina et al., 2003; Gläscher & Adolphs, 2003) or fear-potentiated startle (Funayama et al., 2001), as do at least some patients with unilateral amygdala damage (Angrilli et al., 1996; Gläscher & Adolphs, 2003; LaBar et al., 1995; Funayama et al., 2001; Kubota et al., 2000; Peper et al., 2001; Masaoka et al., 2003). Bilateral amygdala damage also leads to reduced fear-related vigilance (Anderson & Phelps, 2002). The amygdala does not, however, appear to be involved in the *voluntary* production of fearful facial expressions (Anderson & Phelps, 2000), a finding that can be related to the distinction between voluntary and passive or reflexive facial expressions of emotion (Rinn, 1984).

Patient NM (Sprengelmeyer et al., 1999) shows reduced self-report fear experience, as measured by the Fear Survey Schedule (Brown & Crawford, 1988), whereas his scores for comparable questionnaires assessing disgust and anger experience were normal. Patient SM, who, like NM, has bilateral amygdala damage, also reports reduced fear experience. For example, she reports not feeling afraid when shown film clips that normally elicit fear, but does seem to experience other emotions, such as anger, strongly (Adolphs & Tranel, 2000). Masaoka et al. (2003) reported reduced self-report anxiety, an emotion closely related to fear (Izard, 1977), in two patients, following left amygdala resection for drug-refractory epilepsy. Further, when the amygdala is stimulated during surgery in humans, patients frequently report feelings of fear (Halgren, 1992). By contrast, Anderson & Phelps (2002) found that SP, a bilateral amygdala patient, reported no significant differences in the magnitude and frequency of fear experience as measured by the Positive and Negative Affect Scales (Watson et al., 1988), when asked to rate her feelings at the end of each day over the course of a month, although SP does show impaired fear behaviours, e.g. fear-potentiated startle (Funayama et al., 2001).

In general then, patients with (bilateral) amygdala damage show impaired recognition of conspecific fear expressions, reduced fear behaviours and reduced fear experience. A further intriguing link between fear recognition, behaviour and experience comes from two studies of high anxious individuals (who exhibit amygdala hyperactivity (Mathews, Yiend & Lawrence, 2004)), which found that anxiety increased sensitivity to detect fear in morphed facial expressions (Sprengelmeyer et al., 1997a; Richards et al., 2002).

There is a caveat that should be raised at this point. At the beginning of this chapter, we raised the possibility that dissociations in processing of an emotion can occur, not because processing of the emotion occurs in an isolable subsystem, but because of resource artefacts; i.e. processing of fear faces, for example, may simply be differentially sensitive to neurological disease (Shallice, 1988). Consistent with such an interpretation, Rapcsak et al. (2000) found that in a group of patients with various focal lesions, the recognition of fearful facial expressions was disproportionately impaired relative to other emotions, regardless of whether the lesion included the amygdala or not. They attributed these findings to the fact that neurologically intact controls find fear more difficult to recognize than other emotions, and argued that fear recognition impairments were simply an artefact of difficulty level in this group. As noted above, the strongest argument for isolable emotion systems would be evidence for a double dissociation between fear and another emotion.

Selective impairments in disgust processing following damage to the insula and basal ganglia

Following Darwin (1872/1965), Rozin (Rozin & Fallon, 1987; Rozin et al., 2000) proposed that disgust evolved from the mammalian distaste response. Rozin suggests that a core disgust system is constructed from the distaste food rejection system, via a process of secondary adaptation in which the disgust response is attached successively to a variety of things that are offensive within a particular culture. So, according to Rozin, the major event in the cultural evolution of disgust is the expansion or replacement of meanings and elicitors, with the output side of disgust remaining largely intact. Some of these elicitors are likely to be pan-cultural, but many are not (Curtis & Biran, 2001). In Rozin's theory, a typical elicitor of core disgust is *'anything that reminds us that we are animals'*, e.g. bodily waste products. Rozin et al. posit two further domains of disgust elicitors: interpersonal disgust, related to contact with undesirable persons, and moral disgust, related to violations of moral 'purity' (Rozin et al., 2000). In Rozin's theory, disgust becomes the means by which cultures can internalize rejection of an offensive object, behaviour or thought.

Much is now known about the neural structures involved in the distaste response. An index of distaste in rats is Grill and Norgren's (1978) taste-reactivity test, in which distaste is reflected by stereotyped responses including gaping, fluid expulsion, head shaking and forelimb flailing, in response to intra-oral infusion of fluids. In contrast to their effects on fear behaviours, lesions of the rodent amygdala leave intact distaste reactions, whilst impairing food neophobia (Dunn & Everitt, 1988; Galaverna et al., 1993). Instead, damage to the gustatory neocortex, located in agranular insular cortex, impairs distaste reactions (gapes, especially) (Kiefer & Orr, 1992). Distaste reactions also appear to be disturbed by lesions to the globus pallidus, an output nucleus of the basal ganglia, anatomically linked to the gustatory neocortex (Hernádi et al., 1997). In humans, lesions to the presumably homologous area of the gustatory insula impair reactions to bitter tastes, including quinine and citric acid (Pritchard et al., 1999).

As was the case with fear, data from observational learning experiments (Baeyens et al., 1996; Snowden & Boe, 2003), together with evidence for emotional contagion (Lundqvist & Dimberg, 1995), suggest that conspecific distaste/disgust expressions are powerful elicitors of disgust in the viewer (Tomkins, 1963). These data, together with the strong link between distaste and disgust, and with simulationist accounts of emotion recognition, would suggest that lesions to the gustatory insula and basal ganglia (especially the globus pallidus) in humans should lead to impaired disgust reactions, disgust experience and recognition of conspecific disgust expressions.

Evidence for a differential disgust deficit came initially from an investigation of manifest Huntington's disease (HD), an autosomal dominant neurogenetic disorder (Sprengelmeyer et al., 1996, 1997b). HD patients were shown the same forced-choice expression labelling tests that were used with several of the bilateral amygdala patients. The patients with HD showed problems in recognizing several emotions, but a disproportionately severe impairment was found for disgust expressions. Similar deficits were found in recognizing prosodic expressions of disgust. Wang et al. (2003) also found a differentially severe impairment in disgust recognition in Chinese individuals with HD. That study further found that patients with Wilson's disease (WD) had a differentially severe impairment in disgust recognition. Further evidence that HD particularly affects the recognition of disgust came from an investigation of face processing (including facial expression recognition) in people at risk of carrying the mutation responsible for HD (Gray et al., 1997). Participants who were subsequently identified as gene carriers (AR+) were compared with participants who did not carry the gene (AR−). A comparison of the scores revealed just one significant difference for recognition of emotion – the AR+ group made significantly more errors in recognizing facial expressions of disgust than did the AR− group. It should be noted, however, that Milders et al. (2003) failed to find a *differential* deficit in the recognition of facial expressions of disgust in patients with manifest HD and asymptomatic gene-carriers.

Impairments in disgust and, to a lesser extent, anger recognition have been reported in patients with Obsessive Compulsive Disorder (OCD) and in patients with Tourette's syndrome with comorbid OCD (Sprengelmeyer et al., 1997a). Although HD, WD, OCD and Tourette's syndrome are not characterized by focal neuropathology, both HD and OCD patients show pathology in regions of the insula and basal ganglia (Rauch et al., 1998; Thieben et al., 2002).

The strongest evidence for a *selective* impairment in disgust recognition, however, comes from the study of a single case, NK (Calder et al.,

2000b). The damage to NK's brain is lateralized to the left hemisphere and includes the insula, putamen, internal capsule, globus pallidus and, to a lesser extent, the caudate nucleus. On tests of facial and vocal (both prosody and non-linguistic sounds – e.g. retching) expression, NK showed a highly selective disgust deficit in the context of preserved recognition of other emotions.

In addition to a selective disgust recognition impairment, NK also showed abnormal performance on a questionnaire tapping disgust experience, whereas his scores for comparable questionnaires assessing anger and fear experience were normal. The disgust questionnaire was based on Rozin's theory of disgust, measuring disgust sensitivity in several domains relevant to that theory (Haidt et al., 1994). NK showed a significant or borderline reduction in his scores for 5/8 subscales, scoring at or near the minimum on the categories of food, animals, body products, body envelope violation and death, but not on the hygiene, sex or magical (disgust by connotation) categories. This result is notable, as it suggests that NK's disgust impairments relate more to Rozin's core disgust domain (with the exception of hygiene), rather than the interpersonal or moral disgust domains. HD patients have also been administered the disgust scale, and show impairments on the body products, sex, hygiene and magical scales (Sprengelmeyer et al., 1996, 1997b) (with different HD patients showing different patterns of impairment), raising interesting issues about potential differences between their disgust impairment and that of NK. Intriguingly, a recent study (Charash & McKay, 2002) in healthy individuals found that the measure by Haidt et al. of individual differences in disgust sensitivity predicted attentional biases for disgust words, but not fear words, in the emotional Stroop paradigm pioneered by Mathews (Mathews & MacLeod, 1994). This is further evidence for a dissociation between fear and disgust.

Further evidence for a link between disgust recognition and experience comes from the work of Krolak-Salmon et al. (2003). Using depth electrodes implanted during presurgical evaluation of patients with drug-refractory epilepsy, they recorded intracerebral event-related potentials to facial expressions of emotion. The ventral anterior insula was specifically involved in the processing of disgust, but not other (e.g. fear) facial expressions. In addition, when this area was stimulated, patients reported unpleasant sensations in the throat spreading up to the mouth, lips and nose. Earlier stimulation studies of the insula included reports of feelings of nausea, unpleasant tastes and stomach sensations (Penfield & Faulk, 1955).

Adolphs, Tranel & Damasio (2003) have recently reported the case of patient B, who exhibits a disproportionate impairment in the recognition of disgust across a variety of tests, including forced-choice labelling of

Figure 7.1 A double dissociation of the crossover type between the recognition of fear and disgust faces in a forced-choice facial-expression labelling task. Data (Z scores relative to healthy controls) plotted from Sprengelmeyer et al. (1999) (Case NM) and Calder et al. (2000) (case NK). See text for details.

the emotion portrayed in facial expressions, pictures and short vignettes. For example, when told a story about a person vomiting, his descriptions of how the person would feel included 'hungry' and 'delighted'. When describing the experimenter acting out the apparent vomiting of unpalatable food, B reported that 'delicious food was being enjoyed'. As with NK, B reported not feeling disgusted by, for example, food covered with cockroaches. B's pathology, resulting from encephalitis, is rather widespread, but encompasses the insular cortex bilaterally. His basal ganglia, however, appear to be spared (Tranel & Damasio, 1993), suggesting that damage to the insula alone may be sufficient to impair disgust.

In the introduction to this chapter, we argued that the best evidence for isolable emotion systems would be a double dissociation between different emotions following brain damage. Complementary dissociations between fear and disgust deficits can indeed be found, e.g. by comparing patient NM (who has an isolated fear deficit), with patient NK (who has an isolated disgust deficit) (see Figures 7.1, 7.2). These deficits

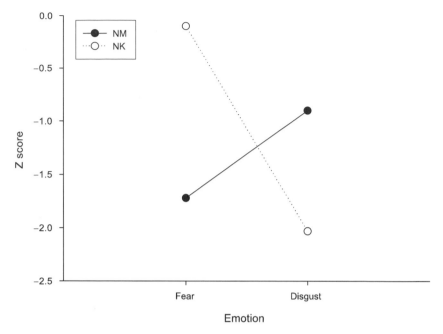

Figure 7.2 A double dissociation of the crossover type between the self-reported experience of fear (as measured by the Fear Survey Schedule) and disgust (as measured by the Disgust Scale). Data (Z scores relative to healthy controls) plotted from Sprengelmeyer et al. (1999) (Case NM) and Calder et al. (2000) (Case NK). See text for details.

encompass the recognition of conspecific emotion expressions, emotion behaviours and emotion experience. Such a double dissociation cannot be explained through different emotions making different levels of demands on the same system (Shallice, 1988), and represents good evidence for isolable emotion systems.

The aim of patient-based neuropsychological work is primarily to test functional (psychological) models, rather than to impute functions to particular structures in the brain (Caramazza, 1992). In recent years, researchers have begun to use functional neuroimaging methods to help impute function to structure, and it is to this literature that we now turn.

Functional neuroimaging studies of fear and disgust

To address evidence for relative regional specialization for different emotions in the human brain, we recently performed a meta-analytic study of regional activation foci reported in 106 functional imaging studies of emotion, including studies of fear (N = 30 studies) and disgust (N =7 studies), which we focus on here (Murphy et al., 2003; see also Phan et al., 2002). Full details of the scope of studies included and detailed results can be found in that paper, but, briefly, studies were chosen that compared activations during emotion conditions, relative to well-matched neutral control conditions using either whole brain $H_2{}^{15}O$ positron emission tomography (PET) or functional magnetic resonance imaging (fMRI) in healthy volunteers. Since studies adopted different analysis methods and significance criteria, all activation foci were accepted when reported as significant by the criteria of the individual studies. The Talairach and Tournoux (1988) atlas was then used as a standard criterion for identifying the anatomical location of activation foci, allowing consistent treatment of all data sets. Given the strong evidence for recognition–behaviour–experience links in emotion, we collapsed data across studies of emotion recognition, emotion behaviour and emotion experience (Murphy et al., 2003).

One of the analyses we conducted examined the neural region that was activated in the highest proportion of studies targeting an emotion (e.g. fear), and the extent to which the same region (e.g. the amygdala) was activated in studies targeting other emotions (e.g. disgust). Figure 7.3 shows the results for studies of fear and disgust. As can be seen, a crossover pattern emerged, implying a double dissociation obtained between the two emotions (Shallice, 2003). The amygdala was the region most often activated in studies of fear, and was much less often activated in studies of disgust. Conversely, the insula/operculum and globus pallidus were most often activated in studies of disgust, but were much less frequently activated in studies of fear. Murphy et al. (2003) found evidence for a remarkable convergence between the areas most often activated for the two emotions and the regions that, when damaged, lead both to selective emotion deficits in humans (amygdala for fear, insula and basal ganglia for disgust), and to their presumed homologues in other mammals (Dunn & Everitt, 1988). Of course, the amygdala was not activated in 100 per cent of fear studies, and likewise the insula and globus pallidus for disgust. There are many reasons for this. For example, some studies may have low statistical power to detect activations; emotion induction methods may have been ineffective in targeting the appropriate emotion in some studies; some studies of emotion recognition may have been contaminated by mis-recognition of the targeted emotion (i.e. confusion with another emotion), and structures such as the amygdala are difficult to image, especially using fMRI (Merbolt et al., 2001). Moreover, as suggested by the neuropsychological data, fear and disgust may themselves not be unitary emotions. Nevertheless, from these results it seems reasonable to conclude that:

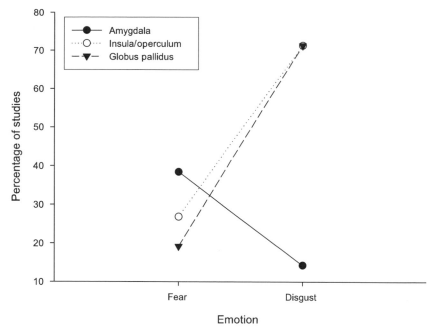

Figure 7.3 Evidence for a double dissociation of the crossover type between fear and disgust in the neuroimaging data. Data represent the percentage of fear and disgust studies that show activation in the region(s) most frequently activated for each individual emotion: the amygdala in the case of fear, and the insula/operculum and globus pallidus in the case of disgust. Plotted from Murphy et al. (2003). See text for details.

1. The imaging data support the neuropsychological data, in that fear and disgust can be doubly dissociated using both methods, and
2. The imaging data have helped to impute function to structure with a precision not possible through the study of brain-damaged individuals alone (Young et al., 2000).

Of course, the amygdala and insula and globus pallidus were not the only regions activated for fear and disgust respectively – merely the regions most frequently activated. In a second analysis, we applied the Kolmogorov-Smirnov (K-S), a non-parametric test for differences between two distributions, to the data set. Though familiarly applied to one-dimensional distributions, the K-S can be extended to those of higher dimensionality. Using the K-S test, the three-dimensional spatial distribution of activation foci across studies of fear was compared with that across studies of disgust. The difference in the spatial distributions of reported activation foci for fear and disgust was highly significant (P = 0.008). This latter finding could be taken as evidence for emotion-specific neurophysiology (LeDoux, 1994) (see Figure 7.4).

Implications for theories of emotion

We have presented evidence for a double dissociation between fear and disgust following brain damage in humans, encompassing not only emotional behaviours and experience, but also the recognition of conspecific emotional expressions, as would be predicted, for example, by simulation theories (Gallese & Goldman, 1998). Additionally, when taken together with the neuroimaging data, we have evidence for at least some degree of relative regional specialization in the brain for these two emotions: the amygdala for fear, and the insula and basal ganglia (especially globus pallidus) for disgust. There is also evidence for homology in mammalian fear and distaste/disgust systems (Griffiths, 1997). To what extent are these data consistent with the theoretical claims of rival theories of the structure of emotions?

The finding of dissociations between different emotions argues strongly against any notion of a *unidimensional, unfractionable* emotion system: only systems that contain a high degree of functional specialization can produce double dissociations of the type seen here.

The data also prove difficult for *low-dimensional* theories of emotion (e.g. Davidson, 1992; Cacioppo et al., 1999; Bradley & Lang, 2000), which argue that broad dimensions, for example valence (pleasant/unpleasant) and arousal (sleepy/activated), or action tendency (approach/withdrawal) are emotion *primitives* or the *fundamental* emotion-relevant dimensions, i.e. are unfractionable. For example, Davidson (1992) argues that '*approach and withdrawal are two dimensions along which emotions differ and these dimensions should properly be regarded as basic*'. Russell (2003) argues that '*core affect*' is a '*neurophysiological state that is consciously accessible as a simple, nonreflective feeling that is an integral blend of hedonic (pleasure–displeasure) and arousal (sleepy–activated) values*' and that '*core affect is primitive, universal and simple (irreducible on the mental plane)*'. Neither of these views readily predicts double dissociations between fear and disgust, as reported here. Both fear and disgust are associated with withdrawal action-tendency, and so a theory that posits action-tendency as an emotion primitive would predict that these emotions would not be dissociated. An approach based on two fundamental dimensions as the foundations of affect would predict that damage to a system coding one or other of these broad dimensions (e.g. arousal) should produce effects on *all* emotions, as the entire emotion space would

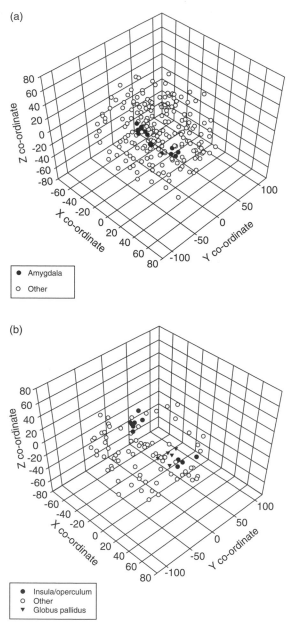

Figure 7.4 Three-dimensional scatterplots showing the distribution of activation foci for contrasts associated with (a) fear and (b) disgust. Filled symbols represent activity in regions most frequently associated with each particular emotion across studies. Plotted from Murphy et al. (2003). See text for details.

be distorted (but see Adolphs, Russell & Tranel, 1999). It is unclear how double dissociations between fear and disgust could arise from a two-dimensional model of emotion space.

This does not imply, of course, that dimensions such as valence are not important components of emotion space, *merely that they are not emotion primitives and are not irreducible or unfractionable*. It is quite possible that high-level systems are involved in computing emotion dimensions such as valence (although see Solomon & Stone (2002) for conceptual problems with the valence concept). For example, Davidson (1992) has proposed the notion of emotion *convergence zones*, located in the prefrontal cortex, which bind together information from widely distributed networks, and Rolls (1999) proposes a role for the frontal cortex in the on-line computation of valence. Indeed there is evidence that prefrontal lesions can result in rather general emotion impairments (e.g. Angrilli et al., 1999; Hornak et al., 2003) and our meta-analysis suggested a rather general role for the medial prefrontal cortices in emotions (Murphy et al., 2003). Selective emotion impairments are not incompatible with the views of Davidson (1992) and Rolls (1999). Nor are they incompatible with *multi-dimensional appraisal* theories, which posit that 'discrete' emotions can be viewed as preferred states or 'attractors' in a state-space defined by multiple ($N > 2$) appraisal dimensions (Scherer & Peper, 2001). There have, however, been few neuropsychological studies *specifically designed* to test the predictions made by particular multi-dimensional appraisal theories (Scherer & Peper, 2001).

One class of theories that the data do appear to support are *categorical* theories of emotion, in which emotion space is viewed as consisting of a collection of discrete categories. We do not suggest, of course, that the data we have described demonstrate that there are 'fear' and 'disgust' centres in the brain, corresponding to the (English-language) vernacular categories of fear and disgust. The fractures we have described do not occur along the 'fault lines' carved out by the English emotion lexicon. Rather, only some instances of what the English language describes as fear are impaired following lesions to the amygdala, and similarly for disgust following insula and basal ganglia lesions. These instances of fear and disgust appear somewhat similar to those proposed by one particular categorical emotion theory, that of Ekman (1977, 1992).

According to Ekman, *affect programmes* direct emotional responses that are brief, often quick, complex, organized and difficult to control. The term affect programme refers to a (neural) mechanism that stores the patterns for these responses, and which then triggers their occurrence. Griffiths (1997) suggests that the system that produces an affect programme has all the properties of a modular system. He also suggests that homologues of the affect programme emotions exist in other mammals, and the current data support the latter claim.

While the affect programme account may turn out to be substantially correct, we would caution against interpreting our data as unequivocal support for a *modular* affect programme theory for several reasons. For a start, the necessary and sufficient conditions for a system to be modular have not been clearly specified (Fodor, 2000; Flombaum et al., 2002). Lyons' (2003) notion of a system might be usefully applied to the results here, where systems are defined (roughly) as being isolable, specialized and internally cohesive. We would argue that the neuropsychological and neuroimaging data point to the existence of particular emotion systems in the sense described by Lyons (2003). These systems are required for, but not necessarily dedicated to, the generation of emotion states (Lambie & Marcel, 2002), and the recognition of conspecific emotion expressions. 'Fear' and 'disgust' systems may well be able to interact (e.g. via convergence zones), but nevertheless would still deserve to be counted as distinct (Lyons, 2003). Whether these systems turn out to be isomorphic with, for example, Ekman's affect programmes is as yet unclear. It may well be that the systems we describe may be further fractionated. We must also be careful not to generalize from fear and disgust to the other affect programme emotions. Only future empirical research will enable us to determine what the granularity (Sterelny & Griffiths, 1999) of emotion systems really is.

NOTE

Our work is funded by the UK Medical Research Council (MRC).

REFERENCES

Adolphs, R., Russell, J. A. & Tranel, D. (1999). A role for the human amygdala in recognizing emotional arousal from unpleasant stimuli. *Psychological Science*, *10*, 167–171.

Adolphs, R. & Tranel, D. (1999a). Preferences for visual stimuli following amygdala damage. *Journal of Cognitive Neuroscience*, *11*, 610–616.

Adolphs, R. & Tranel, D. (1999b). Intact recognition of emotional prosody following amygdala damage. *Neuropsychologia*, *37*, 1285–1292.

Adolphs, R. & Tranel, D. (2000). Emotion recognition and the human amygdala. In J. P. Aggleton (Ed.), *The Amygdala: a Functional Analysis*, 2nd edn, 587–630. Oxford: Oxford University Press.

Adolphs, R., Tranel, D. & Damasio, A. R. (2003). Dissociable neural systems for recognizing emotions. *Brain and Cognition*, *52*, 61–69.

Adolphs, R., Tranel, D. & Damasio, H. (2001). Emotion recognition from faces and prosody following temporal lobectomy. *Neuropsychology*, *15*, 396–404.

Adolphs, R., Tranel, D., Damasio, H. & Damasio, A. (1994). Impaired recognition of emotion in facial expressions following bilateral damage to the human amygdala. *Nature*, *372*, 669–672.

Adolphs, R., Tranel, D., Damasio, H. & Damasio, A. (1995). Fear and the human amygdala. *Journal of Neuroscience*, *15*, 5879–5891.

Adolphs, R., Tranel, D., Hamann, S., et al. (1999). Recognition of facial emotion in nine individuals with bilateral amygdala damage. *Neuropsychologia*, *37*, 1111–1117.

Amaral, D. G., Bauman, M. D., Capitanio, J. P., Lavenex, P., Mason, W. A., Mauldin-Jourdain, M. L. & Mendoza, S. P. (2003). The amygdala: is it an essential component of the neural network for social cognition? *Neuropsychologia*, *41*, 517–522.

Anderson, A. K. & Phelps, E. A. (1998). Intact recognition of vocal expressions of fear following bilateral lesions of the human amygdala. *NeuroReport*, *9*, 3607–3613.

Anderson, A. K. & Phelps, E. A. (2000). Expression without recognition: contributions of the human amygdala to emotional communication. *Psychological Science*, *11*, 106–111.

Anderson, A. K. & Phelps, E. A. (2001). Lesions of the human amygdala impair enhanced perception of emotionally salient events. *Nature*, *411*, 305–309.

Anderson, A. K. & Phelps, E. A. (2002). Is the human amygdala critical for the subjective experience of emotion? Evidence of intact dispositional affect in patients with amygdala lesions. *Journal of Cognitive Neuroscience*, *14*, 709–720.

Anderson, A. K., Spencer, D. D., Fulbright, R. K. & Phelps, E. A. (2000). Contribution of the anteromedial temporal lobes to the evaluation of facial emotion. *Neuropsychology*, *14*, 526–536.

Angrilli, A., Mauri, A., Palomba, D., Flor, H., Birbaumer, N., Sartori, G. & di Paola, F. (1996). Startle reflex and emotion modulation impairment after a right amygdala lesion. *Brain*, *119*, 1991–2000.

Angrilli, A., Palomba, D., Cantagallo, A., Maietti, A. & Stegagno, L. (1999). Emotional impairment after right orbitofrontal lesion in a patient without cognitive deficits. *NeuroReport*, *10*, 1741–1746.

Asahina, M., Suzuki, A., Mori, M., Kanesaka, T. & Hattori, T. (2003). Emotional sweating response in a patient with bilateral amygdala damage. *International Journal of Psychophysiology*, *47*, 87–93.

Baeyens, F., Kaes, B., Eelen, P. & Silverans, P. (1996). Observational evaluative conditioning of an embedded stimulus element. *European Journal of Social Psychology*, *26*, 15–28.

Bechara, A., Tranel, D., Damasio, H., Adolphs, R., Rockland, C. & Damasio, A. R. (1995). Double dissociation of conditioning and declarative knowledge relative to the amygdala and hippocampus in humans. *Science*, *269*, 1115–1118.

Bradley, M. M. & Lang, P. J. (2000). Measuring emotion: behavior, feeling, and physiology. In R. D. Lane & L. Nadel (Eds.), *Cognitive Neuroscience of Emotion*, 242–276. Oxford: Oxford University Press.

Broks, P., Young, A. W., Maratos, E. J. et al. (1998). Face processing impairments after encephalitis: amygdala damage and recognition of fear. *Neuropsychologia*, *36*, 59–70.

Brown, A. M. & Crawford, H. J. (1988). Fear survey schedule-III: oblique and orthogonal factorial structures in an American college population. *Personality and Individual Differences, 9,* 401–410.

Bub, J. (1994). Testing models of cognition through the analysis of brain-damaged performance. *British Journal for Philosophy of Science, 45,* 837–855.

Cacioppo, J. T., Gardner, W. L. & Bernston, G. G. (1999). The affect system has parallel and integrative processing components: form follows function. *Journal of Personality and Social Psychology, 76,* 839–855.

Calder, A. J., Keane, J., Manes, F., Antoun, N. & Young, A. W. (2000). Impaired recognition and experience of disgust following brain injury. *Nature Neuroscience, 3,* 1077–1078.

Calder, A. J., Young, A. W., Rowland, D., Perrett, D. I., Hodges, J. R. & Etcoff, N. L. (1996). Facial emotion recognition after bilateral amygdala damage: differentially severe impairment of fear. *Cognitive Neuropsychology, 13,* 699–745.

Caramazza, A. (1992). Is cognitive neuropsychology possible? *Journal of Cognitive Neuroscience, 4,* 80–95.

Charash, M. & McKay, D. (2002). Attention bias for disgust. *Anxiety Disorders, 16,* 529–541.

Curtis, V.,& Biran, A. (2001). Dirt, disgust and disease. *Perspectives in Biology and Medicine, 44,* 17–31.

Darwin (1872/1965). *The Expressions of Emotion in Man and Animal.* Chicago: Chigaco University Press.

Davidson, R. J. (1992). Prolegomenon to the structure of emotion: gleanings from neuropsychology. *Cognition and Emotion, 6,* 245–268.

Davis, M. (2000). The role of the amygdala in conditioned and unconditioned fear and anxiety. In J. P. Aggleton (Ed.), *The Amygdala: a Functional Analysis,* 2nd edn, 213–287. Oxford: Oxford University Press.

Dunn, L. T. & Everitt, B. J. (1988). Double dissociations of the effects of amygdala and insular cortex lesions on conditioned taste aversion, passive avoidance, and neophobia in the rat using the excitotoxin ibotenic acid. *Behavioral Neuroscience, 102,* 3–23.

Ekman, P. (1977). Biological and cultural contributions to body and facial movement. In J. Blacking (Ed.), *The Anthropology of the Body,* 39–84. London: Academic Press.

Ekman, P. (1992). An argument for basic emotions. *Cognition and Emotion, 6,* 169–200.

Emery, N. J., Capitanio, J. P., Mason, W. A., Machado, C. J., Mendoza, S. P. & Amaral, D. G. (2001). The effects of bilateral lesions of the amygdala on dyadic social interactions in rhesus monkeys (*Macaca mulatta*). *Behavioral Neuroscience, 115,* 515–544.

Fanselow, M. S. & Gale, G. D. (2003). The amygdala, fear, and memory. *Annals of the New York Academy of Sciences, 985,* 125–134.

Flombaum, J. I., Santos, L. R. & Hauser, M. D. (2002). Neuroecology and psychological modularity. *Trends in Cognitive Sciences, 6,* 106–108.

Fodor, J. A. (2000). *The Mind Doesn't Work That Way: the Scope and Limits of Computational Psychology.* Cambridge, MA: MIT Press.

Frank, M. G. & Stennett, J. (2001). The forced-choice paradigm and the perception of facial expressions of emotion. *Journal of Personality and Social Psychology*, *80*, 75–85.

Funayama, E. S., Grillon, C., Davis, M. & Phelps, E. A. (2001). A double dissociation in the affective modulation of startle in humans: effects of unilateral temporal lobectomy. *Journal of Cognitive Neuroscience*, *13*, 721–729.

Galaverna, O. G., Seeley, R. J., Berridge, K. C., Grill, H. J., Epstein, A. N. & Schulkin, J. (1993). Lesions of the central nucleus of the amygdala I: effects on taste reactivity, taste aversion learning and sodium appetite. *Behavioral Brain Research*, *59*, 11–17.

Gallese, V. & Goldman, A. (1998). Mirror neurons and the simulation theory of mind-reading. *Trends in Cognitive Sciences*, *2*, 493–501.

Gerull, F. C. & Rapee, R. M. (2002). Mother knows best: effects of maternal modelling on the acquisition of fear and avoidance behaviours in toddlers. *Behaviour Research and Therapy*, *40*, 279–287.

Gläscher, J. & Adolphs, R. (2003). Processing of the arousal of subliminal and supraliminal emotional stimuli by the human amygdala. *Journal of Neuroscience*, *23*, 10274–10282.

Gray, J. M., Young, A. W., Barker, W. A., Curtis, A. & Gibson, D. (1997). Impaired recognition of disgust in Huntington's disease gene carriers. *Brain*, *120*, 2029–2038.

Griffiths, P. E. (1997). *What Emotions Really Are: the Problem of Psychological Categories*. Chicago: Chicago University Press.

Grill, H. J. & Norgren, R. (1978). The taste reactivity test I. Mimetic responses to gustatory stimuli in neurologically normal rats. *Brain Research*, *143*, 263–279.

Haidt, J., McCauley, C. & Rozin, P. (1994). Individual differences in sensitivity to disgust: a scale sampling seven domains of disgust elicitors. *Personality and Individual Differences*, *16*, 701–713.

Halgren, E. (1992). Emotional neurophysiology of the amygdala within the context of human cognition. In J. P. Aggleton (Ed.), *The Amygdala: Neurobiological Aspects of Emotion, Memory, and Mental Dysfunction*, 191–228. New York: Wiley-Liss.

Hernádi, I., Karádi, Z., Faludi, B. & Lénárd, L. (1997). Disturbances of neophobia and taste-aversion learning after bilateral kainate microlesions in the rat pallidum. *Behavioral Neuroscience*, *111*, 137–146.

Hornak, J., Bramha, J., Rolls, E. T., Morris, R. G., O'Doherty, J., Bullock, P. R. & Polkey, C. E. (2003). Changes in emotion after circumscribed surgical lesions of the orbitofrontal and cingulate cortices. *Brain*, *126*, 1691–1712.

Izard, C. E. (1977). Fear and the forms of anxiety. In C. E. Izard (Ed.), *Human Emotions*, 355–384. New York: Plenum Press.

Kalin, N. H., Shelton, S. E., Davidson, R. J. & Kelley, A. E. (2001). The primate amygdala mediates acute fear but not the behavioural and physiological components of anxious temperament. *Journal of Neuroscience*, *21*, 2067–2074.

Kiefer, S. W. & Orr, M. R. (1992). Taste avoidance, but not aversion, learning in rats lacking gustatory cortex. *Behavioral Neuroscience*, *106*, 140–146.

Kling, A. S., Lloyd, R. L. & Perryman, K. M. (1987). Slow wave changes in amygdala to visual, auditory and social stimuli following lesions of the inferior temporal cortex in squirrel monkey (*S. sciureus*). *Behavioral and Neural Biology, 4,* 54–72.

Krolak-Salmon, P., Hénaff, M.-A., Isnard, J., Tallon-Baudry, C., Guénot, M., Vighetto, A., Bertrand, O. & Mauguière, F. (2003). An attention modulated response to disgust in human ventral anterior insula. *Annals of Neurology, 53,* 446–453.

Kubota, Y., Sato, W., Murai, T., Toichi, M., Ikeda, A. & Sengoku, A. (2000). Emotional cognition without awareness after unilateral temporal lobectomy in humans. *Journal of Neuroscience, 20,* RC97(1–5).

LaBar, K. S., LeDoux, J. E., Spencer, D. D. & Phelps, E. A. (1995). Impaired fear conditioning following unilateral temporal lobectomy in humans. *Journal of Neuroscience, 15,* 6846–6854.

Lambie, J. A. & Marcel, A. J. (2002). Consciousness and the varieties of emotion experience: a theoretical framework. *Psychological Review, 109,* 219–259.

Lane, R. D., Nadel, L., Allen, J. J. B. & Kaszniak, A. W. (2000). The study of emotion from the perspective of cognitive neuroscience. In R. D. Lane & L. Nadel (Eds.), *Cognitive Neuroscience of Emotion,* 3–11. New York: Oxford University Press.

LeDoux, J. (1994). Emotion-specific physiological activity: don't forget about CNS physiology. In P. Ekman & R. J. Davidson (Eds.), *The Nature of Emotion: Fundamental Questions,* 248–251. New York: Oxford University Press.

Lee, G. P., Bechara, A., Adolphs, R., Arena, J., Meador, K. J., Loring, D. W. & Smith, J. R. (1998). Clinical and physiological effects of stereotaxic bilateral amygdalotomy for intractable aggression. *Journal of Neuropsychiatry, 10,* 413–420.

Lundqvist, L.-O. & Dimberg, U. (1995). Facial expressions are contagious. *Journal of Psychophysiology, 9,* 203–211.

Lyons, J. C. (2003). Lesion studies, spared performance, and cognitive systems. *Cortex, 39,* 145–147.

Manning, B. H., Merin, N. M., Meng, I. D. & Amaral, D. G. (2001). Reduction in opioid- and cannabinoid-induced antinociception in rhesus monkeys after bilateral lesions of the amygdaloid complex. *Journal of Neuroscience, 21,* 8238–8246.

Masaoka, Y., Hirasawa, K., Yamane, F., Hori, T. & Homma, I. (2003). Effects of left amygdala lesions on respiration, skin conductance, heart rate, anxiety, and activity of the right amygdala during anticipation of negative stimulus. *Behavior Modification, 27,* 607–619.

Mathews, A. & MacLeod, C. (1994). Cognitive approaches to emotion and emotional disorders. *Annual Review of Psychology, 45,* 25–50.

Mathews, A., Yiend, J. & Lawrence, A. D. (in press). Individual differences in the modulation of fear-related brain activation by attentional control. *Journal of Cognitive Neuroscience.*

Merbolt, K.-D., Fransson, P., Bruhn, H. & Frahm, J. (2001). Functional MRI of the human amygdala? *NeuroImage, 14,* 253–257.

Meunier, M. & Bachevalier, J. (2002). Comparison of emotional responses in monkeys with rhinal cortex or amygdala lesions. *Emotion, 2,* 147–161.

Meunier, M., Bachevalier, J., Murray, E. A., Málková, L. & Mishkin, M. (1999). Effects of aspiration versus neurotoxic lesions of the amygdala on emotional responses in monkeys. *European Journal of Neuroscience*, *11*, 4403–4418.

Milders, M., Crawford, J. R., Lamb, A. & Simpson, S. A. (2003). Differential deficits in expression recognition in gene-carriers and patients with Huntington's disease. *Neuropsychologia*, *41*, 1484–1492.

Mineka, S. & Cook, M. (1988). Social learning and the acquisition of snake fear in monkeys. In T. Zentall & B. Galef (Eds.), *Social Learning: Psychological and Biological Perspectives*, 51–73. Hillsdale, NJ: Erlbaum.

Murphy, F. C., Nimmo-Smith, I. & Lawrence, A. D. (2003). Functional neuroanatomy of emotions: a meta-analysis. *Cognitive, Affective & Behavioral Neuroscience*, *3*, 207–233.

Penfield, W. & Faulk, M. E. (1955). The insula: further observations of its function. *Brain*, *78*, 445–470.

Peper, M., Karcher, S., Wohlfarth, R., Reinshagen, G. & LeDoux, J. (2001). Aversive learning in patients with unilateral lesions of the amygdala and hippocampus. *Biological Psychology*, *58*, 1–23.

Phan, K. L., Wager, T., Taylor, S. F. & Liberzon, I. (2002). Functional neuroanatomy of emotion: a meta-analysis of emotion activation studies in PET and fMRI. *NeuroImage*, *16*, 331–348.

Phelps, E. A., LaBar, K. S., Anderson, A. K., O'Connor, K. J., Fulbright, R. K. & Spencer, D. D. (1998). Specifying the contributions of the human amygdala to emotional memory: a case study. *Neurocase*, *4*, 527–540.

Prather, M. D., Lavenex, P., Mauldin-Jourdain, M. L., et al. (2001). Increased social fear and decreased fear of objects in monkeys with neonatal amygdala lesions. *Neuroscience*, *106*, 653–658.

Pritchard, T. C., Macaluso, D. A. & Eslinger, P. J. (1999). Taste perception in patients with insular cortex lesions. *Behavioral Neuroscience*, *113*, 663–671.

Rapcsak, S. Z., Galper, S. R., Comer, J. F., et al. (2000). Fear recognition deficits after focal brain damage – a cautionary note. *Neurology*, *54*, 575–581.

Rauch, S. L., Dougherty, D. D., Shin, L. M., et al. (1998). Neural correlates of factor-analyzed OCD symptom dimensions: a PET study. *CNS Spectrums*, *3*, 37–43.

Richards, A., French, C. C., Calder, A. J., Webb, B., Fox, R. & Young, A. W. (2002). Anxiety-related bias in the classification of emotionally ambiguous facial expressions. *Emotion*, *2*, 273–287.

Rinn, W. E. (1984). The neuropsychology of facial expression: a review of the neurological and psychological mechanisms for producing facial expressions. *Psychological Bulletin*, *95*, 52–77.

Rolls, E. T. (1999). *The Brain and Emotion*. Oxford: Oxford University Press.

Rozin, P. & Fallon, A. E. (1987). A perspective on disgust. *Psychological Review*, *94*, 23–41.

Rozin, P., Haidt, J. & McCauley, C. R. (2000). Disgust. In M. Lewis & M. Haviland-Jones (Eds.), *Handbook of Emotions*, 2nd edn, 637–653. New York: Guilford.

Russell, J. A. (2003). Core affect and the psychological construction of emotion. *Psychological Review*, *110*, 145–172.

Sato, W., Kubota, Y., Okada, T., Murai, T., Yoshikawa, S. & Sengoku, A. (2002). Seeing happy emotion in fearful and angry faces: qualitative analysis of facial expression recognition in a bilateral amygdala-damaged patient. *Cortex, 38*, 727–742.

Scherer, K. (1993). Neuroscience projections to current debates in emotion psychology. *Cognition and Emotion, 7*, 1–41.

Scherer, K. & Peper, M. (2001). Psychological theories of emotion and neuropsychological research. In G. Gainotti (Ed.), *Handbook of Neuropsychology*, 2nd edn, vol. 5, 17–48. Amsterdam: Elsevier.

Schmolck, H. & Squire, L. R. (2001). Impaired perception of facial emotions following bilateral damage to the anterior temporal lobe. *Neuropsychology, 15*, 30–38.

Scott, S. K., Young, A. W., Calder, A. J., Hellawell, D. J., Aggleton, J. P. & Johnson, M. (1997). Impaired auditory recognition of fear and anger following bilateral amygdala lesions. *Nature, 385*, 254–257.

Shallice, T. (1988). *From Neuropsychology to Mental Structure*. Cambridge: Cambridge University Press.

Shallice, T. (2003). Functional imaging and neuropsychology findings: how can they be linked? *NeuroImage, 20*, S146–S154.

Snowden, C. T. & Boe, C. Y. (2003). Social communication about unpalatable foods in tamarins (*Saguinus oedipus*). *Journal of Comparative Psychology, 117*, 142–148.

Solomon, R. C. & Stone, L. D. (2002). On 'positive' and 'negative' emotions. *Journal for the Theory of Social Behaviour, 32*, 417–435.

Sprengelmeyer, R., Young, A. W., Calder, A. J., et al. (1996). Loss of disgust: perception of faces and emotions in Huntington's disease. *Brain, 119*, 1647–1665.

Sprengelmeyer, R., Young, A. W., Pundt, I., Sprengelmeyer, A., Calder, A. J., Berrios, G., Winkel, R., Vollmöeller, W., Kuhn, W., Sartory, G. & Przuntek, H. (1997a). Disgust implicated in obsessive-compulsive disorder. *Proceedings of the Royal Society of London (Series B: Biology), 264*, 1767–1773.

Sprengelmeyer, R., Young, A. W., Sprengelmeyer, A., et al. (1997b). Recognition of facial expressions: selective impairment of specific emotions in Huntington's disease. *Cognitive Neuropsychology, 14*, 839–879.

Sprengelmeyer, R., Young, A. W., Schroeder, U., et al. (1999). Knowing no fear. *Proceedings of the Royal Society of London (Series B: Biology), 266*, 2451–2456.

Stefanacci, L. & Amaral, D. G. (2000). Topographic organization of cortical inputs to the lateral nucleus of the macaque monkey amygdala: a retrograde tracing study. *Journal of Comparative Neurology, 421*, 52–79.

Sterelny, K. & Griffiths, P. E. (1999). *Sex and Death: an Introduction to Philosophy of Biology*. Chicago: Chicago University Press.

Talairach, J. & Tournoux, P. (1988). Co-planar stereotaxic atlas of the human brain. New York: Thieme.

Thieben, M. J., Duggins, A. J., Good, C. D., et al. (2002). The distribution of structural neuropathology in pre-clinical Huntington's disease. *Brain, 125*, 1815–1828.

Tomkins, S. S. (1963). *Affect, Imagery, Consciousness: vol. 2. The Negative Affects*. New York: Springer.

Tranel, D. & Damasio, A. R. (1993). The covert learning of affective valence does not require structures in hippocampal system or amygdala. *Journal of Cognitive Neuroscience*, *5*, 79–88.

Wang, K., Hoosain, R., Li, X.-s., Zhou, J.-n., Wang, C.-q. & Fu, X.-m. (2002). Impaired recognition of fear in a Chinese man with bilateral cingulate and unilateral amygdala damage. *Cognitive Neuropsychology*, *19*, 641–652.

Wang, K., Hoosain, R., Yang, R.-m., Meng, Y. & Wang, C.-q. (2003). Impairment of recognition of disgust in Chinese with Huntington's or Wilson's disease. *Neuropsychologia*, *41*, 527–537.

Watson, D., Clark, L. A. & Tellegen, A. (1988). Development and validation of brief measures of positive and negative affect: the PANAS scales. *Journal of Personality and Social Psychology*, *54*, 1063–1070.

Young, M. P., Hilgetag, C.-C. & Scannell, J. W. (2000). On imputing function to structure from the behavioural effects of brain lesions. *Philosophical Transactions of the Royal Society of London (Series B, Biology)*, *355*, 147–161.

8   The causal status of anxiety-linked attentional and interpretive bias

Colin MacLeod, Lynlee Campbell, Elizabeth Rutherford and Edward Wilson

Virtually all researchers now would agree that anxiety vulnerability is characterized by distinctive patterns of attentional and interpretive bias, and few would dispute the pivotal role that Andrew Mathews has played not only in establishing this important fact, but also in illuminating the cognitive mechanisms that underpin such effects. Mathews has been directly responsible for the lion's share of those key experimental studies that have served to define each new juncture in the evolution of our understanding about anxiety-linked processing biases. Moreover, when significant advances have been made by other researchers, then those investigators often have been ex-students and/or collaborators of Mathews, whose ideas and methodological approaches build upon foundations that Mathews himself helped to construct. Having ourselves enjoyed the privilege of an ongoing collaborative association with Andrew, we know from personal experience the tremendously constructive impact that his commitment to clarity of theoretical exposition, and to rigour in experimental design and analysis, exerts upon the work of others. Therefore, we are greatly honoured to be included in this volume, which celebrates the achievements and contributions of this distinguished and influential scholar.

Since Mathews' pioneering research in the early 1980s, the literature concerning anxiety-linked processing biases has grown exponentially (cf. MacLeod, 1999; Mathews & MacLeod, 1994). However, despite the scale and diversity of the contemporary research literature, there is one major issue concerning anxiety-linked patterns of attentional and interpretive bias that most researchers probably would agree to be of fundamental importance. Specifically, the theoretical and applied implications of the now common observation that individuals with heightened levels of anxiety vulnerability attend selectively to threatening information, and selectively impose threatening interpretations on ambiguity, depend critically upon the causal nature of this association. Despite their various differences, many influential theoretical accounts of this association assume that these processing biases play a causal role in mediating anxiety vulnerability (e.g. Beck & Clark, 1997; Williams, Watts, MacLeod & Mathews, 1997). Furthermore, this premise also underpins the claim that identification of these cognitive biases lends weight to the rationale behind cognitive therapies for anxiety disorders, which are designed to reduce anxiety vulnerability through the modification of biased cognition (cf. Chambless & Gillis, 1996).

Despite the profound importance of this hypothesis that attentional and interpretive biases play a causal role in the mediation of anxiety vulnerability, few studies have been designed to test it directly. Nevertheless, it is possible to draw indirect inferences concerning their causal status from certain types of experimental studies. In this chapter, we discuss evidence concerning the causal status of such biases that has accrued from four types of experimental approach. We conclude that there is converging support for the hypothesis that attentional and interpretive bias both do indeed causally contribute to anxiety vulnerability, with the strongest support coming from those studies that have adopted the most stringent experimental designs.

The attentional and interpretive characteristics of anxiety vulnerability

Consistent with the hypothesis that anxiety vulnerability is associated with the increased allocation of attentional resources to threatening information, individuals with heightened anxiety vulnerability demonstrate a reduced ability to ignore threatening distractor stimuli. Perhaps the most common experimental demonstrations of this phenomenon have employed the adaptation of the traditional Stroop procedure (Stroop, 1935) that has become known as the emotional Stroop task (MacLeod & Rutherford, 2003; Williams et al., 1997). Participants are shown emotional words in differing ink colours, and must rapidly name the colour while ignoring word content. The common finding that anxiety disordered patients are disproportionately slow to colour-name threatening words provides evidence that the content of such stimuli selectively captures their attention. Such threat interference effects have been observed in generalized anxiety disorder (GAD) (Mathews & MacLeod, 1985), specific phobia (Kindt & Brosschot, 1998), social phobia (Mattia, Heimberg & Hope, 1993), panic disorder (McNally et al., 1994) and post-traumatic stress disorder (PTSD) (Thrasher, Dalgleish & Yule, 1994). This appears to be a characteristic of anxiety vulnerability, rather than emotional pathology, as equivalent effects also are displayed by high trait anxious non-clinical participants (MacLeod & Rutherford, 1992; Mogg et al., 2000).

More direct measures of attentional allocation provide further support for the operation of an anxiety-linked attentional bias to threat. For example, MacLeod, Mathews and Tata (1986) tested GAD patients and non-anxious controls on an attentional probe procedure, within which participants discriminated small dot probes presented to screen locations where either threatening or non-threatening members of a briefly exposed word pair had just appeared. The anxiety patients demonstrated a disproportionate speeding to discriminate probes in the vicinity of the threat words, consistent with their selective allocation of attention towards threat. Variants of this experimental procedure have employed not only emotional words, but also emotional stimuli such as images or tactile sensations, and have confirmed the selective allocation of attention towards threatening information in GAD (Bradley, Mogg, White, Groom & de Bono, 1999), obsessive compulsive disorder (Tata, Leibowitz, Prunty, Cameron & Pickering, 1996), panic disorder and specific phobia (Ehlers & Breuer, 1995). Furthermore, the effect represents a characteristic of anxiety vulnerability rather than clinical dysfunction, having also been observed in high trait anxious non-clinical participants (Fox, 2002; MacLeod & Mathews, 1988).

Evidence that anxiety vulnerability is associated with the negative interpretation of ambiguity is equally compelling (cf. MacLeod & Mathews, 1991). Mathews, Richards and Eysenck (1989) gave GAD patients and non-clinical controls a spelling task that required them to write down auditorily presented words, among which were included threat/neutral homophones, such as groan/grown and die/dye. The anxiety patients demonstrated an elevated tendency to spell the more threatening words, suggesting the operation of a negative interpretive bias. This pattern of biased homophone spelling has been shown to be a function of trait anxiety level (Dalgleish, 1994; Eysenck, MacLeod & Mathews, 1987; Richards, Reynolds & French, 1993).

Priming methodologies lend further weight to the conclusion that anxiety vulnerability is associated with the biased interpretation of anxiety. Using a simple lexical priming procedure, Richards and French (1992) examined the degree to which homograph primes, permitting threatening or non-threatening interpretation (such as stroke or sentence), served to facilitate lexical decisions on targets associated with each of these possible meanings. At prime-target onset asynchronies of 750 ms and above, high trait anxious participants demonstrated disproportionately great facilitation on target words related to the threat meanings of such primes, suggesting that they had selectively imposed the more threatening interpretations on these homographs. Extensions of this priming approach have employed fuller ambiguous text as priming materials, and have continued to find that the processing of target information related to threatening prime meanings is disproportionately facilitated among participants who report heightened susceptibility to anxiety (Hirsch & Mathews, 1997; MacLeod & Cohen, 1993). Such asymmetries in observed patterns of priming are fully consistent with the proposed associated between negative interpretive bias and anxiety vulnerability.

While the evidence reviewed in this section permits the conclusion that anxiety vulnerability is associated with attentional and interpretive bias, it does not serve to illuminate the causal nature of this association. The findings are consistent with the proposal that these processing biases might represent the causal substrate of trait anxiety, operating to influence cognitive representation in ways that directly inflate anxiety responses to stressful situations. However, they also permit the possibility that the reverse causal relationship instead may apply, with vulnerable individuals who frequently experience intense episodes of anxiety coming to develop biased patterns of information processing as a direct consequence of these emotional experiences. Another possibility is that the association between the two factors is not a causal one at all, but rather, cognitive bias and anxiety vulnerability may represent independent consequences of other environmental or temperamental factors. In each of the sections that follow, we review literature that, by advancing our knowledge of the relationship between anxiety vulnerability and cognitive bias, has the potential to shed light upon the causal nature of their association.

Inferring causality from clinical recovery studies

If the attentional and interpretive biases known to characterize anxiety disordered patients causally produce the dysfunctional emotional symptomatology associated with these disorders, then it follows that the successful treatment of clinical anxiety must involve the attenuation of these biases. Should it instead be observed that successfully treated anxiety patients continue to display the same patterns of attentional and interpretive bias as is shown by currently anxious patients, then clearly these biases cannot directly cause the clinical symptomatology. In fact, psychological interventions that effectively alleviate anxiety symptoms do indeed appear to successfully attenuate the biased patterns of processing selectivity normally displayed by anxiety disordered patients.

Using a visual probe task to assess selective orientation to threatening words, Mogg, Mathews and Eysenck (1992) contrasted the patterns of attentional bias observed in current GAD patients and non-clinical controls against those shown by a group of participants whose GAD had been successfully treated by cognitive behaviour therapy. These recovered

GAD patients did not differ from control participants in terms of their attentional response to the emotional stimuli, indicating that effective treatment involved the elimination of their attentional bias. Mathews, Mogg, Kentish and Eysenck (1995) adopted the emotional Stroop task to compare the performance of GAD patients and non-clinical controls, before and after a successful programme of cognitive behaviour therapy. The exaggerated threat interference effect shown prior to treatment by the patients was no longer evident post-treatment. In a subsequent intervention study, Mogg, Bradley, Millar and White (1995) replicated these findings within a different sample of GAD patients. Furthermore, across a twenty-month follow-up period, they observed that the degree to which the treated patients' anxiety symptoms subsequently re-emerged was a direct function of the extent to which their attentional bias to threat re-appeared. Studies of specific phobics also have confirmed that the attentional bias towards feared stimuli commonly shown by such patients is eliminated by psychological treatments that attenuate their emotional symptomatology (e.g. Mogg et al., 1995; van den Hout, Tenney, Huygens & de Jong, 1997). Parallel findings have been obtained for patients suffering from obsessive compulsive disorder (Foa & McNally, 1986) and for social phobics (Lundh & Öst, 2001). Therefore, consistent with the hypothesis that attentional bias to threat causally underpins the dysfunctional emotional symptomology observed in the anxiety disorders, it appears that effective treatment of these clinical conditions involves the remediation of this attentional bias.

There is equally good evidence that treatment efficacy is also associated with removal of the interpretive bias normally displayed by anxiety disordered patients. Mathews et al. (1989) contrasted the patterns of interpretive bias shown on the homophone spelling task by non-clinical controls, current GAD patients and recovered GAD patients. The current patients, relative to the controls, displayed an elevated tendency to spell the homophones in their more threatening manner, but this was not demonstrated by the recovered patients. Similarly, when Eysenck, Mogg, May and Richards (1991) used a false recognition memory measure of interpretive bias for this same purpose, they observed that current GAD patients' inflated false recognition rates for threat disambiguations were no longer evident in recovered patients, who did not differ from non-clinical control participants in their patterns of recognition memory performance. Thus, remediation of clinical symptomatology in these anxiety patients was found to accompany the elimination of interpretive bias.

The hypothesis that biases in attention and interpretation directly cause the emotional dysfunction observed in anxiety disorders could have been challenged by the potential observation that such biases might continue to operate in treated patients who display no evidence of pathological anxiety. The above review indicates that this is not the case, and so the evidence from recovery studies stands consistent with this causal account. Nevertheless, it must be noted that the observed pattern of findings can be accommodated without attributing causal status to these biases. It remains possible that biases in attention and interpretation are merely symptoms of anxiety pathology, which enjoy no special causal status but simply decline together with other facets of symptomatology when treatment is effective. Therefore, while the results of recovery studies do not serve to challenge the potential causal status of attentional and interpretive bias, neither do they permit the firm conclusion that such biases necessarily do play a causal role in the mediation of anxiety vulnerability.

Inferring causality from developmental studies

If anxiety vulnerability represents a direct consequence of attentional and interpretive bias, then these cognitive anomalies should be evident at the earliest points when anxiety vulnerability can be detected. Thus, the association between anxiety vulnerability and selective processing should remain stable even in young children. In contrast, if biased attention and interpretation develop only as a consequence of repeated anxiety episodes, then such effects may not be observed in anxious children.

Developmental studies have served to reveal that attentional bias is indeed a characteristic of anxiety vulnerability even in young children (cf. Gotlib & MacLeod, 1997). Martin, Horder and Jones (1992) first confirmed this in an emotional Stroop study of children with spider phobia aged between six and twelve years. Not only did these investigators demonstrate that, compared to non-anxious control participants, even the youngest children with spider phobia displayed inflated colour-naming latencies on spider-related words, but they also observed that the magnitude of this effect was invariant across the age range studied. In a subsequent replication, Martin and Jones (1995) employed a pictorial version of the emotional Stroop task to study attentional processing in children aged between four and nine years with spider phobia. Once again, increased threat interference effects were evidenced by a selective slowing to name the coloured hues of spider images even in the youngest children with the phobia, and once more this effect was found to remain stable across age.

Evidence of attentional bias in anxious children is not restricted to studies that have examined the attention characteristics of childhood phobias. Moradi, Taghavi, Neshat-Doost, Yule and Dalgleish (1999) employed the emotional Stroop task to compare the patterns of colour-naming interference shown on trauma-related and neutral words by children aged nine to seventeen years, who were either suffering from PTSD or had no such disorder. Regardless of age, the PTSD children evidenced disproportionately long colour-naming latencies on the threat stimuli. In a later study, these same investigators were able to demonstrate that this childhood attentional bias represents a characteristic of anxiety vulnerability, rather than an exclusive symptom of clinical pathology. Moradi, Neshat-Doost, Taghavi, Yule and Dalgleish (1999) compared the emotional Stroop performance of non-disordered children aged between nine and seventeen years, some of whom had a family history of anxiety dysfunction. Across the age range, children from the more vulnerable families displayed significantly elevated colour-naming latencies on threat-relevant words compared to neutral words, which was not the case for children whose family history indicated no heightened level of anxiety susceptibility.

Attentional probe studies have lent further support to the conclusion that attentional bias to threat is evident even in anxious children. Using this approach to compare clinically anxious and non-anxious children, Vasey, Daleiden, Williams and Brown (1995) found that even their youngest anxiety patients, aged nine years, demonstrated a relative speeding to discriminate probes in the vicinity of threatening words. Taghavi, Neshat-Doost, Moradi, Yule and Dalgleish (1999) reported this same finding when examining clinically anxious children as young as eight years of age. Consistent with emotional Stroop findings, probe studies indicate that this tendency to orient visual attention towards threat stimuli is a function of anxiety vulnerability, rather than clinical pathology. Vasey, El-Hag and Daleiden (1996) have observed similar speeding to probes in the vicinity of threat stimuli among high test anxious children, compared to low test anxious children, while Bijttebier (1998) has obtained the same effects in high trait anxious compared to low trait anxious children. Indeed, taking a regression approach, Schippell, Vasey, Cravens-Brown and Bretveld (2003) were able to demonstrate that this biased pattern of probe discrimination latencies is a direct function of children's trait anxiety scores.

Interpretive bias also is a reliable characteristic of anxiety vulnerability even among young children (cf. Vasey & MacLeod, 2001). Taghavi, Moradi, Neshat-Doost, Yule and Dalgleish (2000) presented children aged eight to seventeen years with ambiguous homographs similar to those employed by Richards and French (1992), and required them to construct a sentence using each word. Compared to non-anxious controls, even the youngest clinically anxious participants demonstrated an elevated tendency to construct sentences using the threatening rather than the non-threatening meanings of the homographs. Similar effects have been observed by Hadwin, Frost, French and Richards (1997) in non-clinical children with high levels of trait anxiety. These investigators presented seven- to nine-year-old children aurally with homophones, permitting threat and non-threat interpretations, and directed them to point to pictures that conveyed the meaning of each word. High trait anxious children displayed a heightened tendency to select pictures consistent with the more threatening meaning of the homophones, suggesting that they resolved the ambiguity in a disproportionately threatening manner.

Quite clearly then, the hypothesis that biases in attention and interpretation causally mediate anxiety vulnerability resists disconfirmation from developmental studies. These biases remain strongly associated with both clinical anxiety and trait anxiety even among children, and indeed the association between selective processing and anxiety vulnerability has been found to remain stable across age. Nevertheless, while this observation is consistent with the possibility that attentional and interpretive biases might enjoy the proposed causal status, it does not require the conclusion that they must play this causal role. Instead, it is possible that these patterns of selective processing simply may develop very rapidly in response to the onset of anxiety problems. Thus, the finding that attentional and interpretive biases exist concurrently with anxiety vulnerability in young children does not permit the inference that these biases necessarily precede and precipitate the development of such anxiety.

Inferring causality from emotional prediction studies

In order to test more directly the premise that biases in attention and interpretation precede and precipitate inflated anxiety responses to stress, a small number of studies have been designed to appraise the capacity of initial processing bias measures to predict later emotional reactions to subsequent stressful events. If heightened anxiety reactions to stress do represent the consequence of biased attention and interpretation, then early measures of such processing biases should serve powerfully to predict these future patterns of emotional reactivity.

In an early test of this prediction, MacLeod and Hagan (1992) employed a version of the emotional Stroop task to assess attentional bias in a sample of women undergoing a colposcopy procedure to screen for cervical pathology. This task variant included a backward masking procedure (cf. Turvey, 1973) which, when combined with brief stimulus exposure duration, served to render word content unreportable. Consistent with the contention that anxiety-linked attentional bias operates automatically, in the sense that it is not mediated by conscious awareness of the stimuli, a number of researchers have observed that anxious participants continue to display inflated colour naming latencies for threat words under such exposure conditions (Harvey, Bryant & Rapee, 1996; MacLeod & Rutherford, 1992). MacLeod and Hagan likewise found that, at the time of initial assessment, the magnitude of the threat interference effect under this exposure condition was significantly correlated with trait anxiety scores. The women who later received a diagnosis of cervical pathology were followed up, and the intensities of their negative emotional reactions to this subsequent life event were recorded. The range of questionnaire measures of emotional vulnerability taken during the initial assessment session, including trait anxiety scores, failed to predict individual differences in emotional reactions to the later stressful event. However, the index of threat interference observed on the emotional Stroop task, under the backward masked exposure condition, proved to be a significant predictor of later emotional reactivity, accounting for no less than 25 per cent of the variance in negative emotional reactions to the subsequent diagnosis of cervical pathology. A conceptually similar study reported by MacLeod, Rutherford and Ng (reported in MacLeod, 1995) assessed threat interference effects on the emotional Stroop task, and also took conventional questionnaire measures of emotional vulnerability, in a population of Singaporean high school graduates who, some weeks later, were to travel overseas to commence tertiary studies in Australia. The degree to which participants' state anxiety levels subsequently became elevated, on the day of their arrival in Australia, was better predicted by the initial threat interference measure of attentional bias than by any questionnaire measure of emotional vulnerability.

More recently, Pury (2002) has extended this approach to determine whether early measures of interpretive bias also can predict later emotional reactivity to stressful events. Undergraduate students were required to complete a version of the homophone spelling task introduced by Eysenck et al. (1987), to yield a measure of interpretive bias, some weeks prior to an important examination. Subsequently, Pury assessed the degree to which the experience of this exam served to elicit negative affect in students, using the present moment version of the Positive and Negative Affect Scale (PANAS; Watson, Clark & Tellegen, 1988). Consistent with the researcher's expectation, the proportion of threat spellings provided by participants within the initial homophone task proved to be a powerful predictor of individual differences in the intensity of negative emotional reactions to the subsequent stressful event.

Clearly, the observation that early measures of attentional and interpretive bias do indeed predict later emotional reactivity to subsequent stressful events carries important applied implications, in addition to supporting the potential causal role of these biases in the mediation of anxiety vulnerability. However, while this causal account would have been discredited by the failure to confirm such predictive capacity, this confirmation is insufficient to permit acceptance of the hypothesis that biased selective processing causally underpins susceptibility to anxiety. It remains possible that the observed patterns of cognitive bias, and of emotional reactivity to the stressful events, may both be caused independently by some third individual difference factor that remains stable over time, such as neuroticism, and themselves share no functional relationship.

Inferring causality from bias manipulation studies

Despite the fact that all the findings reviewed above are fully consistent with the proposal that attentional and interpretive bias causally contribute to anxiety vulnerability, none of these observations can serve conclusively to confirm this causal relationship. The basic problem is that, in every case, these findings continue to represent naturally occurring associations between measures of cognitive bias and measures of anxiety vulnerability. If such associations had been found to disappear under certain circumstances, such as following treatment, or in children, or when the measures are rendered temporally disparate, then the causal hypothesis certainly would have been compromised. However, the demonstration that this association remains robust across these various situations cannot resolve its causal nature. Only one methodological approach can definitively establish whether a given variable does indeed causally influence another. Specifically, it is necessary to manipulate the first variable directly, in order to determine whether this also modifies the second. Thus, the most powerful test of the hypothesis that attentional and interpretive bias causally mediate anxiety vulnerability is provided by studies designed to manipulate directly each class of processing bias, in order to test the prediction that this will serve to modify anxiety vulnerability. Such studies have offered strong support for this prediction (cf. Mathews & MacLeod, 2002).

We have created attentional training procedures by introducing contingencies into experimental tasks previously employed only to assess attentional bias, and have examined their impact upon emotional vulnerability. For example, MacLeod, Rutherford, Campbell, Ebsworthy and Holker (2002) report two studies in which a training version of the attentional probe task was employed to manipulate attention bias, before participants' emotional reactivity to a laboratory stressor was assessed. In each of these experiments, students with mid-range levels of trait anxiety were exposed to nearly six hundred attentional probe trials, configured to yield either of two attentional training conditions. In one condition, designed to induce an attentional bias towards threat, the probe stimuli consistently were presented in the vicinity of the threat member of each word pair. The other condition was designed to induce attentional avoidance of threat, by consistently presenting these probes in the vicinity of the neutral word within each pair. Following these training procedures, a block of assessment trials served to confirm that the two participant groups did indeed now exhibit the intended differential patterns of attentional bias, even in response to emotional stimulus words that had not been presented previously in the experimental session. Of greatest importance, however, was the observation that the groups also now differed in their emotional reactivity to a subsequent laboratory stress task, in which they attempted to solve difficult anagrams under timed conditions. Immediately after attentional training, but before encountering this anagram stressor, the two groups reported equivalent affective states, indicating that the attentional training procedure did not directly alter mood per se. However, the magnitude of the negative emotional response to this stressor was found to be attenuated in the group that had been trained to develop attentional avoidance of threat, compared to the group trained to attend toward threat. A second study served not only to replicate this effect, but also to demonstrate that the degree to which the training procedure served to modify the intensity of anxiety responses to the laboratory stressor was a direct function of the degree to which it successfully manipulated attentional bias. Thus, the direct manipulation of attentional bias does indeed serve to modify emotional reactivity, precisely as predicted by the hypothesis that this bias plays a causal role in the mediation of anxiety vulnerability.

We have gone on to deliver extended attentional training procedures of this type to high trait anxious participants, in order to test the prediction that the manipulation of attentional bias will modify their levels of trait anxiety within real world environments. Campbell, Rutherford and MacLeod (2002) have reported two such studies, within which we exposed high trait anxious students to between 6,000 and 7,000 dot-probe attentional training trials, administered within three laboratory training sessions per week across a three-week period. For participants in the experimental condition, the probes consistently appeared in the vicinity of the neutral members of every word pair, with the goal of inducing attentional avoidance of threat. For participants in the control condition, no attentional training contingency was introduced, and so probes appeared equally often within the vicinity of the threat and non-threat words. Parallel findings were obtained across the two experiments, which were identical except for a slight difference in the number of training trials employed. Participants who completed the control condition evidenced no attenuation of their attention bias towards threat, on a standard assessment version of the dot-probe task, by the end of the three-week period, and their trait anxiety scores did not change across this time. In contrast, participants in the experimental condition did indeed demonstrate reduced attentional orientation to threat across the three weeks of attentional training, on a standard assessment version of the dot-probe task, and also evidenced a significant reduction of trait anxiety scores across this same period. Clearly, these findings invite the conclusion that attentional bias does make a causal contribution to trait anxiety.

In order to extend this line of research to clinical populations, we have developed and validated an on-line version of the dot-probe attentional training task (MacLeod, Rutherford, Campbell & Soong, submitted), which can be accessed and implemented in participants' own homes. Using this resource, our student Annie Malcolm now has examined the clinical impact of directly manipulating attentional bias in social phobics (Malcolm, 2003). Participants meeting diagnostic criteria for social phobia completed 384 attentional probe trials each day for two weeks. Once again, the experimental group received the contingency designed to induce attentional avoidance of threat, while the control group received no training contingency. Social anxiety was assessed using the Social Phobia Scale and the Social Interaction Anxiety Scale developed by Mattick and Clarke (1998). Participants in the control condition reported no attenuation of their social anxiety symptoms across this two-week period. In contrast, those social phobics who received the attentional training condition did indeed demonstrate a significant attenuation of their social anxiety symptoms. Therefore, it appears that attentional bias also plays a causal role in the mediation of the clinical symptomatology associated with anxiety pathology.

Studies designed to investigate the emotional impact of directly manipulating interpretive bias have obtained convincing evidence that this pattern of selective processing also contributes causally to anxiety vulnerability. Mathews and his colleagues have successfully developed and validated a number of experimental procedures designed to modify interpretive bias (Grey & Mathews, 2000; Mathews & Mackintosh, 2000). These procedures, which are reviewed more fully by Yiend and Mackintosh within this present volume, involve extended exposure to trials that each initially present ambiguous stimuli that participants then employ to assist in the performance of some subsequent task. A training contingency is built into the session by ensuring that for some participants it consistently is the more threatening interpretations of the initial ambiguity that facilitate such performance, while for other participants it consistently is the less threatening interpretations that facilitate performance. Subsequent assessment trials confirm that the former training condition leads to the acquisition of a tendency to interpret ambiguity selectively in a threatening manner, while the latter condition serves to induce the reverse pattern of interpretive bias.

For example, Grey and Mathews (2000) presented a threat/non-threat homograph at the start of each trial, then displayed a word fragment that participants were required to complete as quickly as possible. Although it was advised that solutions to the fragments always were related to the meanings of the preceding words, in one training condition these solutions actually were all associated with the threatening meanings of the homographs, while in the other training condition they all were associated with the non-threat meanings of these ambiguous words. Following extended exposure to such trials, subsequent assessment trials revealed that participants assigned to the former training condition had acquired a tendency to impose threat meanings upon ambiguity, while those assigned to the latter training condition acquired the reverse pattern of interpretive bias. In another variant of this training procedure, Grey and Mathews required participants to identify whether or not words shown after each ambiguous homograph were related to this initial term. Again, one training contingency ensured that, across all trials, only the threat meanings of homographs ever were pertinent, while the reverse was true for the other training contingency. Once more, participants exposed to the former training condition came to develop an interpretive bias favouring threat resolutions of ambiguity, whereas participants exposed to the latter training condition came to develop a bias favouring non-threatening interpretations of ambiguity.

In a series of studies that further extended this approach to interpretive training, Mathews and Mackintosh (2000) reported that changes to mood state observed during exposure to certain training procedures were consistent with the possibility that biased interpretation might causally influence emotional susceptibility. However, these studies did not expose participants to a stress task following the induction of differential interpretive bias, in order to test directly the prediction that anxiety reactivity to stress would be systematically modified by the manipulation of interpretive bias. Such an approach since has been taken by MacLeod and Mathews' co-supervised Ph.D. student Ed Wilson, and the results strongly support the causal hypothesis (Wilson, MacLeod & Mathews, submitted). Students with mid-range levels of trait anxiety were exposed to either a word fragment completion variant, or a relatedness judgment variant, of the interpretive training procedures introduced by Grey and

Mathews (2000). One group received a training contingency designed to induce a bias favouring threat interpretations of ambiguity, while the other received a contingency designed to induce a bias favouring non-threat interpretations. The efficacy of these training procedures was confirmed by subsequent assessment trials, within which the target patterns of induced interpretive bias were found to be evident on new ambiguous materials. It is of interest to note that the impact of the word fragment training task and the relatedness judgment training task, on interpretive bias, was equivalent regardless of whether this interpretive bias was measured using word fragment assessment trials or relatedness judgment assessment trials. This indicates that the training did indeed modify interpretation, rather than simply shaping performance on a given task. Following the training of differential interpretive bias, participants then were subjected to a laboratory stressor, involving exposure to anxiety-inducing video clips. It was confirmed that the degree to which this subsequent stressor served to elevate anxious mood differed for participants who had been trained to acquire each pattern of interpretive bias. Relative to those who had received the training condition designed to induce a bias favouring threatening interpretations of ambiguity, those exposed to the training condition designed to reduce such a pattern of threat-congruent interpretive bias demonstrated an attenuated tendency to elevated anxiety in response to the video stressor. Thus, the manipulation of interpretive bias does indeed modify emotional reactivity, in precisely the manner predicted by the hypothesis that this pattern of selective processing makes a causal contribution to anxiety vulnerability.

Conclusion and future directions

Although the association between anxiety vulnerability and both attentional and interpretive bias has been established for some considerable time, the theoretical importance of this association, and its potential clinical implications, depend critically upon the causal nature of the relationship. In this short chapter, we have reviewed evidence to support the contention that attentional bias to threat, and interpretive bias favouring threatening resolutions of ambiguity, contribute causally to the mediation of anxiety vulnerability. Such a causal association would be marked by a characteristic signature within various types of experimental data. While the pattern of findings observed in treatment research, developmental research and emotional prediction research all are consistent with this causal signature, we believe the strongest evidence comes from studies that have examined the emotional impact of directly manipulating each pattern of selective processing. The observation that experimental procedures shown to successfully manipulate attentional and interpretive bias also serve to modify anxiety vulnerability not only conclusively establishes the causal status of these processing biases in the mediation of anxiety vulnerability, but also brings us to an exciting new threshold. Specifically, we now are entering into an extended programme of research involving the development and evaluation of novel clinical intervention procedures, designed to attenuate symptomatology in anxiety disordered patients through the therapeutic application of cognitive-experimental procedures capable of directly modifying selective attention and interpretation. There can be no doubt that this research venture will profit handsomely from the ongoing collaborative involvement of our colleague Andrew Mathews. We welcome this opportunity to pay tribute to the remarkable contributions that Andrew already has made to our collective understanding of the cognitive factors that underpin anxiety vulnerability. We also look forward to the key role he is certain to play within the exciting future developments that promise to build so directly upon his rich legacy to date.

REFERENCES

Beck, A. T. & Clark, D. A. (1997). An information processing model of anxiety: automatic and strategic processes. *Behaviour Research and Therapy*, *35*, 49–58.

Bijttebier, P. (1998). Monitoring and Blunting Coping Styles in Children. Unpublished doctoral thesis. Catholic University of Leuven.

Bradley, B. P., Mogg, K., White, J., Groom, C. & de Bono, J. (1999). Attentional bias for emotional faces in generalized anxiety disorder. *British Journal of Clinical Psychology*, *38*, 267–278.

Campbell, L., Rutherford, E. M. & MacLeod, C. (2002). Practice makes perfect: the reduction of trait anxiety through the extended retraining of attentional response to threat. Paper presented at the 36th AABT annual convention, Reno, NV.

Chambless, D. L. & Gillis, M. M. (1996). Cognitive therapy of anxiety disorders. In K. S. Dobson & K. D. Craig (Eds.), *Advances in Cognitive-Behavioral Therapy*, 116–144. New York: Banff.

Dalgleish, T. (1994). The relationship between anxiety and memory biases for material that has been selectively processed in a prior task. *Behaviour Research and Therapy*, *32*, 227–231.

Ehlers, A. & Breuer, P. (1995). Selective attention to physical threat in subjects with panic attacks and specific phobias. *Journal of Anxiety Disorders*, *9*, 11–31.

Eysenck, M. W., MacLeod, C. & Mathews, A. (1987). Cognitive functioning in anxiety. *Psychological Research*, *49*, 189–195.

Eysenck, M. W., Mogg, K., May, J. & Richards, A. (1991). Bias in interpretation of ambiguous sentences related to threat in anxiety. *Journal of Abnormal Psychology*, *100*, 144–150.

Foa, E. B. & McNally, R. J. (1986). Sensitivity to feared stimuli in obsessive-compulsives: a dichotic listening analysis. *Cognitive Therapy and Research*, *10*, 477–485.

Fox, E. (2002). Processing emotional facial expressions. *Cognitive, Affective and Behavioral Neuroscience*, *2*, 52–63.

Gotlib, I. H. & MacLeod, C. (1997). Information processing in anxiety and depression: a cognitive-developmental perspective. In J. A. Burack & J. T. Enns (Eds.), *Attention, Development, and Psychopathology*, *14*, 350–378.

Grey, S. & Mathews, A. (2000). Effects of training on interpretation of emotional ambiguity. *Quarterly Journal of Experimental Psychology*, *53A*, 1143–1162.

Hadwin, J., Frost, S., French, C. C. & Richards, A. (1997). Cognitive processing and trait anxiety in typically developing children: evidence for an interpretation bias. *Journal of Abnormal Psychology*, *106*, 486–490.

Harvey, A. G., Bryant, R. A. & Rapee, R. M. (1996). Preconscious processing of threat in posttraumatic stress disorder. *Cognitive Therapy and Research*, *20*, 613–623.

Hirsch, C. & Mathews, A. (1997). Interpretive inferences when reading about emotional events. *Behaviour Research and Therapy*, *35*, 1123–1132.

Kindt, M. & Brosschot, J. F. (1998). Stability of cognitive bias for threat cues in phobia. *Journal of Psychopathology and Behavioral Assessment*, *20*, 351–367.

Lundh, L.-G. & Öst, L.-G. (2001). Attentional bias, self-consciousness and perfectionism in social phobia before and after cognitive-behaviour therapy. *Scandinavian Journal of Behaviour Therapy*, *30*, 4–16.

MacLeod, C. (1999). Anxiety and anxiety disorders. In M. Powers & T. Dalgleish (Eds.), *Handbook of Emotion and Cognition*. Chichester: Wiley.

MacLeod, C. (1995). Anxiety and cognitive processes. In I. G. Sarason, B. P. Sarason & G. R. Pierce (Eds.), *Cognitive Interference: Theories, Methods and Findings*. Hillsdale, NJ: Erlbaum.

MacLeod, C. & Cohen, I. L. (1993). Anxiety and the interpretation of ambiguity: a text comprehension study. *Journal of Abnormal Psychology*, *102*, 238–247.

MacLeod, C. & Hagan, R. (1992). Individual differences in the selective processing of threatening information, and emotional responses to a stressful life event. *Behaviour Research and Therapy*, *30*, 151–161.

MacLeod, C. & Mathews, A. (1988). Anxiety and the allocation of attention to threat. *Quarterly Journal of Experimental Psychology*, *40A*, 653–670.

MacLeod, C. & Mathews, A. (1991). Cognitive-experimental approaches to the emotional disorders. In P. R. Martin (Ed.), *Handbook of Behaviour Therapy and Psychological Science*. Oxford: Pergamon.

MacLeod, C., Mathews, A. & Tata, P. (1986). Attentional bias in emotional disorders. *Journal of Abnormal Psychology*, *95*, 15–20.

MacLeod, C. & Rutherford, E. (2003). Information processing approaches to generalized anxiety disorder: assessing the selective functioning of attention, interpretation and memory in GAD patients. In R. Heimberg, C. L. Turk & D. S. Mennin (Eds.), *Generalized Anxiety Disorder: Advances in Research and Practice*. New York: Guilford.

MacLeod, C. & Rutherford, E. M. (1992). Anxiety and the selective processing of emotional information. *Behaviour Research and Therapy*, *30*, 479–491.

MacLeod, C., Rutherford, E. M., Campbell, L., Ebsworthy, G. & Holker, L. (2002). Selective attention and emotional vulnerability: assessing the causal basis of their association through the experimental manipulation of attentional bias. *Journal of Abnormal Psychology*, *111*, 107–123.

MacLeod, C., Rutherford, E., Campbell, L. & Soong, L. (submitted). Internet-delivered assessment and manipulation of anxiety-linked attentional bias.

Malcolm, A. (2003). Effect of attentional retraining on social phobia symptoms. Unpublished Master's Thesis, The University of Western Australia, Perth, Western Australia.

Martin, M., Horder, P. & Jones, G. V. (1992). Integral bias in naming of phobia-related words. *Cognition and Emotion*, *6*, 479–486.

Martin, M. & Jones, G. V. (1995). Integral bias in the cognitive processing of emotionally-linked pictures. *British Journal of Psychology*, *86*, 419–435.

Mathews, A. & Mackintosh, B. (2000). Induced emotional interpretation bias and anxiety. *Journal of Abnormal Psychology*, *109*, 602–625.

Mathews, A. & MacLeod, C. (1985). Selective processing of threat cues in anxiety states. *Behaviour Research and Therapy*, *23*, 563–569.

Mathews, A. & MacLeod, C. (1994). Cognitive approaches to emotion. *Annual Review of Psychology*, *45*, 25–50.

Mathews, A. & MacLeod, C. (2002). Induced emotional biases have causal effects on anxiety. *Cognition and Emotion*, *16*, 310–315.

Mathews, A., Mogg, K., Kentish, J. & Eysenck, M. (1995). Effect of psychological treatment on cognitive bias in generalized anxiety disorder. *Behaviour Research and Therapy*, *33*, 293–303.

Mathews, A., Richards, A. & Eysenck, M. (1989). Interpretation of homophones related to threat in anxiety states. *Journal of Abnormal Psychology*, *98*, 31–34.

Mattia, J. I., Heimberg, R. G. & Hope, D. A. (1993). The revised Stroop color-naming task in social phobics. *Behaviour Research and Therapy*, *31*, 305–313.

Mattick, R. P. & Clarke, J. C. (1998). Development and validation of measures of social phobia scrutiny fear and social interaction anxiety. *Behaviour Research and Therapy*, *36*, 455–470.

McNally, R. J., Amir, N., Louro, C. E., Lukach, B. M., Riemann, B. C. & Calamari, J. E. (1994). Cognitive processing of idiographic emotional information in panic disorder. *Behaviour Research and Therapy*, *32*, 119–122.

Mogg, K., Bradley, B. P., Dixon, C., Fisher, S., Twelftree, H. & McWilliams, A. (2000). Trait anxiety, defensiveness and selective processing of threat. *Personality and Individual Differences*, *28*, 1063–1077.

Mogg, K., Bradley, B. P., Millar, N. & White, J. (1995). A follow-up study of cognitive bias in generalized anxiety disorder. *Behaviour Research and Therapy*, *33*, 927–935.

Mogg, K., Mathews, A. & Eysenck, M. (1992). Attentional bias to threat in clinical anxiety states. *Cognition and Emotion*, *6*, 149–159.

Moradi, A. R., Neshat-Doost, H. T., Taghavi, R., Yule, W. & Dalgleish, T. (1999). Performance of children of adults with PTSD on the Stroop color-naming task. *Journal of Traumatic Stress*, *12*, 663–671.

Moradi, A. R., Taghavi, M. R., Neshat-Doost, H. T., Yule, W. & Dalgleish, T. (1999). Performance of children and adolescents with PTSD on the Stroop colour-naming task. *Psychological Medicine*, *29*, 415–419

Pury, C. L. S. (2002). Information-processing predictors of emotional response to stress. *Cognition and Emotion*, *16*, 667–683.

Richards, A. & French, C. C. (1992). An anxiety-related bias in semantic activation when processing threat/neutral homographs. *The Quarterly Journal of Experimental Psychology*, *45A*, 503–525.

Richards, A., Reynolds, A. & French, C. C. (1993). Anxiety and the spelling and use in sentences of threat/neutral homophones. *Current Psychology: Research and Reviews*, *12*, 18–25.

Schippell, P. L., Vasey, M. W., Cravens-Brown, L. M. & Bretveld, R. A. (2003). Suppressed attention to rejection, ridicule, and failure cues. *Journal of Clinical Child and Adolescent Psychology*, *32*, 40–55.

Stroop, J. R. (1935). Studies of interference in serial verbal reactions. *Journal of Experimental Psychology*, *18*, 643–662.

Taghavi, M. R., Moradi, A. R., Neshat-Doost, H. T., Yule, W. & Dalgleish, T. (2000). Interpretation of ambiguous emotional information in clinically anxious children and adolescents. *Cognition and Emotion*, *14*, 809–822.

Taghavi, M. R., Neshat-Doost, H. T., Moradi, A. R., Yule, W. & Dalgleish, T. (1999). Biases in visual attention in children and adolescents with clinical anxiety and mixed anxiety-depression. *Journal of Abnormal Child Psychology*, *27*, 215–223.

Tata, P. R., Leibowitz, J. A., Prunty, M. J., Cameron, M. & Pickering, A. D. (1996). Attentional bias in Obsessional Compulsive Disorder. *Behaviour Research and Therapy*, *34*, 53–60.

Thrasher, S. M., Dalgleish, T. & Yule, W. (1994). Information processing in post-traumatic stress disorder. *Behaviour Research and Therapy*, *32*, 247–254.

Turvey, M. T. (1973). On peripheral and central processes in vision. *Psychological Review*, *80*, 1–52.

Van den Hout, M., Tenney, N., Huygens, K. & de Jong, P. (1997). Preconscious processing bias in specific phobia. *Behaviour Research and Therapy*, *35*, 29–34.

Vasey, M. W., Daleiden, E. L., Williams, L. L. & Brown, L. M. (1995). Biased attention in childhood anxiety disorders. *Journal of Abnormal Child Psychology*, *23*, 267–279.

Vasey, M. W., El-Hag, N. & Daleiden, E. L. (1996). Anxiety and the processing of emotionally-threatening stimuli among high- and low-test-anxious children. *Child Development*, *67*, 1173–1185.

Vasey, M. W. & MacLeod, C. (2001). Information-processing factors in childhood anxiety. In M. W. Vasey & M. R. Dadds (Eds.), *The Developmental Psychopathology of Anxiety*, 253–277. London: Oxford University Press.

Watson, D., Clark, L. A. & Tellegen, A. (1988). Development and validation of brief measures of positive and negative affect: the PANAS scale. *Journal of Personality and Social Psychology*, *54*, 1063–1070.

Williams, J. M. G., Watts, F. N., MacLeod, C. & Mathews, A. (1997). *Cognitive Psychology and Emotional Disorders*. Chichester: Wiley.

Wilson, E., MacLeod, C. & Mathews, A. (submitted). The causal role of interpretive bias in vulnerability to anxiety.

9   The experimental modification of processing biases

Jenny Yiend and Bundy Mackintosh

Introduction

An impressive body of empirical evidence, laid down over the past twenty-five or so years, has firmly established that emotional disorders such as anxiety and depression are accompanied by characteristic cognitive biases in the processing of emotional information. This chapter pays tribute to Andrew Mathews' significant contribution to this accumulated knowledge but also to his continued involvement in the new directions that are building on these solid foundations. On a personal note, Andrew has played a pivotal role in the respective lives and careers of both authors, acting in turn as a nurturing teacher, respected colleague and invaluable friend. Although we can never repay our debt of gratitude, nor match his eloquent style and incisive logic, we can, and do, attempt to highlight his recent work so that the importance of his ongoing contributions to this field are represented in this volume.

Assumptions and observations from clinical practice indicate that cognitive biases must be susceptible to some change since their modification forms an important basis of cognitive therapy. This chapter focuses on the development of experimental techniques to modify cognitive biases and on the assessment of the subsequent effects on mood states and vulnerability to anxiety. Research in this direction has the potential to provide a useful laboratory analogue to aid the investigation of naturally occurring biases, as well as allowing us to address questions of causality (see MacLeod et al., this volume) and explore new treatment possibilities. Before embarking on details of methodology, it is worth considering some of the questions that we have attempted to address on the way.

Modifying cognitive biases

The effectiveness of treatment programmes, particularly Cognitive Behaviour Therapy (CBT), in both ameliorating symptoms and reducing or eliminating cognitive biases has been evident for some time (e.g. Eysenck, Mogg, May, Richards & Mathews, 1991; Mathews, Mogg, Kentish & Eysenck, 1995; Mathews, Richards & Eysenck, 1989; Williams, Mathews & MacLeod, 1996). Treatment frequently proceeds by exposing patients to examples of their particular concerns or by encouraging them to reinterpret situations or events in their lives, a relatively lengthy process that generally spans a number of treatment sessions and 'homework' exercises. Our recent research effort has been directed towards techniques that might modify cognitive biases more directly and in a relatively shorter space of time. The approach taken has been to adapt the very methods previously utilized to establish the existence of biases. Deployment of attention has generally been measured by probing equal numbers of threat or non-threat locations. To induce a bias, the relative frequency with which threat or benign targets are probed has been manipulated, altering expectations of probe locations. Likewise, interpretations of ambiguous words or scripts have been systematically constrained towards either the benign or the threat meaning (see Mathews & MacLeod, 2002). In contrast to clinical treatment, such methods have been successful in inducing attentional or interpretive bias without the participant engaging in conscious effort to assist in the process, nor necessarily being aware that 'training' or 'induction' is taking place.

Consequences of induced biases

The successful induction of cognitive biases, as evidenced by transfer to new material, enables testing of the causal links between bias and anxiety (see MacLeod et al., this volume), but, in addition, further questions arise. For example, is possession of an induced negative bias sufficient to alter anxiety levels alone, and does it also alter vulnerability to subsequent stress? Do differing induction techniques, such as those requiring participants to select and generate an appropriate solution for themselves ('active' methods), compared to those in which the solution is simply presented ('passive' methods), produce distinctive effects? How effectively do induced biases persist over time; do they transfer to novel material and contexts, and does induction technique (e.g. active compared to passive methods) influence any such resilience? Eventually, answers to questions such as these will both enhance our theoretical understanding of the aetiology and maintenance of anxiety and indicate whether induction techniques can provide a significant addition to treatment programmes. For now, we will attempt to update the reader about the current state of understanding of the effects and mechanisms behind bias induction.

Procedures for inducing interpretive bias

Inducing interpretive bias using homographs

A bias in interpretation of emotional ambiguity has been demonstrated using a variety of paradigms, such as recording the spelling choices of auditorily presented homophones, for example dye/die (e.g. Eysenck, MacLeod & Mathews, 1987; Mathews et al., 1989, see also Richards, this volume). In a conceptually similar study (Richards & French, 1992), ambiguous words (homographs) were presented as primes in a lexical decision task, and reaction times to identify words associated with either their negative or benign meanings were taken as a measure of the prime's interpretation. The negative interpretation was more likely to predominate for anxious individuals, reversing a more normal positive bias. Adapting this technique, Grey and Mathews (2000) were able to induce a tendency to select either the negative or the benign interpretation of similar ambiguous words in normal volunteers. In two experiments, active generation of the designated meaning was enforced by presenting a homograph, such as 'batter', followed by a word fragment representing one possible interpretation, either neutral or negative, e.g. 'p-nc-ke' (pancake) or 'ass--lt' (assault). Participants' task on each trial was to press a key as soon as they knew the complete word, and then type in the first missing letter. After many trials involving consistently positive/neutral or negative meanings, transfer to new test items was demonstrated via faster solutions to fragments that maintained the same valence as in training (Experiment 1), or by speeded lexical decision latencies (Experiment 2), as in the task developed by Richards & French (1992).

Finally, to test the importance of the active generation component of this induction technique (here, the fragment completion task), Experiment 3 employed a method that attempted to preclude any active search for valenced meanings. Using a relatedness-judgment paradigm, the positive/neutral or negative associate was presented first, followed by the relevant homograph. The task was to determine, as quickly as possible, whether the two words were related in meaning. Taking the above example of the homograph 'batter', participants saw either 'pancake' or 'assault' first (according to training group), followed by the word 'batter', for which the correct response in both cases would be 'yes' (indicating the words are related). It was intended that presenting the associate prior to the homograph would both ensure that the required meaning was always accessed and reduce the likelihood that alternative meanings would be activated (although this could not, of course, be guaranteed). In lexical decision transfer tasks, training effects were at least as strong using this 'passive' training technique for both old and new homograph primes.

Interpretation training using text

Following the success of homograph training methods, somewhat more naturalistic materials were developed in experiments by Mathews and Mackintosh (2000). Their technique took its origins from that used in Hirsch and Mathews (1997), namely descriptions of social scenarios, with a recognition test akin to that of Eysenck et al. (1991), involving evaluating disambiguating sentences. The procedure consisted of three distinct phases: training, exposure to new ambiguous items, and a subsequent recognition test to assess interpretation of this ambiguous material. During training, participants read three-line descriptions of ambiguous social scenarios in which the last word was a fragment that, when complete, disambiguated the meaning of the prior text. Participants were required to complete the fragment, thereby forcing them into either a negative or positive interpretation, depending on assigned training condition. For example:

> Your partner asks you to go to an anniversary dinner that their company is holding. You have not met any of their work colleagues before. Getting ready to go, you think that the new people you will meet will find you. . . . . . .

A word fragment (b-r-ng/fr-e-dly) constrained the solutions to boring/friendly according to training group.

A comprehension question followed, which required access to the appropriately valenced interpretations, sometimes extending it to emotional implications beyond those already stated. This was intended to reinforce the training-congruent meaning. For example, after the above word completion, the question: 'Will you be disliked by your new acquaintances?' required the response: 'Yes' from negatively trained participants or: 'No' for those positively trained, with feedback given for errors. Typically, the training phase has consisted of fifty to one hundred such scenarios of social situations.

To gauge biases produced by this training, participants were exposed to a new set of ambiguous social scenarios, again requiring a word fragment completion and a comprehension question. However, both the fragment and the question now preserved the ambiguity inherent in the description, allowing later tests of the interpretation taken by each participant. An example test scenario is as follows:

The wedding reception
Your friend asks you to give a speech at her wedding reception. You prepare some remarks and, when the time comes, get to your feet. As you speak, you notice some people in the audience start to . . .
l--gh   *(laugh)*
Did you stand up to speak? (yes/no)

In the recognition phase, participants rated sentences indicating how similar each was to the meaning of the previously seen texts. For each ambiguous test script, four possible sentences required ratings. Two were 'foil' items, providing positive and negative valenced examples, but not closely matched to the original passage meaning. The other two were 'targets' close to the original passage in content, but disambiguated to represent the two alternative (positive versus negative) meanings. For the example above:

As you speak, some people in the audience start to yawn   *(negative foil)*
As you speak, people in the audience applaud your comments   *(positive foil)*
As you speak, people in the audience find your efforts laughable *(negative target)*
As you speak, people in the audience laugh appreciatively   *(positive target)*

Successful training of an interpretive bias should be indicated by higher recognition ratings for targets with the same valence as training, in comparison with targets of the opposite valence. In addition, if training has induced a general priming effect of all congruent material, this should be revealed as an additional consistent recognition difference for same-valence foils.

The results to date using this training technique have proved extremely reliable, as well as robust. We have found significant training effects for both foils and targets, with the latter effect being significantly larger. In addition to analyses of the overall rating scores, signal detection theory was also used to separate sensitivity effects from response biases. Significant effects of training were found on both measures, suggesting that participants were both more sensitive to training congruent interpretations and also generally favoured items of training congruent valence. Over a number of experiments, results suggest that while training may produce a general affective priming, it also produces specific biases in the interpretation of newly encountered ambiguous items. Furthermore, these results are significantly different from those observed in control groups receiving no prior training, and this holds for both negatively and positively trained individuals.

The second main aim of our studies was to test for the influence of induced interpretive bias on anxious mood. The use of more naturalistic material led us to expect that mood effects might result from training, especially as instructions specified that participants should imagine themselves taking part in the social settings. Accordingly, in the experiment described above, state anxiety measures given before and after training showed significant changes in anxious mood, congruent with the direction of training.

Induction through active generation and passive assimilation   The distinction between 'active' training techniques, which require participants to select and generate an appropriate solution for themselves, compared to 'passive' training methods, in which the solution is simply presented, remains a dominant issue and one that we return to later. Grey and Mathews' (2000) success using a passive homograph training technique suggested that an adapted passive text method could provide equally effective induction of bias using social scenarios. This raises the theoretically very important question of the link between induction of the bias and anxious mood. That is, would induction of a bias by passive methods be capable of supporting a change in anxiety to match that of the active generation methods just described? This issue was addressed in a second experiment adapting the material to passive training.

In the adaptation to 'passive' training, the need for participants to generate valenced meaning was removed. The passages were simply presented in completed form, with the fragment and comprehension question incorporated as continuations of the passage. A neutral word fragment and comprehension question were added to provide a match for the format of the previous procedure. The example above became:

Your partner asks you to go to an anniversary dinner that their company is holding. You have not met any of their work colleagues before. Getting ready to go, you think that the new people you will meet will find you boring/friendly. You will (not) be disliked by your new acquaintances. This was followed by a fragment: di-n-er (dinner), and question, 'Did you attend your partner's company Christmas party?' (yes/no).

Ambiguous test and recognition items remained identical. As expected from the outcome with homographs, the training effects persisted under these passive exposure conditions. The recognition of disambiguating target sentences differed significantly in a direction congruent with previous exposure training, in a manner undiminished in comparison with active methods. In contrast, however, congruent state anxiety changes observed with active generation training were quite absent.

Thus, to summarize, various methods of bias induction have been developed by Andrew Mathews, Colin MacLeod and colleagues. Here, we have described in detail only those induction techniques relevant to interpretation biases; for further details of attentional training techniques, the reader is referred to recent reviews, such as Mathews and MacLeod

(2002, see also MacLeod et al., this volume). We have described how both active and passive induction methods provide equally effective vehicles for change in bias, with the former appearing also to support changes in anxiety level. We now turn to consider some of the ongoing themes and questions that have emerged from this research.

Generalization of induced biases

New material

One of the very first empirical questions for researchers attempting the experimental induction of cognitive processing biases was whether, and to what extent, the processes induced would generalize to new situations, and this remains a theme of major interest. The extent of generalization is of theoretical interest because of what it might reveal about the underlying mechanisms that are being altered during induction. It is also of practical importance. There needs to be some degree of generalization beyond specific training procedures if there is to be any therapeutically useful outcome in the longer term.

At the most basic level, it is clear that all methods of induction employed so far, whether focusing on interpretive or attentional biases, result in biased processing that is effectively deployed towards novel stimulus material. This is evident from the test period that usually immediately follows training and invariably uses material not previously presented during training (see previous method sections). The generalization of text-based interpretive training to new material has now been replicated several times (e.g. Mathews & MacLeod, 2002; Yiend, Mackintosh & Mathews, in press; Yiend & Mathews, 2002). Similarly, generalization following homograph interpretation training and attentional training methods have been recently replicated (Wilson, MacLeod & Mathews, submitted; MacLeod et al., this volume).

Thus, the transfer to novel material of processing biases induced using the techniques described here seems to be a robust phenomenon. This deceptively simple level of generalization is critical because it means that participants are not simply learning a fixed response pattern to a specific set of items. Instead, some more generic processing style is being acquired and then spontaneously deployed on new material.

Different tests of the same process

To properly validate the claim that the induction procedure has altered a particular cognitive process, it is necessary to explore the deployment of this process across a variety of different tasks, all of which should show effects of induction. An increasing number of studies looking at induced interpretation bias have now used conceptually similar, but methodologically different, tests of induction procedures. One example is Hertel, Mathews, Peterson and Kintner (2003, see also Hertel, this volume), where participants were given an imagery task, rather than primed lexical decision, following interpretation training with homographs. At test, participants produced and described a self-related image of each word presented, all of which were new emotional homographs. As predicted, subsequent independent ratings of the images produced to the new emotional homographs showed training congruent effects, such that those with negative training produced more threat-related images than those trained in the opposite direction. Indeed, preliminary work in Mathews' laboratory has recently replicated this, finding training congruent effects on a version of this imagery task, again following induction using homographs.

Wilson et al. (submitted) directly explored the transfer of induced interpretive bias across different tasks by using two types of training procedure, which were fully crossed with two corresponding types of test task. Training either required participants to identify whether two words were associated (the emotional homograph and the meaning to be trained: e.g. batter/pancake), or required a fragment completion task (batter/p-nc-k-). At test, the same tasks were used, but without any training contingency, and with new emotional homographs. Results showed no significant task-specific effects. Instead, participants trained to make negative interpretations displayed this on both types of test task, as did those trained in the other direction. This result validates the notion that a task-independent processing style is being acquired during induction, and this bodes well for the therapeutic use of these procedures.

In the case of induction using ambiguous text, only two test tasks have been used to date. Consequently, any conclusions regarding the transfer of these effects must be more cautious. In addition to the recognition task described above, we have developed a test similar to the training procedure itself, which, unlike the recognition test, has the advantage that it can be repeated (see section on Clinical Applications, this chapter, for more details). Results on this test are consistent with those of the recognition test, both within individual subjects as well as across training groups. As such, they represent preliminary evidence that training with ambiguous text also produces effects on interpretation that generalize beyond a specific test task.

In summary, the evidence suggests, at least with interpretive bias training methods, that the processing style being induced carries over to a variety of new tasks, all of which are designed to test for the presence of biases in the interpretation of ambiguity. We therefore suggest that the operation of the induced bias is not task specific, which lends some validity to the notion that training is actually influencing a generic cognitive processing mechanism, rather than an individual task specific process. We must await further data, however, before we can draw similar conclusions as regards attentional training procedures.

From one cognitive process to another

Of course, it is impossible to be sure that a given task reflects only the cognitive process that one might wish to suppose, which brings us to consider the extent to which induced biases might transfer across cognitive operations. It is clearly of theoretical, as well as clinical, interest to know whether training in one process, for example interpretation, would have carry-over effects for other processes, such as memory or attention.

Andrew Mathews and colleagues have addressed this question in pilot work. This suggested that training with homographs involving generation of meanings (see above) did have carry-over effects to an attentional probe task. The latter test involved first showing a homograph alone, and then flanking it with two associates, one corresponding to its negative meaning and the other to its neutral meaning. Responses to probes in the location of either type of flanking word suggested that meanings congruent with prior training did attract attention in trials with previously exposed homographs, but not with new ones. Clearly, there could be task specific or methodological explanations of this failure. Alternatively, it may be that biases in one process are driving the others, and that we have not yet succeeded in identifying that key central effect.

Across modalities

The final variant of generalization that we will consider here is that across modalities. Although this has not been addressed deliberately in experimental work to date, nevertheless some studies do throw some light on this type of transfer, suggesting that training effects do transfer from the visual to the auditory domain. In an experiment using standard visually presented homograph training, Laura Hoppitt, a Ph.D. student working in Mathews' laboratory, has examined responses to novel, auditorily presented homographs and unambiguous emotional words. In response to each homograph, participants had to imagine a scene involving themselves in relation to the word, then speak a one-sentence verbal description of their image into a tape recorder (based on Hertel et al., 2003). Participants' own ratings of their images showed a significant training effect, such that those receiving prior negative training rated their own homograph images as more negative, compared to the same self-ratings of the positively trained groups. The groups did not differ significantly on self-ratings of unambiguous emotional words, confirming that training had resulted in an interpretation bias in the auditory domain, and not merely a response bias favouring all training congruent emotional material.

Similarly, data on how training modulates mood changes on exposure to a stressor (which we will consider in detail in the next section) are relevant to this level of transfer. Training congruent differences in mood responses to subsequent stress have been reported for both attentional and interpretive training techniques. These findings are consistent with the notion that transfer not only occurs across modalities, but also across very different situations. The stress situation has generally been provided by viewing a selection of distressing video clips (e.g. Wilson et al., submitted) or alternatively by presenting an anagram task, in which the majority of items are either very difficult or impossible (e.g. MacLeod, Rutherford, Campbell, Ebsworthy & Holker, 2002). Such stress situations were effective in raising anxiety for all, as indexed by changes in self-rated anxious mood. However, positively and negatively trained groups showed a training congruent differential in their vulnerability, with positive training alleviating and negative training enhancing the stress response. These data suggest that training procedures can have effects which carry over to an entirely different medium, involving real-time sound and vision, and as such, it is perhaps the most impressive demonstration of generalization across modalities. Furthermore, training effects on mood constitute evidence of generalization not just to different materials, cognitive processes or modalities in the conventional sense, but to an entirely different domain, namely that of subjective emotional experience. We therefore suggest that this result warrants the conclusion that not only can generalization occur across modalities, but also across qualitatively different contexts.

Resilience of induced biases

The resilience of induced interpretation bias is also a question of prime importance for any future therapeutic application. If bias induction is to have beneficial consequences for cognitive processing, and perhaps mood, then it is essential to show that our induction techniques produce robust effects. There are several issues of relevance including:

1. How resilient induced biases are over time;
2. To what extent intervening processes may be influential, and
3. Variability within individuals.

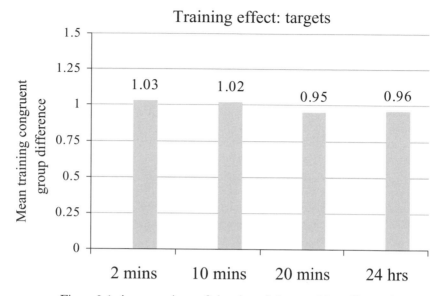

Figure 9.1 A comparison of the size of the cognitive effects of training across different train–test intervals. The index was calculated on the recognition ratings, by summing the mean group differences across positive and negative targets.

One way in which we have explored the latter question is by examining the data of individuals item by item. This revealed that almost every participant appeared to show a clear training effect on most if not all items. To obtain a preliminary feel for decay over time, we have also tested the temporal characteristics of induced interpretation bias (Mathews & Mackintosh, 2000; Yiend et al., in press). The usual two-minute interval between training and test was extended first to ten and then to twenty minutes. Training was effective, and in both conditions training congruent effects were stronger for targets than foils on recognition tests. The extra delay appeared not to reduce the magnitude of induced bias. Interestingly, training-congruent state anxiety effects were, however, dissipated by the delay, helping to confirm that induced biases were not simply a consequence of acquired mood state at the time of testing. Taking this further, Yiend et al. (in press) have established that included biases can be extremely persistent. In one experiment participants returned for testing after a twenty-four-hour interval with minimal loss of the training effect. Thus, here too, despite now having no control over participants' activities in the intervening time, we found persistent training effects. Figure 9.1 illustrates the relative size of training effects across increasing time delays prior to test.

The question of the potential importance of interference, or otherwise, by intervening activities during the delay has yet to be addressed. To date, the consistency, robustness and resilience of training within participants and over time is very encouraging for the possible development of future therapeutic applications.

While these results are very exciting, there is a need for caution. For example, it is not clear at present whether the training-related differential vulnerability to stress (as described earlier) would persist to the same degree. Similarly, it will be important to establish the extent to which interference from intervening training congruent or incongruent processes has the power to alter the consequences of induction. To this end, we are currently attempting to look at the effects of interfering tasks on the deployment of induced biases.

Emotional consequences

One of the most important issues for this programme of research is the emotional consequences of bias induction, whether immediate or delayed, whether latent or manifest. There are at least two reasons for this. First, any mood change that occurs contingent upon the cognitive changes induced by training constitutes direct evidence for the causal connection between maladaptive processing biases and emotional disorders. This frequently assumed connection nevertheless has little direct empirical support, and therefore the contribution that the manipulation of processing biases can make to this question is considerable (see MacLeod et al., this volume). A second, and related, reason is that evidence of emotional consequences of bias manipulation raises the possibility that induction might usefully be developed in future as an additional treatment tool. Given the importance of these issues, we will spend some time considering the data on the emotional effects of bias induction.

Mood change across induction

The first and perhaps most obvious emotional consequences of which we became aware were those occurring across the training procedure itself. In the Mathews and Mackintosh (2000) series, mood change across the session (pre-training – post test) was observed. Subsequently, we have measured anxious mood at multiple times during the experimental session (e.g. Yiend et al., in press). This has revealed that using ambiguous text induction, but not homograph induction, mood change usually occurred across induction itself (i.e. prior to test), in a direction consistent with training direction, so that negatively trained participants became significantly more anxious than the positively trained group. However, this effect soon waned, so that groups no longer differed after a ten-minute or twenty-minute interval (Yiend et al., in press), despite the fact that the induced interpretation bias persisted.

Initial findings (Mathews & Mackintosh, 2000) suggested that mood change during training required the active generation of valenced interpretations and did not occur when passive reading alone was used (see methods described above). This was despite the finding that both methods were successful in producing training-congruent biases in the interpretation of new ambiguous items. However, it appears from Yiend et al. (in press) that while active generation may be a necessary condition for mood change to occur across training, it may not always be sufficient.

Why should training involving a generation procedure sometimes elicit mood change in and of itself, when very similar inductions using homographs or passive reading of text do not? Recall that, during the active generation method, participants have to perform a word completion that disambiguates the meaning of the previous text in the direction of training. We presume that to do this task participants actively have to select from at least two competing meanings of the text and then, having chosen a possible word, have to elaborate sufficiently to verify that it would be an appropriate completion of the text. This represents a considerable amount of processing of the valenced task material, in comparison to the passive reading procedure. Similarly for homograph procedures, although the selection of meaning is integral to the training, there is little opportunity for the elaboration of this, which may mean mood effects do not have chance to develop. Features such as these could account for some of the differences in mood effects between different interpretation training procedures, and indeed this possibility will arise again in the following section.

As far as attentional induction procedures are concerned, there is no evidence to date that the procedure itself leads to mood effects. Despite considerable exposure to valenced items, and the fact that participants clearly learn an association between valence and target location, as demonstrated by test trials, this appears not to influence anxious or depressed mood (MacLeod et al., 2002). This is consistent with the mood data on interpretive induction procedures just described. As with homograph induction, in attentional training there is little time during the procedure for elaborative processing of items, which are usually single words appearing for no more than 500 ms. This lack of opportunity to generate and elaborate on emotional meanings could constitute one reason why little mood change occurs across attentional training procedures.

Although interesting from a theoretical perspective, because of what we might learn about mechanism, mood change across induction is clearly not particularly significant from a clinical point of view, especially given that the mood effects dissipate after ten minutes or so. More important is whether the subsequent deployment of an induced bias could influence mood. This we shall consider next.

Response to a stressor

There is rapidly accumulating evidence that the induction procedures described above can also have latent effects on mood, which become manifest only when participants are exposed to an external stress. Thus, it appears that induced biases can reduce or enhance an individual's vulnerability to stressful situations in a manner analogous to clinically observed variations in natural reactivity (Broadbent & Broadbent, 1988; Mogg, Bradley & Hallowell, 1994; Mogg, Mathews, Bird & Macgregor-Morris, 1990).

The first finding of this sort this was reported by MacLeod et al. (2002; see also MacLeod et al., this volume), using an attentional induction procedure. Participants were given a stressful anagram task (many anagrams were impossible to solve, although participants were not told this) before and after training. On pre-training baselines, neither group differed in emotional response to the anagram stress, but following training there were significant differences according to group assignment. Those trained to attend to threat showed increases in dysphoric mood across the stress, whereas those trained to avoid threat showed little change. Furthermore, a computed index of the size of the induced attentional bias correlated significantly with the magnitude of increased dysphoric mood across the stressor. Although small in magnitude ($r = .33$), this confirms that the extent to which training was successful predicted the ability to cope with post-induction stress.

Similar results have been found following the induction of interpretive biases using homograph training methods. Wilson et al. (submitted; see also MacLeod et al., this volume) trained participants using two different homograph methods (fragment completion and word association). Subsequently, participants were exposed to four short, stressful video clips depicting life-threatening disasters taken from a television programme. Results showed a significant interaction between direction of training and response to the stressful videos. Irrespective of which homograph training method had been used, those trained in a negative direction showed a greater increase in anxious mood while viewing the video than those trained in the opposite direction.

One might be tempted to conclude from the Wilson et al. study that differential reactivity to stress is produced by any form of homograph training. However, recent data we have collected suggests that this is not the case. Our student, Laura Hoppitt, took up the issue raised earlier concerning the importance of active generation and elaboration of meaning during the induction procedure. In one of her studies, 'generation' training participants were, as usual, given a homograph prime followed by a fragment to complete, which corresponded to the direction in which they were being trained (e.g. batter – assault/pancake). In contrast, for 'passive' training, participants saw unambiguously emotional words, corresponding to the direction of their training, followed by related words for completion (e.g. weapons – assault/eggs – pancake). Thus, the passive training condition was essentially an extended period of simple exposure, or priming, in the direction to be trained. In parallel to the findings with generative and passive text training (Yiend et al., in press), both methods produced training-congruent effects on novel homographs, as indexed by reaction times on a lexical decision task. However, when exposed to the same video stress as used in the Wilson et al. (submitted) study, the negatively trained groups responded differently according to the method of training they had received. Those trained using active generation showed a larger anxiety increase than those trained using passive exposure.

Further evidence consistent with this finding was provided by a subsequent experiment by the same student, Laura Hoppitt. She compared the same two training methods, generative and passive, and followed this with an imagery task in which participants had to produce and describe an image in response to novel homograph cue words. Again, the negatively trained groups differed in terms of the degree of change in their state anxiety scores across the imagery task. Those who were trained using the generative procedure became more anxious compared to those who had received the passive exposure induction. It appears from the data discussed that, like the mood effects across training itself, the production of differences in stress vulnerability seems to depend on the specific processes encountered during training. In particular, training must allow the opportunity to select a valenced meaning from amongst competitors and the time to elaborate that meaning. We suggest that, once acquired during training, these processes of selection and elaboration are then unintentionally deployed towards whatever material is subsequently encountered. Whenever possible, selection will favour the direction consistent with prior training, and elaboration will enhance the emotional significance of that selection. In the presence of a stress, these processes will lead to heightened or reduced anxiety.

Towards a clinical application

Throughout this chapter, we have alluded to the potential clinical benefits of the various induction techniques described. In this section, we will review the studies that have been designed to explore directly the possibilities for clinical application.

Several studies of this sort, using attentional training, have been described in detail by MacLeod et al. (this volume). In brief, Campbell, Rutherford and MacLeod (2002) report two separate studies in which high trait anxious participants were either trained positively (i.e. to avoid attending to threat) or were controls (no attentional contingency). After eight to ten sessions spread over a three-week period, they found that the positive group showed significant spontaneous attentional preferences away from threat and, most importantly, a significant reduction in trait anxiety, compared to controls. The same group also report an on-line version of attentional training (MacLeod, Rutherford, Campbell & Soong, submitted), which has shown significant reduction in self-reported symptoms of social anxiety after two weeks of daily training sessions (Malcolm, 2003). This is clearly a promising start towards the development of a clinically useful training tool.

There is also some preliminary data regarding interpretation training. In Mathews' laboratory, with the help of another student, Tom Baker, we have developed a similar multi-session training procedure using emotionally ambiguous text (see also Yiend & Mathews, 2003). Sub-clinically anxious individuals were given positive training on four separate occasions over a period of two weeks, and were compared to a control group who simply read neutral passages. Cognitive measures included the standard recognition test (see earlier procedures section), which was given after the last session and revealed training congruent effects. A second cognitive measure was developed for this study that did not rely on the element of surprise used in the recognition test. The 'ambiguity resolution' test could therefore be repeated throughout training, allowing us to track the course of bias change within subjects. The test involved presenting ambiguous passages and then simply using a direct question (yes/no) to establish participants' spontaneous interpretations. An example follows:

You have just had a new patio laid in your garden and decide to have a barbecue, as the weather is so nice. As your friends arrive, you can see that they have noticed something different. Later, you overhear their
co--ents (comments)
Did your friends have a negative reaction when they saw your new patio? (yes/no)

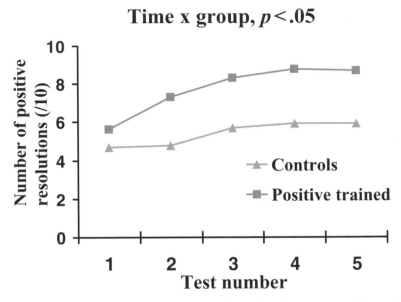

Figure 9.2 High anxious participants' performance on the ambiguity resolution test prior to training (time 1) and following each of four subsequent training sessions (times 2–5).

Items are balanced according to whether a positive or negative response indicates a positive or negative interpretation, and participants accrue a simple total (/10) indicating how many interpretations in each valenced direction are made. The results from this test, administered prior to training (time 1) and subsequently following each session (times 2–5), are shown in Figure 9.2. The figure illustrates the gradual divergence of the groups, with the positively trained making an increasingly larger number of positive interpretations as training progressed.

State anxiety change, which was also measured across each session revealed, as predicted, that the positively trained group became significantly less anxious compared to controls, whose anxiety scores rose. This group difference did not vary significantly across sessions.

These results are encouraging, because they answer one concern, namely the possibility that highly anxious individuals, unlike the unselected participants mostly used to date, might be particularly resistant to the potential benefits of positive inductions. Together with the attentional data, these results show that this concern is unfounded. However, as a postscript, it is worth noting one interesting post hoc finding that struck us when examining the individual participant data in this study.

Surprisingly, a minority of participants displayed an unexpectedly positive bias at the outset (and this bias therefore had little room for, and did not reveal, noticeable change following training). We should therefore not assume that all anxious individuals will be equally suited to positive induction techniques. Instead, future work, especially when aimed towards the clinic, should incorporate an assessment of presenting biases at an individual level. This is one example of how good research is important to help determine the factors influencing the success of potential new clinical approaches.

Conclusions

Hopefully, this chapter has provided a picture of the current state of play within the emerging empirical literature on methods of bias induction. In addition, we have tried to consider both theoretical issues, such as what can be concluded so far about underlying mechanisms driving interpretation training effects, and clinical issues, such as progress towards developing training techniques for possible clinical use.

Throughout most of the chapter, we focused on empirical data. This now shows unequivocally that it is possible to induce biases in interpretation and attention, analogous to those occurring naturally. Biases induced using the techniques described here have been validated by the use of different test tasks, and the data show that they are spontaneously deployed towards novel material. In some cases, there is generalization to different cognitive processes and across modalities. Furthermore, the cognitive effects of induced intepretation bias appear to be very robust, lasting for at least twenty-four hours. Most importantly, induced biases, as well as sometimes producing congruent mood change across training, also produce latent mood effects that emerge in the presence of an external stress. This confirms the implicit assumption of many researchers and clinicians that processing biases are contributing to the variance in individuals' ability to cope with stress.

We also considered some theoretical issues surrounding bias induction. It is now possible to draw some conclusions about the cognitive mechanisms operating during induction procedures. It is clear that training effects are not produced merely by the retrieval of previous episodic memory traces because the same effects are also apparent for new items, for which there could be no such previous trace. In the case of interpretation training, we are in a position to say a little more about possible mechanisms. We initially thought that participants may be learning a specific production rule along the lines of 'respond to ambiguous input by searching for a negative (/positive) meaning where possible'. If so, training involving active generation of the appropriate meaning should enable quick and effective learning of the rule, whereas simple exposure would mean such a production rule was under-specified and cognitive training effects should be weaker. Thus, the absence of any observable cognitive differences between the two training methods suggests that simple priming is sufficient to carry cognitive effects.

Priming could operate in a very general sense by enhancing the accessibility of the entire valence-congruent category. This is suggested by the fact that in the recognition test following text training methods, training congruent foils, as well as targets, are recognized better than non-congruent items. Similarly, following homograph training, Laura Hoppitt's data showed effects on a lexical decision test task using unambiguous primes as well as homograph primes. However, other aspects of the data suggest a more specific priming effect, such as an increased activation of all congruent meanings only when an ambiguous event is encountered. For example, on the recognition test following text training, targets also show significantly larger training effects than foils. Similarly, in contrast to the Hoppitt study, Wilson et al. (submitted) only found training effects following homograph, not unambiguous primes. Clearly, more research is needed to resolve the precise details of the mechanisms driving the cognitive effects of induction, and it is quite possible that these may vary according to the particular method used.

The finding that active and passive interpretation induction techniques do differ with respect to consequences for anxious mood points to the possibility that active induction allows or encourages greater elaboration of emotionally congruent material. This would account for mood effects both across induction and subsequently, as participants trained using active generation may be more likely to engage in extensive processing of emotionally congruent material, which would be more likely to produce effects on mood.

We ended by reviewing some current preliminary work on developing induction methods for possible use in treatment. So far, these have produced promising results for both attentional and interpretive techniques. Analogue sub-clinical populations appear to respond to positive induction methods, showing similar cognitive effects and mood benefits to those found in unselected populations. Work is already under way to test the use of experimental induction on clinical groups (see MacLeod et al., this volume) and ultimately this could produce a new tool for the clinician.

The authors hope that this chapter has given a flavour of the central role that Andrew Mathews continues to play in anxiety research and, in some small way, has paid tribute to his immense capacities as both a researcher and a mentor. It is a privilege and a pleasure to work with him, to experience his enthusiasm, rigour and insight, and to benefit from his generosity in encouraging and acknowledging the contribution of others.

REFERENCES

Broadbent, D. & Broadbent, M. (1988). Anxiety and attentional bias: state and trait. *Cognition and Emotion*, *2*, 165–183.

Campbell, L., Rutherford, E. & MacLeod, C. (2002). Practice makes perfect: the reduction of trait anxiety through the extended retraining of attentional response to threat. Paper presented at the 36th AABT annual convention, Reno, NV.

Eysenck, M. W., MacLeod, C. & Mathews, A. M. (1987). Cognitive functioning in anxiety. *Psychological Research*, *49*, 189–195.

Eysenck, M. W., Mogg, K., May, J., Richards, A. & Mathews, A. (1991). Bias in interpretation of ambiguous sentences related to threat in anxiety. *Journal of Abnormal Psychology*, *100*, 144–150.

Grey, S. & Mathews, A. (2000). Effects of training on interpretation of emotional ambiguity. *Quarterly Journal of Experimental Psychology Section A – Human Experimental Psychology*, *53*, 1143–1162.

Hertel, P. T., Mathews, A., Peterson, S. & Kintner, K. (2003). Transfer of training emotionally biased interpretations. *Applied Cognitive Psychology*, *17*, 775–784.

Hirsch, C. & Mathews, A. (1997). Interpretative inferences when reading about emotional events. *Behaviour Research and Therapy*, *35*, 1123–1132.

MacLeod, C., Rutherford, E., Campbell, L., Ebsworthy, G. & Holker, L. (2002). Selective attention and emotional vulnerability: assessing the causal basis of their association through the experimental manipulation of attentional bias. *Journal of Abnormal Psychology*, *111*, 107–123.

MacLeod, C., Rutherford, E., Campbell, L. & Soong, L. (submitted). Internet-delivered assessment and manipulation of anxiety-linked attentional bias: validation of a free-access attentional probe software package.

Malcolm, A. (2003). Effect of attentional retraining on social phobia symptoms. Unpublished Master's thesis, The University of Western Australia, Perth, Western Australia.

Mathews, A. & Mackintosh, B. (2000). Induced emotional interpretation bias and anxiety. *Journal of Abnormal Psychology*, *109*, 602–615.

Mathews, A. & MacLeod, C. (2002). Induced processing biases have causal effects on anxiety. *Cognition and Emotion*, *16*, 331–354.

Mathews, A., Mogg, K., Kentish, J. & Eysenck, M. (1995). Effect of psychological treatment on cognitive bias in generalized anxiety disorder. *Behaviour Research and Therapy*, *33*, 293–303.

Mathews, A., Richards, A. & Eysenck, M. W. (1989). Interpretation of homophones related to threat in anxiety states. *Journal of Abnormal Psychology*, *98*, 31–34.

Mogg, K., Bradley, B. P. & Hallowell, N. (1994). Attentional bias to threat: roles of trait anxiety, stressful events, and awareness. *Quarterly Journal of Experimental Psychology*, *47*A, 841–864.

Mogg, K., Mathews, A., Bird, C. & Macgregor-Morris, R. (1990). Effects of stress and anxiety on the processing of threat stimuli. *Journal of Personality and Social Psychology*, *59*, 1230–1237.

Richards, A. & French, C. C. (1992). An anxiety-related bias in semantic activation when processing threat/neutral homographs. *Quarterly Journal of Experimental Psychology*, *45*, 503–525.

Williams, J. M. G., Mathews, A. & MacLeod, C. (1996). The emotional Stroop task and psychopathology. *Psychological Bulletin*, *120*, 3–24.

Wilson, E., MacLeod, C. & Mathews, A. (submitted). The causal role of interpretive bias in vulnerability to anxiety.

Yiend, J., Mackintosh, B. & Mathews, A. (in press). The enduring consequences of experimentally induced biases in interpretation. *Behaviour, Research and Therapy*.

Yiend, J. & Mathews, A. (2002). Induced biases in the processing of emotional information. In S. P. Shohov (Ed.), *Advances in Psychology Research*, vol. 13, 43–68. New York: Nova Science Publishers, Inc.

Yiend, J. & Mathews, A. (2003). Training of emotion regulation: inducing biases in the interpretation of ambiguity. *Abstracts of the BABCP 31st Annual Conference*, 42–43, York.

Part III

Clinical perspectives

10 Maintenance mechanisms in social anxiety: an integration of cognitive biases and emotional processing theory

Jonathan D. Huppert and Edna B. Foa

We feel honoured to contribute this chapter to a volume that is devoted to recognizing the unique place that Andrew Mathews has had in the study of anxiety and the anxiety disorders. From the beginning of his career, he set the course for research on anxiety, including psychophysiology, treatment and, most recently, cognitive mechanisms. This chapter will relate predominantly to Mathews' contribution to the cognitive psychopathology of anxiety (see Chapter 1 in this book), attempting to integrate Mathews and Mackintosh's (1998) concepts of anxiety with Foa and Kozak's (1985, 1986; see also Foa & McNally, 1996; Foa & Cahill, 2001) emotional processing theory to further our understanding of social anxiety disorder and its treatment.

Emotional processing theory

Emotional processing theory utilizes information processing concepts to explain the psychopathology and treatment of anxiety disorders. A basic concept in emotional processing theory is the presence of *fear structures* that serve as blueprints for responding to danger (Foa & Kozak, 1986; Lang, 1977). The theory proposes that three kinds of representations are contained in these structures:

1. Information about the stimuli,
2. Information about verbal, physiological and behavioural responses, and
3. The interpretive meaning of these stimuli and responses.

Thus, a fear structure is comprised of an intricate network of associations of the different elements. A normal fear structure contains associations that generally reflect reality accurately (e.g. a car veering towards me → fear (heart rate acceleration, scanning the road, veering my car off the road) → cars coming towards me are dangerous). In general, when a normal fear structure is activated by the individual confronted with a dangerous situation (e.g. a car veering towards the person), it generates fear and leads to adaptive manoeuvring (e.g. moving to safety). In contrast, a pathological fear structure contains associations among the representations of stimulus, response and meaning that do not reflect reality, have excessive response elements (e.g. avoidance), and are more resistant to modification. We propose that the persistence of the fear structure is due to the biases in processing, which interfere with the acquisition of relevant information that is inconsistent with elements of the fear structure.

Foa and Kozak (1985) proposed that specific pathological fear structures underlie the different anxiety disorders, and that successful psychosocial treatment modifies the pathological elements in the structure. Furthermore, each disorder contains elements common to all anxiety disorders (physiological response elements and escape or avoidance responses), as well as disorder-specific elements. For example, the fear structure of patients with panic disorder is characterized by a pathological association between bodily sensations, such as heart palpitations and threat of death; post-traumatic stress disorder (PTSD) on the other hand is characterized by a pathological association between trauma reminders – which are essentially safe situations or images – and danger, or a sense of incompetence. Indeed, Lang and colleagues (e.g. Lang, Davis & Öhman, 2000; Cuthbert et al., 2003) reported different levels of specificity and coherence (strength of association between elements in memory) of the fear structures for PTSD, panic disorder, specific phobia and social anxiety disorder. Physiological reactivity to imagery of feared cues suggested that the physiological and meaning elements are associated within specific anxiety disorders. Other data also suggest a relationship among behavioural responses, meaning and physiological responses (Avero & Calvo, 1999; Kozak, Foa & Steketee, 1988).

Foa and Kozak (1985, 1986) originally proposed that emotional processing can be defined as the modification of the fear structure to replace pathological associations among stimuli, responses and meaning with non-pathological associations. However, recent work on extinction and reinstatement (Bouton, 2000; Rescorla, 2001) suggests that extinction does not eliminate or replace previous associations, but instead creates new associations (e.g. heart palpitations do not mean heart attack) which, under most contexts, will be more readily retrieved than the pathological ones (e.g. heart palpitations mean heart attack). Such a model better accounts for spontaneous recovery in extinction paradigms and relapses after treatment (see Foa & McNally, 1996). The major implication of this reconceptualization is that treatment should include multiple contexts in order to reinforce the non-pathological structure and reduce the likelihood of activating the pathological structure.

Foa and Kozak (1986) proposed that two conditions are necessary for therapeutic emotional processing to occur:

1. Activation of the fear structure, and
2. Incorporation of information that is incompatible with the pathological elements of the fear structure.

Activation occurs when the person encounters stimuli or responses that are represented in the fear structure (and therefore are associated with danger meaning). In general, the greater the match between the evoking experience and the person's fear structure, the greater the activation. Emotional processing theory posits that while activation is a necessary condition for emotional processing, it is not a sufficient condition for modification of the fear structure. Such modification requires the presence of information that disconfirms the erroneous elements in the structure. When such information is unavailable because the individual avoids or escapes the situation, the fear structure will remain unchanged (cf. Solomon, Kamin & Wynne, 1953). Moreover, if the evocative situation contains information that confirms the person's feared consequences, the fear structure will be strengthened. Even when disconfirmatory information is present during the evocative experience, emotional processing occurs only when it is encoded and incorporated into existing knowledge. Foa and McNally (1996) argued that the incorporation of the new information results in a new structure that does not contain the erroneous elements of the original fear structure.

As noted earlier, emotional processing theory posits that specific pathological structures underlie each of the anxiety disorders. It follows that the formation of a new, non-pathological fear structure (i.e. emotional processing) will result in a reduction of symptoms in the corresponding anxiety disorder. Emotional processing can occur as a result of everyday experiences (i.e. natural recovery) or in the context of psychosocial treatment. For example, exposure therapy is designed to ensure that exposure exercises will activate the fear structure and at the same time provide information about the non-threat value of the exercise.

Typically, there is fear decrement during exposure exercises (within session habituation; e.g. Chaplin & Levine, 1981; Foa & Chambless, 1978), as well as decrease in peak intensity across sessions (between-session habituation). Foa and Kozak (1986) perceived these two types of habituation as indicators of emotional processing that are related to but conceptually independent of symptom reduction.

Several studies found evidence for a relationship of between-session habituation and symptom reduction, i.e. treatment outcome (van Minnen & Foa, submitted; Kozak, Foa & Steketee, 1988; Jaycox, Foa & Morral, 1998). However, the relationship between within-session habituation and symptom reduction is more ambiguous. Within-session habituation has been found to be positively related to longer continuous exposure (Chaplin & Levine, 1981; van Minnen & Foa, submitted), and longer continuous exposures have been found to be positively related to symptom reduction in some studies (Chaplin & Levine, 1981; Rabavilas, Boulougouris & Stefanis, 1976; Stern & Marks, 1973) but not others (van Minnen & Foa, submitted). However, no relationship between within-session habituation and symptom reduction has been found (van Minnen & Foa, submitted; Jaycox et al., 1998; Foa et al., 1983; Matthews et al., 1974). Other evidence that within-session habituation is not a necessary condition for improvement includes the finding that people with agoraphobia, who were allowed to escape from their feared situation before the anxiety decreased, improved as much as those who were instructed to stay in the situation until the fear diminished (Emmelkamp, 1974; de Silva & Rachman, 1984; Rachman, Craske, Tallman & Solyom, 1986).

It is possible, then, that within-session habituation is not a reliable indicator of emotional processing. Indeed, reduction of anxiety may be due to factors that impair emotional processing, such as distraction or engagement in safety behaviours. However, the relationship between within-session habituation and outcome is not detrimental to the emotional processing theory because the proposed mechanism underlying symptom reduction is the modification of the relevant erroneous associations through disconfirming information, not through habituation per se. In fact, Foa and Kozak (1986) proposed that within-session habituation is mainly important for patients whose core fear is the erroneous belief that anxiety 'stays forever unless escape is realized'. For these patients, within-session habituation provides the information that disconfirms their erroneous evaluation. Indeed, clinical experience suggests that, in some cases, disconfirming information that had been presented during exposure is incorporated after the exposure exercise. In most cases, this process occurs both within and between sessions.

The fear structure of social anxiety disorder

Social anxiety disorder is characterized by excessive fear of embarrassment or humiliation in interpersonal or other social situations that leads to significant distress and impairment. A cardinal feature of social anxiety disorder is that the core fear is not about physical threat, but interpersonal threat. The specific threat meaning in a pathological fear structure of social anxiety disorder is isolation, ostracization and/or rejection. Thus, social anxiety disorder may be conceptualized as a 'fear of embarrassment'. Phenomenological data suggest that social anxiety disorder can be divided into specific situational fears (e.g. a speech phobia) or more general fears that vary across a number of social situations, including interpersonal and performance realms (Kessler et al., 1998). In terms of the fear structure, patients with more circumscribed fears appear to have more coherent psychophysiological responses to imagery (Cuthbert et al., 2003).

This suggests that those with speech and other circumscribed types of social anxiety have similar fear structures to individuals with specific phobia, except that the core threat is one of rejection (e.g. due to poor performance or exhibiting signs of embarrassment, like blushing or shaking), rather than physical harm. The fear structure underlying generalized social anxiety disorder is characterized by a larger number of stimulus, response and meaning representations, as well as a larger number of associations among these representations. Because individuals with generalized social anxiety disorder comprise the majority of the patients who seek treatment for social anxiety, we will focus on them here.

Below, we present a model of the fear structure of generalized social anxiety disorder that draws on clinical research into the psychopathology of social anxiety disorder, research in social psychology, emotion theory on embarrassment (e.g. Keltner & Buswell, 1997) and direct clinical experience.

Stimuli representations

By definition, the stimuli represented in the fear structure of an individual with social anxiety disorder are circumscribed to people or social situations (e.g. peers, authority figures, or individuals of the opposite sex). For some individuals with social anxiety disorder, the number of stimuli representations is small, circumscribed to a particular context. For others, the fear structure contains a multitude of stimuli and contexts.

Images of oneself in social interactions are stimuli that have gained particular interest recently. For example, Hackmann, Clark and McManus (2000) found that patients with social anxiety disorder had specific recurrent images during social interactions, and that these images appeared to be related to negative social interactions surrounding the onset of the disorder (for a more detailed discussion of these and other findings about imagery and social anxiety, see Hirsch & Clark, this volume).

Representations of verbal, physiological and behavioural responses

Verbal responses can represent anxiety (e.g. hesitations in speech, such as 'ummm' or 'uhhhhh'), or avoidance of poor performance in a social situation (by asking questions, changing topics away from oneself, etc.), or these responses can be an attempt to distract others from signs of one's anxiety (e.g. saying: 'It's hot in here' if the person feels he is noticeably sweating). Physiological responses include heart rate, blushing, sweating and trembling. Some of the physiological responses reflect anxiety (sweating, trembling or shaking), while others reflect embarrassment (blushing). Notably, anxiety is associated with increases in heart rate (Cuthbert et al., 2003), while embarrassment is often associated with decreases in heart rate (Keltner & Buswell, 1997), and either of these experiences may occur in the individual with social anxiety disorder. Behavioural responses include various types of escape and avoidance manoeuvres. As noted by Foa and Kozak (1986), avoidance behaviours may be subtle or of a cognitive nature. Following Salkovskis (1991), Clark and Wells (1995) labelled subtle avoidance behaviours as 'safety behaviours,' emphasizing their cardinal role in the maintenance of social anxiety disorder. Many of these safety behaviors, such as holding a glass tightly, avoiding eye contact, or wearing dark clothing to hide perspiration, can be conceptualized as behavioural responses represented in the fear structure.

Meaning representations of stimuli and responses

Foa and Kozak (1986, 1993) proposed that the meaning of stimuli and responses in the fear structure can be represented in stimuli–stimuli or response–stimuli associations, as well as in evaluations. They emphasized the central role of two cognitive biases, overestimation of the probability of feared harm and exaggerated cost of the negative outcome, in pathological fear structures. This supposition was based partially on Butler and Mathews' (1983) finding that probability and cost of threats were overestimated in anxious groups, and that ambiguous situations were more likely to be interpreted as threatening. Further evidence for the importance of these two cognitive biases in social anxiety comes from more recent research in the area of information processing, which we review below.

With respect to social anxiety disorder, Foa and Kozak (1985) proposed that the exaggerated cost estimates of criticism and social scrutiny are prominent in the pathological fear structure. They further noted that the anxiety responses themselves are associated with threat meaning because they are viewed as drawing criticism, leading to a spiralling of anxiety in social situations. Foa, Franklin and Kozak (2001) further elaborated on this model, proposing that the erroneous meaning of stimuli and responses is influenced by interpretation and judgment biases.

Several studies support the hypothesized relationship between judgment biases about social stimuli and social anxiety disorder. Gilboa-Schechtman et al. (2000) reported that, compared with both anxious and non-anxious controls, patients with generalized social anxiety disorder tended to have greater estimates of probability and cost for unambiguous negative events (e.g. your boss berating you in front of others), greater estimates of negative cost of positive events, and lower estimates of the probability of positive events. Similarly, Foa et al. (1996) found both cost and probability biases in patients with generalized social anxiety disorder, although changes in cost biases were more predictive of change in symptoms of social anxiety after cognitive-behavioural treatment than were changes in probability biases. Consistent with the results of Foa et al. are the findings of Uren, Szabo and Lovibond (2004) that while both cost and probability bias appear to contribute to social anxiety, the former was a stronger predictor of severity. Stopa and Clark's (2000) results further support the relationship between exaggerated cost for negative social events and generalized social anxiety disorder. The primacy of cost over probability could not be tested in their study because the latter was not examined. Interestingly, Uren et al. found that in panic disorder, probability and cost estimates equally predicted the severity of the fear of bodily sensations. Perhaps, then, specific fear structures underlying the anxiety disorders differ in the relative influence that probability and cost estimates have on the threat meaning associated with stimuli and responses.

Two studies examined the hypothesis that the fear structure of social anxiety disorder contains pathological associations between response representations (e.g. heart racing, blushing, sweating) and meaning (e.g. social incompetence). Consistent with this conceptualization, Roth, Antony and Swinson (2001) found that individuals with social anxiety disorder were more likely than controls to interpret their own symptoms of anxiety as pathological (i.e. intense anxiety or some psychiatric problem) and less likely to interpret them as normal. Furthermore, Wells and Papageorgiou (2001a) reported that false feedback regarding pulse rate (e.g. 'Your pulse has increased/decreased') influenced ratings of self-reported anxiety and the strength of their beliefs about an idiosyncratic feared consequence in the expected direction in patients with social anxiety disorder. Thus, perceived strength of responses influences the threat meaning of those responses.

In summary, there are data consistent with the notion that the fear structure of socially anxious individuals is characterized by the pathological associations proposed by Foa and Kozak (1985, 1986). The following aspects distinguish this fear structure from those of other anxiety disorders:

1. The specific stimuli are social, not physical.
2. The structure includes representations of unique physiological responses, such as blushing, in addition to those more commonly associated with anxiety.

3. Specific verbal and behavioural responses are associated with concealing fear responses from others.
4. The meaning of stimuli and response representations is associated with embarrassment, social incompetence and rejection.

Attentional and interpretation biases in social anxiety disorder

The focus of emotional processing theory is to provide a framework for understanding the pathology underlying the different anxiety disorders and the mechanisms by which this pathology is corrected. In its account of the anxiety disorders, emotional processing theory emphasizes the role of judgmental biases; less attention is given to other cognitive biases, such as attentional and interpretation biases. On the other hand, Mathews and colleagues' seminal work has focused on attentional and interpretation biases as the mechanisms underlying the aetiology and maintenance of both normal and pathological anxiety. The cognitive model that emerged from this research is presented in Mathews and Mackintosh (1998) and summarized in Chapter 1. The model states that task demands and the Threat-Evaluation System (TES) compete for attentional resources, and attentional bias towards threat occurs when the TES supercedes the task demands, thereby orienting to the threat stimulus during the parallel processing of threat and neutral stimulus representations. The model suggests that, like attentional bias, interpretation bias also stems from competing resources. However, unlike the competition with task demands in attentional bias, the competition in interpretation bias is between the TES and an appetitive/reward system called the positive evaluation system (PES). It is beyond the scope of this paper to review comprehensively all of the literature on cognitive biases in social anxiety disorder (for recent reviews, see Amir & Foa, 2001; Heinrichs & Hofmann, 2001). The literature on attentional bias and interpretation bias in social anxiety has yielded seemingly conflicting results, many of which may be resolved by Mathews and Mackintosh's model.

Integration of emotional processing and cognitive biases approaches

As noted above, emotional processing theory and Mathews and Mackintosh's (1998) cognitive theory emphasize different aspects of conceptualizing anxiety: the former proposes a model for understanding the maintenance and treatment of different manifestations of pathological anxiety, while the latter proposes a model for understanding interpretation and attentional biases in both clinical and non-clinical anxiety. This difference notwithstanding, the two models share a number of features, a characteristic which facilitates their integration and, in turn, further clarifies processes involved in the maintenance and treatment of social anxiety disorder.

The fear structure and the TES

The concept of 'fear structure' in emotional processing theory is similar to the concept of the TES in Mathews and Mackintosh's cognitive theory. Both concepts suggest that representations of threat stimuli are instantiated in an associative network. Mathews and Mackintosh appear to propose a single threat-evaluation system that is activated by the presence of any threatening stimulus. Foa and Kozak (1986), on the other hand, propose multiple fear structures. Perhaps the most coherent and parsimonious way of integrating the concept of fear structures with the TES is to argue that the TES is comprised of multiple fear structures. Alternatively, the TES may be viewed as comprising a general representation of threat, whereas the stimuli and response elements associated with threat reside in different systems. In either case, the question of how TES accommodates the presence of multiple fears within a single system needs to be explicated.

The proposition of a single threat system would suggest that activation of one fear would lead to increased attention to other feared stimuli. On the other hand, if different fear structures are viewed as relatively independent of one another, then activation of one fear would not lead to increased attention to other feared stimuli. One way to examine this differential hypothesis is through the reactions of individuals with comorbid anxiety disorders. For example, will a patient with comorbid obsessive-compulsive disorder and panic disorder be more attentive to contaminants during a CO_2 challenge that activates their panic disorder fear structure? Another method to examine the generality versus specificity issue is to activate the specific fear of the individual (expecting speech) or a common fear (expecting electric shock) in a patient with social anxiety disorder and testing cognitive biases to social and physical stimuli. The supposition of a general system would lead to the hypothesis that cognitive biases to social threat would be similar in both conditions. The supposition that the fear structures are relatively independent would lead to the hypothesis that under moderate activation, cognitive biases for social threat will be increased after expecting a speech but not after expecting a shock. This kind of research would need to examine the impact of level of activation and the relative similarity across fear structures on the generalization of cognitive biases.

The conceptual relationship between the TES and fear structures informs hypotheses about the associations among judgmental, attentional and interpretation biases. It can be hypothesized that for any stimulus or response represented in a fear structure, estimations of probability and cost are calculated within the TES, and these estimations determine the level of vigilance (attentional biases) and the resolution of ambiguity (interpretation biases). Accordingly, higher probabilities and cost of threat are associated with increased attentional and interpretation biases. Consistent with this hypothesized relationship among the cognitive biases, Mathews and Mackintosh suggest that anxious individuals have more extensive (cf. probability) and higher threat value (cf. cost) representations stored in the TES, partially because they are more sensitive to signals associated with punishment and therefore have stored more information about threat.

By proposing a general TES system, Mathews and Mackintosh (1998) provide an account for the observation that all individuals with anxiety disorder manifest negative cognitive biases more often than do individuals without anxiety disorders. They do not account, however, for the specificity of these biases and the failure to find general biases in individuals with anxiety disorder. Emotional processing theory provides an account for the specificity of the cognitive biases by considering the anxiety disorders as manifestations of specific fear structures that differ in the types of stimuli and/or responses and in their associated meaning. The theory, for example, can account for the observation that physical exercise does not activate the TES in individuals with social anxiety disorder but does activate the TES in individuals with panic disorder (c.f. Schwartz & Kaloupek, 1987). Similarly, the unique physiological responses in social anxiety, such as the blush response, should be less likely to lead to vigilance for fears in non-socially anxious individuals, while it may sensitize unrelated fears in social anxiety. Furthermore, it should be noted that Foa and Kozak (1986) and Mathews and Mackintosh (1998) emphasize the importance of the fear structures/TES potentially operating on two levels of processing (automatic and strategic). Thus, while individuals with social anxiety disorder may be aware of some of the processes that increase their anxiety, they are likely to be unaware of many other such processes.

Application of the integrated model for social anxiety disorder

Emotional processing theory views social anxiety disorder as a manifestation of a pathological fear structure with multiple representations of social situations associated with the threat meaning of being rejected. (We propose that situations that are perceived as irrelevant are not represented in the structure.) The structure includes erroneous associations between stimuli and response representations and their meaning as well as evaluations in the form of exaggerated cost and likelihood of negative social interactions. Thus, most social interactions for a person with generalized social anxiety disorder activate the fear structure. This activation, according to Mathews and Mackintosh, would temporarily sensitize the TES, leading to stronger general cognitive biases. In contrast, emotional processing theory would hypothesize that these biases would increase only for socially relevant material.

The treatment of social anxiety disorder

Modifying the fear structure of social anxiety disorder: special considerations

As noted earlier, Foa and Kozak (1986) suggested that in order to promote emotional processing via exposure therapy (correction of the pathological elements of the target fear structure), the situation that activates the fear structure should incorporate corrective information that is contradictory to the erroneous associations represented in the structure (e.g. people are nice, not nasty). Generally, the corrective information is embedded in the absence of harm during confrontation with the feared situation, object or memory (e.g. giving a speech without the audience booing), thus leading the patients to evaluative changes. Indeed, Hope et al. (1995) found that negative social cognitions decreased significantly after exposure therapy. However, for emotional processing to occur, it is essential that the patient perceive that the feared consequences did not materialize. For a patient with a dog phobia who is confronted with a friendly dog, the absence of negative consequences is obvious. However, because of the nature of social interactions, information disconfirming the patient's belief that others will judge him or her negatively is often obscure (e.g. people do not typically provide unambiguous praise, 'You were absolutely fantastic!', or unambiguous criticism, 'You were totally inadequate!'). A number of factors may interfere with encoding the disconfirming information: the ambiguity of feedback from others, engaging in safety behaviours, attentional bias and interpretation bias. The ambiguity of a social situation stems from the fact that explicit negative feedback during social interactions is censored. Moreover, individuals rarely demonstrate unified enthusiasm after a social interaction. Thus, the absence of open criticism or the presence of some compliments cannot be interpreted as an indication that the individuals involved in a given social interaction greatly and unanimously enjoyed it. Safety behaviours (Clark & Wells, 1995; Salkovskis, 1991), also referred to as subtle avoidance behaviours (Foa & Kozak, 1986), are performed in order to prevent the feared consequences, reinforcing the perception that criticism or rejection would have occurred had such behaviours been unsuccessful. Attentional and interpretation biases lead to selective encoding of social situations as negative, thus further impeding opportunities for emotional processing in the natural environment of the individual with social phobia.

It follows that the goal of treatment is to set up social situations in sessions that will both activate the fear structure and provide unambiguous information that disconfirms the patient's negative perceptions and evaluations. In other words, successful treatment imposes task demands that are sufficiently strong to override the hypervigilance of negative feedback and force the patient to incorporate evidence for the adequate social performance. In this way, disconfirming evidence, either during or after the contrived social situation, is incorporated into the fear structure, thus reducing the probability and cost of negative outcomes.

Accordingly, a number of techniques that have recently been introduced into cognitive behavioural therapies for social anxiety disorder emphasize the elimination of safety behaviours and the encouragement of outward focus (Clark & Wells, 1995). Treatments utilizing these techniques have shown a successful reduction of social anxiety (Clark et al., in press; Wells & Papageorgiou, 2001b). To optimize emotional processing, we have incorporated these techniques with imaginal and in vivo exposure and social skills training into our individualized Comprehensive Cognitive Behavioural Therapy (CCBT; Huppert, Roth & Foa, 2003).

How to overcome difficulties in activating the fear structure of individuals with social anxiety disorder

By definition, individuals with social anxiety disorder, like other phobic individuals, are reluctant to engage in fear evoking situations that may lead to anxiety. Thus, the instructions to confront such situations in vivo or in imagination are threatening. A special complication in the treatment of social anxiety disorder is that patients often view the therapist as a potential source of evaluation and rejection. Thus, engaging in exposures in the presence of the therapist is threatening in and of itself, and sufficient activation can occur through a simple conversation with the therapist or a confederate. If a patient completely refuses to engage in an in vivo situation that would activate even low levels of anxiety, imaginal exposure may be indicated. For details, see the section below. Overall, clinical experience suggests that most individuals with social anxiety disorder have little problem activating their fear structures; as noted above, the problem lies with their difficulties in incorporating disconfirming evidence into their fear structure.

How to overcome the difficulties in disconfirming feared catastrophes of individuals with social anxiety disorder

One obstacle to successful integration of disconfirming evidence into the pathological fear structure of individuals with social anxiety disorder lies in their claim that although the contrived social situations activate fear, they are artificial and, thus, do not reflect the real world. This claim may reflect the perception that while the contrived situation may tap some aspect of the fear, it is not a 'true' representation of their core fear. For example, a conversation with a stooge in the therapist's office is not equivalent to a conversation with a potential date. Despite such protests, positive outcomes of repeated exposure during sessions combined with homework exposures do eventually get incorporated into the patient's fear structure. Another obstacle is that the feedback given in the contrived situation is not viewed as credible. A combination of feedback from the confederate about his or her own anxiety, the patient's anxiety and an estimation of both people's performance increases perceived credibility and facilitates the modification of the erroneous beliefs. Further, corrective information can be provided through video feedback (e.g. Harvey, Clark, Ehlers & Rapee, 2000; Kim, Lundh & Harvey, 2002).

Socially anxious individuals often appear extremely awkward because of their anxiety and safety behaviour (Clark, 2001). It follows that after successful treatment the awkward behaviour will disappear without direct intervention. However, our clinical impression is that some patients continue to exhibit poor social skills after safety behaviours have been dropped, and their perception that others are evaluating them negatively is realistic, thereby strengthening the association between social situations and rejection. We believe that with these patients, social skills training is indicated. This includes both assertiveness training and initiating, maintaining and ending conversations. According to our clinical experience, many patients with social anxiety disorder are not assertive because they perceive their assertive behaviour as aggressive and likely to evoke rejection. Their use of passive behaviours has become so habitual that without social skills training their inappropriate behaviour remains unchanged. Similarly, we have seen patients who have been so isolated because of their social anxiety that they are unable to access the skills required for successful social interactions. Social skills training equips the patient with social behaviours that are likely to result in a positive outcome, which in turn provides disconfirmatory information that modifies their fear structure.

The use of imagery versus in vivo situations: the unique application in social anxiety disorder

Despite evidence for the efficacy of imaginal exposure in the treatment of social anxiety in early studies (e.g. Schwartz & Kaloupek, 1987; Chaplin & Levine, 1981), it has generally fallen into disuse. However, given the importance of imagery in social anxiety disorder (see Hirsch & Clark, this volume), this procedure seems to have a rediscovered relevance in treating this disorder. The specific guidelines for forming the content of the imaginal exposure in the early studies differed from those used successfully with obsessive-compulsive disorder (Kozak & Foa, 1997) and post-traumatic stress disorder (Foa & Rothbaum, 1998). Some methods of imaginal exposure have used positive imagery scripting, positive coping to negative outcomes, or recall of past negative events (Chaplin & Levine, 1981; Schwartz & Kaloupek, 1987). However, Foa and colleagues' way of using imaginal exposure focuses on the exaggerated consequences. The rationale given to the patients for this approach is that socially anxious individuals do not distinguish sufficiently between their thoughts about possible catastrophes (the entire audience laughing at them) and reality (a few people not liking the talk), and, therefore, these thoughts make them extremely anxious. As a result, they attempt to suppress the thoughts, an attempt that increases the frequency and intensity of the catastrophic thoughts (thought suppression paradox, Wenzlaff & Wegner, 2000). The repeated imagery of the feared consequence sharpens the distinction between reality and imagery. This process is similar to that involved in repeatedly watching a scary movie; both increase one's realization that fear, which is a reaction to an imminent threat, is unwarranted. Accordingly, patients are asked to imagine extremely unrealistic negative outcomes (e.g. the patient speaking in public, the audience booing incessantly and shouting the speaker down, and concluding with rotten tomatoes being thrown at the patient). Frequently, the ultimate consequence is rejection and isolation/alienation from others. Our clinical experience with many patients is that such exposures result not only in decreased anxiety and avoidance, but also in boredom or humour.

Imaginal exposure is used in two circumstances:

1. When patients have catastrophic predictions of specific outcomes that are not easily testable or have been repeatedly discounted (e.g. that the audience will evaluate a performance extremely critically), or
2. When patients refuse to confront situations in their hierarchy due to extreme anxiety.

Through repeated exposure to the imagined scenario, the patient learns to tolerate his or her anxiety to the feared scenario, and after some repetitions comes to view the imagined scenario as boring, ridiculous or even funny. Indeed, direct exposure to feared social consequences of the patient can only be achieved in imagination (e.g. the patient being rejected by everyone).

Research with anxiety disorders has shown that repeated imaginal exposure to feared consequences leads to between-session reduction of anxiety (see earlier discussion). Foa and Kozak (1986) proposed that imaginal exposure reduces the exaggerated cost and thereby the estimated probability of the negative outcomes. We suggest that this cognitive process mediates reduction of the anxiety and avoidance of feared situations. In other words, imaginal exposure results in a new, non-threat cognitive structure. This new structure is consolidated through information provided during the contrived, in vivo situations described above. The new associations lower the threshold of the TES during threat situations, thereby decreasing interpretation and attentional biases. Here, we suggest that the same processes take place when imaginal exposure is implemented with socially anxious patients. Indeed, our socially anxious patients exhibit the same pattern of between-session fear reduction and cognitive change.

Modification in the structure of individuals with social anxiety disorder after treatment

After successful treatment for an individual with social anxiety disorder, there are a number of changes that would indicate the formation of a non-pathological social structure. These include reduced:
1. Probability estimates,
2. Cost estimates,
3. Attentional biases,
4. Interpretation bias,
5. Belief that anxiety during social situations remains for ever, and
6. Beliefs about the consequence of social situations (e.g. being rejected).

The first four indicators are changes in information processing that likely lead to the changes in the latter two, as well as a general reduction in symptoms. Furthermore, these changes should also reflect a lowered threshold of the positive-evaluation system (PES) and a higher threshold of the threat-evaluation system (TES), especially in social situations.

Discussion

In this chapter, we have presented a theoretical account of social anxiety disorder that draws on emotional processing theory and Mathews and

Mackintosh's (1998) cognitive model of selective processing in anxiety. How does this revised theory differ from other accounts of social anxiety disorder? Two elaborate theories of social anxiety disorders have been proposed (Clark & Wells, 1995; Rapee & Heimberg, 1997). Both theories account for a variety of the clinical manifestations of the disorder and have made a major contribution to clinical practice. However, emotional processing theory is distinguished in the following ways:

1. It is a general theory of the mechanisms and treatment of pathological anxiety, and thus explains social anxiety disorder within the framework of other anxiety disorders.

2. Consistent with modern learning theories (e.g. Rescorla, 1988), it posits that pathological (erroneous) meaning often resides in associations among representations and does not always involve awareness and recruitment of language processes, such as evaluations and attributions. Thus, it accounts for clinical observations that patients do not always have explanations about their anxiety.

3. Because it conceptualizes meaning in associations among stimuli and/or responses, it accounts for natural recovery and for the efficacy of exposure therapy in the absence of cognitive interventions (e.g. Hope et al., 1995), as well as for the efficacy of cognitive interventions.

4. It explains the efficacy of imaginal exposure to feared catastrophes as a potentially powerful treatment technique.

5. It provides a fuller understanding of social anxiety disorder within an information processing framework and thus generates new hypotheses for future research.

NOTE

We would like to thank Shawn P. Cahill, Jenny Yiend and an anonymous reviewer for their thoughts on earlier drafts of this manuscript.

REFERENCES

Amir, N. & Foa, E. B. (2001). Cognitive biases in social phobia. In S. Hofman & P. M. DiBartolo (Eds.), *From Social Anxiety to Social Phobia: Multiple Perspectives*, 268–280. Needham, MA: Allyn & Bacon.

Avero, P. & Calvo, M. G. (1999). Emotional reactivity to social-evaluative stress: gender differences in response systems concordance. *Personality and Individual Differences*, *27*, 155–170.

Bouton, M. E. (2000). A learning theory perspective on lapse, relapse, and the maintenance of behavior change. *Health Psychology*, *19*, 57–63.

Butler, G. & Mathews, A. (1983). Cognitive processes in anxiety. *Advances in Behaviour Research and Therapy*, *5*, 51–62.

Chaplin, E. W. & Levine, B. A. (1981). The effects of total exposure duration and interrupted versus continuous exposure in flooding therapy. *Behavior Therapy*, *12*, 360–368.

Clark, D. M. (2001). A cognitive perspective on social phobia. In W. R. Crozier & L. E. Alden (Eds.), *International Handbook of Social Anxiety: Concepts, Research and Interventions Related to the Self and Shyness*, 405–430. New York: Wiley.

Clark, D. M., Ehlers, A., McManus, F., Hackmann, A., Fennell, M., et al. (in press). Cognitive therapy vs. fluoxetine in generalized social phobia: a randomized placebo controlled trial. *Journal of Consulting and Clinical Psychology*.

Clark, D. M. & Wells, A. (1995). A cognitive model of social phobia. In R. G. Heimberg, M. R. Liebowitz, D. A. Hope & F. R. Schneier (Eds.), *Social Phobia: Diagnosis, Assessment, and Treatment*, 69–93. New York: Guilford.

Cuthbert, B. N., Lang, P. J., Strauss, C., Drobes, D., Patrick, C. J. & Bradley, M. M. (2003). The psychophysiology of anxiety disorder: fear memory imagery. *Psychophysiology, 40*, 407–422.

De Silva, P. & Rachman, S. (1984). Does escape behavior strengthen agoraphobic avoidance? A preliminary study. *Behaviour Research and Therapy, 22*, 87–91.

Emmelkamp, P. M. G. (1974). Self-observation versus flooding in the treatment of agoraphobia. *Behaviour Research and Therapy, 12*, 229–237.

Foa, E. B. & Cahill, S. P. (2001). Emotional processing in psychological therapies. In N. J. Smelser & P. B. Bates (Eds.), *International Encyclopedia of the Social and Behavioral Science*, 12363–12369. Oxford: Elsevier.

Foa, E. B. & Chambless, D. (1978). Habituation of subjective anxiety during flooding in imagery. *Behaviour Research and Therapy, 16*, 391–399.

Foa, E. B., Franklin, M. E. & Kozak, M. J. (2001). Social phobia: an information processing perspective. In S. Hofman & P. M. DiBartolo (Eds.), *From Social Anxiety to Social Phobia: Multiple Perspectives*, 268–280. Needham, MA: Allyn & Bacon.

Foa, E. B., Franklin, M. E., Perry, K. J. & Herbert, J. D. (1996). Cognitive biases in generalized social phobia. *Journal of Abnormal Psychology, 105*, 433–439.

Foa, E. B., Grayson, J. B., Steketee, G. S., Doppelt, H. G., Turner, R. M. & Latimer, P. R. (1983). Success and failure in the behavioral treatment of obsessive-compulsives. *Journal of Counseling and Clinical Psychology, 51*, 287–297.

Foa, E. B. & Kozak, M. J. (1985). Treatment of anxiety disorders: implications for psychopathology. In A. H. Tuma & J. D. Maser (Eds.), *Anxiety and the Anxiety Disorders*. Hillsdale, NJ: Erlbaum.

Foa, E. B. & Kozak, M. J. (1986). Emotional processing of fear: exposure to corrective information. *Psychological Bulletin, 99*, 20–35.

Foa, E. B. & Kozak, M. J. (1993). Pathological anxiety: the meaning and the structure of fear. In N. Birbaumer & A. Öhman (Eds.), *The Structure of Emotion*, 110–121. Toronto, Canada: Hogrefe, Int.

Foa, E. B. & McNally, R. J. (1996). Mechanisms of change in exposure therapy. In Rapee, R. M. (Ed.), *Current Controversies in the Anxiety Disorders*. New York: Guilford Press.

Foa, E. B. & Rothbaum B. O. (1998). *Treating the Trauma of Rape: Cognitive-behavioral Therapy for PTSD*. New York: Guilford.

Gilboa-Schechtman, E., Franklin, M. E. & Foa, E. B. (2000). Anticipated reactions to social events: differences among individuals with generalized social phobia, obsessive compulsive disorder, and nonanxious controls. *Cognitive Therapy and Research, 24,* 731–746.

Hackmann, A., Clark, D. M. & McManus, F. (2000). Recurrent images and early memories in social phobia. *Behaviour Research and Therapy, 38,* 601–610.

Harvey, A. G., Clark, D. M., Ehlers, A. & Rapee, R. M. (2000). Social anxiety and self-impression: cognitive preparation enhances the beneficial effects of video feedback following a stressful social task. *Behaviour Research and Therapy, 38,* 1183–1192.

Heinrichs, N. & Hofmann, S. G. (2001). Information processing in social phobia: a critical review. *Clinical Psychology Review, 21,* 751–770.

Hope, D. A., Heimberg, R. G. & Bruch, M. A. (1995). Dismantling cognitive-behavioral group therapy for social phobia. *Behaviour Research and Therapy, 33,* 637–650.

Huppert, J. D., Roth, D. A. & Foa, E. B. (2003). Cognitive behavioral therapy for social phobia: new advances. *Current Psychiatry Reports, 5,* 289–296.

Jaycox, L. H., Foa, E. B. & Morral, A. R. (1998). Influence of emotional engagement and habituation on exposure therapy for PTSD. *Journal of Consulting and Clinical Psychology, 66,* 185–192.

Keltner, D. & Buswell, B. N. (1997). Embarrassment: its distinct form and appeasement functions. *Psychological Bulletin, 122,* 250–270.

Kessler, R. C., Stein, M. B. & Berglund. (1998). Social phobia subtypes in the National Comorbidity Survey. *American Journal of Psychiatry, 155,* 613–619.

Kim, H. Y., Lundh, L. G. & Harvey, A. (2002). The enhancement of video feedback by cognitive preparation in the treatment of social anxiety: a single session experiment. *Journal of Behavior Therapy and Experimental Psychiatry, 33,* 19–37.

Kozak, M. J. & Foa, E. B. (1997). *Mastery of Obsessive-Compulsive Disorder: a Cognitive-Behavioral Approach (Therapist Guide).* Boulder, CO: Graywind Publications Incorporated.

Kozak, M. J., Foa, E. B. & Steketee, G. (1988). Process and outcome of exposure treatment with obsessive-compulsives: psychophysiological indicators of emotional processing. *Behavior Therapy, 19,* 157–169.

Lang, P. J. (1977). Imagery in therapy: an information processing analysis of fear. *Behavior Therapy, 8,* 862–886.

Lang, P. J., Davis, M. & Öhman, A. (2000). Fear and anxiety: animal models and human cognitive psychophysiology. *Journal of Affective Disorders, 61,* 137–159.

Mathews, A. M., Johnston, D. W., Sahw, P. M. & Gelder, M. G. (1974). Process variables and the prediction of outcome in behaviour therapy. *British Journal of Psychiatry, 125,* 256–264.

Mathews, A. & Mackintosh, B. (1998). A cognitive model of selective processing in anxiety. *Cognitive Therapy and Research, 22,* 539–560.

Rabavilas, A. D., Boulougouris, J. C. & Stefanis, C. (1976). Duration of flooding sessions in the treatment of obsessive-compulsive patients. *Behaviour Research and Therapy, 14,* 349–355.

Rachman, S. J., Craske, M. G., Tallman, K. & Solyom, C. (1986). Does escape behavior strengthen avoidance? A replication. *Behavior Therapy, 17,* 366–384.

Rapee, R. M. & Heimberg, R. G. (1997). A cognitive-behavioral model of anxiety in social phobia. *Behavior Research and Therapy*, *35*, 741–756.

Rescorla, R. A. (1988). Pavlovian conditioning: it's not what you think it is. *American Psychologist*, *43*, 151–160.

Rescorla, R. A. (2001). Experimental extinction. In R. R. Mowrer & S. B. Klein (Eds.), *Handbook of Contemporary Learning Theories*. Mahwah, NJ: Erlbaum.

Roth, D., Antony, M. M. & Swinson, R. P. (2001). Attributions for anxiety symptoms in social phobia. *Behavior Research and Therapy*, *39*(2), 129–138.

Salkovskis, P. M. (1991). The importance of behaviour in the maintenance of anxiety and panic: a cognitive account. *Behavioural Psychotherapy*, *19*, 6–19.

Schwartz, S. G. & Kaloupek, D. G. (1987). Acute exercise combined with imaginal exposure as a technique for anxiety reduction. *Canadian Journal of Behavioral Science*, *19*, 151–166.

Solomon, R. L., Kamin, L. J. & Wynne, L. C. (1953). Traumatic avoidance learning: the outcomes of several extinction procedures with dogs. *Journal of Abnormal and Social Psychology*, *48*, 291–302.

Stern, R. S. & Marks, I. M. (1973). Brief and prolonged exposure: a comparison in agoraphobic patients. *Archives of General Psychiatry*, *28*, 270–276.

Stopa, L. & Clark, D. M. (2000). Social phobia and interpretation of social events. *Behaviour Research and Therapy*, *38*, 273–283.

Uren, T. H., Szabo, M. & Lovibond, P. F. (2004). Probability and cost estimates for social and physical outcomes in social phobia and panic disorder. *Journal of Anxiety Disorders*, *18*, 481–498.

Van Minnen, A. & Foa, E. B. (submitted). The effects of long versus short imaginal exposure on treatment outcome of PTSD.

Wells, A. & Papageorgiou, C. (2001a). Social phobic interoception: effects of bodily information on anxiety, beliefs and self-processing. *Behaviour Research and Therapy*, *39*, 1–11.

Wells, A. & Papageorgiou, C. (2001b). Brief cognitive therapy for social phobia: a case series. *Behaviour Research and Therapy*, *39*, 653–658.

Wenzlaff, R. M. & Wegner, D. M. (2000). Thought suppression. In S. T. Fiske (Ed.), *Annual Review of Psychology*, vol. 51, 59–91. Palo Alto, CA: Annual Reviews.

11   Mental imagery and social phobia

Colette R. Hirsch and David M. Clark

O wad some Pow'r the giftie gie us
To see oursels as ithers see us!

– Robert Burns, 'To a Louse'

When Robert Burns wrote this verse, he was observing how useful it would be for people to know how they come across to others. In a Festschrift to mark Andrew Mathews' distinguished career, we would like to reflect on how he comes across to his colleagues. Andrew Mathews is a visionary scientist who has made an enormous impact on the field. There are many reasons for the substantial impact his research programme has had over the years. First, Andrew Mathews and colleagues have been adept at devising novel paradigms that capture the essence of a clinical phenomenon while at the same time meeting all the rigorous requirements of experimental psychology. In this way, they have created paradigms and investigative approaches that have become classics in the field. Second, his attention to detail has allowed him to dissect phenomena in a way that enhances our understanding. A well-known example is isolating disengagement from stimuli (rather than lowered detection thresholds) as a key aspect of anxiety related attentional abnormalities (Yiend & Mathews, 2001). Third, while actively pursuing a theoretically driven approach, Andrew does not allow allegiance to one particular position to restrict his thinking and, as a consequence, can happily follow the data wherever they lead. Finally, his willingness to share his ideas and paradigms with others and his generous support of younger researchers has enriched the field and those who work within it.

Some of Andrew's recent research has focused on individuals who do not have an accurate understanding of how others see them. The thesis of this chapter is that inaccurate images of how one appears to others play an important role in social phobia, and that the condition can be substantially ameliorated by procedures that help us 'to see oursels as ithers see us'.

Imagery in anxiety disorders

Several cognitive-behavioural theorists (Beck, 1976; Clark & Beck, 1988; Hackmann, 1999) have suggested that imagery[1] plays a key role in the development and maintenance of anxiety disorders. It is suggested that spontaneous mental images are common, encapsulate patients' distorted beliefs about the dangerousness of feared situations and/or internal states and enhance subjective estimates of danger. Furthermore, it is suggested that although anxiety-related images are often future oriented, they are in part based on memorial representations of past events.

A number of studies have supported the general proposal that negative imagery is common in anxiety disorders. Beck, Laude and Bohnert (1974) interviewed patients with a mixture of anxiety disorders. Spontaneous images were frequently reported, and tended to depict physical and/or psychosocial danger. Subsequent studies focused on specific anxiety disorders. Ottaviani and Beck (1987) interviewed patients with panic disorder and found that they reported a high frequency of images concerned with personal physical or mental catastrophes. De Silva (1986) found that patients with obsessive-compulsive disorder reported images that were similar to their obsessive thoughts and involved themes of death, illness, violence, decay, disaster, sex and blasphemy. Wells and Hackmann (1993) found negative images were common in health anxiety. The themes of the images focused on misinterpretation of symptoms, overestimates of the likelihood of illness or death, and the interpersonal consequences of illness or death. Intriguingly, the latter theme only emerged from a content analysis of images; it had not been evident in earlier analyses (Warwick & Salkovskis, 1990) of negative thoughts.

In the next sections, we focus in more detail on imagery in social phobia. Before doing so, a few words about the nature of social phobia are in order.

Social phobia

Individuals with social phobia fear that if they exhibit symptoms of anxiety or behave in ways which they believe are inept or unacceptable, then this will lead to their embarrassment and rejection by others in social situations (such as: public speaking, meetings, talking to authority figures and working or eating while being observed). As a syndrome, social phobia is the third most common psychiatric disorder, with estimated lifetime prevalence rates of 7–13 per cent (Wittchen, Stein & Kessler, 1999; Kessler, McGonagle, Zhao, Nelson, Hughes, Eshleman et al., 1994) and a typical age of onset in childhood or early adolescence (Schneier, Johnson, Hornig, Leibowitz & Weissman, 1992). Social phobia often results in under-performance at work and can make it difficult for patients to develop and maintain close relationships (Turner, Beidel, Dancu & Keys, 1986; Caspi, Edler & Bem, 1988). The social requirements and demands of society mean that most individuals with social phobia have to regularly enter at least some of the social situations that they find anxiety-provoking. Despite such repeated, naturalistic exposure, the phobia persists. This observation indicates that avoidance alone cannot provide an adequate explanation for the maintenance of social phobia. Some abnormality in the way patients process social situations is also implicated.

A theoretical view of the role of imagery in the maintenance of social phobia

In 1995, Clark and Wells proposed a theoretical account of the maintenance of social phobia that has a strong emphasis on imagery. Figure 11.1 shows the main processes that are hypothesized to occur when someone with social phobia enters a feared situation (see Clark & Wells, 1995; Clark, 2000 for further details of the theory). As a consequence of problematic beliefs about social performance in general and one's social abilities in particular, the patient with social phobia is prone to interpret certain social situations as highly threatening, triggering negative automatic thoughts such as: 'I'll blush', 'People will see I'm anxious', 'I'm being boring' etc. The perception of social danger is accompanied by physiological symptoms of anxiety (e.g. feeling hot, sweating etc.) that often further increase the perceived danger (e.g. 'My face is hot; people will see the blush and think I am weird'). There is also a shift in attention, with relatively less processing of external social cues and enhanced self-focused attention. In this self-focused mode, patients continually monitor their social performance and use internal information to make excessively negative inferences about the way they appear to others. One source of internal information is feelings of anxiety, with patients erroneously thinking: 'Because I feel very anxious, I must look very anxious' (see Mansell & Clark, 1999). A further source of internal information is thought to be spontaneously occurring images and impressions.

It is hypothesized that patients with social phobia use a combination of memories of past aversive social situations and interoceptive information gained from self-focused attention to construct an impression of how they think that they are coming across to other people, which often manifests itself as a self-image.

The self-image is said to be a distorted view of the patient's performance and physical presentation. The image often involves seeing oneself as if from the vantage point of another individual (observer perspective).

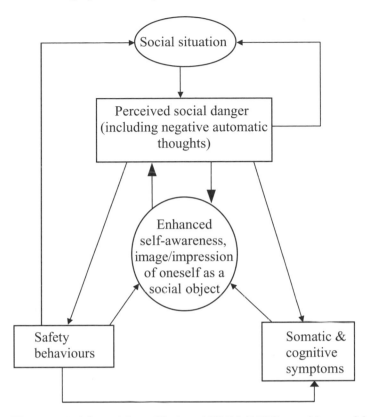

Figure 11.1 Adapted from Clark and Wells' (1995) cognitive model of social phobia.

The content of the image is often a visualization of some aspect of the patient's worst fears. For example, individuals with a fear of blushing typically visualize themselves with much more marked coloration than is actually the case. The occurrence of a negative self-image is said to enhance perceptions of danger and, as a consequence, prompt the use of safety behaviours. Safety behaviours are attempts to prevent or minimize the feared catastrophes (Salkovskis, 1991). Some safety behaviours are mental operations (e.g. memorizing what one has just said and comparing it with what one is about to say, speaking in order to avoid appearing foolish), whilst others are more obvious behavioural manoeuvres (e.g. averting one's face to hide blushing). Safety behaviours can sometimes exacerbate the problem. For example, a self-image that showed a marked hand tremor may prompt a safety behaviour, such as holding a glass very tightly in an attempt to prevent others noticing, but this can aggravate the tremor. Another consequence of some safety behaviours is that the person with social phobia may appear unfriendly or uninterested in others. For example, if the self-image includes sounding boring, a person may adopt the safety behaviour of deliberately saying very little in a conversation. However, others may misinterpret the lack of contribution to the conversation as being aloof, and thus the safety behaviour may have 'contaminated' the social situation. Furthermore, using safety behaviours undermines any potential reduction in negative beliefs, since non-occurrence of catastrophes is attributed to the use of safety behaviours, rather than to the fact that the catastrophe was unlikely to have occurred anyway.

Finally, Clark and Wells (1995) hypothesize that self-imagery may also contribute to problematic post-event processing. When people with social phobia leave social situations, they usually ruminate on their performance in the situation. Since they believe that the self-image is a largely true representation of how they come across and since they do not have external feedback because they were self-focused during the social event, the negative self-image may be regenerated and examined further during this post-event processing. This process results in a further emphasis on negative aspects of the situation and ensures that heightened distress continues for a long time after the social event has finished.

Phenomenology of imagery in social phobia

Initial investigations of the imagery aspects of Clark and Wells' (1995) theoretical account focused on whether the phenomenology of images in social phobia is as envisaged in the theory. In the first study, Wells, Clark and Ahmad (1998) asked patients with social phobia and other non-patient controls to recall recent, anxiety-provoking social and non-social situations, and to generate an image. Whilst holding the image in mind, they were asked whether the image was predominantly from an observer (i.e. as looking at the self from outside) or a field (i.e. as if looking out through one's own eyes) perspective. For social situations, patients with social phobia reported having more of an observer perspective than the control group, who had predominantly a field perspective. The two groups did not differ in their perspective for non-social situations, which was predominately from a field perspective. Hence, in intentional recall and construction of an image, there is a predominance of observer perspective imagery in social phobia.

Coles, Turk, Heimberg and Fresco (2001) built on the study by Wells et al. (1998) by asking patients with social phobia and non-anxious controls to recall three different social situations: namely, the most recent time they felt high, moderate and low social anxiety. Once a given situation was recalled, participants were asked to generate an image of themselves in the situation and then indicate the predominant perspective of the image. In keeping with Wells et al. (1998), individuals with social phobia reported a predominance of observer perspective images for the high-anxiety-provoking social situation, but the images for the moderate and low-anxiety situations were from a predominantly field perspective. The control group had a predominant field perspective for all situations.

A potential problem with the Wells et al. (1998) and Coles et al. (2001) studies is that it is possible that the content of the situations recalled may have differed between the social phobia and control groups. To control for the content of the event, Coles, Turk and Heimberg (2002) conducted a study where patients with social phobia and non-patient controls participated in standardized social situations (a speech and a conversation with a stranger). Patients with social phobia showed a greater observer perspective bias in images constructed immediately after the social event, suggesting that previous findings were not simply a function of patients and controls recalling different events. Intriguingly, the difference in perspective between patients and controls became more marked when participants were asked to recall the event again, three weeks later. This is consistent with the possibility that the observer perspective images of patients with social phobia may be further developed during post-event processing.

Although consistent with aspects of Clark and Wells' (1995) theory, the preceding three studies have limitations. First, participants were asked to generate an image retrospectively. It is possible that images generated in this way may be different from spontaneous images. Second, the content of the images was not assessed, so it is not known whether the images are negative, as required by the theory. To address these issues, Hackmann, Surawy and Clark (1998) conducted a semi-structured interview, in which they asked patients with social phobia and non-patient controls to recall a recent social situation when they felt anxious. They were then asked if at the time of the event they had had any spontaneous imagery.[2] Participants described the content of any imagery, rated its dominant perspective and were asked to assess the extent to which the image seemed distorted. Patients were significantly more likely to report spontaneous images than the controls. The social phobia group's images were from a predominantly observer perspective, whereas the controls had a field perspective for any imagery reported. An independent rater, who did not know which group the image content was from, rated the social phobia group's imagery as more negative than the control group's imagery. In retrospect, patients were able to realize that their images were to some extent distorted. Patients' images seemed to be more a visualization of their feared outcomes, rather than how they actually looked. For example, a young teacher who was anxious about talking with colleagues reported feeling tension around her mouth before asking a question. The tense feelings triggered an image of herself with a twisted mouth 'looking like the village idiot' (Clark, 1997, p. 141). A key finding of the study by Hackmann et al. (1998) was that the proportion of participants who reported experiencing negative, distorted, observer perspective images whilst in the anxiety-provoking social situation was greater in the social phobia (77 per cent) than the control group (10 per cent).

An unexpected observation in the study by Hackmann et al. (1998) prompted a follow-up investigation. Some patients had commented during the semi-structured interview that they experienced a similar image of themselves in many different social situations. To assess whether such recurrent images are common, and to obtain preliminary information about their origin, Hackmann, Clark and McManus (2000) conducted a further semi-structured interview study. All patients with social phobia reported recurrent images. When asked whether a particular event was associated with the first occurrence of the image, 96 per cent of patients were able to identify a specific, embarrassing or humiliating experience. Often, the event was from many years ago. Dating of the events indicated that they tended to cluster around the onset of the social phobia. It could be the case that patients with social phobia develop an image of their anxious social self on the basis of early, traumatic social experiences, and that this image is repeatedly reactivated in subsequent anxiety-provoking situations, without being substantially updated in the light of experience.

A further aspect of the study by Hackmann et al. (2000) involved assessing the modalities of self-images. The modality most frequently reported was visual, evident in 86 per cent of images, but 82 per cent of images included body sensations and/or perceptions and 32 per cent involved auditory aspects of the image. The images often comprised more than one modality. For example, of those who reported visual aspects to the image, 74 per cent noted that other modalities were also present.

In summary, people with social phobia report experiencing negative images of themselves performing poorly in social situations. These images comprise a variety of modalities, may be experienced from an observer-perspective and are often linked to an aversive social experience that may date back to around the time of the onset of the disorder.

Causal status of imagery in social phobia

The phenomenological studies reviewed above indicate that negative imagery is common in social phobia, and that the content of the images is broadly in line with Clark and Wells' (1995) theoretical account. However, it could be argued, in line with a common criticism of cognitive accounts (see Rosenhan & Seligman, 1995, p. 128), that the images are epiphenomena that have no causal role in social anxiety. To establish a causal role, it is necessary to manipulate imagery experimentally and demonstrate that such manipulations can modulate aspects of social anxiety.

A causal role for imagery in eliciting anxious mood

To date, two studies have experimentally manipulated imagery and investigated the effects of the manipulation on anxious mood. Both have provided support for the causal hypothesis. Hirsch, Clark, Mathews and Williams (2003a) asked patients with social phobia to have two conversations with a stranger, one while holding their usual negative self-image in mind and the other while holding a less negative (control) self-image in mind. Half the patients had the images elicited by semi-structured interview, based on a memory of a time when they felt anxious (negative image) or felt relaxed (control image) in a social situation. The other patients had the images elicited on the basis of the image they had of themselves during an earlier conversation with a stranger prior to (negative image) or after (control image) cognitive preparation and video feedback (see 'negative imagery as a target for treatment' section below for more details of cognitive preparation and video feedback). Compared to the control image, when participants held their usual negative image in mind during the experimental conversations (irrespective of how the images were elicited) they reported more anxiety, as assessed by the state form of the Spielberger State Trait Anxiety Inventory (STAI: Spielberger, Gorsuch, Lushene, Vagg & Jacobs, 1983) completed retrospectively in relation to how they felt during the conversation.

Hirsch, Meynen and Clark (2004) asked high social anxiety volunteers to have conversations with a person whom they had never previously met and who did not know that the study related to social anxiety or imagery. During one conversation, the socially anxious volunteers held a negative self-image in mind, while during the other conversation they held in mind a less negative (control) self-image. The images were elicited using the semi-structured interview used by Hirsch et al. (2003a). Once again, the negative imagery condition was associated with significantly higher levels of anxious mood (as assessed by STAI).

A causal role for imagery in perceptions of one's social performance

In addition to investigating the impact of negative imagery on patients' anxiety during a social situation, Hirsch et al. (2003a) also assessed patients' perception of their own performance and, for an objective assessment of the performance, an assessor rated videotapes of the patients. When patients held their negative image in mind during the conversation, they rated their anxiety symptoms as being more visible to others and their performance as poorer, compared to when they held the control image in mind. For both conversations, patients underestimated their performance relative to an independent assessor, who rated a videotape of the conversation. This suggests that the patients based their judgments of how they appear on information that was not available to the assessor, and this information may have included their self-image. In keeping with this, the patients' underestimation of their own performance was greater in the negative image condition, as compared to the control condition.

A more critical rating of self-performance and observable anxiety was also evident for the high socially anxious individuals reported by Hirsch et al. (2004), who believed that they came across less well and showed more symptoms of anxiety when holding the negative image in mind than when holding the control image in mind. Once again, imagery also influenced the extent to which individuals underestimated their performance. In particular, the discrepancy between individuals' ratings of their own performance and their conversational partners' ratings of them was significantly greater in the negative image condition.

A causal role for negative imagery in contamination of social situations

In addition to the increased anxiety and more critical self-assessment of performance, negative imagery appears to be associated with observable changes in patients' performance and the quality of the interaction. Hirsch et al. (2003a) report that an assessor observed poorer performance and more symptoms of anxiety when patients held a negative image in mind than when they held the control self-image in mind. This effect was also evident in the study by Hirsch et al. (2004). The conversational partner rated the socially anxious person's performance more critically in the negative image condition than in the control condition. Furthermore, both the conversational partner and the socially anxious participant themselves rated the quality of the conversation as poorer in the negative image condition, as compared to the control condition.

The more critical evaluation of the anxious individuals by other people must be based on observable changes in their behaviour. Clark and Wells (1995) suggested that greater use of safety behaviours may lead to more negative evaluations by others. Consistent with this suggestion, Hirsch et al. (2004) found that socially anxious participants reported using more safety behaviours in the negative image condition and there was a significant correlation between self-reported use of safety behaviours and ratings of the quality of the conversation made by the conversation partner.

In summary, studies which have manipulated the content of self-imagery in social phobia have demonstrated that negative imagery increases anxiety, results in the person themselves overestimating how evident their symptoms of anxiety are and how poorly they came across, and is associated with greater use of safety behaviours. In addition, it impacts adversely on objective measures of anxiety symptoms and performance, and the social situation flows less well. Further research is required to determine the extent to which any negative imagery needs to be self-referential in order to produce these effects, and to clarify the exact mechanism whereby images effect objective measures of performance and the quality of the interaction.

A causal role for negative imagery in blocking benign inferences

Research using self-report questionnaires has demonstrated that people with social phobia tend to make negative interpretations of ambiguous social events (Amir, Foa & Coles, 1998; Stopa & Clark, 2000). However, questionnaire studies do not distinguish between two clinically and theoretically relevant alternatives. The interpretations may be generated at the time that the ambiguous social information is initially encountered (i.e. on-line), or only later during post-event processing (i.e. off-line). Research utilizing an 'on-line' processing paradigm has indicated that while non-clinical controls generate benign inferences, people with social phobia do not. Hirsch and Mathews (2000) asked patients with social phobia and non-clinical controls to read descriptions of job interviews which included emotionally ambiguous points in the text, where both benign and threat inferences could be generated. At other points in the text, sentences were designed to ensure that all readers should arrive at the same inference. Whilst reading the descriptions, participants also performed lexical decisions, which involve indicating whether a string of letters (known as a probe) is an English word or not. When the lexical decisions were presented at points of emotional ambiguity, non-clinical volunteers endorsed words corresponding to benign interpretations as rapidly as they did in the baseline condition. In contrast, these same participants were significantly slower to endorse probe words corresponding to a socially threatening inference. Since the baseline was designed to provide an estimate of latencies when an inference had almost certainly been made, this implies that non-anxious participants made benign, but not threat inferences. In contrast, patients with social phobia did not show any such evidence of on-line inferences at points of emotional ambiguity. In an ambiguous context, participants with social phobia were significantly slower to endorse words corresponding to either threat or benign interpretations than they were in the baseline condition. It was concluded that social phobia is associated with a failure to generate any on-line emotional inferences in ambiguous social situations.

One possible explanation for this finding is that the negative self-imagery in social phobia may prevent the generation of benign on-line inferences. To explore this possibility, Hirsch, Mathews, Clark, Williams and Morrison (2003b) allocated low-socially anxious volunteers to either a negative image group, who were trained to generate and hold a negative self-image in mind, or a control group, who performed a control imagery task that did not manipulate self-imagery. Following negative image training, or the control task, volunteers completed the text-based task used by Hirsch and Mathews (2000). Data from the control group replicated earlier findings of a benign inferential bias for non-anxious individuals. In contrast, the negative image group lacked any benign inferences and also reported higher levels of state anxiety. These data were interpreted as showing that when non-socially anxious people hold a negative image in mind, this blocks their normal benign inferential bias. Since individuals with social phobia have spontaneous negative imagery, this may explain their lack of a benign inferential bias. The normal benign inferential bias demonstrated by individuals without social phobia may sustain a benign feedback cycle that could serve to maintain self-esteem, and even help prevent clinical levels of social anxiety from developing; negative imagery evident in social phobia may be preventing this benign bias from operating, which could be disadvantageous for patients with social phobia.

In summary, negative self-imagery appears to have a causal role in the maintenance of social phobia. It increases anxiety, results in spontaneous use of more safety behaviours and makes the person underestimate their performance and overestimate how evident anxiety symptoms are. Furthermore, others observe more anxious symptoms and evaluate performance more critically, social situations are contaminated and benign inferences are blocked.

Origins of negative imagery

Given that negative imagery appears to be problematic for people with social phobia, it is pertinent to speculate about the origins of such imagery. This issue can be considered in three ways. First, why do patients with social phobia construct images? Second, what is the experiential basis of the image? Third, once images are established, what stimuli trigger them?

With respect to why images may be constructed, people with social phobia are concerned to know how they come across in social situations, since they fear that others will judge them harshly if they exhibit symptoms of anxiety, or behave in an embarrassing way. One way of finding out how one comes across is to observe other people's reactions. This requires good eye contact and involvement in a social interaction, both of which are extremely threatening for patients with social phobia. Constructing a self-image may be a less threatening (but unfortunately less accurate) way of collecting the information.

With respect to experiential origins, the study by Hackmann et al. (2000) suggests that the image may be synthesized from a memory of an earlier traumatic social experience that has been laid down at the time of the event. Due to decreased processing of external information, and perhaps cognitive avoidance due to its distressing content, the image and memory are not subsequently updated with more current and realistic information. Given the personally traumatic nature of the memory, aspects of the memory structure may be similar to traumatic memories reported by individuals with post-traumatic stress disorder (PTSD), including the multi-sensory aspects of the social images, akin to intrusive memories in PTSD.

Traumatic memories in PTSD can be triggered by a range of stimuli, including low-level sensory input that matches aspects of the sensory experience evident during the traumatic event (Ehlers & Clark, 2000); this may also apply to images in social phobia. When people with social phobia are in a social situation, they may experience physical sensations, emotional reactions or other stimuli that have a similarity to the original traumatic event. If so, then this may trigger the memory of the original traumatic event in the form of a negative image. Other triggers for imagery in social phobia may be consequences of high levels of self-focused attention; this will result in patients having increased awareness of interoceptive information, such as heart rate, feeling hot and other such phenomena, which may be perceived as symptoms of anxiety. If they notice the interoceptive information, then they may infer that the physiological phenomena they are perceiving will be observable to other people (e.g. feeling hot in the face could be seen by others as blushing); if this matches salient aspects of their self-image, then this may trigger negative self-imagery at that time.

In summary, it is postulated that individuals with social phobia construct self-images because they need to know how they are coming across to others. The image may be based on an early traumatic social experience and can be triggered by a range of stimuli, particularly those that match aspects of an earlier traumatic social event, or involve interoceptive stimuli that match salient aspects of the image. Further research is required to clarify these issues.

Negative imagery as a target for treatment in social phobia

Given negative imagery's detrimental impact on individuals with social phobia, procedures for successfully dealing with negative images should have a useful therapeutic effect. Video feedback is a potentially powerful way of helping patients to discover that their self-images are distorted. Rapee and Hayman (1996) demonstrated that showing people with social phobia, or high social anxiety, videotapes of themselves in a prior social situation enables them to observe that they come across less poorly than they believed they had done. Clark and Wells (1995) noted that some patients process videos in ways that are likely to undermine the effectiveness of the procedure. In order to address this, Clark and Wells (1995) developed a way of preparing patients for the video feedback that was intended to maximize the opportunity for the patients to identify differences between their self-image and the way they actually came across. The preparatory instructions involved participants:

1. Predicting in detail what they would observe on videotape,
2. Forming an image of how they thought they would come across on videotape, and
3. Watching the videotape as though they were watching a stranger, paying particular attention to what was actually evident on the videotape, rather than how they felt whilst watching it.

Harvey, Clark, Ehlers and Rapee (2000) assessed the effectiveness of the preparatory instructions by asking volunteers to give a short presentation and then watch the presentation on videotape, following either no instructions or the preparatory instructions. With no instructions, observing the video led to improved ratings of social performance, but this effect was significantly greater in the preparatory instructions condition. Kim, Lundh and Harvey (2002) replicated the results of Harvey et al. (2000) and showed that the benefits of video feedback with preparatory instructions generalized to a subsequent social situation where they felt less anxious and believed that they came across better during a second speech, as compared to a second speech following video feedback without preparatory instructions. Spurr and Stopa (2003) further explored the conditions under which video feedback is likely to be helpful, and found that it was associated with greater change in self-ratings of performance if socially anxious individuals had adopted an observer perspective in the original interaction. Presumably, this is because the video would be more discrepant from the information that was available to participants at the time of the interaction.

In addition to video feedback, there are several other ways in which patients with social phobia can be helped to counteract the effects of negative imagery. One such technique is to facilitate an external focus of attention during social interactions, so that the patient processes environmental cues, rather than internal sensations during the interaction. Wells and Papageorgiou (1998) demonstrated that patients with social phobia reported less anxiety when they were externally focused in a social situation, as compared to when they were not instructed to have their attention focused externally (when they would have been likely to be more self-focused). This finding was replicated by Woody and Rodriguez (2000). Therapeutically, these findings translate into a need to get patients to shift their attention externally, with a further benefit of being able to gather information about others' reactions to them.

Another clinically useful technique involves asking patients with social phobia to recall and hold in mind the realistic image of themselves that they saw on videotape when in subsequent social situations, since this can counteract the aversive impact of the negative image. This can be supplemented by requiring patients to switch between the 'video image' and the negative image; this enables them to observe that the negative image increases their anxiety (Hirsch et al., 2003a).

Other techniques detailed in Clark and Wells (1995) that address negative imagery have not been experimentally examined, but clinical observations suggest that they are therapeutic. For example, it is clinically useful to demonstrate to patients that even if they did come across in the manner represented in their image, people would not interpret this in as critical a manner as they predict. This can be done through the use of surveys, where other people are asked what they think about a person exhibiting a given symptom of anxiety (e.g. blushing), whether their opinion of the person would change and if they would remember seeing the symptom in the long term. The survey is constructed with the patient to address their idiosyncratic concerns about their feared symptoms. The survey is given to other people by the therapist, patient or both individuals and the patient then collates the information so that they can draw their own conclusions. Another clinically useful technique involves the therapist modelling being in a real social situation (e.g. local shops or cafés) whilst exhibiting an exaggerated form of the feared symptom (e.g. putting blusher all over their face so that they are more red than is physically possible). The patient observes other reactions to the therapist. Then the patient repeats this exercise themselves and monitors others' reactions to them very closely. This provides data that others either do not notice symptoms that are perfectly visible (and prominent in the self-image), or that they do not react critically (if at all) to them. It also enables them to realize that being in a social situation whilst exhibiting an extreme version of the symptom is tolerable. The clinical validity of this technique could be investigated experimentally in future research.

There is growing interest in restructuring early traumatic memories (Smucker, Dancu, Foa & Niederee, 1995; Arntz & Weertman, 1999). In keeping with the literature on restructuring traumatic memories, the memory of the traumatic social situation, which may form the basis of the negative image, can be targeted therapeutically using imagery rescripting. The main aim of the approach is to update the image in the light of subsequent adult experiences and discussions during therapy. The general approach involves getting the patient to close their eyes, recall the original event and describe it as if it were happening now. The therapist then discusses with the patient their assumptions and beliefs about their own and the other person's/people's behaviour and what they would have liked to have done differently. The patient then closes their eyes for a second time and the scenario is imagined again, but this time the situation unfolds differently because:

1. They respond differently or appraise the situation differently in the memory;
2. They enter the memory as their adult self and help their younger self, and/or
3. Another individual enters the memory and responds as they would have liked to have happened during the original event.

Clinical observation suggests that this procedure can result in negative images no longer intruding spontaneously into consciousness.

In summary, there a number of therapeutic techniques that can either directly address the negative image or enable new information to be gained which in turn will challenge the validity and catastrophic nature of the negative images, such that the patient realizes that the image is not a realistic representation of how they come across, and that even if it were to be accurate others would not judge them harshly for it. All of these techniques are incorporated in a recently developed cognitive therapy programme. Two randomized controlled trials have evaluated the programme. The results suggest that it is an effective treatment. In the first trial, Clark, Ehlers, McManus, Hackmann, Fennell, Campbell et al. (2003) compared cognitive therapy alone with:

1. Selective serotonin reuptake inhibitor (fluoxetine) plus self-exposure instructions, and
2. Placebo medication plus self-exposure instructions.

All three treatments were associated with significant improvements, but cognitive therapy was superior to both medication groups. The overall pre-treatment to post-treatment effect size for cognitive therapy was large (2.14). In the second trial, Stangier, Heidenreich, Peitz, Lauterbach and Clark (in press) compared individual cognitive therapy with group cognitive therapy and a wait list control condition. Both versions of cognitive therapy were superior to the wait list. On some measures the individual treatment was superior to the group treatment. The difference may be partly because it is easier to focus on the idiosyncratic nature of the patients' fears and their negative images in the individualized version than in the group treatment.

Conclusions

Negative self-imagery is common in social phobia, and is often associated with aversive social experiences. The research presented here indicates that negative self-imagery appears to have a causal role in maintaining the disorder by increasing state anxiety, enhancing unrealistically critical self-appraisals, and having a detrimental effect on performance and the social situation in general. Treatment techniques that attempt, directly or indirectly, to modify negative self-imagery appear to have a useful therapeutic effect, confirming Robert Burns' view about the value of seeing 'oursels as ithers see us'.

NOTES

1. For the purpose of this chapter, imagery will be defined in keeping with Hackmann (1998a) as a cognitive activity that is not of purely verbal or abstract form, which can involve a number of sensory modalities.
2. Some individuals said that it was more of an impression than an image. For the purpose of this chapter, image is used to refer to both impressions and images.

REFERENCES

Amir, N., Foa, E. B. & Coles, M. E. (1998). Negative interpretation bias in social phobia. *Behaviour Research and Therapy, 36*, 945–957.
Arntz, A. & Weertman, A. (1999). Treatment of childhood memories: theory and practice. *Behaviour Research and Therapy, 37*, 715–740.
Beck, A. T. (1976). *Cognitive Therapy and the Emotional Disorders*. New York: International Universities Press.
Beck, A. T., Laude, R. & Bohnert, M. (1974). Ideational components of anxiety neurosis. *Archives of General Psychiatry, 31*, 319–325.
Caspi, A., Elder, G. H., Jr & Bem, D. J. (1988). Moving away from the world: life-course patterns of shy children. *Developmental Psychology, 24*, 824–831.

Clark, D. M. (1997). Panic disorder and social phobia. In D. M. Clark & C. G. Fairburn (Eds.), *Science and Practice of Cognitive Behaviour Therapy*, 119–153. Oxford: Oxford University Press.

Clark, D. M. (2000). A cognitive perspective on social phobia. In R. Crozier & L. Alden (Eds.), *International Handbook of Social Anxiety*. Chichester: Wiley.

Clark, D. M. & Beck, A. T. (1988). Cognitive approaches. In C. G. Last & M. Hersen (Eds.), *Handbook of Anxiety Disorders,*. 362–385. Elmsford: Pergamon.

Clark, D. M., Ehlers, A., McManus, F., Hackmann, A., Fennell, M., Campbell, H., Flower, T., Davenport, C. & Louis, B. (2003). Cognitive therapy vs. fluoxetine in generalized social phobia: a randomised control trial. *Journal of Consulting and Clinical Psychology, 71*, 1058–1067.

Clark, D. M. & Wells, A. (1995). A cognitive model of social phobia. In R. G. Heimberg, M. Liebowitz, D. Hope & F. Schneier (Eds.), *Social Phobia: Diagnosis, Assessment and Treatment*, 69–93. New York: Guilford.

Coles, M. E., Turk, C. L. & Heimberg, R. G. (2002). The role of memory perspective in social phobia: immediate and delayed memories for role-played situations. *Behavioural and Cognitive Psychotherapy, 30*, 415–425.

Coles, M. E., Turk, C. L., Heimberg, R. G. & Fresco, D. M. (2001). Effects of varying levels of anxiety within social situations: relationship to memory perspective and attributions in social phobia. *Behaviour Research and Therapy, 39*, 651–665.

De Silva, P. (1986). Obsessional-compulsive imagery. *Behaviour Research and Therapy, 24*, 333–350.

Ehlers, A. & Clark, D. M. (2000). A cognitive model of posttraumatic stress disorder. *Behaviour Research and Therapy, 38*, 319–345.

Hackmann, A. (1999). Working with images in clinical psychology. In P. Salkovskis (Ed.), *Comprehensive Clinical Psychology, 6*, 301–318. Oxford: Elsevier.

Hackmann, A., Clark, D. M. & McManus, F. (2000). Recurrent images and early memories in social phobia. *Behaviour Research and Therapy, 38*, 601–610.

Hackmann, A., Surawy, C. & Clark, D. M. (1998). Seeing yourself through others' eyes: a study of spontaneously occurring images in social phobia. *Behavioural and Cognitive Psychotherapy, 26*, 3–12.

Harvey, A. G., Clark, D. M., Ehlers, A. & Rapee, R. M. (2000). Social anxiety and self-impression: cognitive preparation enhances the beneficial effects of video feedback following a stressful social task. *Behaviour Research and Therapy, 38*, 1183–1192.

Hirsch, C. R., Clark, D. M., Mathews, A. & Williams, R. (2003a). Self-images play a causal role in social phobia. *Behaviour Research and Therapy, 41*, 901–921.

Hirsch, C. R. & Mathews, A. (2000). Impaired positive inferential bias in social phobia. *Journal of Abnormal Psychology, 109*, 705–712.

Hirsch, C. R., Mathews, A., Clark, D. M., Williams, R. & Morrison, J. (2003b). Negative self-imagery blocks inferences. *Behaviour Research and Therapy, 41*, 1383–1396.

Hirsch, C. R., Meynen, T. & Clark, D. M. (2004). Contamination of social situation with negative imagery. *Memory*, *12*, 496–506.

Kessler, R. C., McGonagle, K. A., Zhao, S., Nelson, C. B., Hughes, M., Eshleman, S., Wittchen, H. U. & Kendler, K. S. (1994). Lifetime and 12-month prevalence of DSM-III-R psychiatric disorders in the United States; results from the National Comorbidity Survey. *Archives of General Psychiatry*, *51*, 8–19.

Kim, H.-Y., Lundh, L. & Harvey, A. (2002). The enhancement of video feedback by cognitive preparation in the treatment of social anxiety. A single session experiment. *Journal of Behaviour Therapy and Experimental Psychiatry*, *33*, 19–37.

Mansell, W. & Clark, D. M. (1999). How do I appear to others? Social anxiety and processing of the observable self. *Behaviour Research and Therapy*, *37*, 419–439.

Ottaviani, R. & Beck, A. T. (1987). Cognitive aspects of panic disorders. *Journal of Anxiety Disorders*, *1*, 15–28.

Rapee, R. M. & Hayman, K. (1996). The effects of video feedback on the self-evaluation of performance in socially anxious subjects. *Behaviour Research and Therapy*, *34*, 315–322.

Rosenhan, D. L. & Seligman, M. E. P. (1995). *Abnormal Psychology*, 3rd edn. New York: Norton.

Salkovskis, P. M. (1991). The importance of behaviour in the maintenance of anxiety and panic: a cognitive account. *Behavioural Psychotherapy*, *19*, 6–19.

Schneier, F. R., Johnson, J., Hornig, C. D., Liebowitz, M. R. & Weissman, M. M. (1992). Social phobia: comorbidity and morbidity in an epidemiologic sample. *Archives of General Psychiatry*, *49*, 282–288.

Smucker, M. R, Dancu, C., Foa, E. B. & Niederee, J. L. (1995). Imagery rescripting: a new treatment for survivors of childhood sexual abuse suffering from posttraumatic stress. *Journal of Cognitive Psychotherapy*, *9*, 3–17.

Spielberger, C. D., Gorsuch, R. L., Lushene, R. E., Vagg, P. R. & Jacobs, G. A. (1983). *Manual for the State-trait Anxiety Inventory*. Palo Alto: Consulting Psychologists Press.

Spurr, J. M. & Stopa, L. (2003). The observer perspective: effects on social anxiety and performance. *Behaviour Research and Therapy*, *41*, 1009–1028.

Stangier, U., Heidenreich, T., Peitz, M., Lauterbach, W. & Clark, D. M. (in press). Cognitive therapy for social phobia: individual versus group treatment. *Behaviour Research and Therapy*.

Stopa, L. & Clark, D. M. (2000). Social phobia and interpretation of social events. *Behaviour Research and Therapy*, *38*, 273–283.

Turner, S. M., Beidel, D. C., Dancu, C. V. & Keys, D. J. (1986). Psychopathology of social phobia and comparison to avoidant personality disorder. *Journal of Abnormal Psychology*, *95*, 389–394.

Warwick, H. M. C. & Salkovskis, P. M. (1990). Hypochondriasis. *Behaviour Research and Therapy*, *28*, 105–117.

Wells, A., Clark, D. M. & Ahmad, S. (1998). How do I look with my mind's eye: perspective taking in social phobic imagery. *Behaviour Research and Therapy*, *36*, 631–634.

Wells, A. & Hackmann, A. (1993). Imagery and core beliefs in health anxiety: contents and origins. *Behavioural and Cognitive Psychotherapy*, *21*, 265–273.

Wells, A. & Papageorgiou, C. (1998). Social phobia: effects of external attention on anxiety, negative beliefs, and perspective taking. *Behavior Therapy*, *29*, 357–370.

Wittchen, H.-U., Stein, M. B. & Kessler, R. C. (1999). Social fears and social phobia in a community sample of adolescents and young adults: prevalence, risk factors and co-morbidity. *Psychological Medicine*, *29*, 309–323.

Woody, S. R. & Rodriguez, B. J. (2000). Self-focused attention and social anxiety in social phobics and normal controls. *Cognitive Therapy and Research*, *24*, 473–488.

Yiend, J. & Mathews, A. (2001). Anxiety and attention to threatening pictures. *Quarterly Journal of Experimental Psychology*, *54*, 665–681.

12 Experimental cognitive psychology and clinical practice: autobiographical memory as a paradigm case

J. Mark G. Williams

It is the sixth session of cognitive therapy for depression. The patient, Julie, is talking about some difficulties with her mother.

JULIE: I always find that I get upset when my mother talks to me like that.

THERAPIST: You find it difficult?

JULIE: Oh yes. I don't know why – it's been going on a long time.

THERAPIST: Can you give me an example of such a time, when it was difficult for you?

JULIE: It's always the same thing. She rings me about something fairly harmless, and then I tell her something; then she starts to tell me what I should do.

THERAPIST: Can you describe such a time?

JULIE: It's often late at night, when I'm tired. I don't have the energy to fight back.

THERAPIST: Can you tell me about a particular time, perhaps something that happened recently?

JULIE: The sort of thing she'll say is: 'Why don't you ask Charlie to help?' – things like that – she undermines me all the time.

What is going on here? The therapist is asking for more detail about her patient's recurrent situation, and although more detail of a sort is emerging, it is not yet episodic information. That is, this patient, even after three prompts, is not identifying a particular occasion. Perhaps she doesn't want to be more specific. Yet this is six sessions into the therapy, and she has disclosed issues that are much more 'sensitive' that these phone calls. Perhaps, then, she does not understand. Perhaps. But soon the therapist will give up asking for details and move on, maybe to elicit thoughts. And if this happens, potentially important opportunities will have been missed. First, most psychotherapies involve some retrieval of past events (distant or recent) in order to reorder, recode or reinterpret them in some way (depending on the model of therapy). If specific events are not retrieved, they are less likely to be able to be recoded; they will tend to remain categorized and schematic, and still justifying the conclusions to which they first gave rise (my mother interferes; I cannot cope with her, etc.).

Second, most structured psychotherapies involve asking patients to complete diaries, in which they record activities, emotions, thoughts and beliefs. This is likely to prove difficult if the patient is not able to encode or retrieve events in their daily lives in a specific way. In an early study, Wahler and Afton (1980) found that mothers who had been referred for help with their problem in coping with 'difficult' children often could not retrieve specific examples of their children's behaviour, remaining schematic and over-general. They concluded that these mothers were failing to encode specific instances, and found that such mothers failed to benefit from the parent training programme. Where a mother did benefit (and diaries were an important part of assisting the encoding process) the degree to which she became more specific was associated with the degree of improvement (see also Wahler & Sansbury, 1990).

These clinical observations were important in focusing our experimental work, which I shall describe in this chapter. The aim of this chapter is to examine a phenomenon, over-general memory, that was originally described in the context of experimental cognitive psychology research, but which we believe has important parallels in these clinical observations. The research on memory aims to understand how normal memory processes can become impaired, what causes it, and what consequences it has. In so doing, we aim to see how it may inform clinical practice.

Our line of research on this problem started with a serendipitous finding while conducting a study on mood-congruent memory in suicidal patients. We were surprised that in many of their responses to both positive and negative cue words (e.g. *happy, safe, interested; angry, hurt, clumsy*), patients failed to respond by giving a specific memory. Instead, on about half the occasions, they responded with a memory that gave a category that summarized a number of similar events (e.g. I used to walk the dog every morning) (see Figure 12.1a).

Subsequent research found that this occurred despite ample practice, clear instructions and using different types of cues (words, scenarios, free descriptions, 'activity' cues, see Williams, 1988).

We also found that over-general memory did not arise from general semantic processing impairment, assessed using Baddeley's semantic processing speed test (Baddeley et al., 1992). The results are shown in Figure 12.1b. As might be expected, both hospital groups were relatively slow, yet it was only the suicidal group that showed the over-general memory, not the hospital controls (Williams & Broadbent, 1986).

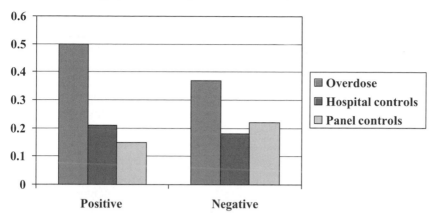

Figure 12.1a Proportion of responses that were over-general (Williams & Broadbent, 1986).

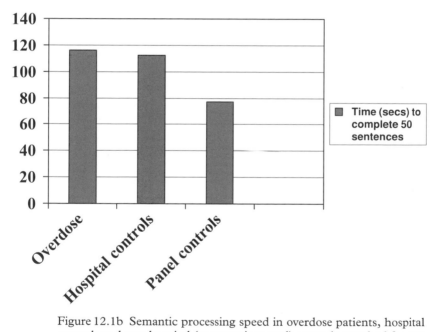

Figure 12.1b Semantic processing speed in overdose patients, hospital controls and non-hospital (community panel) controls matched for age and educational level (Williams & Broadbent, 1986).

The retrieval of generic events when specific events are requested is not unique to emotionally disturbed people; it can occur during retrieval of other information (Pillemer et al., 1988; Pillemer, 1998), and when participants are asked to retrieve self-referential memories (Singer & Moffitt, 1992). Indeed, it is important for all people to have both general and specific information available in memory. For most purposes, in conversation with others and for generic problem solving, general summaries of a large number of instances will suffice. If we were constantly retrieving specific information in most situations, it would impair our progress on a task, and probably make other people avoid us. However, people need to move fluently through their memory, drawing on the appropriate level of specificity or generality as the task requires. Subsequent research has shown that, in the emotional disturbance we were studying, the retrieval of generic information was a relatively long-term cognitive style of which patients were unaware, and which did not readily respond to increased efforts to exert strategic control.

Early and recent studies

In a review chapter written in 1994 and published two years later, I drew together the research published at that time (Williams, 1996). To structure this chapter, I shall summarize the state of play at that time, and then say what has happened over the last ten years.

By the mid-1990s, although the phenomenon had originally been described in suicidal patients, it had become clear that categoric memory was a reliable characteristic of major depression (Moore, Watts & Williams, 1988; Williams & Scott, 1988; Puffet, Jehin-Marchot, Timsit-Berthier & Timsit, 1991; Kuyken & Dalgleish, 1995; Kuyken & Brewin, 1995).

Studies published since then have endorsed this view (Goddard, Dritschel & Burton, 1996; Wessel et al., 2001), as well as replicating the finding for suicidal patients (Williams et al., 1996; Pollock & Williams, 2001). It appeared at that time as if depression was a key feature, since this effect did not occur in generalized anxiety disorder (GAD) (Burke & Mathews, 1992), and its appearance in obsessive-compulsive disorder was wholly accounted for by the co-occurrence of major depression (Wilhelm, McNally, Baer & Florin, 1997).

More recent data have confirmed that over-general memory is not a feature of individuals with anxiety. First, high scores on neuroticism and/or trait anxiety are not associated with over-general memory (Merckelbach, Muris & Horselenberg, 1996).

Second, patients with anxiety disorders (including panic disorder with or without agoraphobia, social phobia, specific phobia, generalized

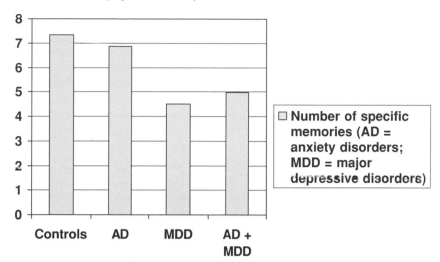

Figure 12.2 Number of specific memories in depressed, anxious and mixed groups of patients, and matched controls (Wessel et al., 2001).

anxiety disorder and obsessive-compulsive disorder) have been confirmed as showing normal memory by Wessel et al. (2001). The results were clear-cut, and are shown in Figure 12.2. Lack of specificity in this study was associated with a diagnosis of depression, but not anxiety.

However, the association with depression is complex in that over-general memory does not appear to be state-dependent. This conclusion comes from two types of studies: those that have examined people when in remission, and those that have examined the correlations, within a patient group, between over-generality and severity of depression. First, patients remain over-general when they have recovered. This had been shown in recovered suicidal patients (Williams & Dritschel, 1988) and recovered depressed patients (Brittlebank et al., 1993; Mackinger, Pachinger, Leibetseder & Fartyacek, 2000; Peeters, Wessel, Merckelbach & Boon-Vermeeren, 2002 and Nandrino et al., 2002, for recurrent depression only).

The second type of study uses correlational analysis. Early studies showed that the level of over-generality, unlike other memory deficits and biases associated with depression, does not correlate with severity of mood (Williams & Broadbent, 1986; Kuyken & Brewin, 1995). This lack of correlation with severity of mood has now been found: by Williams et al. (1996) for both specificity of the past and the future, in suicidal and control participants; by Phillips and Williams (1997) in a group of elderly patients attending a memory clinic; by Hutchings et al. (1998) in a sample of mothers whose children had been referred to Child Guidance;

by Jones et al. (1999) in a group of patients with a diagnosis of border-line personality disorder; and by Peeters et al. (2002) in patients with major depression. In addition, Williams et al. (2000), who reported a significant decrease in the proportion of categoric memories in a group who had received mindfulness-based cognitive therapy (compared to a treatment-as-usual control, see Teasdale, this volume), found that change in mood did not correlate with change in such categoric memories. Finally the study by Wessel et al. (2001) of ninety-three outpatients (depressed and anxious, and mixed anxiety and depression) found no correlation between self-rated depression and specificity of memory.

The three studies that have reported significant correlations have obtained conflicting results. Orbach et al. (2001) analysed the responses of children (N = 22) mean age 14 at interview) who had been victims or witnesses of physical abuse some years before (confirmed by social workers' reports). They found significant positive correlation ($r = 0.41$) between higher depression on the Beck Depression Inventory (BDI) and greater number of categoric responses. However, Swales, et al. (2001) found that although disturbed adolescents (N = 26; mean age 14 years) were, in general, more categoric than matched controls, nevertheless, within the disturbed group, there was a significant correlation between increased *specificity* and both depression (BDI) scores ($r = 0.4$) and hope-lessness (Beck Hopelessness Scale, Beck et al., 1974; $r = 0.55$). This is in the opposite direction to that of Orbach et al. As the authors point out, it may have been due to the fact that in Swales et al., the investigator had a therapeutic relationship with the participants, so that there were other aspects of the situation that might promote more specific retrieval in the more distressed patients – for example, the fact that some of these events may have been talked about before in therapy.

Finally, Ramponi, Barnard and Nimmo-Smith (in press) found an association more like that of Orbach et al. (2001). They studied adults (community volunteers, sixteen of whom had scores above a cut-off of nine on the BDI). They found that more depression was associated with less specific ($r = -0.60$) and more categoric ($r = 0.34$) memories (whole group correlations), but both depression and over-general memory also correlated with rumination in this study, raising the possibilility that it may have been rumination rather than mood that was responsible for the over-generality in memory. A link between memory and rumination has now been established in a series of studies by Ed Watkins and John Teasdale (Teasdale, this volume; Watkins, et al., 2000; Watkins and Teasdale, 2001). In these experiments, ruminative thinking is either experimentally exacerbated (with instructions to think about the causes and consequence of mood) or reduced (using distraction, 'decentring' or experiential focusing). When rumination is experimentally reduced, then autobiographical memory becomes more specific. This strongly suggests that over-general memory and ruminative thinking are closely bound together in a vicious circle, either one of which might exacerbate the other.

In summary, the balance of evidence suggests that over-general memory is not mood-state dependent, but does vary with level of depressive ruminative thinking.

The causes of over-general retrieval: what damages the memory mechanism?

Although many early studies prior to 1996 had found that depression seemed to be a key factor in the aetiology of this deficit in memory, by that time there had also been a number of studies (for example, in Vietnam veterans) that showed that the occurrence of past trauma is at least as important a precursor of categoric memory as is depression (McNally, Lasko, Macklin & Pitman, 1995; McNally, Litz, Prassas, Shin & Weathers, 1994; Brewin et al., 1999).

Subsequent studies have endorsed the role of past trauma, though there is some uncertainty whether memories of or thoughts about the trauma should still be intruding in order to produce categoric retrieval. For example, Henderson et al. (2002) found that female students who report a history of sexual abuse tend to retrieve more categoric memories.[1] There was no relation between intrusions on the Impact of Events Scale and degree of specificity in memory, however. This contrasted with Kuyken & Brewin (1995), who found that those who experienced a greater frequency of avoidance of intrusive thoughts and memories were more categoric, and Brewin et al. (1999), who found that greater avoidance and number of intrusions correlated with more over-general memories.

Not all studies since 1996 have found that trauma is significant. Wessel et al. (2001) found that depression played a larger role than past trauma in predicting level of over-general memory. However, the authors point out that the trauma in this study may not have been sufficiently severe. This conclusion would be consistent with the studies by De Decker (2001), who found an association between trauma history and specificity of memory in adolescents referred for emotional problems, and in children whose trauma had been living through the Bosnian war. She found no evidence in her studies, though, that problems in retrieving specific memories were related to self-rated intrusion by, or avoidance of, memories or thoughts about the trauma, similar to the results of Henderson et al. (2002). These studies suggest that the intrusion and avoidance may simply be the result of having more severe trauma, and it is the severity of trauma that is related to over-general memory, rather than the continued intrusion or avoidance of the memories.

The differences between studies is not just an issue with which memory paradigm is used to test memory. Sabine Schonfeld and Anke Ehlers at the Institute of Psychiatry in London have found that post-trauamatic stress disorder (PTSD) sufferers have over-general memories, whether word cues, picture cues or involuntary recall is used as the paradigm to assess retrieval (Schonfeld & Ehlers, 2003). Furthermore, trauma itself, although it may be necessary to produce over-general retrieval, is clearly not sufficient, for in her studies, as in McNally's earlier studies of PTSD, matched controls were used who had suffered similar traumas but had not developed PTSD. This raises the possibility that a tendency to retrieve autobiographical memories over-generally might predate a trauma, and make some people more vulnerable than others to develop PTSD if it occurs.

What mechanisms underlie over-generality in memory?

Descriptions theory

The phenomenon of over-general memory has been explained within a 'descriptions theory' (Norman and Bobrow, 1979; Burgess & Shallice, 1996). According to this theory, voluntary retrieval is 'a process in which some information about a target item is used to construct a description of the item and this description is used in attempts to recover new fragments of information' (Williams & Hollan, 1981, p. 87). The descriptions framework has influenced a number of models of event retrieval (Conway 1990; Reiser, Black & Abelson 1985; Williams & Hollan, 1981), and has been the framework in which the phenomenon of over-general memory has been most often explained (Williams, 1996).

Norman & Bobrow's theory assumed that a person encodes only a limited amount of possible information (an incomplete list of properties or a partial image). To encode or retrieve an event from memory, a partial description is formed that provides an initial entry point into the memory, the description acting as an index for the memory. Burgess & Shallice (1996) elaborate the model, suggesting that autobiographical memory retrieval needs the sub-processes of 'descriptor', 'mediator' and 'editor', and that when the cognitive system is in 'retrieval mode' the preferred level of entry is the 'general event'.

Memory retrieval, then, involves both a strategic aspect and a more direct, 'associative' component. The strategic aspect is a staged process in which an individual first derives an intermediate description of the to-be-recalled information, and then uses the description to derive indices to search for candidate episodes that fit the description. The associative component is analogous to lower-level routines involving a large variety of sensory and conceptual content in long-term store (LTS). Co-occurrence of different patterns of activation across domains results in associative links being established, and these patterns of activation may be reinstated by any cue or collection of cues that activates one of the elements above a certain threshold.

Categoric memory as truncated search

Williams & Dritschel (1988, 1992) suggested that over-general responses in autobiographical memory represent the output of these intermediate descriptions. All individuals have some strategic control over how much of the memory 'hierarchy' needs to be searched in order to meet the requirements of the task specificity. Suicidal, depressed and PTSD patients access an 'intermediate description' but stop short of a specific example. Their memory appears to abort the search for a specific event prematurely, when only the general description stage has been reached. It is this truncated search (called by Conway & Pleydell-Pearce, 2000, a *dysfacilitation* of the retrieval process) which appeared to be responsible for over-general memory responses. Such dysfacilitation would result in a memory output which, having failed to access a specific event, results in further attempts at retrieval. After a number of such failed iterations, a more highly elaborated network of categoric intermediate descriptions are hypothesized to exist. In future attempts at retrieval, an initial cue is likely to activate an intermediate description that simply activates other self-descriptions. The term 'mnemonic interlock' has been coined to describe this phenomenon, and recent data using think-aloud procedures while participants are retrieving support the operation of such a system (Barnhofer et al., 2002).

What is not yet clear is the extent to which mnemonic interlock results from deficits that arise during the retrieval specification process (e.g. due to reduced capacity, preventing a person from escaping from the descriptions stage of retrieval), or from the fact that general descriptions may produce less affect than specific responses, at least for some memories, and so remaining at the level of more general information reduces the impact of potentially emotional material. Such an *affect-gating hypothesis* would be consistent with current models of PTSD (Foa & Kozak, 1986; Ehlers & Clark, 2000; Brewin, 2001) and models of autobiographical memory (Conway & Pleydell-Pearce, 2000). These models converge on the view that intrusive images/memories and flashbacks arise from the relatively automatic activation of mnemonic material related to the trauma (for example, the 'situationally accessible memories' of Brewin et al., or Conway and Pleydell-Pearce's 'direct retrieval'). This direct activation of event-specific knowledge interrupts concurrent processing and results in a number of strategies to exercise top-down control, to attempt to avoid such high-risk situations and memories.

Until recently, there was no independent evidence to suggest that an affect-gating mechanism might explain the results. At a minimum, any affect-gating theory requires that, at some point, a person who tends to retrieve memory more specifically would risk experiencing greater affective disturbance. Otherwise, there is no motivation for the negative reinforcement of a less specific retrieval style. Raes et al. (2003) showed just such evidence. They found that degree of mood disturbance following experimental manipulation of frustration using a puzzle task (in which the participants – student volunteers – thought they were doing badly) was greater in those participants with a more specific retrieval style.

Clinical consequences of over-general recall

Reduced problem solving

Experimental cognitive psychology methods have become an important way of helping us to understand the psychological processes underlying the biases and impairments we see in the clinic. But can it go beyond theoretical understanding, and help us see more clearly the practical consequences of the biases and impairments? Is there a link between what we see in the clinical laboratory and the phenomena we see in the world of clinical practice? By the late 1980s and early 1990s, a number of studies had found that over-generality in retrieval style had a number of detrimental effects on other aspects of a person's functioning. Since then, other studies have replicated and extended these early results.

One of the first matters to be studied in relation to memory was the issue of problem solving. Understanding this was a matter of some urgency, since of all the detrimental effects that non-specificity of autobiographical memory has on cognition, its effect on problem solving is likely to have the greatest implications for the prevention of suicidal behaviour, and it was suicidality that we had been studying when we first came across over-generality in this way. One of the most commonly found aspects of suicidal thinking is that the person feels they have run out of coping options: they simply do not know what to do. It is under these circumstances that, if they have heard of someone else harming themselves, or if it has happened to a friend or family member, or if they have seen a television programme involving self-harm, then they are very likely to conclude that this is the only thing they can do to cope with or escape (at least for a while) from their difficulties.

Several studies have examined the hypothesis that problem solving becomes inhibited because suicidal people truncate their memory search at the descriptions stage, then attempt to use these intermediate descriptions as a database to try and generate solutions. The database is restricted because the lack of specific information gives too little help to the individual in generating coping options for current problems.

The data show that low specificity of autobiographical memory is associated with impairment in problem solving, both in depression (Goddard et al., 1996, 1997) and specifically in suicidal patients (Evans et al., 1992; Sidley, et al., 1997). Furthermore, suicidal patients show greater impairment in autobiographical memory than psychiatric controls matched for level of depression, and, correspondingly, show greater deficits in problem solving (Pollock & Williams, 2001).

However, all the studies that have examined the relations between memory and problem solving have been correlational. Although each has taken account of the possibility that general cognitive sluggishness to respond might have affected both variables, producing spuriously high correlations between them, it remains possible that both specificity of memory and quality of problem solving performance might be determined by other factors. The data are still unclear on this issue. Goddard et al. (2001) found that asking participants to retrieve a specific memory before completing the MEPS did not enhance problem solving performance. On the other hand, our own data (Williams, Eade & Wallace, in preparation) suggest that manipulation of memory specificity using high or low imageable cue words in an induction phase of an experiment does affect problem solving effectiveness on the MEPS in the test phase, with the induction of more specific memories producing more effective problem solutions.

Over-generality prolongs affective disturbance

A second major consequence of non-specificity in memory is that it predicts the persistence of affective symptoms once depressed (assessed using the Hamilton scale; Brittlebank, Scott, Williams and Ferrier, 1993). One study, using the Beck rather than the Hamilton scale, did not replicate this finding (Brewin et al., 1999), but Dalgleish et al. (2001) used both Beck and Hamilton in their group of people suffering Seasonal Affective Disorder, and found that memory over-generality predicted persistence of depression on the Hamilton but not on the Beck, suggesting an association of memory with somatic symptoms of depression. Further work will be need to clarify this point.

Harvey, Bryant and Dang (1998) found that those who had less specific recall of events surrounding a trauma were more likely to find that their acute stress became chronic. Furthermore, the specificity of autobiographical memory, assessed in women during pregnancy, predicts affective disturbance following childbirth (Mackinger, Loschin & Leibetseder, 2000a).

A recent replication of these predictive results was made by Peeters, Wessel, Merckelbach and Boon-Vermeeren (2002). They assessed twenty-five out-patients (mean age 41.5 years), all of whom met DSM-IV criteria for major depressive disorder. They excluded any who had a diagnosis of bipolar disorder, organic brain disease, substance abuse and treatment with ECT within six months. Following Brittlebank et al. (1993), they followed up the patients at three and seven months, assessing both autobiographical memory and severity of mood. The results showed, first, that despite significant clinical improvement in mood at three months and at seven months, memory remained non-specific across the course of the study (and, if anything, went in the less specific direction, with the overall proportion of specific memories being 46 per cent at the outset and 41 per cent at seven months). Second, they found that specificity of memory in response to negative cue words significantly predicted the persistence of symptoms, with greater over-generality predicting more persistent depression. Note that, unlike Brittlebank et al., this was found for negative rather than positive memories. This pattern, in which significant effects are sometimes shown more on negative than on positive memories, may be explicable in terms of the particular settings (cueing conditions) in which participants are tested. Mackinger et al. (2000b) suggested that greater over-generality is likely to be found for the valence condition that is mood-incongruent (that is, if mood is euthymic, more over-generality will be found in response to negative cues, but if mood is depressed, more over-generality will be found in response to positive cues). However, there has been no systematic study of this possibility.

Finally, Mackinger et al. (in press) have found that over-general retrieval predicts how many depressive symptoms remain following three weeks of in-patient detoxification therapy in sixty-five alcohol dependent men, even after taking account of initial depression, mental status and degree of alcohol dependence.

Over-generality for the past makes the future vague and difficult to plan for

A third consequence of over-generality in memory is perhaps the most subtle, but may turn out to have the largest impact. We have found that over-general memory makes it hard to imagine a specific future (Williams et al., 1996). This study found that, first, suicidal people were poorer at producing specific events that might happen to them in the future (positive or negative events) and that this difficulty was correlated with over-generality in memory. Of course, such correlations do not indicate the direction of cause. So Williams et al. also conducted an experimental manipulation of memory-retrieval style. In a second experiment, they randomly allocated student participants to two conditions, A and B. They gave instructions to participants to use the cue words to give either specific events (in condition A) or categories of events (in condition B). In a third experiment, they used high or low imageable cue words to induce specific or categoric memories. Results from both experiments showed that these manipulations had the predicted effect. Participants were induced to generate specific or categoric memories in the study phase. Each experiment then had a second, test phase, in which all participants were given a new set of cues, and asked to come up with some event that might occur in the future. Those participants whose memory had been induced to be categoric now tended to produce general future events (e.g. to the cue *compliment* – 'a friend might'). Those participants whose memory had been induced to be specific, tended to give specific future events (e.g. *compliment* – 'my husband may give me a compliment next week when I have my hair done'). These experiments show that over-general recall can have a causal link to the ease with which a person plans their future.

These results have implications beyond depression and psychopathology. It is well known within health psychology (for example, in Azjen's development of the theory of reasoned action) that in order to change one's behaviour, one needs to go beyond having general intentions, and instead have specific 'implementation' intentions (Ajzen, 1998). For example, it is not enough to say: 'I'll start to exercise next week'. One needs to specify what day and time the exercise regimen will start. Our data suggest that such planning will be undermined by the tendency to retrieve the past in an over-general way.

A striking illustration of this was provided in a small study that Judy Hutchings and colleagues carried out in North Wales (Hutchings et al., 1998). They were interested in how over-generality in the memory of mothers whose children had been referred to the Child Guidance Clinic might affect the outcome for the child, as he or she went through their treatment (that is, to replicate the results of Wahler and Afton (1980); see earlier). Twenty-six mothers and their children entered the study. However, the main part of the study could not be carried out, since ten out of the twenty-six mothers did not even attend the Child Guidance Clinic for their first appointment. When they looked at the memory scores for the mothers who did not attend this first appointment, they turned out to be substantially lower than the mothers who had attended. In fact, the

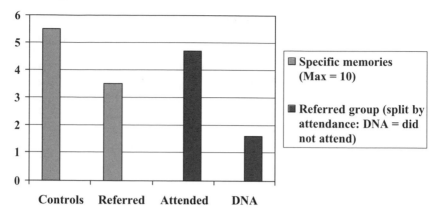

Figure 12.3 Number of specific memories in control mothers whose children attended the University Nursery, compared with mothers whose children have been referred to Child Guidance (last two bars show referred mothers who did or did not attend the appointment; Hutchings et al., 1998).

memory of the mothers who had attended was not different from a control group of mothers whose children attended the University Nursery (see Figure 12.3). Although autobiographical memory over-generality was associated with socio-economic deprivation, the memory score predicted attendance better than the score on a social deprivation scale. These data suggest that the inability to retrieve specific memory, although described most extensively in experimental laboratory tasks, assesses something very important about everyday functioning. They remind us that the inability to solve problems affects others in the close family, and not just the person we are testing in the lab, or seeing for therapy.

Concluding remarks

The patient with whom this chapter started is clearly not an isolated case. In doing psychotherapy, we rightly attend closely to the beliefs, attitudes and explanations that patients use to describe themselves, their world and their future. Our research suggests that the way patients use their evidence base, their memory for events in their lives, may make an important contribution to the maintenance of their difficulties. If we miss these signs, we risk missing an aspect of their processing that may be creating more difficulties for them.

Autobiographical memory is the domain in which one of the most important aspects of psychological functioning (memory) intersects with a person's sense of 'self' (the autobiography). There is no type of psychological problem or its treatment that does not involve both domains to some extent, so we might expect research at this intersection to yield important findings. The research reviewed here is pointing to the fact that some individuals are considerably handicapped by an aspect of their memory that appears benign. We have found that a treatment approach that focuses on moment to moment awareness and in encouraging non-avoidance (MBCT, see Teasdale, this volume) can help patients to be more specific in their memory.

1. Note that, in all cases where a correlation with abuse is reported, the memories being asked for in the experiments do not concern abuse.

REFERENCES

Ajzen, I. (1998). *Attitudes, Personality and Behavior*. Chicago, IL: The Dorsey Press.

Baddeley, A. D., Emslie, H. & Nimmo-Smith, I. (1992). *The Speed and Capacity of Language Processing (SCOLP) Test*. Bury St Edmunds, Suffolk: Thames Valley Test Company.

Barnhofer, T., Jong-Meyer, R., Kleinpass, A. & Nikesch, S. (2002). Specificity of autobiographical memories in depression: an analysis of retrieval processes in a think-aloud task. *British Journal of Clinical Psychology, 41*, 411–416.

Brewin, C. R. (2001). A cognitive neuroscience account of PTSD and its treatment. *Behaviour Research and Therapy, 39*, 373–393.

Brewin, C. R., Reynolds, M. & Tata, P. (1999). Autobiographical memory processes and the course of depression. *Journal of Abnormal Psychology, 108*, 511–517.

Brittlebank, A. D., Scott, J., Williams, J. M. G. & Ferrier, I. N. (1993). Autobiographical memory in depression; state or trait marker? *British Journal of Psychiatry, 162*, 118–121.

Burgess, P. W. & Shallice, T. (1996). Confabulation and the control of recollection. *Memory, 4*, 359–411.

Burke, M. & Mathews, A. (1992). Autobiographical memory and clinical anxiety. *Cognition and Emotion, 6*, 23–35.

Conway, M. A. (1990). *Autobiographical Memory*. Milton Keynes: Open University Press.

Conway, M. A. & Pleydell-Pearce, C. (2000). The construction of autobiographical memories in the self memory system. *Psychological Review, 107*, 261–268.

Dalgleish, T., Spinks, H., Yiend, J. & Kuyken, W. (2001). Autobiographical memory style in Seasonal Affective Disorder and its relationship to future symptom remission. *Journal of Abnormal Psychology, 110*, 335–340.

De Decker, A. (2001). Autobiographical memory in traumatized adolescents. Unpublished Ph.D. Thesis, University of Leuven.

Ehlers, A. & Clark, D. M. (2000). A cognitive model of posttraumatic stress disorder. *Behaviour Research and Therapy*, *38*, 319–345.

Evans, J., Williams, J. M. G., O'Loughlin, S. & Howells, K. (1992). Autobiographical memory and problem solving strategies of parasuicide patients. *Psychological Medicine*, *22*, 399–405.

Foa, E. B. & Kozak, M. (1986). Emotional processing of fear: exposure to corrective information. *Psychological Bulletin*, *99*, 20–35.

Goddard, L., Dritschel, B. & Burton, A. (1996). Role of autobiographical memory in social problem solving and depression. *Journal of Abnormal Psychology*, *105*, 609–616.

Goddard, L., Dritschel, B. & Burton, A. (1997). Social problem solving and autobiographical memory in depressed students. *British Journal of Clinical Psychology*, *36*, 449–451.

Goddard, L., Dritschel, B. & Burton, A. (2001). The effects of specific retrieval instruction on social problem-solving in depression. *British Journal of Clinical Psychology*, *40*, 297–308.

Harvey, A. G., Bryant, R. A. & Dang, S. T. (1998). Autobiographical memory in acute stress disorder. *Journal of Consulting and Clinical Psychology*, *66*, 500–506.

Henderson, D., Hargreaves, I., Gregory, S. & Williams, J. M. G. (2002). Autobiographical memory and emotion in a non-clinical sample of women with and without a reported history of childhood sexual abuse. *British Journal of Clinical Psychology*, *41*, 129–141.

Hutchings, J., Nash, S., Williams, J. M. G. & Nightingale, D. (1998). Parental autobiographical memory: is this a helpful clinical measure in behavioural child management? *British Journal of Clinical Psychology*, *37*, 303–312.

Jones, B., Startup, M., Jones, R. S. P., Heard, H., Swales, M. & Williams, J. M. G. (1999). Dissociation and over-general autobiographical memory in borderline personality disorder. *Psychological Medicine*, *29*, 1397–1404.

Kuyken, W. & Brewin, C. R. (1995). Autobiographical memory functioning in depression and reports of early abuse. *Journal of Abnormal Psychology*, *104*, 585–591.

Kuyken, W. & Dalgleish, T. (1995). Autobiographical memory and depression. *British Journal of Clinical Psychology*, *34*, 89–92.

Mackinger, H. F., Leibetseder, M. F., Kunz-Dorfer, A. A., Fartacek, R. R., Whitworth, A. B. & Feldinger, F. F. (in press). Autobiographical memory predicts the course of depression during detoxification therapy in alcohol dependent men. *Journal of Affective Disorders*.

Mackinger, H. F., Loschin, G. G. & Leibetseder, M. M. (2000a). Prediction of postnatal affective changes by autobiographical memories. *European Psychologist*, *5*, 52–61.

Mackinger, H. F., Pachinger, M. M., Leibetseder, M. M. & Fartyacek, R. R. (2000b). Autobiographical memories in women remitted from major depression. *Journal of Abnormal Psychology*, *109*, 331–334.

McNally, R. J., Lasko, N. B., Macklin, M. L. & Pitman, R. K. (1995). Autobiographical memory disturbance in combat-related posttraumatic stress disorder. *Behaviour Research and Therapy*, *33*, 619–630.

McNally, R. J., Litz, B. T., Prassas, A., Shin, L. M. & Weathers, F. W. (1994). Emotional priming of autobiographical memory in post-traumatic stress disorder. *Cognition and Emotion*, *8*, 351–367.

Merckelbach, H., Muris, P. & Horselenberg, R. (1996). Correlates of over-general memories in normal subjects. *Behavioural and Cognitive Psychotherapy*, *24*, 109–115.

Moore, R. G., Watts, F. N. & Williams, J. M. G. (1988). The specificity of personal memories in depression. *British Journal of Clinical Psychology*, *27*, 275–276.

Nandrino, J.-L., Pezard, L., Poste, A., Reveillere, C. & Beaune, D. (2002). Autobiographical memory in major depression: a comparison between first episode and recurrent patients. *Psychopathology*, *35*, 335–340.

Norman, D. A. & Bobrow, D. (1979). Descriptions: an intermediate stage in memory retrieval. *Cognitive Psychology*, *11*, 107–123.

Orbach, Y., Lamb, M. E., Sternberg, K. J., Williams, J. M. G. & Dawud-Noursi, S. (2001). The effect of being a victim or witness of family violence on the retrieval of autobiographical memories. *Child Abuse and Neglect*, *25*, 1427–1437.

Peeters, F., Wessel, I., Merckelbach, H. & Boon-Vermeeren, M. (2002). Autobiographical memory specificity and the course of major depressive disorder. *Comprehensive Psychiatry*, *43*, 344–350.

Phillips, S. & Williams, J. M. G. (1997). Cognitive impairment, depression, and the specificity of autobiographical memory in the elderly. *British Journal of Clinical Psychology*, *36*, 341–348.

Pillemer, D. B. (1998). *Momentous Events, Vivid Memories*. Cambridge, MA; London: Harvard University Press.

Pillemer, D. B., Goldsmith, L. R., Panter, A. T. & White, S. H. (1988). Very long term memories of the first year in college. *Journal of Experimental Psychology; Learning, Memory and Cognition*, *14*, 709–715.

Pollock, L. R. & Williams, J. M. G. (2001). Effective problem solving in suicide attempters depends on specific autobiographical recall. *Suicide and Life Threatening Behavior*, *31*, 386–396.

Puffet, A., Jehin-Marchot, D., Timsit-Berthier, M. & Timsit, M. (1991). Autobiographical memory and major depressive states. *European Psychiatry*, *6*, 141–145.

Raes, F., Hermans, D., de Decker, A., Eelen, P. & Williams, J. M. G. (2003). Autobiographical memory specificity and affect-regulation: an experimental approach. *Emotion*, *3*, 201–206.

Ramponi, C., Barnard, P. & Nimmo-Smith, I. (in press). Recollection deficits in dysphoric mood: an effect of schematic models and executive mode? *Memory*.

Reiser, B. J., Black, J. B. & Abelson, R. P. (1985). Knowledge structures in the organization and retrieval of autobiographical memories. *Cognitive Psychology*, *17*, 89–137.

Schonfeld, S. & Ehlers, A. (2003). *Changes in Autobiographical Memory in Patients with PTSD*. Paper presented at 3rd Autobiographical Memory and Psychopathology meeting, Le Lingely, Belgium, May 2003.

Sidley, G. L., Whitaker, K., Calam, R. M. & Wells, A. (1997). The relationship between problem solving and autobiographical memory in parasuicide patients. *Behavioural and Cognitive Psychotherapy*, 25, 195–202.

Singer, J. A. & Moffitt, K. H. (1992). An experimental investigation of specificity and generality in memory narratives. *Imagination, Cognition and Personality*, 11, 233–257.

Swales, M. A., Williams, J. M. G. & Wood, P. (2001). Specificity of autobiographical memory and mood disturbance in adolescents. *Cognition and Emotion*, 15, 321–331.

Teasdale, J. D. & Barnard, P. J. (1993). *Affect, Cognition and Change: Re-modelling Depressive Thought*. Hove: Erlbaum.

Wahler, R. G. & Afton, A. D. (1980). Attentional processes in insular and non-insular mothers: some differences in their summary reports about child problem behaviors. *Child Behaviour Therapy*, 2, 25–41.

Wahler, R. G. & Sansbury, L. E. (1990). The monitoring skills of troubled mothers: their problems in defining child deviance. *Journal of Abnormal Child Psychology*, 95, 144–149.

Watkins, E. & Teasdale, J. D. (2001). Rumination and over-general memory in depression: effects of self-focus and analytic thinking. *Journal of Abnormal Psychology*, 110, 353–357.

Watkins, E., Teasdale, J. D. & Williams, R. M. (2000). Decentering and distraction reduce over-general autobiographical memory in depression. *Psychological Medicine*, 30, 911–920.

Wessel, I., Meeren, M., Peeters, F., Arntz, A. & Merckelbach, H. (2001). Correlates of autobiographical memory specificity: the role of depression, anxiety, and childhood trauma. *Behavior Research and Therapy*, 39, 409–421.

Wilhelm, S., McNally, R. J., Baer, L. & Florin, I. (1997). Autobiographical memory in obsessive-compulsive disorder. *British Journal of Clinical Psychology*, 36, 21–31.

Williams, J. M. G. (1988). General and specific autobiographical memory and emotional disturbance. In M. Gruneberg, P. Morris & R. Sykes (Eds.), *Practical Aspects of Memory: Current Research and Issues*. Chichester: John Wiley.

Williams, J. M. G. (1996). Autobiographical memory in depression. In D. Rubin (Ed.), *Remembering our Past: Studies in Autobiographical Memory*. Cambridge: Cambridge University Press.

Williams, J. M. G. & Broadbent, K. (1986). Autobiographical memory in attempted suicide patients. *Journal of Abnormal Psychology*, 95, 144–149.

Williams, J. M. G. & Dritschel, B. H., (1988). Emotional disturbance and the specificity of autobiographical memory. *Cognition and Emotion*, 2, 221–234.

Williams, J. M. G. & Dritschel, B. H. (1992). Categoric and extended autobiographical memories. In M. Conway, D. Rubin, H. Spinnler & W. Wagenaar (Eds.), *Theoretical Perspectives on Autobiographical Memory*, 391–412. Dordrecht, Boston & London: Kluwer Academic Publishers.

Williams, J. M. G., Eade, J. E. & Wallace, P. (in preparation). Fifty ways to lose a lover: interpersonal problem solving depends on memory specificity.

Williams, J. M. G., Ellis, N. C., Tyers, C., Macleod, A. K. & Rose, G. (1996). Specificity of autobiographical memory and imageability of the future. *Memory and Cognition*, 24, 116–125.

Williams, J. M. G. & Scott, J. (1988). Autobiographical memory in depression. *Psychological Medicine, 18*, 689–695.

Williams, J. M. G., Teasdale, J. D., Segal, Z. V. & Soulsby, J. (2000). Mindfulness-based cognitive therapy reduces over-general autobiographical memory in formerly depressed patients. *Journal of Abnormal Psychology, 109*, 150–155.

Williams, M. D. & Hollan J. D. (1981). Processes of retrieval from very long-term memory. *Cognitive Science, 5*, 87–119.

13   Mindfulness-based cognitive therapy

John D. Teasdale

One of Andrew Mathews' most important contributions to our field has been the demonstration that anxiety is associated with an attentional bias towards threat-related material. This bias provides a plausible basis for understanding the origins and maintenance of anxiety-related disorders in terms of self-perpetuating, interacting processes: selective attention to threat means that experience is more likely to be interpreted in threatening ways; these interpretations will generate further anxiety; that anxiety will reinforce the attentional bias, and so on.

From this perspective, it might seem counterproductive, even foolish, to train anxious patients to deliberately focus their attention towards unpleasant aspects of their experience. And yet this is a central component of the application of mindfulness training to emotional disorders, and there is encouraging evidence (reviewed by Baer, 2003) that such training can reduce symptoms of generalized anxiety disorder (GAD) and panic.

Clearly, there is more than one way we might attend to unpleasant aspects of our experience. For example, we might attend to our unpleasant experience as if we were a scientist, curious about the precise nature of the constellation of thoughts, feelings and body sensations that comprise the experience; or, we might attend to the unpleasant experience as revealing an aspect of ourselves that we loathe and despise; or, indeed, we might attend to the unpleasant experience as a potential threat to our physical or mental well-being. In this chapter, I will consider how mindfully attending to unwanted experience may alleviate, rather than exacerbate, emotional disorders. Mindfulness, here, means 'paying attention in a particular way: on purpose, in the present moment, and nonjudgmentally' (Kabat-Zinn, 1994, p. 4).

My work in this area has been conducted in a close collaboration with Zindel Segal and Mark Williams. Together, we have developed a novel treatment programme, mindfulness-based cognitive therapy for depression (MBCT) (Segal, Williams & Teasdale, 2002). MBCT was designed to reduce relapse and recurrence in patients with recurrent major depressive disorder. (Relapse and recurrence both refer to the return of symptoms of major depression following a period of being well: relapse refers to an onset occurring after a relatively short period; recurrence refers to an onset after a longer period.)

Historically, the development of MBCT sprang from attempts to understand:

1. The processes mediating depressive relapse/recurrence,
2. The way that conventional cognitive behaviour therapy for depression (CBT) (Beck, Rush, Shaw & Emery, 1979) reduced relapse/recurrence by disrupting those processes, and
3. The nature of mindfulness training.

Cognitive vulnerability to relapse and recurrence

Individuals who have experienced episodes of depression in the past are at a substantially greater risk of onset of episodes of major depression in the future than those without such experience (Judd, 1997). If we were to design an intervention to reduce this greater risk, it was important to identify the cognitive processes mediating this vulnerability; these processes would be the targets that the intervention sought to change.

We adopted the differential activation hypothesis of cognitive vulnerability (Teasdale, 1988). This hypothesis proposes that individuals who have recovered from major depression differ from individuals who have never experienced major depression in the patterns of thinking activated when they experience mild depressed mood (dysphoria) (and also see Persons & Miranda, 1992). Specifically, the differential activation hypothesis suggests that, in recovered depressed patients, the thinking activated by dysphoria shows similarities to the negative thinking patterns previously present in depressive episodes. These patterns commonly involve globally negative views of the self, and a hopeless view of the future, and are assumed to maintain depression. Reactivation of such thinking by dysphoria in those with a history of major depression makes it more likely that dysphoria will progress, through escalating self-perpetuating cycles of cognitive-affective ruminative processing (Teasdale, 1988, 1997), to more intense and persistent states, increasing risk of onset of a further episode of major depression.

Studies comparing the patterns of thinking activated by dysphoria in those with and without a history of major depression support the differential activation account; recovered depressed patients show greater activation of globally negative views of the self and dysfunctional attitudes (Ingram, Miranda & Segal, 1998). They also show a greater tendency to respond ruminatively to their depressed mood (Spasojevi & Alloy, 2001).

What is reactivated?

Our best hypothesis was that it is actually a whole processing configuration, or 'mind' (Teasdale, 1997), which gets 'wheeled in' in states of dysphoria in depression-prone individuals. This configuration is characterized by habitual ruminative thought patterns revolving around a globally negative view of self, reinforced by feedback loops involving the effects of depression on the body (Teasdale et al., 1995). Consistent with this hypothesis, a ruminative style of responding to depression ('repetitively focusing on the fact that one is depressed; on one's symptoms of depression; and on the causes, meanings, and consequences of depressive symptoms', Nolen-Hoeksema, 1991) is consistently associated with more persistent and intense depressed states, and a negative self-focus is characteristic of depression (Ingram, 1990; Pyszczynski & Greenberg, 1987).

Analyses of rumination (e.g. Pyszczynski & Greenberg, 1987) suggest that it involves a process that continually monitors and evaluates conceptual representations of the current situation against conceptual representations of what is desired, required, feared or expected. In depressive rumination, the goal of such processing is to get rid of current depressive experiences and to avoid future depressed states. In many situations, such discrepancy-based processing can be effective in achieving goals and solving practical problems. However, in depressive rumination, such processing is disastrously counterproductive. We can identify a number of features that distinguish maladaptive rumination from adaptive discrepancy-based problem solving. First, rumination tends to focus on aspects of the self, both our affective experience and our more enduring views of self, whereas adaptive problem solving tends to focus on states of the world. Second, rumination tends to involve relatively automatic, habitual patterns of cognitive processing, often occurring unattended, 'at the back of the mind'. By contrast, adaptive problem solving is more likely to involve intentional, deliberate, cognitive processing. Third, as discussed in more detail later, the avoidance motivation underlying rumination is an important factor, making it particularly counterproductive as a response to negative self-states.

Essentially, rumination tries to 'think' a way out of emotional difficulties by dwelling on conceptual representations of current emotional and self-states, previous negative experiences and anticipated problems if current states of mind persist. There is a tragic mismatch between these cognitive strategies and what is required to change the self-perpetuating states of mind that underpin persistent negative affect. Discrepancies between current and desired self-states may motivate attempts to reduce these discrepancies, but they also fuel the generation of further undesired negative affect (Higgins, 1987). In this way, attempts to solve affective problems by endlessly thinking about them can serve merely to keep the individual locked into the state from which they are trying to escape.

From this perspective, the key task in relapse prevention is to disengage from these relapse-engendering states of mind into alternative states that are not so maladaptive. How was this to be achieved? Knowing that CBT is effective at reducing depressive relapse (e.g. Evans et al., 1992), an obvious starting-point to answering this question was to ask how that approach achieved these effects.

How does cognitive therapy reduce relapse and recurrence of depression?

At the time that Zindel Segal, Mark Williams and I considered this central question, it was generally assumed that CBT had its effects through changes in belief in the content of negative thoughts and dysfunctional assumptions – these, of course, are its explicit aims. We proposed an alternative (Teasdale et al., 1995). We suggested that, in the course of CBT, as a result of repeated experiences of responding to depressed mood with the following trained sequence, patients made a general shift in their mode of processing negative thoughts and feelings:

1. Make a deliberate pause.
2. Identify negative thoughts as they arise.
3. Stand back from them to evaluate the accuracy or adaptiveness of their content.

This mode of processing differed from the ruminative, relapse-related mode in at least two important respects. First, in contrast to the habitual ('automatic') quality of the ruminative cognitive mode, patients switched to a conscious, intentional mode. Second, rather than, as in the ruminative mode, seeing negative thoughts and feelings as necessarily valid reflections of reality, or identifying with them as aspects of the self, patients switched to a mode within which they could see such thoughts and feelings from a different perspective, simply as passing events in the mind that might or might not correspond to reality. The importance of such 'distancing' or 'decentring' had previously been recognized in discussions of CBT (e.g. Beck et al., 1979), but usually as a means to the end of changing belief in thought content. By contrast, our analysis suggested that this shift in relationship to thoughts and feelings might actually be the vehicle of therapeutic change, rather than merely the means to belief change.

A trial of CBT for residual depression provided evidence consistent with our alternative view. Teasdale et al. (2001) found that CBT reduced extreme response style in relation to depressive material, and that these changes mediated the reduction in relapse by CBT observed in that trial. The measure of extreme response style ('black and white thinking') used in this study was simply the number of times that an individual used the response options 'Totally agree' or 'Totally disagree' in answering a number of questionnaires, irrespective of whether the response was to items with positive or negative content. All these questionnaires used the same seven-category response format. Extreme response style ('Totally agree' or 'Totally disagree') was interpreted as a marker of a rapid, relatively automatic processing mode in which the initial dysfunctional products of schematic processing were immediately accepted, without being subjected to further reappraisal. In this way, these data supported the suggestion that CBT had its effects through teaching patients to switch from an 'automatic' ruminative mode into a more intentional mode, in which thoughts and feelings could be interpreted in other ways.

Using data from this same trial, Teasdale et al. (2002) found that CBT led to an increase in patients' ability to view negative feelings and thoughts from a decentred perspective. Early relapse was associated with failure to see such thoughts and feelings from a decentred perspective. Together with the evidence from the effects of CBT on extreme response style, these findings lent preliminary support to our view that CBT worked to prevent relapse by teaching patients, implicitly, to switch to an intentional cognitive mode, in which negative thoughts and feelings were viewed from a decentred perspective.

The attraction of this alternative view was that it gave us the freedom to consider alternative approaches that, while fostering a shift in the mode of processing of negative thoughts and feelings, might, unlike CBT, have no elements explicitly directed at changing belief in thought content. To understand our thinking here, it will be helpful to look more closely at the concept of cognitive mode. Much of this thinking was worked out within a comprehensive information-processing framework, Interacting Cognitive Subsystems (ICS) (Teasdale, 1997, 1999; Teasdale & Barnard, 1993; Teasdale et al., 1995). Here, I shall present the essence of these ideas without recourse to ICS terminology.

Modes of mind

We can think of the mind as an assembly of interacting components. Each of these components receives information arising from the world of the senses, or from other components of the mind. Each component processes the information it receives and passes the transformed information on to other components. These components then do the same again, and pass on more information. We can think of the workings of the mind as a continuous flow and exchange of information between its components. If we could look into the mind, we would notice that, over time, there were certain recurring patterns in the interactions between its components. For a while, one pattern would predominate, and then, in response to changes in the external or internal worlds, a shift would occur so that those same components of mind that previously interacted in one pattern would now do so in a different configuration. This would then prevail for a longer or shorter time until a further shift occurred, either back to the original pattern of interaction or to yet a further configuration. In this way, we could see the activity of the mind as continually shifting between recurring or evolving patterns of interaction between its components – a little like the way that, in a car driving through a busy city, there is a continuous sequence of shifts up and down between gears.

We can think of recurring patterns of interaction between mental components as modes of mind, loosely analogous to the gears of a car. Just as each gear has a particular use (starting, accelerating, cruising etc.), so each mode of mind has a characteristic function. In a car, a change of gear can be prompted either automatically (with an automatic transmission, by a device that detects when the engine speed reaches certain critical values) or intentionally (with a manual gear shift, by the driver making a decision to change gear). In the same way, modes of mind can change either automatically (triggered in response to the processing of particular kinds of information) or intentionally (by the individual consciously choosing to rehearse a particular intention or to deploy attention in a particular way).

Equally, just as a car cannot be simultaneously in two gears at the same time because both gears require exclusive access to a single engine, so the mind cannot at the same time be in two modes that require exclusive use of the same mental components. Operating in certain modes of mind automatically precludes being in certain other states of mind at the same time. Using the analogy of mental gears, the task of relapse prevention could be seen as giving patients skills to change mental gears so that, at times of potential relapse, they could recognize the mental gear that supports rumination, disengage from it and shift to a more functional, incompatible mental gear, or cognitive mode. Mindfulness training offers a way to do that.

What is mindfulness and how is it relevant to reducing vulnerability to relapse/recurrence?

Relapse-related rumination involves a particular cognitive mode, characterized by habitual ('automatic') processing routines, focused on conceptual-level representations ('thinking about'), directed at getting rid of or avoiding unwanted self-states. The idea of cognitive modes suggests that it is not just *what* is processed that determines whether relapse ensues, but *how* that material is processed. In other words, the problem with relapse-related rumination is not just that processing is dominated by negative self-related material, but that this material is processed within a particular cognitive mode. Viewed from this perspective, one way to pre-empt the establishment of relapse-related processing would be to establish a cognitive mode different from that of depressive rumination, and then process depression-related and other material within that alternative cognitive mode.

Mindfulness can be seen as just such an alternative cognitive mode. As already noted, mindfulness has been defined as 'paying attention in a particular way: on purpose, in the present moment, and nonjudgmentally' (Kabat-Zinn, 1994, p. 4). Mindfulness has been afforded central importance within many religious and spiritual traditions. The Buddhist tradition, in particular, has developed methods of cultivating mindfulness through meditation, and these methods have been in use for two and a half thousand years. It is only relatively recently that mindfulness training has been applied in clinical contexts. This has largely been through the work of Jon Kabat-Zinn and his colleagues. These workers have developed a mindfulness-based stress reduction (MBSR) programme (Kabat-Zinn, 1990) that is accessible to the average citizen in purely secular health care settings. The MBSR programme and related interventions have now been applied to a wide range of clinical problems (Baer, 2003).

If we consider Kabat-Zinn's definition of mindfulness, we can see that on each component of this definition, mindfulness as a cognitive mode provides an exact antithesis to the ruminative cognitive mode that dominates relapse-related processing. First, mindfulness is intentional ('on purpose'), in contrast to the 'automatic' (in the sense of running off highly practised habitual cognitive routines) quality of rumination.

Second, mindfulness is experiential, focusing directly on present experience, in contrast to the predominantly conceptual emphasis of rumination, which focuses on thoughts *about* experience, most of which are oriented to the past or future. Further, when thoughts about the past, future or present are processed within the mindful mode they are treated as mental events occurring in the present moment, to which attention can be directed as objects of experience, rather than identified with as self, or automatically treated as valid reflections of reality. Relating to thoughts simply as mental events in this way embodies the decentred perspective on internal experience. As noted earlier, our analysis of the mechanism of action of CBT had suggested that the effects of CBT in preventing relapse/recurrence were mediated through teaching patients to adopt this perspective with respect to patterns of negative thinking reactivated by dysphoria at times of potential relapse/recurrence.

Third, the non-judgmental characteristic of mindfulness means that pleasant and unpleasant experiences are treated simply as that, as experiences. This stands in contrast to treating them conceptually, as 'good things' or 'bad things', as they would be in goal-related discrepancy-based ruminative processing, the core of which is the constant evaluation of conceptual representations of experience against conceptual representations of desired and undesired goal states.

Finally, the emphasis within mindfulness training on being fully present, open to and accepting of the content of moment-by-moment experience, whether it is pleasant, unpleasant or neutral, is of obvious relevance to reducing the cognitive and experiential avoidance (Hayes, et al., 1996) which often seems an important contributor to relapse.

In summary, our analysis suggested that risk of relapse and recurrence would be reduced if patients who have recovered from episodes of major depression could learn, first, to be more aware of the ruminative cognitive mode that rendered them vulnerable at times of potential relapse/recurrence, and, second, to learn how, at such times, to disengage from that mode and shift to an alternative, incompatible cognitive mode ('mental gear'). Mindfulness training offered a means to each of these ends, providing awareness of dysfunctional modes, the means to switch modes, and a more adaptive cognitive mode within which depression-related material could be processed. In the longer term, repeatedly shifting to a decentred perspective with respect to negative thoughts and feelings would, we hypothesized, also create alternative metacognitive representations, in which such thoughts and feelings would be seen simply as events passing through the mind. We assumed that these representations would mediate more enduring reductions in risk of relapse and recurrence, over and above any use of mindfulness skills as coping devices.

Having presented the ideas behind MBCT, let us now look at it in more detail.

Mindfulness-based cognitive therapy (MBCT)

MBCT is designed to teach patients in remission from recurrent major depression to become more aware of, and to relate differently to, their thoughts, feelings and bodily sensations. The programme teaches skills that allow individuals to disengage from habitual ('automatic') dysfunctional cognitive routines, in particular depression-related ruminative thought patterns, as a way to reduce future relapse and recurrence of depression.

MBCT is a manualized group skills training programme (Segal et al., 2002) that draws heavily on the mindfulness-based stress reduction programme developed by Kabat-Zinn (1990), and integrates it with compatible elements of CBT. Unlike CBT, in MBCT there is little emphasis on changing belief in the *content* of negative thoughts; rather, the emphasis is on cultivating greater mindfulness with respect to thoughts, feelings and bodily sensations. Such mindfulness involves:

1. An intentional, rather than habitual (automatic), mode of processing;
2. A shift to a decentred relationship to thoughts and feelings, so that these are no longer identified with as aspects of the self, or as necessarily accurate reflections of reality, but are treated as objects of attention in much the same way that we might attend to sounds arising and passing away; and
3. A stance of radical acceptance towards unpleasant thoughts, feelings and bodily sensations that pre-empts habitual response tendencies to escape, avoid or 'fix' unpleasant emotional states; although motivated by a desire to get rid of unwanted states, such responses actually act to maintain them (Hayes, Wilson, Strosahl, Gifford & Follette, 1996).

Aspects of CBT included in MBCT are primarily:

1. The sharing of a cognitive model that provides a way of understanding depression, depressive relapse and relapse prevention;
2. Exercises designed to facilitate the shift to a decentred relationship with negative thoughts, and
3. The skilful use of activities in the service of mood regulation.

Because, unlike CBT, there is little explicit emphasis in MBCT on changing belief in the content or specific meanings of negative automatic thoughts, training can occur in the remitted state, using everyday experiences as the objects of practice.

The MBCT programme

After an initial individual orientation session, the MBCT programme is delivered by an instructor in eight weekly two-hour group training sessions, involving up to twelve recovered recurrently depressed patients. During this period, the programme includes daily homework exercises. Homework invariably includes some form of guided (taped) or unguided awareness exercises, directed at increasing moment-by-moment non-judgmental awareness of bodily sensations, thoughts and feelings, together with exercises designed to integrate application of awareness skills into daily life.

A core feature of the programme involves facilitation of an aware mode of being, characterized by greater freedom and choice, in contrast to a mode dominated by habitual, overlearned automatic patterns of cognitive-affective processing. For patients, this distinction is illustrated by reference to the common experience, when driving on a familiar route, of suddenly realizing that one has been driving for miles 'on automatic pilot', unaware of the road or of other vehicles, preoccupied with planning future activities or ruminating on a current concern. By contrast, mindful driving is associated with being fully present in each moment, consciously aware of sights, sounds, thoughts and body sensations as they arise. When mindful, the mind responds afresh to the unique pattern of experience in each moment, rather than reacting mindlessly to fragments of a total experience with old, relatively stereotyped, habitual patterns of mind. Increased mindfulness allows early detection of relapse-related patterns of negative thinking, feelings and body sensations, so allowing them to be 'nipped in the bud' at a stage when this may be much easier than if such warning signs are not noticed, or are ignored. Further, entering a mindful mode of processing at such times allows disengagement from the relatively automatic ruminative thought patterns that would otherwise fuel the relapse process. Formulation of specific relapse/recurrence prevention strategies is also included in the later stages of the programme.

Following the initial eight weekly group meetings, follow-up meetings are scheduled at increasing intervals.

Evaluating MBCT

Two clinical trials have evaluated the effects of MBCT on the subsequent experiences of major depression of recurrently depressed patients, in recovery at the time of entry to the trial. Choice of an appropriate design for the initial evaluation of a novel intervention, such as MBCT, is influenced by a number of factors. At the time we planned the first trial, there was no published evidence that any psychological intervention, initially administered in the recovered state, could prospectively reduce risk of recurrence in major depression. Given this situation, the first priority was to evaluate whether MBCT was of *any* benefit in reducing relapse/recurrence; if benefits were observed, subsequent research could compare MBCT with other psychological interventions, including controls for attention-placebo factors, and with alternative approaches to prevention, such as maintenance pharmacotherapy.

We used a simple additive design in which patients who continued with treatment-as-usual (TAU) were compared with patients who, additionally, received training in MBCT. Such a design does not allow any reduction in rates of relapse and recurrence for patients receiving MBCT to be attributed unambiguously to the specific components of MBCT, rather than to non-specific factors, such as therapeutic attention or group participation. However, this design was the most appropriate to answer the question that was of primary interest to us: does MBCT, when offered in addition to TAU, reduce rates of relapse and recurrence compared to TAU alone?

The first trial (Teasdale et al., 2000)

At three different treatment sites, a total of 145 patients, currently in remission or recovery from major depression, were randomized to continue with TAU or, additionally, to receive MBCT. To enter the trial, patients had to have experienced at least two previous episodes of major depression, the most recent two episodes occurring within the preceding five years. All patients had previously been treated with antidepressant medication but had been well and off medication for at least three months before entering the trial. None had previously received CBT.

After baseline assessments and randomization to treatment condition, patients entered an initial seven-week treatment phase, after which they were followed up for a year. The primary outcome variable was whether and when patients experienced relapse or recurrence of major depression, as assessed by bimonthly clinical interviews.

The sample was stratified on number of previous episodes of major depression (two versus three or more). Before conducting the main statistical analyses, we checked that the relative effects of MBCT and TAU were the same in patients in these different strata. When we did this, we found a significant interaction of treatment by number of previous episodes, indicating that the treatments were differentially effective in these two groups of patients. In patients with three or more previous episodes (who made up 77 per cent of the total sample) MBCT significantly halved relapse/recurrence rates (MBCT 37 per cent versus TAU 66 per cent), but in patients with only two previous episodes, MBCT showed no reduction in relapse/recurrence (MBCT 54 per cent versus TAU 31 per cent; this difference, based on samples of thirteen and sixteen, was non-significant). For the patients recruited to this trial, the benefits of MBCT were restricted to those with more extensive histories of depression.

In TAU patients, risk of relapse and recurrence over the study period increased in a statistically significant linear relationship with number of previous episodes: two episodes, 31 per cent; three episodes, 56 per cent; and four or more episodes 72 per cent. In patients receiving MBCT, there was no significant relationship between number of previous episodes and risk of relapse/recurrence: 54 per cent relapsed in the two-episode group; 37 per cent relapsed in the three or more episodes group. MBCT apparently eliminated the increased risk of relapse in patients with three or more previous episodes of depression.

The most important finding of this trial was that, in participants with three or more previous episodes of depression, MBCT almost halved relapse/recurrence rates over the follow-up period, compared to TAU. Because patients were seen in groups, this benefit was achieved for an average investment of less than five hours of health professional time per patient, making MBCT a cost-efficient approach to prevention of depression.

The finding that MBCT reduced relapse and recurrence in patients with three or more previous episodes of depression, but not in patients with only two previous episodes, is of particular interest with respect to the theoretical background to MBCT (Segal et al., 1996; Teasdale et al., 1995). MBCT was specifically designed to reduce the effects on relapse and recurrence of patterns of depressive thinking reactivated by dysphoria. Such dysphoria-linked thinking, it was assumed, resulted from repeated associations between the depressed state and negative thinking patterns. The strengthening of these associations with repeated episodes was assumed to contribute to the observed increased risk of further episodes with every successive episode experienced. In particular, it was assumed that negative thinking reactivated by dysphoria contributed to the increasingly autonomous nature of the relapse/recurrence process with multiple episodes: environmental provoking events have been found to play a progressively less important role in onset with increasing number of episodes (Post, 1992).

This account suggests that, in this trial:

1. The greater risk of relapse/recurrence in those with three or more episodes than in those with only two episodes (apparent in TAU) was attributable to autonomous relapse/recurrence processes involving reactivation of depressogenic thinking by dysphoria.

2. Prophylactic effects of MBCT arose, specifically, from disruption of those processes at times of potential relapse/recurrence. Consistent with this analysis, MBCT appeared to have no prophylactic effects in those with only two previous episodes, and the rate to which relapse/recurrence was reduced by MBCT in those with three and more episodes (37 per cent) was similar to the rate of relapse/recurrence in those with only two episodes receiving TAU (31 per cent).

Alternatively, it is possible that the differences in response to MBCT of patients with three or more versus only two previous episodes were not solely the result of differences in previous experience of depression, but also reflected the fact that they came from different base populations, with distinct psychopathologies. In this case, in this trial, the number of previous episodes might have been a marker of particular psychopathologies, rather than (or as well as) the cause of the observed differential response to MBCT. Consistent with this possibility, patients with only two previous episodes were significantly older when they experienced their first episode of depression than individuals with three or more episodes.

The second trial (Ma & Teasdale, 2004)

A second trial was conducted to address a number of issues raised by the first trial. The same basic design was employed, but this time all seventy-five patients were recruited at one treatment site. A primary aim of this trial was to see whether the relapse prevention effects of MBCT observed by Teasdale et al. (2000) for patients with three or more previous episodes of depression (who, in this second trial, again made up three-quarters of the total sample) could be replicated. The new results showed that they could; again, MBCT halved relapse/recurrence rates compared with TAU (36 per cent versus 78 per cent), this time for the investment of less than three hours' instructor time per patient, on average. (The reduction in average instructor time from the first trial reflected a reduction in the number of follow-up sessions, and the fact that the initial induction interview was combined with the initial assessment interview.) MBCT does, indeed, appear to offer a cost-efficient and efficacious approach to prevention in this group of patients.

A second aim was to see whether further evidence could be obtained of differential response to MBCT in a group of patients with three or more episodes versus a group with only two (recent) episodes. Again, the earlier findings were replicated; the difference in relapse/recurrence rates between MBCT (50 per cent) and TAU (20 per cent) in patients with just two episodes was significantly different from, and in the opposite direction to, the difference in relapse rates between MBCT and TAU in patients with three or more episodes. As in the first trial, the difference in relapse/recurrence rates between MBCT and TAU in patients with two episodes was, itself, non-significant.

A third aim was to test the hypothesis that MBCT is specifically effective in preventing relapses mediated by autonomous, internal processes (such as reactivation of patterns of negative ruminative thinking by dysphoria) rather than relapses provoked by stressful life events, and that this can account for its ineffectiveness in the group of patients with only two previous episodes. Consistent with this view, in patients with three or more episodes, the difference in the percentage of patients relapsing in the TAU and MBCT groups was greatest in relapses occurring in the absence of any obvious provoking life events (TAU 26 per cent, MBCT 4 per cent), and least in relapses associated with severe life events, where there was actually no difference (7 per cent versus 7 per cent). Further, this differential effectiveness of MBCT for different types of relapse could account for the failure of MBCT to benefit patients with only two episodes. In contrast to patients with three or more episodes, nearly all the relapses in patients with only two episodes were associated with severe life events, and these were just the kind of relapses that, within the three or more episodes group, MBCT was ineffective at reducing.

A final aim of the second trial was to seek evidence to clarify, using our selection criteria and recruitment procedures:

1. Whether the patients recruited with only two episodes were from the same base population as those recruited with three or more episodes, and simply at an earlier point in their depressive career, or
2. Whether these two groups actually represented distinct populations with different psychopathologies.

As in the first trial, patients with three or more episodes were found to have an earlier onset of first depression than patients with only two episodes. They also reported more adverse childhood experiences. Both differences support the hypothesis that, in the context of the selection criteria used in these trials, patients with three or more episodes and patients with two episodes came originally from distinct populations.

Together, these two trials suggest that MBCT is a cost-efficient and efficacious intervention to reduce relapse/recurrence in patients with recurrent major depressive disorder who, following a reportedly adverse childhood, have experienced three or more previous episodes of depression, the first of which was relatively early in their lives. MBCT appears to be most effective in preventing relapse/recurrence that is unrelated to environmental provocation. This finding is consistent with MBCT having its effects, as intended, through the disruption of autonomous, relapse-related cognitive-affective ruminative processes reactivated by dysphoria at times of potential relapse. The apparent failure of MBCT to prevent relapse in the particular group of patients with only two previous episodes that were studied in these trials appears to reflect the fact that these patients originated from a different base population, with normal reported childhood experience, later initial onset of major depression, and relapse/recurrence predominantly associated with major life events. MBCT appears to be contra-indicated for this group.

Adaptive and maladaptive forms of self-attention

Having described the development and evaluation of MBCT, let us now return to the question posed at the beginning of this chapter: how can we reconcile the fact that selectively attending to negative material is part of the psychopathology of emotional disorders with the fact that training patients to attend to unpleasant information in mindfulness-based clinical programmes appears to be helpful? If we focus analysis at the level of the content processed by specific cognitive operations, then, indeed, these facts seem anomalous. However, this problem resolves if we focus analysis at the level of cognitive modes – wider, integrated configurations of processing operations that cut across specific contents. From this perspective, the effects of specific pieces of information depend on *how* that information is processed within such wider configurations: to understand the effects of deploying attention to particular material, we need to recognize that attention is never deployed in isolation, but always as part of a wider processing configuration. Depending on the overall cognitive mode within which attention is deployed, the effects of attending to the same material may vary from the maladaptive to the adaptive.

A recent study by Watkins and Teasdale (in press) gives direct support to this position. Depressed patients were instructed to self-focus attention in one of two conditions for eight minutes. The aspects of the self that patients focused on were the same in both conditions; the conditions differed in *how* patients were asked to focus their attention. In 'analytical' self-focus, patients thought about those aspects, their causes, meanings and consequences, much as they might in rumination. In the 'experiential' condition, patients focused their attention directly on the experience of those aspects, much as they might in mindfulness training. The effects of the two conditions were compared on a measure of over-general autobiographical memory, high scores on which have been associated with the persistence of clinical depression (Williams, 1996). Analytical self-focus maintained patients' elevated scores on over-general autobiographical memory. By contrast, experiential self-focus significantly reduced these scores. Such evidence demonstrates that, even when attention was focused on identical topics in the two forms of self-attention, different modes of attention had very different effects – maladaptive in one case, adaptive in the other.

The analytical and experiential conditions in Watkins and Teasdale's study differed in the level of representation to which attention was directed. A study by Trapnell and Campbell (1999) suggests that other differences were probably of equal, or greater, importance. These workers distinguished two modes of self-focus, rumination and reflection. Both modes emphasized conceptual processing, but the modes differed strikingly in their patterns of association: rumination was correlated with neuroticism, whereas reflection was correlated with openness to experience, a measure of psychological health. Trapnell and Campbell suggested that the crucial difference between rumination and reflection was their underlying motivations: rumination is neurotically motivated (e.g. by anxiety), whereas reflection is philosophically or epistemically motivated (e.g. by curiosity).

Trapnell and Campbell's (1999) suggestion has important implications for our consideration of ruminative analytical self-focus and experiential mindful self-focus. It suggests that, in understanding why one is maladaptive and the other is adaptive, the fundamental difference may not be the level of representation that controls processing so much as its underlying motivations. I suggested earlier that the ruminative cognitive mode uses analytical, conceptual processing in the service of an underlying avoidance motivation – to get rid of depression and to avoid its future adverse consequences and recurrence. By contrast, mindfulness, with its emphasis on non-judgment and radical acceptance, has a more approach-based underlying motivation, akin to curiosity and openness to novelty. (Approach here is used in the sense of turning towards, or being positively oriented to, rather than in the sense of striving to attain a valued goal.)

The distinction between approach and avoidance motivations is fundamental, rooted in our biological apparatus, and has widespread ramifications (Elliot & Thrash, 2002). A recent study by Friedman and Forster (2001) provides compelling evidence of the way that, depending on the underlying motivation with which an apparently trivial behaviour is performed, our whole information processing system can be swung, quite automatically, into an approach-dominated mode or an avoidance-dominated mode, with very different effects on cognitive function. Completion of a paper-and-pencil maze was used to prime an underlying approach or avoidance motivation. In both conditions, a cartoon mouse was shown trapped inside a maze with the instructions: 'Find the way for the mouse'. In the approach condition, a piece of Swiss cheese was shown lying outside the maze, in front of a brick wall containing an entry for the mouse. In the avoidance condition, instead of Swiss cheese, an owl was shown above the maze, ready to swoop down and capture the mouse unless it could escape the maze and retreat through the entry. Although solving the maze took less than two minutes, the condition with which the maze was performed powerfully affected scores on a subsequent measure of creativity; participants who had completed the cheese maze generated significantly more creative uses for a brick than participants who had completed the owl maze. Friedman and Forster concluded that the cues in the two mazes, through association, had 'switched on' two very different cognitive modes, the 'risky', explorative style of the approach mode, fostering creativity, relative to the risk-averse style of the avoidance mode.

This line of reasoning suggests that a crucial difference between the attention paid to unpleasant material in affective disorders and in mindfulness training is that, in those disorders, attention is deployed as part of a wider cognitive mode with an underlying avoidance motivation. By contrast, in mindfulness, attention is deployed as part of a wider cognitive mode with an underlying approach motivation. If this analysis is correct, it suggests that, for mindfulness training to have beneficial effects, it is crucial that the cognitive mode trained should have an underlying approach motivation. This is well-recognized by experienced teachers within the meditation tradition from which clinical applications of mindfulness have been derived, e.g.

The quality of transforming attention is one of curiosity and interest. Burglars may have wonderful concentration, a soldier going into battle may be remarkably focused, and a stalker may have a highly developed single-pointedness. But there is a real difference between the concentration of obsession and preoccupation, and the attention of mindfulness. Mindful attention is light, gentle, warm; above all it is dedicated to understanding and freedom. It is both single-pointed, and open and receptive in the same moment (Feldman, 2001, p. 177).

Helping patients to learn to attend in this way is not necessarily easy, particularly when it is remembered that much of what they will be asked to attend to will be unpleasant and unwelcome, and that the main vehicle through which this quality of attention is communicated is the quality of attention which the mindfulness instructor embodies in this teaching. It is for this reason that, unusual as it may seem, it is widely recommended that potential instructors of mindfulness-based clinical interventions should, themselves, learn mindfulness on a personal basis before attempting to teach it to patients (e.g. Segal et al., 2002, p. 324). Equally, such reasoning suggests that the clinical outcomes of mindfulness-based procedures may be powerfully affected by the qualities of the instructors.

Conclusions

Our theoretical analyses of the processes mediating the onset of depressive episodes in patients with recurrent major depression, and of the processes through which cognitive behavioural therapy (CBT) reduced depressive relapse and recurrence led us to design mindfulness-based cognitive therapy (MBCT). This programme draws heavily on mindfulness-based stress reduction (MBSR), as developed by Jon Kabat-Zinn and colleagues, and integrates it with aspects of CBT for depression. The results of our trials suggest that this integration yielded a cost-efficient preventative programme that can be effective in substantially reducing risk of relapse and recurrence in patients with three or more previous episodes of depression.

In developing MBCT, the generic MBSR programme was modified to increase its relevance to the particular target of preventing relapse and recurrence in major depression. Taken with the results from smaller, or less controlled, evaluations suggesting the effectiveness of the generic MBSR programme in treating a range of disorders (reviewed by Baer, 2003), the effectiveness of MBCT suggests that mindfulness-based clinical interventions may hold considerable therapeutic promise, either alone, or in combination with other forms of intervention. In particular, CBT and mindfulness-based approaches offer complementary, and therefore potentially synergistic, approaches to emotional disorders, suggesting that the general strategy of combining them may be relevant to a wider range of problems, beyond relapse prevention in recurrent depression.

REFERENCES

Baer, R. A. (2003). Mindfulness training as a clinical intervention: a conceptual and empirical review. *Clinical Psychology: Science and Practice, 10,* 125–143.

Beck, A. T., Rush, A. J., Shaw, B. F. & Emery, G. (1979). *Cognitive Therapy of Depression.* New York: Guilford.

Elliot, A. J. & Thrash, T. M. (2002). Approach–avoidance motivation in personality: approach and avoidance temperament and goals. *Journal of Personality and Social Psychology, 82,* 804–818.

Evans, M. D., Hollon, S. D., DeRubeis, R. J., Piasecki, J. M., Grove, W. M., Garvey, M. J. & Tuason, V. B. (1992). Differential relapse following cognitive therapy and pharmacotherapy for depression. *Archives of General Psychiatry, 49,* 802–808.

Feldman, C. (2001). *The Buddhist Path to Simplicity: Spiritual Practice for Everyday Life.* London: Thorsons.

Friedman, R. S. & Forster, J. (2001). The effects of promotion and prevention cues on creativity. *Journal of Personality and Social Psychology, 81,* 1001–1013.

Hayes, S. C., Wilson, K. G., Strosahl, K., Gifford, E. V. & Follette, V. M. (1996). Experiential avoidance and behavioral disorders: a functional dimensional approach to diagnosis and treatment. *Journal of Consulting and Clinical Psychology, 64,* 1152–1168.

Higgins, E. T. (1987). Self-discrepancy: a theory relating self and affect. *Psychological Review, 94,* 319–340.

Ingram, R. E. (1990). Self-focused attention in clinical disorders: review and a conceptual model. *Psychological Bulletin, 109,* 156–176.

Ingram, R. E., Miranda, J. & Segal, Z. V. (1998). *Cognitive Vulnerability to Depression.* New York: Guilford.

Judd, L. J. (1997). The clinical course of unipolar major depressive disorders. *Archives of General Psychiatry*, *54*, 989–991.

Kabat-Zinn, J. (1990). *Full Catastrophe Living: The Program of the Stress Reduction Clinic at the University of Massachusetts Medical Center*. New York: Delta.

Kabat-Zinn, J. (1994). *Wherever You Go, There You Are: Mindfulness Meditation in Everyday Life*. New York: Hyperion.

Ma, S. H. & Teasdale, J. D. (2004). Mindfulness-based cognitive therapy for depression: replication and exploration of differential relapse prevention effects. *Journal of Consulting and Clinical Psychology*, *72*, 31–40.

Nolen-Hoeksema, S. (1991). Responses to depression and their effects on the duration of depressive episodes. *Journal of Abnormal Psychology*, *100*, 569–582.

Persons, J. B. & Miranda, J. (1992). Cognitive theories of vulnerability to depression: reconciling negative evidence. *Cognitive Therapy and Research*, *16*, 485–502.

Post, R. M. (1992). Transduction of psychosocial stress into the neurobiology of recurrent affective disorder. *American Journal of Psychiatry*, *149*, 999–1010.

Pyszczynski, T. & Greenberg, J. (1987). Self-regulatory perseveration and the depressive self-focusing style: a self-awareness theory of reactive depression. *Psychological Bulletin*, *102*, 122–138.

Segal, Z. V., Williams, J. M. G. & Teasdale, J. D. (2002). *Mindfulness-based Cognitive Therapy for Depression: A New Approach to Preventing Relapse*. New York: Guilford.

Segal, Z. V., Williams, J. M., Teasdale, J. D. & Gemar, M. (1996). A cognitive science perspective on kindling and episode sensitisation in recurrent affective disorder. *Psychological Medicine*, *26*, 371–380.

Spasojevi, J. & Alloy, L. (2001). Rumination as a common mechanism relating depressive risk factors to depression. *Emotion*, *1*, 25–37.

Teasdale, J. D. (1988). Cognitive vulnerability to persistent depression. *Cognition and Emotion*, *2*, 247–274.

Teasdale, J. D. (1997). The relationship between cognition and emotion: the mind-in-place in mood disorders. In D. M. Clark and C. G. Fairburn (Eds.), *Science and Practice of Cognitive Behaviour Therapy*, 67–93. Oxford: Oxford University Press.

Teasdale, J. D. (1999). Emotional processing, three modes of mind and the prevention of relapse in depression. *Behaviour Research and Therapy*, *37*, S53–S78.

Teasdale, J. D. & Barnard, P. J. (1993). *Affect, Cognition and Change: Re-modelling Depressive Thought*. Hove: Erlbaum.

Teasdale, J. D., Moore, R. G., Hayhurst, H., Pope, M., Williams, S. & Segal, Z. V. (2002). Metacognitive awareness and prevention of relapse in depression: empirical evidence. *Journal of Consulting and Clinical Psychology*, *70*, 275–287.

Teasdale, J. D., Scott, J., Moore, R. G., Hayhurst, H., Pope, M. & Paykel, E. S. (2001). How does cognitive therapy prevent relapse in residual depression: evidence from a controlled trial. *Journal of Consulting and Clinical Psychology*, *69*, 347–357.

Teasdale, J. D., Segal, Z. V. & Williams, J. M. G. (1995). How does cognitive therapy prevent depressive relapse and why should attentional control (mindfulness) training help? *Behaviour Research and Therapy*, *33*, 25–39.

Teasdale, J. D., Segal, Z. V., Williams, J. M. G., Ridgeway, V. A., Soulsby, J. M. & Lau, M. A. (2000). Prevention of relapse/recurrence in major depression by mindfulness-based cognitive therapy. *Journal of Consulting and Clinical Psychology*, *68*, 615–623.

Trapnell, P. D. & Campbell, J. D. (1999). Private self-consciousness and the five-factor model of personality: distinguishing rumination from reflection. *Journal of Personality and Social Psychology*, *76*, 284–304.

Watkins, E. & Teasdale, J. D. (in press). Adaptive and maladaptive self-focus in depression. *Journal of Affective Disorders.*

Williams, J. M. G. (1996). Depression and the specificity of autobiographical memory. In D. Rubin (Ed.), *Remembering our Past: Studies in Autobiographical Memory*, 244–267. Cambridge: Cambridge University Press.

14   Clinical difficulties to revisit

Gillian Butler

When helping people with complex problems to take a constructive hold on their lives, it sometimes helps if you can fit things together. When analysing biases in emotional processing, it is important to pay close attention to fine detail. Both activities contribute to the development of a science, and the detailed work led and inspired by Andrew Mathews has played a significant part in bringing them closer together. We now know that experimentally established processing biases play a causal role in mediating vulnerability to anxiety, and that selectively manipulating the interpretive bias can modify anxious responses to stress (Mathews & MacLeod, 2002; MacLeod et al., this volume; Yiend & Mackintosh, this volume). Clinicians often behave as if they understand cause and effect. Discovering how it really works, even on a small scale, is of enormous clinical, as well as academic value. It is also the product of Andrew's open-minded curiosity, enthusiasm and ability to keep worrying away at unsolved problems without letting preconceptions intrude, which I valued as a Ph.D. student – and still value as a clinician working in a field in which science and practice are supposedly closely related.

Starting-points

For cognitive therapists, the work on anxiety disorders provides the paradigm example of a successful research and development strategy. It has produced the evidence for the evidence-based practice that providers supposedly offer. As a direct result, we now have working models to guide the treatment of panic disorder, social phobia, obsessive-compulsive disorder (OCD), health anxiety and post-traumatic stress disorder (PTSD) (Clark, 1999). These are testable models, subject to refinement as research findings continue to accumulate (Hirsch & Clark, this volume; Teasdale, this volume), and they are largely the product of the cognitive specificity hypothesis which suggests that each disorder has distinct cognitive characteristics with clear implications for the development of specific clinical techniques.

290

The success of the strategy generally underpins the decision of researchers to continue with it. For example, Arntz (1999) said that his aim was: 'to advocate the development of theoretical models of personality disorders that can be empirically tested [. . .] The field can learn a lot from the work that has been done in the area of anxiety disorders' (p. S98). The strategy he then recommended was to identify the specific (dysfunctional) cognitive characteristics associated with each personality disorder so as to devise specific intervention techniques to change them.

Earlier approaches to the practice of cognitive behavioural therapy (CBT) (e.g. Beck, Rush, Shaw & Emery, 1979; Beck, Emery & Greenberg, 1985) describe a much more general approach: identify what someone is thinking, re-examine those thoughts so as to identify an alternative way of seeing things, and then use behavioural experiments to test the ideas out. The initial, unrefined treatment method has advantages that we may have lost sight of in the rush to develop specific models for specific conditions. Using it, therapists could (and did) deal with the anger, irritation, frustration or hopelessness of the anxious person 'all in the same breath', so to speak. Its disadvantage – or one of them – was that it did not address specific maintaining factors (such as self-focused attention) directly or precisely. But this problem has been solved over the last decade by the development of specific models for specific conditions. The productivity has been phenomenal, as is illustrated by Wells' (1997) book: *Cognitive Therapy of Anxiety Disorders: A Practice Manual and Conceptual Guide*. The title is revealing. With a precise conceptual guide in hand, you can apply the practice manual presented in the book. Treatment protocols derived from specific models are presented here with little associated debate.

I am not arguing for a return to the *status quo*, but I do not think that we have quite as many answers as Wells' (1997) book suggests – as would also be implied by the range of issues covered in this book. Clinicians still have problems treating people who suffer from anxiety, and it is not yet clear where they should look for answers to them. This may be partly because they have lost touch with cognitive science – if indeed they ever were as closely in touch as was sometimes supposed. Or they may not have found its products easy to assimilate, especially when facing the challenge of helping someone whose problems are less than straightforward. Four of the difficulties that clinicians continue to face are described next.

The problem of effectiveness

First, despite the claims, as clinicians we only make a big difference to relatively few people. Westbrook and Kirk (in press) analysed data from 1,267 patients treated with CBT in the NHS psychology outpatient

Table 14.1 *Outcome following cognitive therapy in routine clinical practice (N = subset for whom start and end data were available)*

Measure	N	Reliably improved %	Recovered %	Effect size**
BDI	559	47.9	34.3	1.15
BAI*	321	49.5	31.5	0.94

* The BAI was introduced later than the BDI, hence the smaller N. The loss rate for data was equivalent on the two measures.
** The difference between the two scores divided by their standard deviation.

Table 14.2 *Benchmarking comparisons*

Mean scores	Oxford NHS sample	Persons: private practice sample	TDCRP research sample
N	127	45	40
Start BDI	25.6	21.7	26.8
End BDI	13.6	11.7	10.2
N (completers)	127	23	40
Reliably improved	52%	57%	50%
No reliable change	43%	43%	47%
Reliably deteriorated	5%	0%	3%

service in Oxford between 1987 and 1998. The patients suffered from a range of disorders, and did not have formal diagnoses. Their problems were relatively chronic (mean reported onset twelve years before the current referral), and about half had previously received treatment from the mental health services. Table 14.1 shows data from a subset, for whom start and end data were available on Beck's standard measures of depression and anxiety, and for whom scores at the start of treatment were greater than ten (outside the normal range) on either measure. By the end of treatment, only about half the patients were reliably improved, and only one-third had recovered (into the normal range). On average, patients received thirteen sessions of CBT, with 10 per cent having more than twenty sessions.

Comparing these data with others does not change the picture. The benchmark chosen for this comparison was Persons, Bostrom and Bertognolli (1999), which compares outcomes for depressed patients treated in Persons' private practice to outcomes from two major research trials: Murphy, Simons, Wetzel and Lustman (1984), and the NIMH Treatment of Depression Collaborative Research Program (TDCRP:

Elkin, Shea et al., 1989). Comparing treatment for depression in our NHS sample with two of these samples still suggests that only half the patients completing treatment are reliably improved by the end of treatment (Table 14.2). These data also show that there is no reliable change in BDI scores for just over 40 per cent of the patients, whatever the source of the sample. Hence the claim that we only make a big difference to relatively few people. Maybe clinicians delivering routine services are less well trained than those working in research trials, but maybe they are also faced with more complex, or less circumscribed problems.

The problem of comorbidity

Comorbidity has become more obvious as scarce resources have increasingly been allocated to those with the most distressing problems, and it has many forms. Patients may have more than one type of anxiety, they may be depressed as well as anxious (or have other 'dual' diagnoses), and/or they may have been anxious all their lives, and fulfil criteria for one of the personality disorders. An illustrative case follows.

Eliza's presenting problems

- frequent panic attacks, at home and elsewhere.
- agoraphobia: alone, she could just walk to local shops.
- social anxiety: avoidance of strangers and intimacy; severe self-consciousness; fear of rejection and a 'need to please'.
- worry (GAD): recent concerns included her family, health, finances, ex-partner, a new relationship and her future.
- mild obsessionality: she used reassuring (verbal) rituals in 'bad' situations, repeating certain phrases a set number of times.
- dental phobia (avoided throughout adulthood).

In addition she was moderately depressed and had low self-esteem. Her thoughts are reflected in the following statements: 'I don't trust my own judgment any more'; 'I'm responsible for all the family'; 'It's frightening to confront all your demons'; 'People like us don't succeed'; 'I've got a fluid sense of myself. I don't know who I am'. These statements are not typical of someone suffering from an anxiety disorder for which one of the standard protocols would readily apply.

A surprising clinical approach to the problem of comorbidity was described by Craske (1998). Having identified the main problem and the associated protocol to start with, this problem usually improves, and others may also diminish, but somewhat less. So the second step mentioned then was to select, after a decent interval, a second target problem and to repeat the process. This approach seems theoretically unnecessary and practically long-winded, but it illustrates well the influence of thinking in terms of differentiating features of anxiety states. Similarly, Williams, Watts, MacLeod and Mathews (1997) explore differentiating features of anxiety and depression. However, to solve the problem of comorbidity efficiently we need to think more in terms of commonalities (Mineka, Walsh & Clark, 1998), and it appears that we now know enough about differences to do so (Hertel, 2002; this volume; Mogg and Bradley, 1998; this volume).

Technical problems

Some people do not benefit from completing Dysfunctional Thought Records (DTRs). One common reason for this is that their thoughts refer straight back to their beliefs. When re-examining their thoughts, all they can 'see' is the evidence for them and none against, and the worse they feel. In this case, looking for evidence confirms current biases and the process ends by closing rather than opening the mind. Presenting new information is not useful when the 'mental crusher' in operation transforms incoming information to fit with old schema. Changing it involves making metaphorical changes, like making a new opening in the head, or creating a new drawer for the internal filing cabinet. The metaphors that clinicians use, though useful in practice, reveal gaps in our understanding of the processes involved.

In addition, the standard way of using DTRs focuses attention on the past. Patients start by thinking of a recent time when they felt distressed, then proceed with identifying and re-examining their thoughts. In essence, something 'bad' has to happen before they can start working on it. But anxious patients need another way of thinking about the future – a way of 're-setting' the system in advance, so that they can meet future threats, risks and worries with (more) equanimity. There is nothing in the DTR that directly counteracts the instantaneous, automatic appraisal that triggers anxiety, and which might even be 'cognitively impenetrable', or proceed out of awareness (Öhman and Mineka, 2001).

Lastly, some people are unable to find any alternative, more functional perspectives – even when their therapist is able to produce a seam of open-minded, Socratic questions with which to prompt them. Or when they do find them, they easily lose sight of them again. The explicit methods used in therapy are not always effective in changing what may be an implicit, or automatic process.

The paradigm example of when these problems arise is when people do not have a store of functional material to draw upon. Their experience has not provided it, but has provided something else instead: in Eliza's case, a childhood that exposed her to the terror of her father during his panic attacks, and to the distance and incompetence of her mother, that separated her socially from contemporaries, and a first adult relationship marked by extreme physical abuse. Hearing her story, it seems not surprising that she reacts 'automatically' to perceived threats or risks.

A problem of identity

Cognitive therapy has thrived on the twin notions that therapists should believe what their patients say, and take care to understand what they personally mean by it. The assumption is that reliable reporting is both possible and meaningful. So we tend to believe the horrific stories we sometimes hear. Nevertheless, in some cases it is not possible literally to believe what our patients say. For example: 'I do not exist', 'I am not a person', 'I'm just an object'.

The problem here is in one sense straightforward, and it has a straightforward solution: work instead on what the patient means by what they say, just as we would when someone declares: 'I never, ever do anything right' or: 'I always have been, and always will be a complete failure.' However, there is also a real problem of identity to which cognitive therapists have not yet seriously turned their attention. This makes it hard to help people like Eliza to make fundamental changes in the way they see themselves. She said: 'I have a fluid sense of myself; I don't know who I am'. If you don't know who you are, how can you know what you think? For Eliza, the 'fluidity' was confusing. It undermined a sense of constancy and stability, and made it hard to 'reflect' as well as react. Her experience had provided little opportunity to develop or to express opinions, and interactions with others were dominated by neglect and threat. Living in self-protective, vulnerable mode had apparently prevented self-discovery.

These four problems: insufficiently effective treatments, comorbidity, problems with techniques and problems of identity, cause tensions as well as difficulties for clinicians. The essence of cognitive therapy is reflected in its emphasis on keeping an open mind – so as to remain constantly curious and interested in understanding someone else's perspective, in seeing things from their point of view, and in seeking with them to find another way of seeing things that is helpful (and in fitting things together theoretically: making a formulation which reflects the range of difficulties experienced and the different levels at which they impinge). One of the by-products of model-building and protocol development is a (largely unintended) emphasis on the right way of doing things. This tends to close the mind, and to make reference to a hypothetical rule book. The attempt to reduce uncertainty is admirable, but the claim to have succeeded in reducing it is exaggerated. Our knowledge remains insufficient; uncertainties abound. Despite our models, we are nowhere near reducing them sufficiently to write a rule book.

The pressure on clinicians is still to explain more than they know: to answer questions such as: 'How come?', 'Why me?', 'What shall I do?' So they try to make sense, to fit things together, and they offer supposedly causal explanations along the lines of: 'It is not that people like you can't change, or that you don't exist, but that you come to think this way *because of* what happened to you.' It would be better if clinicians (and their patients) were able to put their causal explanations onto a solid foundation. The wide-ranging and enduring vulnerabilities of people like Eliza are not yet amenable to proper causal analysis, and clinicians are still seeking solutions.

Hierarchical thinking

Cognitive therapists structure their thinking about cognitions hierarchically: at the lowest level are the many automatic thoughts, positive, negative and neutral, that represent the 'stream of consciousness'. Higher up come assumptions; above them, beliefs and, finally, representations of schema (variously described).

An obvious point follows: changing cognitions at a higher level in the pyramid will affect a broader range of cognitions lower down. So, in cases of comorbidity, working at higher levels of cognition should enable therapists to target related problems simultaneously rather than successively. For example, working on Eliza's sense of vulnerability, and working to understand the idiosyncratic flavour of this vulnerability, she started to change slowly. Her comment was: 'It's like moving on all fronts at once' as – metaphorically speaking – she learned a new language for describing her experiences (past and present). The initial strategy was to ensure that all the work was relevant to changing her underlying sense that 'people like us can't change', whatever the associated feelings. In order to do this work, it is important to work on underlying meanings. As Teasdale said: 'You can't change things by thinking at a single level of cognitive architecture' (1997), and the proliferation of multi-level theoretical approaches (Teasdale and Barnard, 1993; Brewin, Dalgleish and Joseph, 1996; Power and Dalgleish, 1997) now provides ways of thinking more coherently about the different levels.

Understanding meaning

Here, I shall introduce Stella, whose difficulties will provide us with material to illustrate some of the points to follow. Her problems resulted from parental neglect and sexual assault as a child. They included: severe depression with serious suicidal intent; self cutting; pervasive anxiety, especially in social situations; anger, shame and frustration; atypical eating problems; disturbed behavioural patterns, such as not keeping herself warm, giving away her personal belongings and sleeping fully clothed on the floor for only three to four hours a night. About herself she said: 'I am a piece of shit.' In order to help Stella, it helps to assume that in some way, or at some level, it all makes sense.

Even though the heart of the matter in cognitive therapy is in the meaning of an event, clinicians appear to have thought little about meaning. They behave as if it is all the same to them whether they are talking about the significance of what someone says, or about its implications, about what someone means by what they say, or about their intention in saying it. Meaning is many things, not just one, and people use it to do many things: for example, to resolve an issue, or to process it (leave it behind); to test out reactions to it, or to elicit the kind of reaction needed at an earlier time. Psychologists interested in changing meaning have not yet explored the different processes implied by these distinctions.

Here, I shall focus on metaphor, as one of the most important (and ubiquitous) tools for conveying meaning inherent in our various languages. We cannot communicate without using metaphor, and yet it is imagery, rather than metaphor, that has grabbed the attention of researchers (e.g. Hackmann 1998; Hirsch and Clark, this volume). This is surprising, as images, which supposedly reflect meaning, are usually communicated through language, and therefore through metaphor.

Cognitive therapists appear to make a number of assumptions about the use of metaphor that those who study the subject, and tease out the way it works – linguists and literary theorists, as well as philosophers – might consider to be inaccurate, or simple-minded, or downright wrong. For example:
- Metaphors are only loosely related to facts: one step, or more, away from precision; not literally true; different from straightforward rational thinking.
- Metaphors are 'optional extras', or embellishments. They reflect imaginative, not concrete, thinking.
- Using metaphor is 'good': a sign of being creative and imaginative.

But, as George Eliot (1872) said: 'the quickest of us walk about well wadded with stupidity'.

Why do we use metaphor?

According to Pribram (1990): 'Existential understanding is essentially private, whereas scientific understanding is essentially and eminently shareable'. The feelings that reflect what it was like to be a child in a dysfunctional, or overtly harmful, family are, in these terms, essentially private. However, understanding of them is often achieved by using metaphor. Metaphor can make private matters communicable. One way it does this is by making reference to something shareable. When Stella said 'I am a piece of shit', she was referring to herself as an object (or heap) – with no feelings; something that could be acted upon by others – for their purposes, and also as a disgusting, potentially harmful object, that should be disposed of.

Aspects of experience that are poorly delineated are likely to become the targets of metaphor, for example abstract concepts, mental activities and emotions. And there are patterns, conventions and cultural variations in the metaphors that we use. We talk about time as if it were money: we waste it, save it, squander it, lose it, or owe it to each other. We describe our thinking as straight, crooked or contorted, using one type of metaphor, and as lucid or obscure, using another. Emotions may bubble up, spill over, explode, paralyse us, go cold or flat, take us over or carry us away.

The point is that the metaphor is as literal as we can get. In an analysis of a passage in *Middlemarch* which 'ultimately turns on the emotional disappointment of a young ardent woman married to the wrong, cold husband', George Eliot points out that if Dorothea had been 'required to state the cause' of her crying, 'she could only have done so in some such general words as I have used' because 'to have been driven to be more particular would have been like trying to give a history of the lights and shadows'.[1]

So when it is hard to find words in which to describe our experiences, metaphor becomes an essential tool. Pictorial imagery is another, but it is an optional one, and using it as a means of communication usually involves metaphor. A patient drew a picture to reflect the feelings that she could not at that time speak about. She described the picture in terms of the aftermath of an earthquake. Using this metaphor, she was able to 'step outside' her intense distress and to 'reformulate' her experiences and current difficulties (nightmares, flashbacks, dissociative episodes and problems in daily functioning) more compassionately. Communicating about our subjective experiences is not easy, and both metaphor and pictures (drawings) help to convey what we mean. Using metaphor has many functions, which should be distinguished. Some of the essential ones are listed below.

1. Metaphor clarifies meaning: it describes or explains what we mean. It is not 'loosely related to facts', or opposed to the literal, but (e.g. when talking about emotions) brings us close to understanding someone else's experience – e.g. Stella's as 'a piece of shit', or a message on an

envelope, given me by a patient, to describe her experience of cognitive therapy:

Pity me
That the heart is slow to learn
What the swift mind beholds at every turn

2. Metaphor adds something to what is conveyed, such as an evaluation or judgment. Eliza described her mother as 'constantly cutting me down to size'.
3. Metaphor uses language efficiently. A patient talking about whether she was ready for discharge said: 'I'm standing, but I'm not yet walking.'
4. Metaphor can provide distance, a way of talking about something indirectly, for example, 'I have to wear my pain on my sleeve' said by someone who had not disclosed that she was cutting her arms.

Metaphor performs these (meaningful) functions by making the abstract concrete, by asserting likeness relationships, by stepping out of one framework into another, and also by drawing on different aspects of meaning, including the implicational level. There are also conventions for doing these things that we could make better use of if we understood them better. So, contrary to the assumption attributed to therapists above, metaphor is not an 'optional extra'. It pervades our language, and provides a necessary tool for communicating about abstract and subjective matters. In order to talk about these things, it helps to make them concrete, and there are standard ways of doing this, which make them clearer, not foggier. Dominant metaphors provide common ground within a particular culture: life as a journey, for example. Less dominant ones, such as life as a 'gift', may raise other issues: should you repay the giver? Did you deserve it?

Whether a metaphor 'works' will depend on what it means to someone: there will be cultural and individual variations (Lakoff, 1987). So, using metaphor is not always 'good'. A metaphor may be 'dead', and its internal logic may not fit. Time may be thought of as an asset, like money, that you can invest in, but you cannot put it in the bank to use later. Metaphors will be unhelpful if outdated; they may be mixed, misleading or muddling, or draw on the wrong logic. For example, a patient spoke of herself as being 'eaten up' by hatred of her abusive ex-husband, from whom she separated fourteen years previously, as if her hatred was a parasite inside her. She thought of therapy as 'getting it out of her system', and wanted to do this by talking about it. This made her worse. She was helped instead by using a different metaphor: the hatred was a dynamic force which 'wore her out', and 'used up all her resources'. Working to replenish her resources, and to divert her energy into more productive activities, was more helpful.

Therapists who do not pay attention to the metaphors used by their patients will be in more trouble than those that do: stuck with a single perspective; more focused on literal meaning; less clear about what is being described; less able to change affect, as well as cognition; more likely to miss the implications and significance of what is said; less aware of judgments and evaluations; less able to help someone push back the boundaries of their understanding, and less able to understand their view of themselves as a person (or lack of such a view).

Equally, therapists who suppose that using metaphor, or imagery, is always relevant and likely to be helpful, are wrong. The value of metaphor will depend on its precise meaning and on its accessibility to the recipient. Without research into how, when and where metaphor (as well as, instead of or in combination with imagery) can be used to change the various aspects of meaning, we may continue to operate as at present: well wadded with stupidity.

Philosophers and linguists, amongst others, have made numerous useful distinctions that potentially contribute to a therapist's understanding of metaphor, and of meaning. We should learn from them, rather than attempt to write a protocol-driven rule book, and start to explore the psychological (as opposed to philosophical or linguistic) processes involved in their use. Would generating specific types of metaphor influence attentional or interpretive biases? Or mood states? Or contribute to the development of new cognitive habits? Or help people attend to painful material in a more accepting and less avoidant way?

Understanding problems of identity

There are still major gaps in our understanding of other people's thinking processes. When the techniques that we use as cognitive therapists let us down, sometimes this is because we are working with people who have a non-existent, or poorly developed, sense of self. These are some of the statements that I have heard patients make about themselves:

I have no value; I'm both here and not here; I'm not real; there's no real me; I'm a non-person; I don't really exist; I don't know how to be me – what it would mean to be me; There's no one there; there's no space for me.

So far, cognitive therapists have not taken these statements seriously, and this may be one reason why they still have the problems listed above. If you have no stable, identifiable sense of yourself, then of course it is hard to answer Socratic questions, to fill in DTRs and to keep hold of the new idea that only a short while ago seemed so helpful. It is as if there was nowhere to put it. These difficulties occur when working with people who have suffered greatly over long periods, especially during their childhoods, but they also occur in less extreme forms in others. If we could resolve them, then we might be able to make a bigger difference to more people.

Cognitive therapists need to think more about the self (or selves), and this is what I have been doing with the patients described here. The work owes much to others (e.g. Linehan, 1993; Hayes, Strosahl and Wilson, 1999), and also to the patients concerned. When, in contrast with cases of single incident trauma, there is no 'life to reclaim' it has helped instead to think in terms of creating a sense of self, so that (metaphorically speaking) there is somewhere for the new information to reside. When this work goes well, patients' comments reflect this process: 'I feel more connected' 'It's all beginning to link up', 'When that happens, I have a sense of 'me', and during the transition period: 'I keep losing the feeling of connectedness, and I don't know how to get it back', 'The feeling of being real comes and goes'. The processes can only be described metaphorically – hence the need to understand how metaphor works, and the general principles that govern our attempts to communicate about ourselves and our subjective experiences.

Working with Stella (an exceptionally able person intellectually) raised numerous questions about the processes involved in change. Her statement: 'I am a piece of shit' literally meant that she thought of herself as an object. She had no wishes or intentions, could make no claim on others, could be used by anyone for whatever purpose they had in mind, and she claimed no longer to have feelings (though she still engaged in behaviours intended to numb the pain or make herself tough). She also thought of herself as a disgusting, repellent object, and behaved as if obliged to remove herself from others (unless thoroughly disguised as an apparently functioning person). It was because she believed that contact with her was harmful (but did not want to harm others) that she had decided to kill herself. When wearing the disguise of a person, she was adamant that she was 'not herself' – 'not real'. It took a while to grasp that Stella really thought of herself as an object. I had understood that her statement was metaphorical, but had thought of it as similar to saying: 'I'm a rat.' Her choice of metaphor clarified much about her behaviour: objects don't own things, have feelings or make plans for themselves. Her metaphor explained, as precisely as she was able, her sense of herself and of her own value.

The first significant change she made was to think of herself as a human being – as part of the human race. For Stella, the meaning of being a human being changed over time. At first, it meant just that she had skin (rather than feathers, scales or fur), and that she had a right to live, rather than an obligation to separate herself from others. She described it as 'a head thing', and the cognitive part of the work at this stage involved exploring the meaning (reference, significance, implications) of being a human being instead of an object. Later, she wrote: 'I chose another identity that I wanted to develop in place of a piece of shit; I decided I wanted to be a human being, which for me means someone with intrinsic value, with the potential for good and bad behaviour, who can learn from mistakes, and is of equal worth to every other person on the planet.' Many factors probably contributed to this belief change, including re-formulating her history in terms of the consequences of her experiences; acknowledging the pain they caused; using experiential techniques, such as imagery re-scripting; being consistently treated as a human being, deserving of respect and understanding, and reflecting explicitly on all of these activities and their significance. Their relative value is, of course, unknown.

Achieving this belief change sounds ideal, but it was not. Stella became distressed when she could not answer standard Socratic questions, such as: 'What does doing your work say about you?' In her work, broadly in the educational field, she acted in accordance with a strong value system (respecting the rights of the child, striving to include everyone), but for her this was an astonishing discovery. She had not thought of these values (or of any values) as hers. To her list of the qualities of a human being she added: consciousness, of thoughts and of decisions; self-determination: you can choose what kind of human being to be (not like my mother); inconsistency: being inconsistent is human. It does not mean I am a fake . . . but she said: 'I still do not know who I am.'

The next step for Stella was marked by discovering that she was not just a human being; she was also a person. Identifying some of the rules she lived by helped her to draw this conclusion, for example: 'You should never hurt anyone else.' This rule became clear shortly after her baby was born. Stella described the difference to her of being a person in this way: 'A *human being* walks upright, has skin, and is part of the species. A *person* has identity, interests and values.'

The process of 'becoming' a person was diverse and emotional. In general, Stella tried to behave in accordance with her interests, inclinations and values, which forced her to think about numerous self-denying and self-punishing behaviours. She said: 'If I'm a non-person, I don't see any need to hold values, or to apply them to my own life.' As a person, she started to fight the impulse to give away her clothes and the books she needed for work, and to fight the need to make herself tough by going hungry or cold, and sleeping on the floor. Behaving differently produced an obvious contradiction: 'I don't believe in punishment as a way of dealing with anything' and: 'I have to punish myself.' She commented that being a human being had been like having a committee in her head, whereas being a person enabled her to attend to her wishes, wants and needs, as if she had 're-set' part of her original cognitive framework, and was learning new habits of thinking. However, it also felt contradictory and dangerous. It precipitated many sad, confused and angry images and memories.

When distressed, her former inflexible patterns of thinking and behaving re-emerged. Stella readily lost the new-found flexibility of allowing herself to be a person. As a musician, she had loved improvising, and derived emotional consolation from it. She used this as a metaphor for what she was now doing, and explained to me that improvisation had structure, provided for example by a key signature and/or a time scheme. So she needed background structure also: a routine for the baby, sleeping only at night, and in a bed, and then she could start to improvise for her own life – for her 'self'. But how would she know what this would be like? She asked: 'If I'm a person, then how do I know who I am?' She started by making choices of plants for her home, but discovering preferences was alarming. Aged twelve, she remembered wanting to disappear, because: 'If you appear, you have to appear *as* something' and: 'If you don't know who you are, then nothing seems right. It all feels like pretending.'

Feeling valued by people with values similar to hers at work provided real glimpses of being a person. Then, at a conference, she was talking to a colleague when someone asked: 'Where did you two meet?' She was greatly distressed by being unable to answer, saying: 'I can't tell a story.' This defined the next step: using the word 'I' in a story about herself – not a story of the details of what happened to her, but a condensed overview that encapsulated the meaning – the significance and implications – to her of her experiences. A self has continuity, and can tell a story. It can assert itself: not only have preferences, but also seek to express them: ' "I" can plan ahead. Being "I" has enabled thinking about the future for the first time'. Having a sense of ourselves allows us to look back on our former selves – something that Stella was at first unable to do – as well as forward to a future that concerns us.

Alain de Botton, in his novel *The Art of Travel* (2002), describes what needs to happen when people tell a story: there needs to be condensation and overview, and less (not more) attention to detail, so that the meaning becomes clear. If this process is correctly described, it contrasts markedly with methods of 'reliving' used following Type 1 trauma.

The work with Stella suggests something about the stages, as well as the content of change. Another patient wrote: 'I have been thinking deeply about why I seem to miss my mum so very much. I think that because I so desperately wanted her to approve of me and to show that she loved me, or even liked me a little, I tried to replicate every detail of her. I think I tried to eliminate myself, so I became more like her. I don't think I allowed myself to have an identity of my own. I just wanted to be her, so she would show me some affection. Maybe that is why I feel so empty without her. I lost my identity when she died.' Developing her identity reduced this sense of sadness, and when she had done so she wrote: '. . . I now realize that you have to look backwards in order to move forwards, but you can only successfully do this if you look back from a position of strength . . . To look backwards without this strength will simply reinforce [the] negative viewpoint [. . .] to look back with a strong self-image is a release, [and brings] freedom to make my own decisions to move forward.' For her, at least, it was important to develop a sense of identity – the strong self-image – before looking back.

Using metaphors to clarify and to change thinking about private experience, and helping someone develop a sense of self, are ways of working with the significance to people of events, and of thinking coherently about their implications. The difficulty is that doing this work, it is hard to keep focused. One option is to keep a coherent strand of behavioural work going at the same time (for the sake of clarity, and for its impact). Eliza, working on her sense of being permanently vulnerable to both internal and external threats, turned taking her five-year-old son to judo class into a paradigm behavioural experiment (Bennett-Levy, Butler et al., 2004). On the basis of her beliefs she predicted what would happen. On the basis of her observations, she re-evaluated those beliefs. Stella established elements of a daily routine for herself and drew conclusions about herself as a person. Thus, the work progressed at two distinct levels: at a deeper level of meaning and at a more immediate, often behavioural, level, and it appeared (at least partially), and often painfully, to change habits of thinking and to re-set an original information processing bias. How did this happen?

Concluding speculations

In the context of the work described in this book, it is interesting to think about whether attentional and interpretive biases played a causal role in the mediation, and also in the moderation, of vulnerability to anxiety for Eliza and for Stella. In both cases, their reported experiences might have contributed to the development of an attentional bias and descriptions of their original problems were consistent with the operation of such a bias. Their daily lives were motivated by avoidant and protective attitudes, and the ability to reflect on their circumstances, and to be curious, were markedly lacking.

It is possible that the style of cognitive therapy, as well as its content, contributed to shifting this bias (and helped to create new habits of thought), and that it did so by drawing attention to different things and by encouraging a different way of attending to ongoing experience. Agenda-setting helps people to segment their problems, to attend selectively to aspects of their difficulties, and to select what to work on. Socratic questioning invites people to focus on aspects of their experience, to reflect, and to be curious about what they observe. Collaboration implies that both parties contribute and that both contributions are valued. Formulation work enables people to make links, normalize maintenance processes and define implications for change. Exchanging feedback, and explicitness, reflect a stance of acceptance and openness, a willingness to explore and to share ideas. Treating people with respect, consistency, openness and curiosity, and reflecting on the meaning of so doing, potentially impacts on their sense of value, or identity. Just as in mindfulness-based treatments (Teasdale, this volume), qualities of the practitioner and of the interaction between practitioner and patient may be crucial, and as we now know, habits of attending selectively can be established in one set of situations and later revealed in others (Mathews & MacLeod, 2002; see also MacLeod et al., this volume). It has always been mysterious that spending a few hours with someone can make any difference at all. If doing so affects what they attend to, and the way in which they attend (i.e. non-judgmentally), then maybe that is not so surprising As Goldfried said: 'Our role as therapists is to focus a clinical spotlight on aspects of [clients'] lives about which we believe a better awareness would lead to positive benefits. In this sense, we as therapists are "attention deployers" . . .' (Goldfried, 1995, p. 223).

NOTE

1. I owe this example to Christopher Butler.

REFERENCES

Arntz, A. (1999). Do personality disorders exist? On the validity of the concept and its cognitive-behavioural formulation and treatment. *Behaviour Research and Therapy*, 37, S97–S134.
Beck, A. T., Emery, G. & Greenberg, R. C. (1985). *Anxiety Disorders and Phobias: A Cognitive Perspective*. New York: Basic Books.
Beck, A. T., Rush, A. J., Shaw, F. & Emery, G. (1979). *Cognitive Therapy of Depression*. New York: Guilford.

Bennett-Levy, J., Butler, G., Fennell, M., Hackmann, A., Mueller, M. & Westbrook, D. (2004). *The Oxford Guide to Behavioural Experiments in Cognitive Therapy*. Oxford: Oxford University Press.

Brewin, C., Dalgleish, T. & Joseph, S. (1996). A dual representation theory of posttraumatic stress disorder. *Psychological Review*, *103*, 670–686.

Clark, D. M. (1999). Anxiety disorders: why they persist and how to treat them. *Behaviour Research and Therapy*, *37*, S5–S27.

Craske, M. G., Farchione, T., Tsao, J. & Mystkowski, J. (1998). Comorbidity and panic disorder. Paper presented at the EABCT annual conference, Madrid, September 1998.

De Botton, A. (2002). *The Art of Travel*. London: Hamish Hamilton.

Eliot, G. (1872). *Middlemarch*, chapter 20.

Elkin, I., Shea, M. T., Watkins, J. T., Imber, S. T., Sotsky, S. M., Collins, J. F., et al. (1989). National Institute of Mental Health Treatment of Depression Collaborative Research Program: general effectiveness of treatments. *Archives of General Psychiatry*, *46*, 971–982.

Goldfried, M. (1995). Toward a common language for case formulation. *Journal of Psychotherapy Integration*, *5*, 221–244.

Hackmann, A. (1998). Working with images in clinical psychology. In A. S. Bellack & M. Hersen (Eds.), *Comprehensive Clinical Psychology*, *6*, 301–316. Oxford: Elsevier.

Hayes, S. C., Strosahl, K. D. & Wilson, K. G. (1999). *Acceptance and Commitment Therapy*. New York: Guilford.

Hertel, P. T. (2002). Cognitive biases in anxiety and depression: introduction to the Special Issue. *Cognition and Emotion*, *16*, 321–330.

Lakoff, G. (1987). *Women, Fire and Dangerous Things: What Categories Reveal about the Mind*. Chicago: University of Chicago Press.

Lakoff, G. & Johnson, M. (1980). *Metaphors We Live By*. Chicago: University of Chicago Press.

Linehan, M. (1993). *Cognitive-Behavioural Therapy for Borderline Personality Disorder*. New York: Guilford.

Mathews, A. & MacLeod, C. (2002). Induced processing biases have causal effects on anxiety. *Cognition and Emotion*, *16*, 331–354.

Mineka, S., Walsh, D. & Clark, L. A. (1998). Comorbidity of anxiety and unipolar mood disorder. *Annual Review of Psychology*, *49*, 377–412.

Mogg, K. & Bradley, B. P. (1998). A cognitive-motivational analysis of anxiety. *Behaviour Research and Therapy*, *37*, 595–604.

Murphy, G. E., Simons, A. D., Wetzel, R. D. & Lustman, P. J. (1984). Cognitive therapy and pharmacotherapy: singly and together in the treatment of depression. *Archives of General Psychiatry*, *41*, 33–41.

Öhman, A. & Mineka, S. (2001). Fears, phobias and preparedness: toward an evolved module of fear and fear learning. *Psychological Review*, *108*, 483–522.

Persons, J. B., Bostrom, A. & Bertognolli, A. (1999). Results of randomized controlled trials of cognitive therapy for depression generalize to private practice. *Cognitive Therapy and Research*, *23*, 535–548.

Power, M. & Dalgleish, T. (1997). *Cognition and Emotion: From Order to Disorder*. Hove: Psychology Press.

Pribram, K. H. (1990). From metaphors to models: the use of analogy in neuro-psychology. In D. H. Leary (Ed.), *Metaphors in the History of Psychology*. Cambridge: Cambridge University Press.

Teasdale, J. D. (1997). Preventing depressive relapse: applying ICS to ACT. Paper presented at BABCP conference in Canterbury.

Teasdale, J. D. & Barnard, P. J. (1993). *Affect, Cognition and Change*. Hove: Erlbaum.

Wells, A. (1997). *Cognitive Therapy of Anxiety Disorders: A Practice Manual and Conceptual Guide*. Chichester: Wiley.

Westbrook, D. & Kirk, J. (in press). The clinical effectiveness of cognitive behaviour therapy: outcome for a large sample of adults treated in routine practice. *Behavioural and Cognitive Psychotherapy*.

Williams, J. M. G., Watts, F. N., MacLeod, C. & Mathews, A. (1997). *Cognitive Psychology and Emotional Disorders*, 2nd edn. Chichester: Wiley.

Index

Cognition, Emotion and Psychopathology

This edited collection is a tribute to Andrew Mathews, distinguished researcher in cognition and emotion. It presents a 'state of the art' account of the cognitive-clinical literature and sets an agenda for future work. The book is structured around theoretical, empirical and clinical approaches. Theoretical topics covered include learning theory, attentional processes and repression, while the discussion of empirical work covers areas such as cognitive training, ambiguity resolution and functional imaging. The final section examines work with a clinical perspective, including imagery, social anxiety, autobiographical memory and mindfulness-based cognitive therapy. The list of contributors includes some of the leading researchers in the field and will ensure that this book appeals to a broad international readership in cognitive science, neuroscience, clinical psychology, psychiatry and the study of emotion.

JENNY YIEND is a Research Fellow at the Department of Psychiatry, University of Oxford. She was previously a research assistant at the MRC Cognition and Brain Sciences Unit in Cambridge.

Andrew Mathews